Operations of Life and Health Insurance Companies

Second Edition

LOMA (Life Office Management Association, Inc.) is an international association founded in 1924. LOMA's mission is to help companies in the insurance and financial services industry improve their management and operations through quality education, research, information sharing, and related products and services. Among its activities is the sponsorship of the FLMI Insurance Education Program, an educational program intended primarily for home office and branch office employees.

The **FLMI Insurance Education Program** consists of two levels—Level I, "Fundamentals of Life and Health Insurance," and Level II, "Functional Aspects of Life and Health Insurance." Level I is designed to help students achieve a working knowledge of the life and health insurance business. Level II is designed to further the student's career development by providing a more detailed understanding of life and health insurance and related business and management subjects. Upon the completion of Level I, the student is awarded a certificate. Upon the completion of both levels, the student is designated a Fellow of the Life Management Institute (FLMI) and is awarded a diploma.

Operations of Life and Health Insurance Companies

Second Edition

Kenneth Huggins, FLMI/M
Robert D. Land, FLMI, ACS

LOMA

FLMI Insurance Education Program
Life Management Institute LOMA
Atlanta, Georgia

Textbook Project Team:

Authors	Kenneth Huggins, FLMI/M, and Robert D. Land, FLMI, ACS
Project Manager	Katherine C. Milligan, FLMI, ALHC
Project Editor	Jeanne Michel Jones, FLMI, ALHC, ACS
Administrative Support	Sharon Bibee
Typography	Peirce Graphic Services, Inc.

ISBN 0-939921-41-3

Library of Congress Catalog Card Number 92-81826

Printed in the United States of America

Contents

CHAPTER 7   ACTUARIAL FUNCTIONS FOR INDIVIDUAL LIFE INSURANCE

Acknowledgments

No textbook is produced by a single person. No matter how much work authors put into a book, there are always others who provide valuable assistance that make publication of the book possible. Such is certainly the case with *Operations of Life and Health Insurance Companies* (2nd edition), which required the combined efforts of a large number of people. At this time, I would like to offer my thanks and the thanks of LOMA to the individuals who gave their time and energy to the development of this textbook.

My foremost thanks go to the members of the textbook development panel, who reviewed the outline for the entire book and each chapter as it was completed. They oversaw the project from the beginning to end and made invaluable contributions. Their critical judgment, patience, and technical expertise were essential to the book's accuracy and completeness. The members of the textbook development panel are listed below.

TEXTBOOK DEVELOPMENT PANEL

Kathryn P. Ciurczak, FLMI
Manager, Office Services
Mutual Benefit Life Insurance Company

Robert W. Gidlow, FLMI, CLU
Assistant Vice President
Hartford Life Insurance Company

William J. Hazlewood, FLMI, CLU, CHFC
Marketing Vice President
Mercantile and General Life Reassurance Company of Canada

Operations of Life and Health Insurance Companies

Donald J. Lindo, FLMI, CLU, ChFC
Principal
The Miller Group

Lawrence B. Ruark, Ph.D., FLMI, CLU
Senior Policy Forms Analyst
Sun Life Assurance Company of Canada

John E. Schroeder, FLMI
Senior Auditor
Country Life Insurance Company

I would also like to extend my sincere appreciation to the following individuals whose knowledge added to the quality and technical accuracy of selected chapters of the text that had their attention:

Paul D. Adornato, CLU
Senior Vice President
MassMutual Life Insurance Company

Harriet M. Grayson
Second Vice President
MassMutual Life Insurance Company

Louis J. Higdon, FLMI, CLU
Assistant Vice President
State Farm Insurance Companies

Vance F. Howard, FLMI
President and Chief Operating Officer
North American Company for Life and Health Insurance

Donald Joshua, LL.B., FLMI
Consultant, Pension Services
ManuLife Financial

SPECIALIST REVIEWERS

Besides the members of the development panel listed above, specialists in many fields reviewed each of the topical areas discussed in the book:

marketing, actuarial, underwriting, customer service, claim administration, investments, accounting, legal operations, human resources, and information systems. These experts reviewed the material in their area of specialization and provided a valuable perspective and much new information.

Marketing

David M. Dobbin, FLMI
Manager, Product Development and Support
The Prudential Assurance Company Ltd.

Patricia J. Lavelle, FLMI/M, CPCU, ALHC
Special Claim Coordinator
Colonial Penn Group

Actuarial

Warren A. Carter, ASA, MAAA
Second Vice President
TIAA-CREF

Gerald R. Chapman, FSA
Assistant Actuary
Minnesota Mutual Life Insurance Company

Elaine R. Shute, FLMI
Manager, Group Operations Planning
Confederation Life Insurance Company

Underwriting

W. Wayne Key, Jr., M.D.
Medical Director
Life Insurance Company of Virginia

D. Stephen Martin, FLMI, AALU
Vice President, Underwriting
AIG Life Insurance Company

Customer Service

Ted Johnson, Jr., FLMI
Director, Life and Health Policy Service
USAA Life Insurance Company

Dennis E. McKenna, FLMI/M, ACS
Senior Quality Service Consultant
The Prudential Insurance Company of America

Harry L. Ruppenthal
Director, Policyowner Service
Northwestern Mutual Life Insurance Company

Ursula Wanko, FLMI, CLU, FALU, ALHC
Assistant Vice President
Westfield Companies

Patricia A. Winne
Director of Client Services
MassMutual Life Insurance Company

Claim Administration

James B. Hiers, III, FLMI, ALHC, HIA
Manager, Group Claims
Munich American Reassurance Company

Thomas P. O'Donnell, FLMI, ALHC
Life Claims Officer
Sun Life Assurance Company of Canada

William G. Wanless, FLMI, ALHC
Consultant, Group Legal and Contract Services
London Life Insurance Company

Investments

Connie Caycedo, FLMI
Manager, Investment Co.
Cotton States Life and Health Insurance Company

Ron Gadbois, FLMI, CFA
Vice President and Chief Financial Officer
The Equitable Life Insurance Company of Canada

Wayne Gates
Senior Vice President
John Hancock Freedom Securities

Accounting

Andrew Archer, CA, CPA
Accounting Director
Manufacturers Life Insurance Company

Alan E. Close, CPA, FLMI
Associate Controller
Northwestern Mutual Life Insurance Company

Legal

Steven F. Abba, FLMI, CLU, ALHC
Assistant Vice President
Mercantile and General Reinsurance Company

Muriel L. Crawford, J.D., FLMI, CLU, ChFC, CEBS
Attorney
Hancock, Rothert & Bunshoft

Human Resources

Lura A. Kamiya, FLMI, SPHR, ACS
Second Vice President, Human Resources
Covenant Life Insurance Company

Helen A. Wylde, FLMI, ALHC
Vice President, Administration
Commercial Union Life Insurance

Information Systems

Nancy F. Dudgeon, FLMI/M, ALHC, ACS
Assistant Vice President, Life Reinsurance
Administrative & Information Services
Manufacturers Life Insurance Company

Ron Raffan, FLMI
Manager, Investment Business Systems Division
Prudential Insurance Company of America

Because of their expertise in particular areas, the following individuals also reviewed selected portions of the text.

Gilbert H. Forst
President and Chief Executive Officer
Savings Bank Life Insurance Fund

Jacques Guilmette
Director, Health and Disability Claims Control
Sun Life Assurance Company of Canada

Kevin Hennosy
State Public Affairs Manager
National Association of Insurance Commissioners

Jean Olson
Senior Manager, Member and Examination Service
National Association of Insurance Commissioners

Richard A. Peters
Vice President and Secretary
Savings Bank Life Insurance Company of Massachusetts

Peter L. Tedone, CLU
Vice President
The Savings Bank Life Insurance Company

LOMA REVIEWERS

Textbook authors at LOMA are fortunate to have many fellow staff members who are knowledgeable about industry trends and practices in a diverse array of subject matters. I would like to thank the following LOMA staff members who gave valuable input on this second edition.

Jane Lightcap Brown, FLMI, ALHC
Senior Associate, Education Division

Susan Conant, FLMI, CEBS, HIA
Senior Associate, Education Division

Sean Schaeffer Gilley, FLMI, ALHC, HIA, ACS
Senior Associate, Education Division

Dennis W. Goodwin, FLMI, ACS, HIA
Manager, Curriculum Department

Jean Crooks Gora
Senior Research Associate, Research Division

Gail Haney
Senior Research Associate, Employee Selection and Research Services Unit

Harriett E. Jones, J.D., FLMI
Senior Associate, Education Division

Barbara Kruse
Manager, Employee Selection and Research Services

Ernest L. Martin, Ph.D., FLMI
Director, Examinations

Brian K. McGreevy, J.D., FLMI
Manager, International Programs, and Counsel

Ann Purr, FLMI, ACS, CSP
Manager, Information Management Resources

Zoila Galarza Vega, CCP, SPHR
Senior Personnel Associate

Many other people contributed to this second edition. Alexa Selph copyedited the final manuscript and prepared the index. Sharon Bibee compiled the glossary and provided excellent assistance throughout the project. Robert H. Hartley, FLMI, ALHC, and Elizabeth A. Mulligan, FLMI, ACS, of LOMA's Education Division staff researched and adapted much of the material for the INSIGHT sections. Dani L. Long, FLMI, ALHC, made many valuable contributions to these sections as well.

As co-author of the second edition, I am indebted to Kenneth Huggins, FLMI/M, for the excellent first edition of this text. Thanks also go to Jeanne Michel Jones, FLMI, ALHC, ACS, who edited every draft of the manuscript, and Katherine C. Milligan, FLMI, ALHC, who supervised the entire project.

Robert D. Land

The purpose of *Operations of Life and Health Insurance Companies* is to describe life and health insurance companies—how they are organized, how they operate, and the environment in which they operate. The first three chapters describe the place that life and health insurance maintains in the North American economy, the various types of organizations that provide insurance, and examples of the internal organization of insurance companies.

Most of the remaining chapters in the book describe the major functions performed in a life and health insurance company. The emphasis throughout the text is on what the function is, who does it, and how they do it.

Operations of Life and Health Insurance Companies is designed to illustrate typical functions and organizational structures; thus, the grouping of functions and operations used in this book may not correspond exactly with those used in any company with which you are familiar. The book does not describe any particular company, and it does not set forth any descriptions as models to be followed.

Some companies combine into one department the functions that are described here as being the functions of two departments. Other companies might assign to several departments the functions that are described in this book as belonging to only one department. Nevertheless, the same basic functions are necessary for all companies to operate. Similarly, the names and duties of any particular department or job may vary from one company to another. Every attempt has been made to find and use the most commonly accepted terms for departments, jobs, and functions. Alternate terminology is offered when it is appropriate.

As you compare this book's descriptions of various functions and departments with the departments in your own company, you will probably notice that in most cases the differences are not in *what* is done but in *where* it is done. For example, all life and health insurance companies have a policy issue unit. In this book, policy issue is included as part of the discussion of the underwriting functions. In some companies, however, policy issue is part of the customer service function; in others, it is a department by itself. Regardless of its location, the functions and activities of policy issue are essentially the same.

NEW FEATURES FOR THE SECOND EDITION

A number of new features distinguish this second edition of *Operations of Life and Health Insurance Companies* from the first. Lists of learning objectives and key terms have been added to each chapter to help students focus their study. Also, the text now includes INSIGHTS—excerpts from industry publications, LOMA activity reports, and other sources—that are designed to highlight company operations and discuss trends in the life and health insurance industry. These INSIGHTS should help students to get a better feel for insurance operations and, in some cases, to put a human face on the array of functions and processes that define a company's operations.

The second edition of *Operations* also includes some content changes from the first edition. Industry data has been updated, to 1990 where available. More information has been included on corporate-level operations, such as the benefits and drawbacks of joint ventures and the motivations of an insurer that enters the international marketplace. The material on information systems has an expanded, company-wide approach. The marketing, claim administration, underwriting, and human resources chapters have been enhanced. Issues such as self-managed work teams, reengineering, and the flattening of the organizational pyramid are also introduced.

Because of these types of changes, the second edition of *Operations of Life and Health Insurance Companies* should be an improved guide to understanding insurance company operations in the 1990s.

SUGGESTIONS FOR STUDYING THIS BOOK

If you are reading this book to prepare for an FLMI examination, you may find it helpful to follow these suggestions for studying the material.

First, review the table of contents to get an overview of the material that you will be covering. Before reading each chapter, read and think about each of the learning objectives so that you will begin to understand the relative importance of the subjects covered in the chapter. Next, scan through the chapter to familiarize yourself with how the information is presented. By looking at the headings and figures, you'll get an idea of how various subjects relate to each other. Then, return to the beginning of the chapter and start your reading.

As you read, look for the material that will help you meet the learning objectives presented at the beginning of the chapter. Pay special attention to the key terms highlighted in ***bold italics*** and to the definition or explanation that follows. These important terms are defined again in the glossary at the end of the book. Study carefully the figures and the INSIGHTS, which enhance your understanding of the concepts presented in the chapter. Reinforce your learning through making notes—either on a separate sheet or in the text's margins—and highlighting or underlining important material.

USING LOMA-PUBLISHED STUDY AIDS

LOMA-published study aids provide a helpful means of review and reinforcement of assigned material. (Study aids are designed to *supplement*, not to replace, the assigned textbook[s]. There is no substitute for reading the assigned material.) Study aids typically provided for FLMI texts include Student Guides and Test Preparation Guides, each of which is described below.

Student Guides

Student Guides reinforce your learning of the material covered in the text by providing you with a comprehensive review of important topics covered. Each Student Guide identifies and reviews key learning objectives for each chapter, provides an outline and an overview of each chapter, and leads you through structured note-taking and other types of exercises covering each chapter. Student Guides also help you to recognize and remember key terms and concepts. Most students find it helpful to read a chapter in the text, work through the exercises in the Student Guide covering that chapter, and then answer the practice questions covering that chapter in the Test Preparation Guide.

Test Preparation Guides (TPGs)

Test Preparation Guides provide practice in answering the types of questions that appear on FLMI examinations. After an extensive explanation of how to study for and take examinations, each TPG provides from 3 to 10 sample questions (and answers) for each chapter assigned. Finally, a comprehensive examination similar in construction to an actual FLMI examination gives you a chance to test yourself. (Text references and an answer key are given for the practice test.)

LOMA recommends that you use all of the study aids that are available. **Studies have indicated that students who use LOMA study aids consistently perform significantly better on FLMI Program examinations.** Consult the current LOMA Insurance Education Catalog for a list of the study aids that accompany this text.

Chapter 1

Insurance Companies and Their Environment

After reading this chapter, you should be able to

- Describe the role that life and health insurance companies play in a nation's economy
- Discuss the regulatory environment in which insurers operate
- Identify recent demographic changes and changes in economic conditions that affect the ways insurance companies operate
- Discuss how and why consumers' attitudes toward the financial services industry have changed
- Describe how insurance companies have changed their product offerings to accommodate changes in economic conditions

Providing life and health insurance protection for almost 190 million policyowners in the United States and Canada requires the skills, energy, and creativity of millions of people who work for insurance companies. In this book, we will describe the ways in which these companies are established and how they are organized. We will also look at the many different functional areas of an insurance company, the types of work conducted in each area, and the way that these functional areas relate to each other. This first chapter describes the environment in which insurance companies operate. We begin by looking at the important role that the life and health insurance industry plays in the economy.

THE ROLE OF INSURANCE COMPANIES IN AN ECONOMY

Life and health insurance companies play major roles in the national economies of the United States and Canada. By providing protection from the risk of economic loss, insurance companies offer policyowners, insureds, beneficiaries, and annuitants a measure of financial security. People who are adequately insured can pursue their goals in life, knowing that if they die or become disabled, their families or businesses will not be subjected to undue financial hardships. Furthermore, life and health insurance companies manage a large portion of the retirement funds in the United States and Canada, thereby helping people accumulate funds for the time when they are no longer working.

In addition to providing protection from the risk of economic loss, life and health insurers employ many people in these two countries. At the end of 1990, more than 2,500 life and health insurance companies in the United States and Canada provided jobs for about 1.5 million people, not including the sales force. Life and health insurance sales and support functions provided another 680,000 jobs.

Life and health insurance companies are actually part of the larger financial services industry, which can generally be segmented into three groups: deposit-type institutions, contractual savings institutions, and other types of financial services companies.[1]

- At *deposit-type financial institutions*—such as commercial banks, savings and loan associations, mutual savings banks, and credit unions—customers can maintain savings and checking accounts and secure mortgage, business, and consumer loans.
- *Contractual savings institutions* include insurance companies and pension funds. Contractual savings institutions help provide financial security to their customers.
- Other types of financial services institutions include finance companies, which provide small loans but do not accept deposits, and mutual funds, which provide a savings and investment vehicle for consumers. Also, some government agencies, such as the Department of the Treasury, sell bonds and Treasury bills for consumers to purchase as investments.

Life and health insurance companies are among the most important financial institutions in North America. In 1990, their assets totaled more than $1.5 trillion. As financial institutions, life and health insurers take some of the money that their customers pay in the form of premiums and invest in business and industry. The insurance industry has for many years been a leader in investing in social programs as well. Thus, investments made by insurers not only help provide funds that businesses need to operate and expand but also may help improve the quality of life. As shown in Figure 1-1, life and health insurers are among the most important sources of funds

Figure 1-1
Sources of funds in the U.S. money and capital markets, 1990.

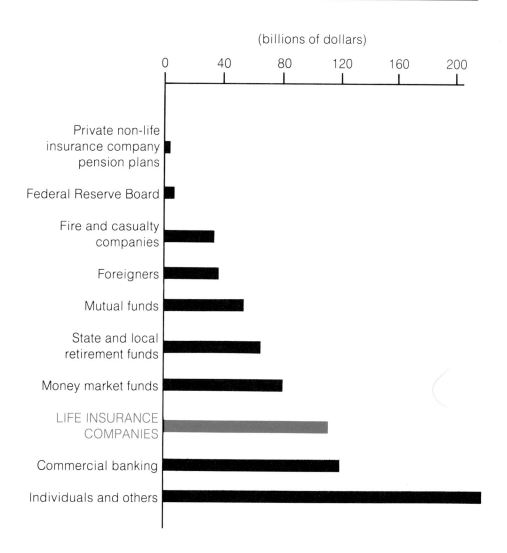

Source: 1991 Life Insurance Fact Book Update (Washington, D.C.: American Council of Life Insurance, 1991), p. 45.

used for economic growth. INSIGHT 1-1 provides some examples of socially responsible investing by insurers.

INSIGHT 1-1

Social Investing by Life Insurance Companies

Over the past few decades, an investment trend known as Socially Responsible Investing (SRI) has been catching the attention of investors, including life and health insurers. In the 1960s and 1970s, investors concerned about the Vietnam War avoided weapon systems manufacturers. In the 1970s, private investors, university endowment funds, and pension funds started demanding that, because of human rights issues, their investments should be pulled from companies with ties to South Africa. Today, the list of consumer concerns has expanded to include the environment and nuclear energy.

The idea of investing your values along with your money is not a new one. Church organizations in the 1920s refused to invest in "sin" stocks of alcohol, tobacco, and gambling-related securities.

However, people don't invest only for altruistic reasons; they invest for profit. By following standard investment principles that hold true for successful investing in almost any market, investors who characterize themselves as socially responsible are finding that they can have it all. As a result, SRI is becoming the fastest-growing investment market in the country.

Examples of social investing by life insurance companies are numerous:

- In 1991, Security Benefit began offering to purchasers of their Variflex Variable Annuity an opportunity to place the funds in a special Social Awareness Series of investments. The Series' objective is to seek high total returns with investments that meet certain social criteria established for the Series.

  The criteria include avoiding investments in any company that has economic ties to South Africa, engages in nuclear energy production, or has production practices that pollute the environment. The Series looks for companies that have fair and unbiased labor practices and that engage in proper use of natural resources.

- New York Life has invested $8.5 million over a four-year period to finance a partnership with IDEC Pharmaceuticals Corp. in LaJolla, California. The funds are used to study a particular type of therapy for AIDS-related complications.

- Insurers contributed heavily to health care and social programs in 1989, according to a recent report published by the life and health industry's Center for Corporate Public Involvement (CPI). The report, "Social Report of the Life and Health Insurance Business," says social investments by insurance companies for health care facilities topped $100 million in 1989. The "Social Report" defines social investments as project investments that would not otherwise be made under the estab-

lished lending standards of an insurance company, but which are considered for social reasons.
- Life and health companies deposited

$243 million in minority financial institutions, and invested $19 million in minority businesses in 1989.

Source: Adapted with permission from an Activity Report submitted to LOMA by Lisé White of Security Benefit Life, September 1991; "Insurance Industry's Social Contributions: A 'Remarkable' Record," *Council Review,* July 1989, p. 10; and "Current Trends," "Major Support Given to Programs in 1989," *Resource,* January 1991, p. 38.

Life and health insurers offer a wide range of insurance products. Products such as term life insurance, whole life insurance, universal life insurance, variable universal life insurance, medical expense insurance, disability income insurance, annuities, and group life and health insurance and retirement plans are designed to protect consumers from the risk of economic loss. Some of these products also help consumers save money for the future. In addition, some life and health insurers offer noninsurance products, such as mutual funds, designed to help people invest their money.

Throughout much of the twentieth century, life and health insurance companies operated in a fairly stable economy, and traditional insurance products reflect that economic stability. In periods of greater economic stability, level-premium whole life insurance policies were the most popular type of life insurance policies, and today they still represent a large portion of life insurance sales. *Level-premium whole life insurance policies* provide a specific amount of insurance protection for as long as the insured lives; a *level premium* remains the same for each year of the premium payment period.

As part of their pricing structure, whole life policies accumulate a *cash value,* which is the amount of money that an insurance company guarantees to the policyowner if the policyowner cancels the coverage and surrenders the policy to the insurance company.[2] Policyowners can borrow against the policy's cash value. The cash value accumulates because insurance companies invest a portion of the premiums that are received for whole life insurance policies. On these investments the companies earn *interest,* which is money that is paid for the use of money. Insurers guarantee that a portion of the policy's premium and a portion of the interest earnings will be used to fund the cash value of each policy.

Until the early 1970s, the interest rates that were guaranteed to policyowners on the cash values of their level-premium whole life policies were usually 3 to 5 percent. These interest rates were about the same that banks and savings and loan associations paid on their customers' accounts.

Therefore, a life insurance policy, through its cash value, provided a savings vehicle that could compete with the savings vehicles of other financial institutions. Such policies also gave insurance companies a predictable source of money that they could invest to earn more money both for themselves and their customers.

Changing Economic Conditions

In the early 1970s, economies around the world experienced a period of intense *inflation,* which is a condition of rising prices. This inflation eventually caused an increase in the cost of using money, and interest rates rose significantly. The increased inflation and rising interest rates of the 1970s challenged the competitiveness and profitability of level-premium whole life insurance products for several reasons.

First, because of the increased cost of living and doing business throughout the 1970s and early 1980s, insurance companies found that the cost of operating was reducing their profit margins. Salaries of employees rose. So did the cost of equipment and rent for office space. Unfortunately, most insurers were holding long-term investments that provided fixed rates of income which were not keeping up with inflation.

An insurance company of the 1960s, for example, would typically place its premium income in 20-year investments earning 6 to 8 percent interest each year. When inflation was no more than 2 or 3 percent per year and the interest rates guaranteed on a policy's cash value were 3 to 5 percent, insurance companies could operate successfully while earning 6 to 8 percent interest on their investments. However, when inflation rose and interest rates increased to 12, 15, or even 20 percent in the 1970s and early 1980s, insurance companies were still holding their 20-year investments that were now earning noncompetitive rates of interest. Of course, insurance companies began investing new income in higher-earning, shorter-term investments, but they still had billions of dollars in the older, long-term, relatively low-interest investments. Therefore, as the costs of operating an insurance company increased rapidly, the interest income earned by the company remained relatively stable.

Policy loans, policy surrenders, and disintermediation

As they found that they could earn 10 or 15 percent interest at other financial institutions, consumers began borrowing money from the cash values of their life insurance policies at the guaranteed policy-loan interest rate of 5 to 6 percent and depositing that money elsewhere to earn much higher interest (see Figure 1-2). To provide these 5 and 6 percent policy loans, insurance companies were forced to use money that they might otherwise have placed in high-yielding investments. In addition, because policy loans do not need to be repaid, companies' cash flows were affected adversely. By 1981, life and health insurers in the United States were investing 9.3 percent of their assets in policy loans; in comparison, the average percentage of U.S. life insurance company assets invested in policy loans from 1945 to 1985 was roughly 5.7 percent. In Canada, where insurance companies could adjust their policy-loan interest rates on policies issued after 1968, conditions were not quite as bad. Policy loans in Canada rose to just 5.2 percent of company assets.

Not only were policyowners borrowing money on the cash values of their whole life policies, they were also surrendering their policies. The surrender rate on insurance policies rose for two main reasons. First, inflation drove up the cost of living so much that many policyowners felt that they could no

Figure 1-2
U.S. rate of inflation vs. policy loans as a percentage of life and health insurance company assets, 1960-1990.

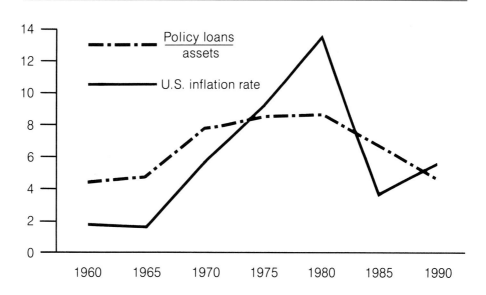

*The measure of inflation used is the yearly change in the Consumer Price Index (CPI).

Source: *Life Insurance Fact Book Update* (Washington, D.C.: American Council of Life Insurance, 1991), p. 44; *Statistical Abstract of the United States 1991*, p. 474.

longer afford life insurance; they needed the money to pay for day-to-day living expenses. Second, with other financial institutions offering significantly higher interest rates on customer deposits or investments, many policyowners decided that they should surrender their insurance policies, take the cash value, and put it into more profitable investments. This process of removing money from one financial intermediary in order to earn a higher yield somewhere else (generally with another financial intermediary) is called *disintermediation.*

Disintermediation, through policy loans or policy surrenders, became a major problem for life and health insurers throughout the 1970s and into the 1980s. In fact, in 1981, some life and health insurance companies found themselves in what was, for them, a new situation: rather than being lenders on the basis of their steady positive cash flow from premium income and interest on investments, many insurers became borrowers. Companies found that policy loans and surrenders were requiring them to pay out larger amounts of cash than were readily available. These insurers had plenty of assets, but only a small portion was in cash. Their assets were, for the most part, low-yielding, long-term investments that could be sold for cash only at a great loss, because the value of fixed-income investments decreases as interest rates increase. As a result, many companies had serious cash flow problems that led them to borrow money from other financial institutions in order to meet the demand for cash caused by policy loans and surrenders.

The rising cost of health care

The inflation that affected so many areas of the North American economy was also reflected in the rapidly increasing cost of health care. Between 1960 and 1990, the cost of health care in the United States rose from $27.1 billion to $666.2 billion per year (see Figure 1-3). The enormous increase in the cost of health care occurred for a number of reasons:

- More people are seeking health care now than sought it 30 years ago.
- Medical treatments are more extensive, sophisticated, and effective than ever before. The technology required for many of these treatments is extremely expensive, especially when the treatments are first introduced to the public.
- AIDS and its related diseases require expensive and often long-term treatment.
- The cost of training health care professionals, such as doctors, nurses, and laboratory technicians, is much greater than it was 30 years ago.
- Doctors and other health care professionals are increasing the charges

Figure 1-3
U.S. National Health Expenditure (N.H.E.) vs. N.H.E. as a percentage of
Gross National Product (GNP).

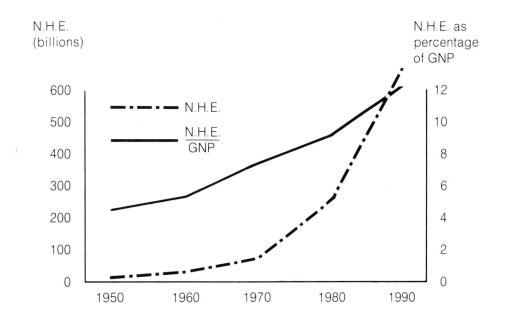

Source: U.S. Department of Health and Human Services, Health Care Financing
Administration.

for their services in order to pay greatly increased premiums for
malpractice insurance.
- People are living longer and thus need more health care.
- Little competition exists among health care providers. Therefore, the
marketplace does not place many restraints on health care costs.
- When a significant part of a person's medical expenses is paid by an
insurance company, neither the patient nor the health care provider
has much incentive to control costs.

For these reasons and many others, the cost of health care has risen steadily
and quickly for the last few decades. The costs have risen so much, in fact,
that consumers, health insurers, employers, and the federal government
frequently express an inability and unwillingness to continue to pay for such
high costs.

We have already examined one important aspect of an insurance company's environment: economic factors. Because noneconomic aspects of the environment change constantly as well, insurance companies that hope to succeed must anticipate and adapt to environmental changes. Among the other environmental factors to which insurance companies must respond are regulatory factors, population trends, and technological developments.

REGULATION OF FINANCIAL INSTITUTIONS

Until recently, the different kinds of financial institutions performed fairly distinct roles in the economy, and these roles were generally restricted by state, provincial, and federal laws. Regulations pertaining to the different kinds of financial institutions had, in effect, erected barriers that guaranteed that one kind of institution could not participate in activities that were specifically assigned to another kind of institution. Banks, for example, could not sell certain kinds of investment products that were offered by brokerage houses, and brokerage houses could not offer checking accounts. In most cases, neither banks nor brokerage houses could sell life insurance.

In Canada, the community of financial institutions was divided into the "four pillars"—banks, insurance companies, brokerage firms, and trust companies. The activities and responsibilities of each type of institution were clearly delineated, and legal restrictions separated the four pillars.

Since the middle 1970s, however, the regulatory barriers separating financial institutions have been breaking down, both in the United States and Canada. Inflation and rising interest rates helped hasten this breakdown in the United States. The crisis of disintermediation that struck the life insurance industry also struck other kinds of financial institutions. Particularly affected were depository institutions, such as banks and savings and loan associations, which were prohibited from offering savings accounts that earned more than 4 to 5.5 percent interest. These institutions found that depositors were withdrawing their money and investing it in money market funds that were earning much higher rates of interest.

Depository institutions began asking regulators for permission to offer products that could earn higher rates of interest and thereby allow them to compete with the investment institutions. In 1980, the Depository Institutions Deregulation and Monetary Control Act became law in the United States. Among other things, this act provided for the eventual removal of all interest ceilings on customer deposits in banks and other depository institutions. Then, in 1982, the Depository Institutions Deregulation

Committee voted to allow depository institutions to offer their customers money market accounts that were similar to and competitive with the money market funds being offered by investment institutions, such as brokerage firms.

As of 1991, the competitive relationships between depository institutions and insurance companies had not changed as much as the relationships between depository institutions and investment institutions. However, pressures to change these relationships continue. Some commercial banks were still interested in selling all kinds of insurance, including life and health insurance, and a few life and health insurers have expressed interest in offering the sorts of depository accounts and other services available in banks and other types of depository institutions.

In Canada, pressures to deregulate financial institutions have also been accumulating. In 1984, Quebec made it legal for insurers incorporated in that province to apply for licenses that would allow participation in stock brokerage and trust company activities. In addition, Canadian officials proposed establishing a new class of banks, called *Schedule C banks*, which could be owned by another corporation, such as an insurance company.

The distinctions that once separated financial institutions from one another are now less clear. What were once related but separate types of financial businesses could possibly become one integrated financial services industry. The pressures caused by an unpredictable economy, a movement toward less regulation, and advances in computer technology have forced all financial institutions to reconsider their primary economic roles and the means by which they serve their customers. Today, it is difficult to tell how the regulation of banks, insurance companies, and investment firms may change, but clearly these financial institutions are entering a new phase of their development.

Deregulation or Reregulation

The recent movement to deregulate more and more industries in the United States and Canada has advocates in both business and government. The primary argument for deregulation is that it can increase competition, which is considered essential in order for businesses to operate in their most efficient manner. Open competition, advocates of deregulation say, means that the companies best suited to provide services and products can provide them at the lowest prices and in the most convenient manner for consumers. Open competition weeds out the inefficient companies, leaving the best-qualified companies to provide products and services for the public. Prices then seek their own levels, and the economy tends to be more stable and healthy. Since the mid-1970s, these and other arguments have been used to advocate the continuing deregulation of the financial services industry as well as other industries.

On the other side of the regulation question are those people in business and government who say that financial institutions are too closely involved with the public trust to be left unregulated. Many of these advocates of regulation agree that financial institutions are changing and that past regulations are no longer adequate for controlling these evolving institutions. However, they believe that some regulation is still needed. In many cases, they assert that new regulations should be developed to meet the needs of the emerging financial services industry. They support these arguments by pointing to recent and well-publicized failures throughout the savings and loan segment of the financial services industry. Such failures occurred, say the advocates of reregulation, because (1) traditional regulations had become inadequate for today's sophisticated financial industry and (2) the institutions that failed competed so aggressively that they disregarded the caution required of institutions that hold the public's trust.

These opposing positions on regulation are widespread in the financial services industry. The types of compromises that will be made between these two positions and the shape of the financial services industry in years ahead are both ongoing issues.

REGULATION OF THE INSURANCE INDUSTRY

Each type of financial institution is subject to specific regulation. The functions that the life and health insurance industry performs—providing consumers with protection against economic loss and offering consumers opportunities to save and invest money—have placed the industry in a special position of public trust. Thus, insurance regulation has two primary goals: (1) to assure that insurance companies remain solvent and can pay their debts and claims when they come due and (2) to assure that insurance companies treat consumers fairly and ethically.

Insurance Regulation in the United States

Insurance regulation began in the United States more than 140 years ago when, in 1851, New Hampshire became the first state to establish a full-time board of insurance commissioners. The purpose of this board was to examine the activities of life insurance companies. Other states soon followed this lead, and in 1858, Elizur Wright, generally considered the first important figure in American life insurance, became Massachusetts insurance commissioner. During Wright's tenure, Massachusetts passed a number of laws to guarantee the ethical and sound financial operation of insurance companies.

Landmark regulatory decisions

In 1869, the U.S. Supreme Court made a landmark decision affecting the regulation of insurance. An agent in Virginia, Samuel B. Paul, had challenged the right of Virginia to require the licensing of insurance agents. His contention was that, under the federal constitution, commerce among the states was subject to regulation by Congress, not by the states. In its ruling on the case, *Paul v. Virginia,* the Supreme Court stated that an insurance policy was a contract of indemnity, not a transaction in commerce. Therefore, an insurance policy was not subject to federal regulation. This decision affirmed the role of the states as the source of all insurance regulation, a view that held until 1944.

In 1944, in the case of *United States v. South-Eastern Underwriters Association,* the Supreme Court reversed its earlier decision. In this case, the court stated that insurance is, in fact, commerce and that insurance business conducted across state lines is interstate commerce, subject to federal regulations.

This new decision posed major problems for the insurance industry, because it cast doubt on all the state insurance laws that had been enacted up to that time. Because no federal insurance laws existed, invalidation of the state statutes would have left much of the industry unregulated.

To remedy this situation, Congress passed legislation in 1945 that is now generally known as the McCarran-Ferguson Act. This act declared that the regulation of insurance by the states was in the public interest and that silence by Congress regarding insurance legislation should not be regarded as a barrier to state regulation. Insurance regulation was left to the states as long as Congress considered state regulation to be adequate. Although life and health insurance companies continue to be regulated by the states under the umbrella of the McCarran-Ferguson Act, Congress has retained the right to enact legislation if it feels that state regulation is inadequate or not in the public interest. Repeal of the McCarran-Ferguson Act is also discussed from time to time by government and insurance industry analysts.

State insurance departments

The state regulatory structure calls for an insurance department in each state. These state insurance departments, directed by insurance commissioners or state superintendents, hold the primary legal authority over insurance company operations. Among their responsibilities, state insurance departments

- issue certificates and licenses authorizing insurance companies to operate in the state
- license agents to sell insurance and revoke licenses when warranted
- review the Annual Statements of insurance companies
- assure that policy forms include the required provisions and are printed in the proper format
- make on-site examinations of insurance companies
- maintain an office for receiving and acting on consumer complaints
- ensure that insurance companies observe rules affecting policy reserve maintenance and investment activities

The National Association of Insurance Commissioners (NAIC)

The *National Association of Insurance Commissioners (NAIC)* is a nongovernmental organization that has an important influence on insurance regulation. The NAIC tries to foster uniformity in state regulation and cooperation among state insurance departments by developing model bills and regulations on which states may base their insurance legislation. Although the NAIC has no regulatory authority, the recommendations of the NAIC and the actions taken at its meetings carry great weight with state insurance commissioners, state legislatures, and the insurance industry.

For example, in 1988, an NAIC committee was formed to identify a minimum standard for state financial regulation of insurers. As a result of the committee's work, the association adopted the NAIC Financial Regulation Standards in September 1989. The standards provide a basic outline of the minimum levels of resources and authority each regulatory jurisdiction needs to have in place for effective solvency regulation. Building upon those standards, the NAIC adopted in June 1990 the Financial Regulation Standards and Accreditation Program. The program is designed both to implement a system of peer review and to encourage compliance with the standards.

The zone system for company examinations. The NAIC has also established a zone system for examining insurance companies that operate in more than one state. This system was developed because if each insurance department were to examine every insurer in the state, some insurance companies could be examined by dozens of states during the same period. In order to eliminate this duplication of effort and to reduce the workload of state insurance departments, the NAIC developed the zone system of examination.

Figure 1-4
Map of the four NAIC zones.

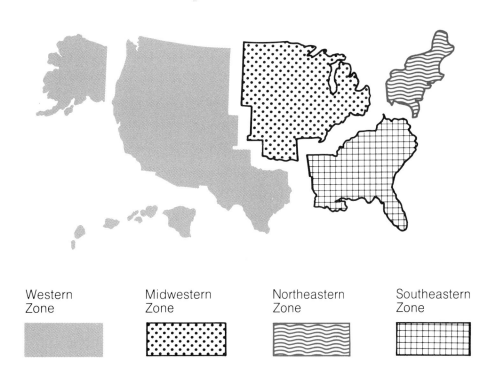

| Western Zone | Midwestern Zone | Northeastern Zone | Southeastern Zone |

Source: National Association of Insurance Commissioners.

Under this system, the United States is divided into four zones (see Figure 1-4). Each zone has a pool of insurance examiners, supplied by the insurance departments of the states within that zone. Each insurance company that has its home office in the zone is examined by one or more examiners from the state of domicile. Examiners from other states in the zone may also participate. The examiner-in-charge is from the company's home state.

If the company receives as much as $1 million in premiums or 20 percent of its total premiums from another zone, that zone can assign an examiner, known as a *zone examiner,* to the examination team. Zone examiners serve two major functions: (1) They provide the commissioners outside the home zone with an independent check on the quality of the examination, and (2) they provide the examination team with information about the regulations of the states outside the home zone.

An insurance company is typically examined every three to five years. The examination can take from three to six months or, in the case of a very large company, a year or more. The examiner-in-charge has wide discretion in conducting the examination. Obviously, the examiners cannot review every transaction that has occurred since the last examination. Areas of concentration are determined by the examiner-in-charge, and statistical sampling and computer audit techniques are utilized in appropriate areas. Because audits by certified public accountants are now required for most insurers, their work is taken into consideration in planning the examination. Actuaries or actuarial examiners generally participate when their expertise is required.

When the examination is completed, the examiner-in-charge, in consultation with the zone examiners, drafts a written report. Zone examiners record their concurrence by signing the report. The examiner-in-charge then submits the report to the insurance commissioner of the company's home state. At that time, the company has an opportunity to review the draft report. If company management and the examiner-in-charge have different opinions about statements or recommendations made in the report, the home-state commissioner holds hearings and determines whether changes to the report are appropriate. The final report is then adopted by the commissioner and becomes a matter of public record.

The Securities and Exchange Commission (SEC)

The *Securities and Exchange Commission (SEC)* is charged with regulating the marketing of investment products. Life and health insurers that sell products with qualities of investment products as well as of insurance products are subject to regulation by the SEC. For example, to a certain extent the SEC regulates companies that market ***investment-based life insurance products***—those in which the cash value and benefit level can fluctuate according to the insurer's investment earnings and in which policyowners accept the risk of sharing in the insurer's investment gains and losses. Only insurance agents who are SEC-certified as well as state-licensed can sell these products. Such products, sometimes called *nonguaranteed products*, include variable annuities, variable life insurance, and variable universal life insurance. Through its various reporting requirements, the SEC also affects the operations of publicly held stock companies.

The Internal Revenue Service (IRS)

The *Internal Revenue Service (IRS)* has no legislative power over insurance companies. However, through its interpretation and administration of the

Internal Revenue Code, the IRS significantly influences the way in which insurance companies do business. Both individual taxation and corporate taxation affect the types of products a company markets, the investment strategies it uses, and the corporate structure it establishes.

Insurance Regulation in Canada

The primary areas of Canadian insurance regulation parallel many of those found in the United States. These areas include registration of companies, licensing of agents, filing of Annual Statements, and examination of companies. The major difference is that in Canada the regulations are handled by both the federal government and the provincial governments, with the federal government taking a more direct role than in the United States.

In 1867, the confederation of the four provinces of Ontario, Quebec, New Brunswick, and Nova Scotia formed the Dominion of Canada. Modern Canadian insurance regulation dates from that time. In 1868, the first federal Insurance Act provided that companies could be registered with the federal government's Minister of Finance in Ottawa, Ontario. Federally registered companies were required to deposit funds with the ministry as reserves and submit annual reports on company operations. Federal incorporation, however, was not required. A Canadian company could—and still can— choose to operate without federal incorporation. An insurer can incorporate in any of the provinces in which it chooses to operate. Today, however, most Canadian insurance companies are federally incorporated and are licensed to do business in all provinces.

In 1932, a period of disputes between the provinces and the federal government in Canada ended with a Privy Council decision that most operational jurisdiction over insurance companies would rest with the provinces. Today, Canadian federal insurance laws are primarily concerned with company solvency. The provinces have jurisdiction over the terms of insurance policies, the rights of policyowners and beneficiaries, and the licensing of agents.

Current federal and provincial regulation

In order to do business in Canada, federally incorporated insurers are required to obtain from the Minister of Finance a certificate of registry. Although provincially incorporated insurers are not required to register, they may obtain a certificate of registry. Most of these insurers are, in fact, federally registered.

The federal government in Canada has the primary responsibility for ensuring the financial stability of both federally registered and provincially registered insurers. Federally registered insurers, which make up the majority of insurance companies in Canada, are required by law to

- register each year with the Office of the Superintendent of Financial Institutions (OSFI)
- submit to the OSFI an Annual Statement, which presents the company's assets and liabilities as of year's end and the company's income and expenditures during the year
- file with the OSFI a semiannual statement, the *movement of securities return,* which details transactions involving securities and loans made during the previous six months
- be examined by the OSFI at least once every three years to verify compliance with federal insurance statutes

The provincial insurance departments are responsible for licensing insurance companies and their agents, enforcing provincial insurance laws relating to policy contracts, and approving promotional material for the sale of equity-based insurance products. Canadian companies' marketing of equity-based products is supervised by the provincial insurance departments, and companies that want to sell investment funds can do so only with the approval of the provincial securities commissions.

Each provincial insurance department also has complete responsibility for examining those companies that are not federally registered. The federal government has agreed to supervise companies incorporated by some of the smaller provinces that do not have the resources to supervise insurers adequately. The provinces generally retain the right, however, to supervise the operations of any insurer that operates within the province. The provincial superintendents require only a short form of the Annual Statement from federally registered companies.

The Canadian Council of Insurance Regulators

The *Canadian Council of Insurance Regulators (CCIR)* in Canada, formerly known as the Association of Superintendents of Insurance, is similar to the NAIC in the United States. The CCIR develops model insurance legislation that it encourages provincial legislatures to adopt. Its efforts help make insurance regulations uniform in the common law provinces, which are those provinces with laws based on English common law. All Canadian provinces except Quebec are common law provinces. Quebec law is based not on English common law, but on the old French Civil Code. Consequently, basic insurance laws in Quebec have differed from those in the rest of

Canada but, since 1977, the Quebec Insurance Act has brought Quebec insurance law closer to the insurance statutes of the other provinces.

CHANGING POPULATIONS AND THEIR INSURANCE NEEDS

Many changes have occurred in the populations of the United States and Canada during the past 25 years:

- The average age of the two nations' populations is higher now than it was 25 years ago.
- A larger percentage of families is headed by single parents, many of whom are working women.
- Families tend to be smaller than they were 25 years ago, and in many families, both parents work outside the home.
- A larger percentage of people in each country has a college or university education.

Because of these types of changes, insurance companies must continually reevaluate their customers' changing needs and design new products to meet those needs, as INSIGHT 1-2 shows.

INSIGHT 1-2

Insurers React to Demographic Change

One of the major challenges facing the life insurance industry of the 1990s involves adjusting to changing demographics. How the industry responds to changes in life expectancy, as well as social and cultural norms and values will shape the success of the industry in the twenty-first century.

In the United States, Canada, and other affluent countries, the average life span is increasing. Clearly, this change modifies the population's needs for financial products and thus profoundly affects the insurance industry.

A young population traditionally has asked, "How will I be able to provide for my family if I die?" or "How will I pay the hospital bills if my children are sick?" When people live longer, these questions do not disappear; instead, new questions are raised as a result of new needs. Now the questions include, "How can I prepare for my retirement?" or, "If I am in a nursing home for an extended period of time, how can I ensure that my family will not be financially devastated?"

As a result of the general aging of the

population, analysts predict significant growth in sales for retirement income, annuities, and long-term-care products. Further new products that serve these same needs are already emerging.

Insurance companies are starting to invest more dollars in developing products for nursing home care, custodial care, and long-term-care insurance. Systems will have to be able to adapt rapidly to the changing products and not restrict their introductions because of administrative limitations.

Social and cultural issues will also affect the insurance market of the '90s. Affluent family units are becoming smaller, while poor families continue to have a larger number of children. The result is a delineation of family sizes along income lines. The result for the insurance industry means promoting different products for "haves" and "have-nots."

Pensions are another growing area of concern. In an effort to reduce expenses, businesses have been paring back elaborate defined-benefit or defined-contribution pension plans offered to all employees. At the same time, reduced employee loyalty to a given employer is encouraging increased job-hopping, resulting in the forfeiture of most or all accrued pension benefits. This could lead to the mandating of portable pension plans. In the United States, the Social Security system must soon deal with the large, aging "baby boom" generation, which will be followed by a small "baby bust" generation responsible for footing the bill for the boomers' benefits. Although Social Security benefits will continue, in one form or another, the need for supplemental products for those who can afford to buy them will grow.

Another major demographic change is the growing number of single people. Products need to be made available in units of one, not just packaged in familylike units or conditions. For example, many single women want and need maternity benefits— a product that was, at one time, available only to married women. Disability income insurance for working women came about when the assumption was dispelled that all women are cared for by their husbands. Joint mortgage protection products are needed by co-owners of homes, whether or not these co-owners are married.

Women continue as a growing force in the workplace, with the issue of child care becoming correspondingly more pressing as a result. Cafeteria plans are growing in popularity with employers, and one of the future growth areas for benefits is child care.

Source: Adapted with permission of the publisher from Gary W. Neace, "Insurance Directions into the 1990s," Resource, July 1990, pp. 37-38; and Sara Carlin, "The Future of Health Care," Resource, February 1991, p. 10.

Maturing Population

In 1970, the median age of the U.S. population was 28.0 years— that is, as many people were over age 28 as were under age 28. In 1990, the median age was 32.7 years. Between 1990 and 2000, the 45- to 54-year-old age group is expected to increase by 46 percent, while the number of people age 25-34 is expected to decrease by 15 percent. Comparable changes are occurring in the Canadian population.

This steady maturing of the population in the United States and Canada creates several opportunities for insurance companies. A growing proportion of the population consists of people between the ages of 35 and 54. These people generally have families, careers, and significant financial responsibilities. To protect their families and expanding financial resources, these people are more likely than others to purchase life and health insurance. Therefore, this age group is an ideal market for insurance and other financial products.

Changes in the death rate

The death rate of people who are 50 to 70 years old has been steadily decreasing. Many people in this age group are less concerned about dying unexpectedly than they are about living longer than their present incomes can support them. Therefore, this age group is usually less interested in buying life insurance. Their children are grown, their houses may be paid for, and they have fewer concerns about the economic losses caused by unexpected death. However, these people are becoming more interested in guaranteeing that they have enough money to live adequately in their later years.

To respond to this need, insurance companies are developing more products that are intended to provide individuals with the income they need to live comfortably long after they retire. For example, insurance companies are providing many types of annuities that may be used in retirement plans, such as Individual Retirement Accounts (IRAs) and Keogh plans in the United States and Registered Retirement Savings Plans (RRSPs) in Canada. Insurers are also interested in this market because people between the ages of 50 and 70 typically have more disposable income than other age groups. Such income can be used to purchase annuities and other products that can, for example, provide funds for the education of children and grandchildren.

Another effect of the declining death rate among older people is a decrease in the cost of life insurance. The cost of life insurance is based in part on the death rate, called the ***mortality rate,*** which is the frequency with which death occurs among a defined group of people. As the mortality rate declines among insureds, insurance companies receive fewer claims, and more insureds are alive for longer periods of time to pay for the cost of insurance. Therefore, the cost of insurance can be reduced, thus making it more attractive and more affordable to a larger number of people.

The Changing Family

In the 1950s and 1960s, most families in the United States and Canada included a husband who worked full-time outside the home and a wife who stayed at home raising children and managing the household. By the early 1990s, only a small percentage of families matched that description. The family is changing in many ways, and these changes affect the types of life and health insurance products that are required to cover families' needs.

Growing divorce rate

It is estimated that half of all marriages entered into after 1985 will end in divorce. In Canada, one out of three first marriages and one out of four succeeding marriages end in divorce. Divorce often disrupts a family's financial condition because the divorced man and woman must often economize in order to maintain separate households. Many things that the couple formerly owned in common must be sold and the cash divided in order to assure a financially equitable divorce. Quite often under these circumstances, life insurance policies are surrendered or allowed to lapse, even though the need for insurance still exists. Thus, an increasing divorce rate can significantly affect insurance companies' sales and persistency rates.

Women and the changing family structure

More women are in the work force than ever before. In fact, women made up 45 percent of the employed labor force in the United States in 1990 (see Figure 1-5). As a result, an increased number of families are likely to have two incomes. Because planning a family budget and allocating two incomes is complicated, families now are more concerned with financial planning and management, which makes them likely insurance customers. Two-income families need protection for both wage-earners—the wife as well as the husband—and some life and health insurers have developed joint life insurance products specifically for these families.

The increase in the number of working women, coupled with the high divorce rate discussed earlier, also means that an increased number of families have a woman as the sole head of the household. In fact, almost one-third of all households in the United States were headed by women in 1990. These women, too, represent a growing market for insurance products.

Figure 1-5
Percentage of men and women in the employed civilian labor force, 1960-1990.

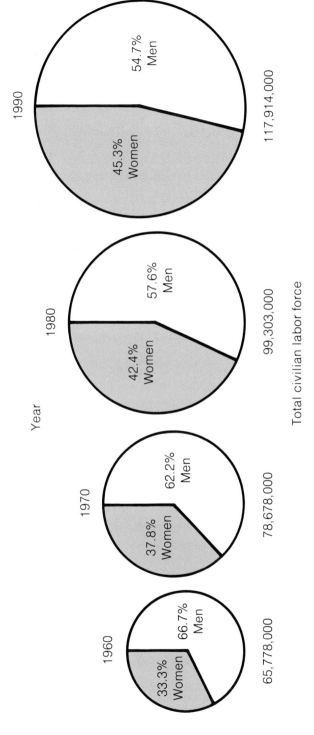

1990
54.7% Men
45.3% Women
117,914,000

1980
57.6% Men
42.4% Women
99,303,000

1970
62.2% Men
37.8% Women
78,678,000

1960
66.7% Men
33.3% Women
65,778,000

Year

Total civilian labor force

Source: Statistical Abstract of the United States 1991.

More Affluent and Knowledgeable Consumers

As a whole, the populations of the United States and Canada have achieved higher levels of education than ever before. Typically, well-educated people tend to have higher-paying jobs than do members of the population as a whole. People with higher incomes and more formal education are likely to recognize their need for financial security and take the necessary steps to obtain that security. These consumers want sophisticated products to satisfy their need for security and are willing to shop around for the best insurance products that they can find. They are also willing to exchange their current insurance products for products that appear to provide better value.

In many cases, therefore, insurance companies are now faced with a more affluent and knowledgeable consumer who expects insurance products to be flexible enough to meet a variety of needs and inexpensive enough to provide for those needs at a reasonable cost. Inexpensive term life insurance, cash management accounts, and investment-based insurance products are just a few of the financial products that insurance companies provide for such consumers.

Changing attitudes and consumerism

As consumers have become more knowledgeable about their financial needs and about insurance, they have started to demand more from the insurance industry. Also, in the wake of serious problems experienced in the savings and loan industry in the United States and losses in the junk bond and real estate markets during the late 1980s and early 1990s, consumers have become increasingly concerned about the stability of all companies in the financial services industry, including insurance companies.

In response to such concerns, insurance companies and regulatory agencies have tried to anticipate and address consumers' needs. Insurance companies now develop policy documents that are easier to read and understand. Insurers also provide their agents with ongoing training, which is required in many jursidictions. Many insurance companies are emphasizing quality throughout their organization and focusing on excellent customer service to assure that questions are answered quickly and correctly and that appropriate action is taken on customer requests. The state and provincial insurance departments that regulate the insurance industry have established consumer "hotlines," which insurance customers can call to register complaints and ask questions about insurance policies, prices, and procedures.

In addition, both the American Council of Life Insurance (ACLI) and the Canadian Life and Health Insurance Association (CLHIA) provide consumers with insurance industry information. Rating agencies such as the A.M. Best Company publish, among other things, an annual rating of insurance companies in the United States and Canada. Other rating agencies include Moody's Investor Services and Standard & Poor's. Consumer advocacy groups also have private services that rate insurers according to such criteria as premiums charged, dividends paid, and number of complaints filed against specific companies.

TECHNOLOGICAL CHANGES

Because of the ongoing revolution in computer technology, the age we live in is often referred to as the *Age of Information*. Computers continue to change the way that people work and manage their lives. Our complex systems of credit cards and automated teller machines could not operate without computers. Insurance companies could not offer many of their newer products without computers, nor could they provide quick and adequate service to their customers. Insurers could not plan timely investments or handle their complex accounting systems without computers.

More information is being exchanged in business than ever before, and insurance companies have a high demand for fast and accurate information transfer. Through office automation and data communication systems, insurance companies are establishing networks that (1) transmit information quickly within the company, from one department to another; (2) allow insurance agents and employees in regional offices to exchange information immediately with the home office, even if the home office is thousands of miles away; and (3) allow policyowners to receive information about their policies immediately or within a very short time.

Computer technology today is far more powerful, more accessible, and less expensive than ever before, and it changes how insurance companies operate. These changes will be described more fully throughout this book, particularly in Chapter 16, where information systems are discussed.

RESPONDING TO CHANGES AND CHALLENGES

Life and health insurers have taken a number of innovative steps to meet the challenges posed by changing environmental factors. In response to this changing environment, insurers are changing the products offered, reorganizing company operations, marketing products more effectively and in a more focused manner, using advanced technologies, and undertaking new business ventures. These responses to change are subjects discussed here and throughout this book.

Changing Life Insurance Products

Fixed-benefit, fixed-premium policies, which guarantee specific interest rates or cash values, lost their appeal for many consumers during the 1970s and early 1980s. However, insurers could not simply increase the interest-rate guarantees in their cash value products unless they could be certain of earning those increased rates of interest in the future. The answer for many insurers included developing new insurance products, modifying current products, and enhancing in-force policies.

Offering new products

Most of the new products introduced since the late 1970s shift investment risk from the insurer to the policyowner. In this way, an insurer can provide competitive interest-rate earnings when its investments are doing well. On the other hand, an insurer is not committed to offer such returns when investment experience is less favorable. This strategy protects the company from losses and allows policyowners to realize improvements in investment income. In most cases, insurers still offer some minimum interest-rate guarantees in these contracts, but these guarantees are far below the rates that are paid initially. For example, an insurer might sell an insurance contract based on current earnings of 10 percent interest but guarantee only that interest earnings will never drop below 4.5 percent.

In addition to providing the opportunity for potentially higher investment returns, some life insurance products now allow policyowners to change the premium amount or projected death benefit of their policies. In this way, an in-force policy can be adapted to the policyowner's changing financial circumstances. Canceling the policy and purchasing a new one to meet new needs is often not necessary.

One of the products that insurers developed in the late 1970s to meet the needs created by the changing interest rate environment was universal life insurance. *Universal life insurance* provides for variable interest-rate assumptions and flexibility in the premium amounts and death benefits. From 1977, when it was first introduced, to 1990, universal life insurance grew to represent almost 20 percent of all whole life insurance in force in the United States.

Other products designed to give policyowners more flexibility and investment income include adjustable life insurance, variable life insurance, and variable universal life insurance.

Modifying current products

Besides designing new products to meet the economic challenges of the 1970s and 1980s, insurers have also modified traditional cash-value products to overcome the problems associated with fluctuating interest rates. For example, in some of these revised whole life policies, insurers specify a guaranteed maximum premium rate and charge a lower rate as long as their investment returns remain above a certain level. This type of plan is generally called an *indeterminate premium plan*. In addition, to counteract disintermediation, insurers in the United States began to include a varying policy loan interest rate in their whole life policies, much as Canadian insurers have included in their policies. In this way, insurers can let their policy loan interest rates fluctuate according to the prevailing interest rates in the economy. Also, tax laws that do not allow a deduction for interest paid on a policy loan discourage such loan activity.

Enhancing in-force policies

By developing new products and modifying the structure of others, insurance companies have answered some of the concerns that consumers expressed about life insurance products. However, such actions do not affect policies that are already in force. Therefore, some insurers have enhanced or updated in-force policies in order to keep policyowners from surrendering these policies or allowing them to lapse. For example, some insurers allow policyowners to increase the death benefit of their in-force policies without having to pay a higher premium rate. In this way, insurers can make in-force policies more attractive to their owners. In addition, companies that offer participating policies can increase their dividend rates on in-force policies, thereby reducing policyowners' total premium outlay on level-premium policies and staying competitive with newer, more cost-efficient policies.

Responding to Rising Health Care Costs

As a result of the expressed concerns of consumers, health insurers, employers, and government, a number of steps are now being taken to control the cost of health care. Insurers are among the leaders in proposing ways to control costs.

Among other approaches, insurance companies are (1) urging employers to promote "wellness" programs for their employees, thus preventing potential health problems; (2) paying insurance benefits for at-home health care to reduce hospital expenses; (3) requiring second opinions on certain types of nonemergency surgery, thereby avoiding some surgery that may be unnecessary; and (4) paying the full cost of outpatient surgery to discourage unnecessary hospital stays.

Health maintenance organizations (HMOs), which first appeared in the United States in the 1930s but received federal sponsorship in the 1970s, are considered one way to contain health care costs. ***Health maintenance organizations*** provide comprehensive health care services for people in a specified geographic area; people enrolled in an HMO pay fixed, periodic dues in return for the right to health care services. At some HMOs, a fixed fee per visit is also charged. HMOs place great emphasis on maintaining the good health of their members, thereby controlling health care costs by preventing illness. Many routine preventive procedures, such as annual checkups, are provided for HMO members at little or no cost. HMOs have a strong economic incentive to reduce costs and keep their members healthy because these organizations receive a fixed income regardless of the services rendered. Many insurance companies have now established or own HMOs, as well as preferred provider organizations.

A ***preferred provider organization (PPO)*** is a group of hospitals and physicians that contract with employers, insurers, and other organizations to provide comprehensive health care services for individuals at discounted fees. By negotiating with organizations for contracts, PPOs add a competitive element to providing health care services. Proponents of PPOs believe that competition will help control health care costs.

Reorganizing Company Operations

Life and health insurance companies are taking a number of steps to ensure that they remain vital and successful in a changing environment. We will mention here a few organizational changes that insurers are making. More changes will be discussed in later chapters.

Increased emphasis on employee authority and responsibility

For years, many insurance companies operated with a centralized organizational structure that provided numerous levels of slightly increasing supervision and authority. Most suggestions had to go through a number of different levels of authority before receiving final approval. This structure made detecting possible problems or errors more likely, but it also tended to slow the decision-making process. In addition, the authority to make decisions was moved away from the people who were most directly affected by those decisions.

Today, more companies are organized with fewer levels of supervision. Increased authority and responsibility have been given to the people most directly involved with any particular activity. Companies believe that such a decentralized structure

- results in quicker and better decisions
- enhances quality because employees have an increased sense of personal accountability
- helps make their employees more satisfied and productive
- improves internal communication
- improves competitiveness by reducing the cost of supporting several layers of management

With a more productive staff, companies can become more responsive to changes in the economy and to the needs of their customers.

Subcontracting of services

In their quest to operate more efficiently, some insurance companies have found that they can reduce their operating costs, and thus the cost of their products, if they do not try to do all the work themselves. For example, instead of administering its own claims, an insurance company may find that hiring an outside organization that specializes in claim administration is more cost-effective. Similarly, an insurance company may hire an outside organization to underwrite policies, design products, or manage investments.

Changing methods of distribution

Insurance companies are always looking for more effective ways to market their products. For example, instead of training their sales personnel to sell all products to all of their clients, some companies use specific distribution systems to sell certain products to certain types of customers. Insurance distribution systems are discussed in Chapters 4, 5, and 6 of this text.

KEY TERMS

level-premium whole life insurance
   policy
level premium
cash value
interest
inflation
disintermediation

investment-based life insurance product
mortality rate
universal life insurance
health maintenance organization
   (HMO)
preferred provider organization (PPO)

NOTES

1. David S. Kidwell and Richard L. Peterson, *Financial Institutions, Markets, and Money*, 4th ed. (Chicago: Dryden Press, 1990).
2. In the United States, the cash value is also paid to a policyowner who allows a whole life policy to lapse.

If you are reading this book to prepare for an FLMI examination, you will want to reinforce your knowledge of the material in this chapter by using LOMA-published study aids. Consult the current LOMA Insurance Education Catalog for a list of the currently offered study aids that accompany this text. (For a description of the types of LOMA study aids provided, see page xxvii of this text.) ***Studies have indicated that students who use LOMA study aids consistently perform significantly better on FLMI Program examinations.***

Chapter 2

Formation of Life and Health Insurance Companies

After reading this chapter, you should be able to

- Describe the differences between a stock insurance company and a mutual insurance company
- Explain which form of business—a sole proprietorship, a partnership, or a corporation—is the most appropriate for an insurer
- Compare the procedures for establishing an insurance company in the United States and Canada
- Give reasons why an insurance company would mutualize or demutualize
- Describe the differences between mergers and acquisitions
- Distinguish between a conglomerate, a spin-off, a holding company, and a subsidiary
- Define *strategic alliance* and give some reasons an insurer enters into one
- Identify organizations other than stock and mutual life insurance companies that can sell life insurance products

As is the case with most organizations engaged in commerce, an insurance company must first legally establish itself as a business before it can begin selling its products. In this chapter, we will study the two basic forms of life and health insurance companies: stocks and mutuals. We will look at how each form is established, how stocks and mutuals differ from each other, and how and why insurance companies change from one form to the other. We will then learn how insurers as corporate entities merge with, acquire, hold, and form alliances with other companies. Finally, we will describe some organizations other than stock and mutual insurers that can provide life insurance.

STOCKS AND MUTUALS

The two most common types of commercial insurance companies are stock companies and mutual companies. A **stock insurance company** is owned by people who purchase shares of the company's **stock,** which represents ownership in a company. The owners of stock, called **stockholders** or *shareholders*, are eligible to receive a portion of the company's earnings through periodic payments known as **dividends.** The price of a company's stock can also rise or fall, resulting in capital gains or losses for a stockholder when the stock is sold.

Certain stockholders, called *common stockholders*, vote on company affairs and are ordinarily granted one vote per share of stock. Common stockholders elect the company's directors and influence company operations by voting on matters of company policy. Normally, however, common stockholders are not involved in day-to-day operations; such operations are controlled by company executives who are appointed by the board of directors. Another class of stockholders is known as *preferred stockholders*. Preferred stockholders must be paid their dividends before common stockholders are paid theirs, but preferred stockholders generally do not have voting rights regarding the company's directors or company policy.

In a **mutual insurance company,** the policyowners are the owners of the company, and they theoretically control the company. Mutual companies do not issue stock and thus do not have stockholders. However, each policyowner in a mutual company is eligible to vote in elections of the company's board of directors on the basis of one vote for each policyowner, regardless of the amount of insurance or the number of insurance policies that the policyowner owns. As in a stock company, executives appointed by a board of directors control a mutual company's day-to-day operations.

Participating and Nonparticipating Policies

All mutual and some stock companies in the United States issue a type of insurance policy called a **participating policy,** also called a *par policy*, under which the policyowner shares in the insurance company's surplus. **Surplus** is the amount by which a life insurance company's assets exceed its liabilities and capital. **Capital** is the amount of money invested in a company by its owners or stockholders.

The amount of surplus that is available for distribution to policyowners is called the **divisible surplus.** A policyowner's share of the divisible surplus is called a **policy dividend** and is payable to owners of participating policies at the end of the policy year. The policy dividend is considered a return of part of the premiums that these policyowners paid to keep their policies in force for that year. Policy dividends should not be confused with the stock dividends paid to a stock company's shareholders. Stock dividends are available only from a stock company and are payable only to holders of the company's stock.

Most of the policies sold by stock companies in the United States are **nonparticipating policies,** also called *nonpar policies,* under which the policyowner does not share in company surplus. However, some stock companies do offer participating policies and, in rare instances, a mutual company can sell nonpar policies along with its par policies. In some states, mutual companies can offer only participating policies.

Canadian companies, whether stock or mutual, tend to offer both par and nonpar policies. For a Canadian stock company to sell participating policies, at least one-third of the directors must be elected by participating policyowners. If only nonparticipating policies are sold, the company's charter may provide for directors to be elected by the policyowners or by designated classes of policyowners. Some stock companies in the United States have revised their charters to permit policyowners to elect a certain number of directors. Generally, however, policyowners can elect only a minority of a stock company's board of directors.

Proportion of Stock Companies to Mutual Companies

Most newly formed life and health insurance companies in the United States and Canada take the form of stock companies, primarily because stock companies are easier to establish than are mutual companies. The founders of a stock company can raise the money needed to establish the company by selling shares of stock in the firm that is being created. After the company has started doing business, additional funds can be raised by selling more shares in the company. Organization as a stock company also makes mergers easier because one company can easily buy the stock of another.

On the other hand, to establish a mutual insurance company, the company's organizers must find a specific number of people who are willing to submit an application and pay the first premium to a company that does not yet legally exist. Finding investors who are willing to purchase stock is much easier and more practical.

At the end of 1990, there were 2,270 life and health insurance companies in the United States. Of these, 2,153, or 95 percent, were stock companies, while 117 companies were mutuals. Mutual companies, however, held 45 percent of the assets of all U.S. life and health insurance companies, while stock companies held 55 percent of the assets. Figure 2-1 compares the

Figure 2-1
Percent of assets and in-force insurance held by mutual and stock life and
health insurance companies in the United States in 1990.

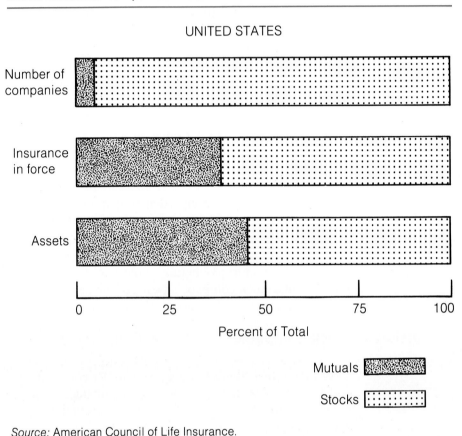

Source: American Council of Life Insurance.

number of mutual and stock companies in the United States and the amount
of assets held by each type of company. Figure 2-2 provides the same
information for Canada. The reason that the small percentage of mutual
companies holds a disproportionate share of the assets is that the average
mutual company is far older than the average stock company. For example,
in 1989, 70 percent of stock companies had been in business less than 25
years. In contrast, 21 percent of U.S. mutuals had been in business over 100
years. Older companies that have done business for 100-plus years have had
time to accumulate more assets than younger insurance companies.

Of the 163 life insurance companies operating in Canada at the end of
1990, 123 were stock companies, and 40 were mutual companies. Canada has
a higher proportion of mutuals to stocks than the United States because of a
1957 amendment to the federal Canadian and British Insurance Companies
Act. This amendment provided a specific procedure for *mutualization,* which
is the process of changing a stock company to a mutual company. With the

Figure 2-2
Percent of assets and in-force insurance held by mutual and stock life and health insurance companies in Canada in 1990.

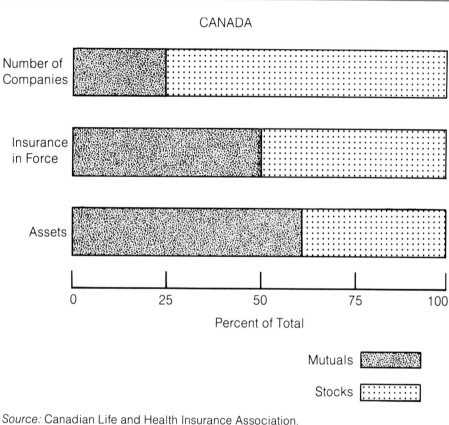

Source: Canadian Life and Health Insurance Association.

passage of the 1957 amendment, Canadian stock companies were encouraged to become mutual companies in order to avoid takeover by foreign firms. A mutual company that has no stock to sell cannot be bought by another company as a stock company can. Through mutualization, many Canadian companies have successfully avoided takeovers.

THE STRUCTURE OF LIFE AND HEALTH INSURANCE COMPANIES

A business may take one of three basic forms—*sole proprietorship, partnership,* or *corporation.*

A **sole proprietorship** is a business that is owned—and usually operated—by one person, the *sole proprietor*. The size of the business is limited by the amount of money that the owner can personally raise. All the debts of the business are the debts of the owner. If the business fails, its **creditors**—people or organizations that have loaned money or extended credit to the business—can recover money owed to them from the sole proprietor's personal property. Although the owner can leave the assets and the liabilities of the business to someone else, continuing the operation of a sole proprietorship after the owner's death is often difficult.

A **partnership** is a business that is co-owned by two or more people. As in a sole proprietorship, the size of a partnership is limited by the amount of money that the co-owners can personally raise. Furthermore, each general partner is responsible for the debts of the whole business, not just for a proportionate share based on that partner's original investment in the business. An unwise decision by one general partner can thus jeopardize the personal funds of all other general partners. A partnership ends with the death or withdrawal of any general partner, and the remaining partners must form a new partnership if they want to continue the business.

Because of the need for permanence and stability among insurance companies, insurance laws in the United States and Canada prohibit sole proprietorships and partnerships from issuing life and health insurance. All commercial insurance companies in the United States and Canada are corporations. Defined in 1819 by U.S. Supreme Court Chief Justice John Marshall, a **corporation** is "an artificial being, invisible, intangible, and existing only in contemplation of the law." Based on the definition given by Chief Justice Marshall, corporations have two major characteristics that set them apart from sole proprietorships and partnerships.

First, corporations are considered to be distinct legal entities, which means that a corporation, apart from its owners, can be a party in a legal action. Any legal actions involving a corporation affect only the assets and liabilities of the corporation itself. The owners of a corporation, unlike the owners of sole proprietorships and partnerships, are not personally liable for the debts of the corporation. If a corporation goes bankrupt, the corporation's creditors must be satisfied with the assets of the corporation only. The creditors cannot legally require the owners of the corporation to pay the corporation's debts out of their own personal property. This feature of limited liability is important to potential owners, especially if a company has to incur large debts in the course of doing business.

Second, a corporation continues beyond the death of any or all of its owners. This feature gives a corporation a stability that sole proprietorships and partnerships cannot guarantee. Furthermore, a corporation that is well managed can survive the personal misfortunes of any of its owners. This fact is reassuring to people who might invest in the corporation or buy its products.

Incorporating in the United States

The exact requirements for incorporating a business vary from state to state. The usual procedure is for the people who want to form a corporation to file proposed articles of incorporation with a state official, often the secretary of state. These articles describe the essential features of the proposed company, including its name, the type of business in which it will engage, the initial investment being made in the company, and the number of shares of stock. The organizers of the corporation must pay a filing charge, which is usually based on the number of authorized shares of the company's stock. The filing then becomes a matter of public record.

If no objections are raised and if the organizers have complied with all legal requirements, the state then issues a charter. This corporate **charter** is the legal contract that creates the corporation and contains the terms specified in the articles of incorporation. In addition, all pertinent state laws regarding incorporation automatically become a part of the charter. If the corporation, once in business, violates any condition included in its articles of incorporation, it breaches its contract with the state and risks losing its charter.

A company incorporates only once, in a state of its choosing. The company is then said to be *domiciled* in the state in which it is incorporated. Later, the insurer may file applications with other states to do business in those states. From the point of view of any state, a **domestic corporation** is one that is incorporated under the laws of that state; a **foreign corporation** is one that is incorporated under the laws of another state; and an **alien corporation** is one that is incorporated under the laws of another country. These distinctions play an important part in the manner in which states regulate corporations.

Most businesses in the United States are incorporated by a state government, but some types of businesses are incorporated under federal law. For example, national banks and quasi-government agencies, such as the Pension Benefit Guaranty Corporation, are incorporated under federal law.

Establishing Life and Health Insurance Companies in the United States

A life and health insurance company established in the United States must be chartered under the laws of the state in which it is established. To extend its operations to another state, the company must obtain a license to do business there and comply with any requirements that that state has about contracts and operations.

Each state has minimum financial requirements that the organizers of a life insurance company must meet before they can establish the company. In New York, for example, organizers planning to establish a stock life insurance company must have (1) at least $2 million from the sale of stock and (2) a surplus of at least $4 million or 200 percent of its capital, whichever is greater. This surplus usually comes from money that the organizers have borrowed.

Anyone planning to establish a mutual company in New York must (1) secure a minimum of 1,000 applications for life insurance, each application being for a face amount of not less than $1,000; (2) receive from each applicant the full amount of one annual premium, with the sum of all premiums equaling at least $25,000; and (3) begin operations with an initial surplus of at least $150,000.

The purpose of such restrictions on the entry of new companies into the life and health insurance business is to assure that new companies are financially stable. However, the New York requirements are among the most stringent in the United States. Other states require less initial capital for an insurance company to be established. In Arizona, for example, $300,000 in capital and $180,000 in surplus are needed to start a stock life insurance company. In practice, insurance regulators want potential insurers to have capital and surplus levels in excess of these minimum requirements. A company that has excess amounts of capital and surplus can demonstrate better that it has enough funds to operate an insurance business in a financially sound manner.

Incorporating in Canada

A company may be incorporated under the Canada Business Corporations Act of the federal government or similar legislation in any of the provinces. If a company plans to operate in a number of provinces, it usually seeks incorporation under the Canada Business Corporations Act, thereby obtaining the right to transact business in any province once the company is licensed. A company that plans to operate in only one province will incorporate under the laws of that province.

Establishing Life and Health Insurance Companies in Canada

A Canadian insurance company can incorporate either through the use of *letters patent* or through a *memorandum of association*. Insurance companies that wish to incorporate through the federal government or only in the provinces of Quebec, New Brunswick, Prince Edward Island, or Manitoba use **letters patent,** in which the applicant petitions the appropriate government agency for incorporation. An insurance company that wishes to incorporate only in the provinces of British Columbia, Alberta, Saskatchewan, Ontario, Newfoundland, or Nova Scotia must use a ***memorandum of association,*** which is a document that contains the fundamental terms for registering for incorporation.

Life and health insurance companies seeking federal incorporation must comply with the Canadian and British Insurance Companies Act, which specifies the authorized initial value of a company's stock and the amount of money that investors must pledge to put toward the purchase of shares. The amount of money required depends on the kinds of insurance to be sold and is subject to the requirements of the federal superintendent of insurance. Companies seeking provincial incorporation must comply with various provincial acts, each of which specifies the amount of capital required for incorporation.

Life and health insurance companies in Canada must be licensed by every province in which they do business. In addition, most insurers are also federally licensed, although federal licensing is not necessarily required. To obtain a federal license, a company must (1) file a certified copy of its charter and a statement of its financial condition with the federal department of insurance and (2) deposit with the federal government certain types of government securities with a market value of at least $100,000. About 83 percent of Canadian life and health insurance companies, providing 89 percent of the life insurance coverage in force in Canada, are federally licensed. Each year, every insurance company doing business in Canada must obtain government certification of its right to continue to do business.

Regulation is the responsibility of both the federal and provincial governments. The vast majority of insurers are regulated for solvency by the federal superintendent. Provincial legislation regarding solvency applies only to those provincially licensed companies that are not also federally licensed. The provinces concern themselves primarily with licensing companies and agents and with administering legislation concerning policy contracts.

In Canada, a company incorporated under Canadian law is known as a ***resident corporation,*** and a company incorporated under the laws of another country is known as a ***nonresident corporation.***

MUTUALIZATION AND DEMUTUALIZATION

A stock insurance company can convert to a mutual company, and a mutual company can convert to a stock company. In both cases, the process is time-consuming and expensive, but for various reasons companies sometimes decide to change their form. Earlier in this century, several stock life and health insurance companies converted to mutual companies for two primary reasons: (1) to gain freedom from the demands of stockholders and (2) to avoid being taken over by other companies. As mentioned earlier in this chapter, companies are bought when investors acquire company stock, but because a mutual company has no stock, an acquiring company has nothing to buy. Thus, by becoming mutuals, some insurance companies felt that they could protect themselves from control by outside interests.

However, for reasons mentioned below, a mutual company today is more likely to consider converting to a stock company—a process called *demutualization.* One study showed that between 1930 and 1987, 125 mutual companies converted to stock ownership, although many of these conversions involved relatively small companies or immediate acquisition by another company.[1] In the late 1980s, though, some larger companies began looking at the benefits and drawbacks of demutualization. For a description of one company's demutualization process, read INSIGHT 2-1.

INSIGHT 2-1

Chronology of NWNL's Demutualization

Northwestern National Life Insurance Co. (NWNL) became the second major life insurance company to demutualize, following UNUM in 1986. NWNL completed most of its conversion process in 1988. Before its conversion, NWNL was a hybrid stock and mutual company, an unusual situation made possible by Minnesota law.

The following chronology of events describes NWNL's demutualization process. The comments are by John H. Flittie, NWNL's senior vice president and chief financial officer.

MAY 1987
Informal study begins

"We recognized at the time that this study—and actual implementation of the plan, if events so evolved—would have to be accomplished with a sense of urgency. We could not afford to let the process last for years because our people resources were limited and could not be diverted for a long period of time from the opportunities of our basic business."

SEPTEMBER 1987
Presentation of informal study to management
Commitment to major study
Full-time task force formed
Consultants hired

"The process could not have been successful without the complete, and very visible, commitment of the chief executive officer and chief operating officer. The CEO appointed a special committee of the board of directors to oversee the reorganization. Another key was top management's willingness to form a task force of senior professionals in the organization, commit them virtually 100 percent for the duration of the project, and give them a very loose rein in cutting across organizational fences.''

DECEMBER 1987
Initial presentation of concepts to NWNL board of directors
Board request for more information
Board forms reorganization committee
Initial discussion with Minnesota Commissioner of Commerce

''We received excellent cooperation from the Minnesota Commissioner of Commerce, who oversees insurance matters. Prior to our public announcement, in January 1988, that we were considering demutualization, our CEO met with the commissioner to advise him of the announcement and to determine how he wished us to proceed during the study period. John Pearson, our CEO, suggested that we would like to work with the commissioner's staff so that neither party would be surprised at the end.''

JANUARY 1988
Formal report to Board
Board authorizes development of a conversion plan for review
Public announcement

FEBRUARY-APRIL 1988
Commissioner hires advisors
Task force work continues

-Staff work
-Meetings with board committee
-Meetings with advisors
Working draft of plan discussed with advisors
Request for Private Letter Ruling from IRS

''The commissioner retained very qualified advisors from the legal, accounting, actuarial, and investment banking professions at our expense (as in the case of state insurance department examinations). These advisors assisted him and his staff in determining that the conversion plan was in accordance with Minnesota statutes, that it was fair to policyholders, and that it left the company financially capable of carrying out its obligation to its policyholders. The commissioner's advisors had complete access to the task force and its data, to the general corporate records, and to their counterparts among our consultants. Their attitudes were constructive, as we all realized that in many areas, we were plowing new ground.''

MAY 1988
Preliminary discussions with SEC

JULY 1988
Plan of conversion filed with commissioner
Mailing of announcement and notice of hearing to policyholders and shareholders

''Shareholder concerns were simple: dilution of their existing interest and the impact on the company's earnings power. Since their vote was also necessary, it was vital for the plan to address these concerns.''

AUGUST 1988
Public hearing
Ruling by administrative law judge

"The public hearing gave all policy-holders and shareholders an oppor-tunity to come forward and be heard. It also created a public record of the background and rationale for the plan of conversion and presented evidence of its fairness to both policyholders and shareholders."

SEPTEMBER 1988
Preliminary order by commissioner
Proxy and prospectus filed with SEC

OCTOBER 1988
IRS Private Letter Ruling received
Board approves plan
SEC clearance obtained
Mailing of proxy and statement of preliminary equity share amounts to policyholders
Mailing of proxy to shareholders

"The SEC process went smoothly, al-though our registration statement did receive full review over approximately six weeks as a 'one-of-a-kind' trans-action. Several months before filing, we submitted a position paper on various accounting and financial information presentation issues to the SEC for its informal comment. The help of our audit firm's SEC specialists was invaluable in this regard."

NOVEMBER 1988
Follow-up mailings and phone calls soliciting proxies
Meeting with stock analysts

"The biggest surprise of the process was how little reaction we had from both policyholders and shareholders—and the fact that the reaction we did get was overwhelmingly positive."

DECEMBER 1988
Approval by policyholders and shareholders at special meeting of company
Confirmations of final amounts and form of payment mailed

"The key issues we dealt with from the policyholder standpoint were:

1) Who would share in the distribution?

2) How much would policyholders receive in the aggregate?

3) How would the aggregate amount be split among eligible policyholders?

4) What form would the distribution take—cash, stock, or other?

5) How would participation rights be maintained for mutual policyholders?"

JANUARY 1989
Commissioner signs order approving plan
New holding company formed

FEBRUARY 1989
Cash and stock distributed to policyholders

"The Minnesota statute provided min-imal specific direction, particularly as to the amount of the aggregate distribu-tion. This resulted in the need for NWNL and its board to ascertain and be able to demonstrate that the plan was fair to policyholders in all regards. The final resolution of the aggregate distribution issue was based on a market value approach.''

MARCH 1989
Public offering of senior notes to finance cash distribution

Source: Adapted with permission of the publisher from John H. Flittie, ''NWNL Looks at Life After Demutualization,'' *Resource,* July/August 1989, pp. 21-22, 24-25.

Benefits of Becoming a Stock Company through Demutualization

By converting to a stock company, a mutual company can benefit in a number of ways, including the following:

- *More flexible corporate structure.* Life and health insurance companies in the United States can buy other companies, such as brokerage firms or property and casualty insurers. Stock companies have greater flexibility than mutual companies in buying and operating other types of companies. A stock insurance company can buy companies that are not in the insurance business without necessarily restricting those companies to regulations meant only for insurers. However, if a mutual company buys a different type of company, that company must conform to the regulations that affect a mutual insurance company. Some analysts believe that, in today's business environment, the ability to establish holding companies provides stock companies with a competitive edge.
- *Access to the capital market.* Stock companies can increase their capital by selling additional shares of stock. The cash that stock companies receive from selling stock can then be used to buy other companies or to pay for expansion and improvements. The wealth of many mutual companies lies largely in their accumulated surplus, but mutuals are limited in the ways that they can use their surplus.
- *Added ability to attract management.* To attract top-level managers, stock companies can offer shares of company stock as part of their executive compensation package, whereas mutuals do not have this option.
- *More active interest of the company's owners.* Stock companies are owned by their stockholders, who tend to take a more active interest in company operations than do the policyowners who own mutual companies. Some executives believe that, because of the scrutiny of stockholders, the management of stock companies tends to be more aggressive, growth-oriented, and adaptable to changes in the economy than that of mutuals.

Difficulties of Demutualizing

As with most business decisions, the decision to demutualize has disadvantages as well. Some mutual companies have considered demutualization but have not proceeded with the lengthy and complicated process for a number of reasons.

First, regulations on demutualization are inconsistent from state to state. Not all states specifically allow demutualization, and, thus, these states have no guidelines for the process. Many states have no regulations that address demutualization directly, while some states have specific regulations forbidding demutualization. In Canada, federal insurance laws do not provide for demutualization.

Second, demutualization requires the distribution of a mutual company's surplus among its policyowners. The mutual company must find an equitable and efficient way to distribute this surplus. The company must also seek the legal opinions of regulators and find answers to several difficult questions. Two of the most difficult questions are discussed below:

- *Which policyowners should share in the surplus?* Some authorities believe that all of a company's policyowners, living and dead, have contributed to surplus; therefore, all policyowners and their heirs should share in its distribution. Other authorities believe that only current policyowners should participate in the distribution. Still others believe that only people who have had policies in force within three to five years before the conversion should participate in the distribution. Policyowner advocates, regulators, and the management of mutual companies must reach a feasible solution to these conflicting approaches.
- *Should policyowners receive cash, shares of stock in the converted company, or both cash and stock?* All of these options present problems for the converting company. A company that distributes its surplus in the form of cash can deplete its surplus to such an extent that once it becomes a stock company it may be too weak to attract additional capital. A company that distributes its surplus in the form of stock may dilute its pool of shareholders excessively. For example, a large mutual with $40 billion in assets may have as many as three million policyowners. To distribute shares to each of these policyowners would leave the company with three million shareholders. In comparison, an established stock company with $40 billion in assets would probably have 35,000 to 40,000 shareholders. Most authorities, though, believe that a mutual company converting to a stock company should probably offer its policyowners both cash and shares of stock.

A third reason companies have not pursued the demutualization process is that the legal, printing, and postage costs of conversion to a stock company are usually enormous and difficult to estimate in advance.

Fourth, the morale of the converting company's employees could decline because of uncertainty about the new direction of the company. Demutualization involves changes in direction and policy that may confuse employees. The process must be handled to minimize disruption of the workplace and any negative effect on employee morale.

MERGERS, ACQUISITIONS, HOLDING COMPANIES, AND STRATEGIC ALLIANCES

Life and health insurers merge with one another, purchase and sell corporations, and are purchased and sold. For a variety of reasons, they also enter into alliances with other companies. Some insurance companies are owned by other insurance companies; others are owned by noninsurance companies. Changes in the financial services environment have caused many insurance companies to consider a number of activities and transactions that can help them obtain a competitive edge. The next section of this chapter will discuss some of these transactions.

Mergers

A *merger,* called an *amalgamation* in Canada, occurs when two or more corporate entities are legally joined. One may be absorbed by the other, with only one continuing in existence. In cases in which an entirely new company is formed by merging two or more companies, the merger is called a *consolidation.* The basic purpose of a merger or consolidation involving a life and health insurance company is to form a stronger company that has more efficient and more profitable operations.

Benefits of mergers

Life and health insurance companies have many reasons for merging with other companies. A weak company may seek a stronger partner to overcome financial difficulties or to obtain enough surplus to help it expand. Another company may need new products and services to offer its customers, but rather than spend the time and money to develop these new products and services itself, the company can seek a partner whose products, sales force, or territories complement its own. For example, a company selling ordinary insurance may merge with a company that sells group insurance, or a company that concentrates in the Midwest may merge with a company that concentrates in the Southeast. Some insurance companies buy investment brokerage firms in order to be able to offer customers a wider range of financial services and to gain access to the customers of the brokerage firms.

Companies also merge to obtain the advantages of economies of scale. **Economies of scale,** which exist because some operations are more efficient when done on a large scale, are said to be present when a company's unit costs decrease as its size of operations increases. If two companies merge, they should be able to become more efficient and thereby reduce their unit costs and, possibly, lower the prices of their products.

Besides achieving greater economies of scale, a company can benefit in other ways by participating in a merger and forming a larger company. For example, customers often feel that larger companies are more stable than smaller ones. Furthermore, companies that appear to be growing find it easier to attract and keep good management personnel.

Drawbacks to mergers

Mergers are not without their problems. Some of these problems are discussed below.

- To effect a merger, the companies involved in the merger often incur enormous legal and accounting costs.
- The employees of merging companies often experience a great deal of anxiety about the merger. They wonder if their jobs will be eliminated or changed. They also wonder if the management style of the new company will be different from the previous management style. Some employees leave the company during the transition rather than wait to see how their jobs fit into the new structure. Allaying these anxieties and dealing with employee turnover can cost the merging company a large amount of time and money, including temporary loss of business.
- If the merging companies are headquartered in different locations, one of the companies may have to relocate, which could mean that some employees would resign and the company would have to hire new employees at the new location. The company that is moving may have to provide severance pay to certain employees, relocate key employees, and sell buildings that it owns in the old location.
- Contracts between the merging companies and their agents may need to be rewritten to reflect changes caused by the merger.

The merger process

As stated previously, the merger process is complicated. The list below presents the major steps needed to merge two life and health insurance companies.

1. Possible merger partners must be located and evaluated.
2. The financial status of the two companies are usually appraised by an independent actuarial firm or an investment banking firm.
3. A merger proposal that is acceptable to the boards of directors of the merging companies must be developed.
4. The owners of the merging companies must approve the merger. In a merger of stock companies, the approval of at least two-thirds of the stockholders of each company is required to complete the merger. A mutual company usually must have the approval of two-thirds of its policyowners.
5. In the case of a stock company, those stockholders who vote against the merger must be paid a fair market value for the forced surrender of their stock if the merger eventually takes place.
6. The regulatory authorities of the states and provinces in which the merging companies are domiciled must approve the merger.
7. The final merger document must be filed with the appropriate officials of the state or province in which the new or surviving company will be domiciled.
8. The assets and liabilities of all merging companies must be transferred to the new or surviving company, and policyowners of the nonsurviving company must be notified of the change.
9. In the United States, licenses and a new or amended certificate of incorporation must be issued for the new or surviving company. In Canada, the necessary memorandum of association or letters patent are required.

Acquisitions

An *acquisition* occurs when one company buys a controlling interest in another company, usually by purchasing a percentage of the acquired company's stock. Ownership of more than 50 percent of the acquired company's stock generally gives the purchaser a *controlling interest* in the acquired company. Practical control of a company's operations can take place with as little as 10 percent of a company's stock, if the remaining stock is widely distributed. Sometimes the stock is held only as an investment, and the management team of the acquired company continues to direct the company. In other cases, new management or the management of the acquiring company takes over the operation of the acquired company.

Life and health insurance companies can purchase a controlling interest in other companies, including other insurance companies. However, as we've stated, mutual insurers have no stock and cannot be acquired, although they can acquire stock companies. Stock companies, on the other hand, can be both the acquirers and the acquired. In Canada, a life and health insurance company is not allowed to own more than 30 percent of the shares of another Canadian life and health insurer. Canadian law also restricts the nonresident ownership of a Canadian life insurance company to 25 percent of company stock. This provision has the effect of requiring nonresidents to incorporate a new company if they want to enter the Canadian market rather than take over a Canadian company.

Friendly and hostile takeovers

One company can acquire another company through either a friendly takeover or a hostile takeover. In a *friendly takeover,* the acquiring company makes an offer to purchase a company, the company to be purchased agrees to the acquisition, and both companies settle on a buying price. The board of directors of the target company must approve the offer and then recommend in a public announcement to its stockholders that the offer be accepted. In the United States, once the stockholders approve the acquisition, both companies must obtain the approval of the insurance commissioners of the states in which the companies are domiciled and then file all required legal documents with the secretary of state, the insurance department in the state of domicile of each insurance company involved, and often the Securities and Exchange Commission (SEC).

A *hostile takeover* occurs when the management of a company refuses an acquisition offer, but the acquiring company continues with its takeover attempt despite the wishes of the target company's management. In a hostile takeover, the acquiring company makes a *tender offer,* in which the acquiring company tries to buy a controlling share of the target company directly from the target company's stockholders. Under the procedures of a tender offer, a U.S. company that is seeking the acquisition files a document with the SEC. The document states the acquiring company's intent to offer to buy the target company's stock. This document also reveals (1) the reasons for the acquisition, (2) any plans to liquidate the target company or sell a major share of its assets, and (3) the source of funds for the acquisition. No more than half of the funds to be used for the acquisition can be borrowed funds. Then the acquirer makes a public announcement in which it offers to purchase the stock of the target company at a specified price, which is usually higher than the market value. Sometimes the acquiring company states that it will pay the price in the tender offer only if it can buy a certain percentage of the target company's stock within a certain period of time.

Hostile takeovers often result in long legal and financial battles. Sometimes the target company makes a counteroffer and tries to buy enough shares of the prospective purchaser's stock to control it. If the target company does not make a counteroffer, the board of directors of the target company often tries to persuade stockholders that the takeover is not good for the long-term value of the company's stock. The target company may even try to buy enough of its own stock to assure that it maintains a controlling interest. If a target company thinks it cannot prevent a hostile takeover, it may seek a purchaser more to its liking, called a *white knight*.

If a takeover attempt succeeds and the required number of shares is purchased, the acquiring company then controls the majority of the stock and can elect a new board of directors and decide on management policy.

Leveraged buyouts (LBOs)

A more recent approach to acquisitions in the insurance industry is the leveraged buyout. In a ***leveraged buyout (LBO),*** one company acquires another company in a transaction that is financed primarily through borrowing. The borrowed funds are paid back in a specified period of time with money generated by the operations of the acquired company or through a sale of the acquired company's assets.

Holding Companies

When one company is acquired by another company, the acquired firm becomes a ***subsidiary.*** The company that owns the subsidiary is called a ***holding company*** and has a controlling interest in the subsidiary. Originally, the holding company concept was used to acquire a group of companies in the same or related lines of business in order to maximize expertise and market presence in that field. Now, the holding company arrangement is also used to control subsidiaries in widely differing industries. In this way, the holding company can diversify its interests and protect itself from the risks involved in concentrating on just one kind of business.

A ***conglomerate*** is a group of unrelated businesses under the control of a holding company (see Figure 2-3). Many businesses that make up conglomerates are subsidiaries that previously had been independent

Figure 2-3
Corporate structure of a conglomerate that includes insurance companies.

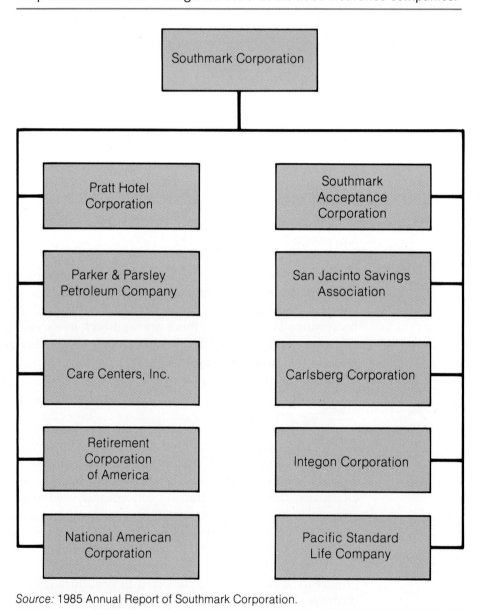

Source: 1985 Annual Report of Southmark Corporation.

companies with their own traditions, identities, and management. These businesses continue to operate as separate corporate entities, often under their own corporate titles. Operating decisions are ordinarily left with the management of each subsidiary, but decisions about the allocation of financial resources and long-range planning are made by the management of the holding company itself.

The trend toward holding companies

Starting in the late 1960s, a number of stock life and health insurance companies became subsidiaries of other corporations. In several cases, the acquiring companies were property and casualty insurance companies faced with declining profits and a need for new products to increase their earnings. In other cases, the acquiring firms were conglomerates, attracted by the large cash flows generated by life and health insurance companies.

Some life and health insurance companies have found that forming a holding company offers several benefits over operating independently. These benefits include (1) diversification of services provided, (2) fewer restrictions on investments, and (3) greater flexibility in raising capital.

Not only are many insurance companies buying other companies in order to achieve the advantages of creating holding companies, but some insurance companies are actually letting portions of their own companies "spin off" to form subsidiary corporations. *Spin-offs* are former units or departments of a company that operate as independent companies, although their parent company is their primary customer. Spin-offs can, however, offer their services to other individuals or organizations. For example, the pension department of an insurance company might be allowed to spin off and form a pension management firm, or the investment department might spin off and form a brokerage house whose primary client is its own holding company. Such spin-offs are established under the assumption that, freed from the restrictions of operating within a larger company, a subsidiary tends to be managed in a more aggressive and competitive manner. Spin-offs also may be designed to utilize excess resources, to take advantage of unusual expertise in a certain area, or to seize perceived profit opportunities.

Upstream and downstream holding companies

Holding companies may be formed either upstream or downstream from the company that forms them, as shown in Figure 2-4. In the *upstream* arrangement, a holding company is formed by the parent company, which in turn is controlled by the holding company. The holding company is then in

52

Operations of Life and Health Insurance Companies

Figure 2-4
Upstream and downstream holding companies.

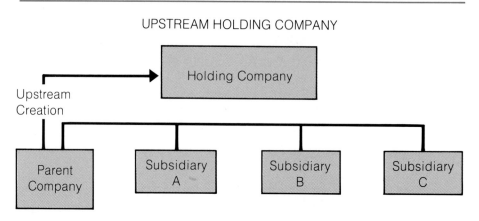

UPSTREAM HOLDING COMPANY

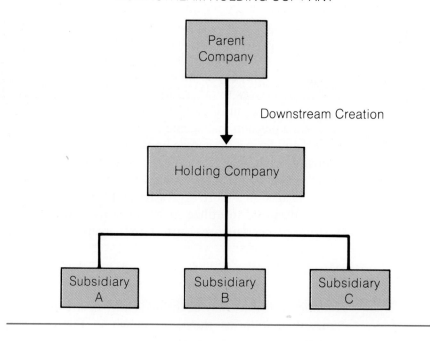

DOWNSTREAM HOLDING COMPANY

a position to create or acquire additional subsidiaries. In the ***downstream*** arrangement, the parent company establishes a holding company, which then creates or acquires subsidiary firms while the parent company remains independent.

A stock life and health insurer can form either an upstream or a downstream holding company. A mutual insurer, because it cannot be controlled by another company, can form only a downstream holding company. Some mutual companies feel that this restriction limits their ability to compete with other companies. This restriction is another factor that causes some mutuals to consider demutualization.

Regulatory Concerns

In the 1960s, when noninsurance companies acquired a sizable number of life and health insurers, regulatory authorities expressed concern about the trend and considered forbidding the acquisition of a life insurance company by a nonlife holding company. However, a more moderate approach was chosen. Regulators established procedures to assure that purchasers of insurance companies would manage them with due respect for the rights of policyowners and beneficiaries. As mergers, acquisitions, and the creation of holding companies continue, regulators are particularly concerned that the assets and liabilities of any insurance subsidiary be separated from the assets and liabilities of holding companies and other subsidiaries.

Regulators in the United States are acutely aware that a holding company could raid the surplus of an insurance subsidiary to help finance either the holding company's operations or the operations of other subsidiaries. As a result, some states have passed laws to protect the insurer's surplus. The provisions commonly included in such state laws are summarized below:

- The state insurance commissioner must approve the acquisition of an insurance company by another company.
- A mutual company may not invest more than 5 percent of its assets or 50 percent of its surplus in subsidiaries.
- An insurance company subsidiary must disclose in its Annual Statement any financial transactions with its parent holding company and report as liabilities any expenses paid by the parent.
- Extraordinary distributions of dividends to the parent company that would weaken the financial position of the insurance subsidiary are prohibited.
- Insurance companies must be operated by their own full-time personnel.

- Insurance companies cannot file consolidated statements with noninsurance companies.

Strategic Alliances[2]

Insurance companies also have a long tradition of strategic alliances with outside firms, such as third-party administrators and securities firms. In recent years, insurers have significantly expanded both the number and scope of their alliances. Among insurers' alliance partners are foreign insurance companies (discussed further in Chapter 17), other domestic insurers, commercial banks, technological firms, and medical firms.

A *strategic alliance* can be defined as a prolonged relationship involving risk and reward sharing by two or more independent firms that are pursuing individual strategic goals. Through a strategic alliance, a life insurance company can gain the resources or expertise of other firms and still retain its own independence.

Current conditions make strategic alliances particularly attractive for insurers. Life and health insurance companies face constant technological change, new products and competitors, increased competition from traditional competitors, and the globalization of financial markets. By cooperating with other firms in a systematic manner, they can dramatically increase their ability to respond to the changing environment. INSIGHT 2-2 describes a strategic alliance formed by two insurers to provide group life and health insurance products.

INSIGHT 2-2

Insurers Combine Forces in Group Market

Great-West Life and The New England (TNE) recently formed a joint venture under which Great-West will provide administrative support services for TNE large group life and health products. The companies expect the arrangement to increase profits and to expand their employee benefits market.

"We view it as a major opportunity, and we're excited and committed to it. It shows every indication of working quite well," said Alan Maclennan, senior vice president of group life and health at Great-West Life.

Under the arrangement, which involves TNE's group life and health products for over 25 lives, Great-West provides a wide range of services. These services include billing and collection, policyholder administration, claim payments, and underwriting. TNE provides the group life and health products, which are sold under the TNE name by its employee benefits representatives to TNE clients. Both companies share the financial results of the joint venture.

Herbert F. Clark, TNE senior vice president, employee benefits group, stated, "TNE wanted to remain in this marketplace on an ongoing and stronger basis. We wanted to continue to serve our customers, and we wanted to be a bigger player. It was also clear to us that we had a lot of untapped potential from an agency distribution system which we could capture."

In the spring of 1987, TNE had entered into a pilot joint venture with a second party serving as the administrator. This joint venture covered the company's small group insurance products for under 25 lives. The pilot exceeded the company's expectations and prompted TNE to actively pursue a joint arrangement for its group life and health products for over 25 lives.

For Great-West, the joint venture will lead to greater economies of scale and increased profits. "Historically," Maclennan explained, "business at Great-West has been consistently profitable with some ups and downs. The opportunity to share in the profits of an additional block of business attracted us."

Both companies stress they aren't consolidating sales organizations. Both will continue to sell insurance and pension products individually. The arrangement, explained Clark, "is not a merger. They're still our clients and products, and the products are sold under The New England name by its producers." Each company keeps separate group offices, marketing identities, and employee benefits organizations. To the customer, the joint venture is invisible.

There are several factors that enhance the joint agreement. In terms of geographic location, TNE has a greater proportion of business east of the Mississippi, while Great-West is stronger on the West Coast. TNE is primarily an individual operation, and Great-West is known as a group organization. Both companies see these differences as bringing strength to the joint arrangement.

The arrangement also provides employment opportunities for Great-West employees. According to Maclennan, the company had to create a fairly sizable organization at its head office in Denver to accommodate the venture. The creation of this new area coupled with the fact that Great-West assumed responsibility for TNE's existing claim offices gave Great-West employees numerous advancement opportunities.

"Everyone at TNE and Great-West had a tremendous commitment to quality," Clark summarizes. "Both sides came out winners."

Source: Adapted with permission of the publisher from Chris Breston, "Insurers Combine Forces in Group Market," *Resource,* September/October 1988, pp. 25-26.

Insurance companies have a variety of motivations for entering strategic alliances, including

- accessing new geographical markets
- gaining new distribution channels
- maximizing return on existing operations
- upgrading customer service
- enhancing a product line

Insurance industry strategic alliances usually take one of two forms: joint ventures or partnerships. In a joint venture, two or more companies together undertake an enterprise in which each company has partial ownership. The reasons for entering joint ventures tend to differ from the reasons for entering partnerships. Joint venture participants often view a venture as a way to invest in a new business or technology. If a particular venture is successful, one of the companies may try to buy it or the companies involved may merge some or all of their operations.

In contrast, firms that enter into strategic partnerships often do not want to merge with or acquire other companies. In fact, this partnership differs from the legal form of partnership discussed in Chapter 1. Instead, in the strategic type of partnership, insurers, which are corporations, want specific services from their strategic partners and are not directly involved in those companies' other operations. Even so, a contractual relationship typically exists between the two companies.

In a time of constant change, strategic alliances offer a flexible and cost-efficient way of doing business. In a strategic alliance, participants can move quickly into new and potentially profitable situations.

OTHER ORGANIZATIONS THAT MARKET LIFE AND HEALTH INSURANCE

Besides the more than 2,400 stock and mutual companies providing life and health insurance in the United States and Canada at the end of 1990, other types of organizations provide consumers with life and health insurance products and services. More than 160 fraternal benefit societies operate in the United States and Canada, while savings banks in certain states can offer life insurance and annuity products. In addition, under specific circumstances, other banks can be involved in the life and health insurance business.

Fraternal Benefit Societies

Fraternal benefit societies are organizations formed to provide social and insurance benefits to their members. In such societies, members often share a common religious, ethnic, or vocational background, although some fraternals, including some of the largest, are open to the general public.

Fraternal benefit societies began to offer life insurance protection in the last half of the nineteenth century because low-income farmers and laborers could not afford the life insurance protection offered by commercial companies. This form of insurance benefit proved immensely popular, and by the end of the century, fraternal societies provided slightly more than half of the life insurance in force in the United States. However, as commercial insurers changed their marketing and underwriting practices, the percentage of insurance in force with fraternal societies steadily declined. (However, read INSIGHT 2–3 to see how a fraternal society can also respond to changes in the marketplace.) Today, fraternal societies in the United States and Canada control more than $26 billion in assets and about $175 billion of the life and health insurance in force, which is still less than 2 percent of the in-force coverage.

INSIGHT 2-3

New England Fraternal Discovers New Direction

In the early 1980s, members of the 88-year-old Union Saint-Jean-Baptiste (USJB) believed their fraternal society was losing its focus. "We discovered, in effect, that we had no formal direction," says A. Robert Mailloux, president of the fraternal. To correct this problem, members of USJB spent three years producing a new strategic plan for the fraternal, a plan whose main components consisted of a mission statement and a new product portfolio to reflect the changing needs of the members.

"As a fraternal benefits society, we market not only insurance," Mailloux explains. "We market the fraternal, which happens to include the insurance. We had to find a way to reorganize our thinking and our entire reason for being, and to bring it all together and develop a mission for the overall corporation." The new mission statement provides a focus for the society:

> The purpose of Union Saint-Jean-Baptiste, a fraternal benefits society, is to provide financial security to its members while offering the opportunity to participate in an organization whose primary objective is to support the Franco-American heritage.

To accomplish its mission, the fraternal concentrated on three areas—internal operations, membership, and product portfolio. The company took an in-depth look at its internal operation and decided both restructuring and modernizing were needed. New computer hardware and software were necessary to place its data processing function "in the twentieth century," says Mailloux. Specifically, USJB sought software capable of handling routine insurance services, such as billing and reserve calculation, as well as software capable of tracking members within the fraternal's 120 councils in New England. "We found that many systems could handle traditional insurance administration-type activities," comments Mailloux. "There were few that could take this one more step and track our membership. This was very critical to us."

Along with upgrading its data processing system, USJB established an aggressive educational approach as part of its internal restructuring. Today, USJB employees are encouraged to pursue the FLMI designation, and new employees are required to complete the first two FLMI courses. Technical personnel are encouraged to take college courses.

To address the membership issue, USJB used a number of surveys to profile its membership. These surveys highlighted two membership problems. First, the older fraternal members, though highly dedicated to and supportive of USJB, felt unrecognized by the fraternal for their loyalty. To acknowledge these members, the company developed a recognition program, which includes special mailings to the members thanking them for their support.

The second problem, according to Mailloux, was that the fraternal had not developed a means to attract and retain the newer, younger member. "We did not want to lose sight of the older members because they're the loyal backbone of our society," Mailloux recalls. "But we had to develop programs simultaneously to attract new members from an insurance and fraternal point of view." Membership in the fraternal, which reached its height of 78,280 members in 1953, had declined significantly in recent decades.

To attract and retain members, USJB decided it needed to update its insurance product portfolio. "We discovered that for the insurance environment we were in," Mailloux continues, "our product portfolio was inadequate from a member needs point of view." To meet these needs, USJB redesigned and introduced a number of products. Today, the fraternal's products include an interest-sensitive whole life product; a mortgage term product; a five-year renewable and convertible term product, and a universal life product. In addition, USJB offers annuities and specialty products for children and older members.

To complement its new product offerings, the fraternal society also emphasized and developed its member benefits, such as its 6,000-volume library highlighting the genealogy and history of the French in North America, its educational assistance program for members, Project FAITH (Franco-American Interest in the Handicapped), and the summer Heritage Camp for members aged 14 to 18.

"But we still have some areas to address," Mailloux points out. "To stay at the status quo is to regress." Mailloux foresees the fraternal's continuing to penetrate the family marketplace along with refining its distribution network in the New England region.

"Our market," he says, "is certainly larger than our membership. We want to continue to support the marketplace and offer services and programs that address the marketplace, while not losing sight of the society's mission.

"The more we communicate with our membership," he concludes, "the stronger we'll become."

Source: Adapted with permission of the publisher from Chris Breston, "New England Fraternal Discovers New Direction, But Retains Tradition," Resource, September/October 1988, pp. 22-24.

Characteristics of fraternal benefit society insurance

Fraternal insurers operate through a lodge system whereby only lodge members are permitted to own the fraternal society's insurance. Some fraternal societies offer insurance to people who are not society members at the time of application, but the applicants automatically become members of the society once their policies are issued.

Like mutual companies, fraternals have no capital stock and exist only to benefit members and their beneficiaries, as well as the public at large. Each fraternal is managed by a governing body elected by the members in accordance with the society's bylaws.

In Canada and the United States, provincial and state laws require fraternal societies to use an *open contract.* Under this type of contract, the society's charter, constitution, and bylaws become a part of the insurance contract, and any amendments to them automatically become amendments to the insurance contract. No such amendment, however, can destroy or diminish benefits that the society is contractually obligated to pay. In contrast, commercial insurance companies use *closed contracts,* under which the terms of the insurance policy constitute the entire agreement between the policyowner and the insurer.

In the United States, the National Fraternal Congress of America, in conjunction with the NAIC, has developed a Uniform Fraternal Code. This code defines a fraternal benefit society and provides for nonforfeiture benefits, settlement options, a grace period, an incontestability clause, and the licensing of full-time fraternal life insurance agents. In Canada, fraternals are registered under the same law that applies to stock and mutual companies. Each fraternal society is required to file an annual valuation report issued by an actuary, who must certify in the report that the fraternal's policy reserves are adequate. U.S. and Canadian fraternal societies are subject to the same laws regarding investments as commercial insurers.

Taxation of fraternal societies

The distinctive features of fraternal benefit societies, especially their charitable acts, are generally cited as the basis for the favorable tax status that they enjoy. In the United States, fraternal organizations are exempt from federal income tax and from all state and municipal taxes with the exception of taxes and assessments on real estate and office equipment. In Canada, fraternal societies are subject to federal income tax on the net investment and premium income from their life insurance business. Each province also levies a 2 percent premium tax on premiums received from policies issued in the province. Generally, these provincial taxes do not apply to fraternals' health insurance business, which gives them a slight edge over stock and mutual companies. The fraternal societies in Canada are subject to local taxes on real estate and to provincial sales taxes on equipment and supplies.

Banks

In the United States, banks have historically been allowed to sell *credit life insurance,* which is a type of life insurance designed to pay off a debt to a creditor if the debtor-insured dies. In addition, national banks, which are regulated by the Office of the Comptroller of the Currency, can sell life insurance if they are located in a town of under 5,000 people.

Banks in Delaware have also made some inroads into the life insurance industry. Banks that are chartered by the state of Delaware can sell insurance on an interstate basis as long as such activity is allowed in those states. In towns of under 5,000, Delaware banks can sell insurance from branches. However, most banks in Delaware must establish separate companies to underwrite insurance on an interstate basis—that is, a separate and distinct company must be created to accept the risk presented by the insurance that is placed in force. Delaware's state-chartered banks that are insured by the Federal Deposit Insurance Corporation (FDIC) can underwrite insurance only to the extent of national banks as discussed earlier. In addition, one bank—Citibank—is allowed to underwrite insurance within Delaware to residents of Delaware.

Savings banks in Connecticut, Massachusetts, and New York are allowed to sell and underwrite insurance and annuity products. Savings bank life insurance (SBLI) policies are typically participating policies.

- Savings banks in Connecticut wholly own a life insurance company that can issue policies and annuities on the lives of people who live or work in Connecticut. At the end of 1990, 56 of the 57 savings banks in Connecticut offered SBLI. The maximum amount of coverage that can be purchased from all banks is $100,000 for ordinary insurance and $200,000 for group insurance.
- In 1992, Massachusetts changed the structure of its savings bank life insurance system. The Savings Bank Life Insurance Company of Massachusetts is now a stock life insurance company owned by savings banks. The present voluntary limit for ordinary life insurance coverage is $500,000.
- In New York, the Savings Bank Life Insurance Fund is a not-for-profit organization within the New York State Banking Department. The Fund is managed by unpaid trustees who are also trustees of savings banks. These trustees are appointed by the Superintendent of Banks with the consent of the Governor. The Fund is responsible for the conduct of the System's business, and its activities are similar to a life insurance company's home office. The maximum amount of individual insurance that can be issued on one life is $50,000. Also, up to

$350,000 of group yearly renewable and convertible term insurance can be purchased by customers of savings banks.

KEY TERMS

stock insurance company	nonresident corporation
stock	demutualization
stockholder	merger
dividend	consolidation
mutual insurance company	economies of scale
participating policy	acquisition
surplus	controlling interest
capital	friendly takeover
divisible surplus	hostile takeover
policy dividend	tender offer
nonparticipating policy	leveraged buyout (LBO)
mutualization	subsidiary
sole proprietorship	holding company
creditor	conglomerate
partnership	spin-off
corporation	upstream holding company
charter	downstream holding company
domestic corporation	strategic alliance
foreign corporation	fraternal benefit society
alien corporation	open contract
letters patent	closed contract
memorandum of association	credit life insurance
resident corporation	

NOTES

1. David F. Babble and Ransom B. Jones, "Not Whether, But When," *Best's Review* 88, no. 9 (January 1988), p. 54.
2. The next section of this chapter has been adapted with permission from Jean C. Gora, "Strategic Alliances on the Increase," *Resource* XVI, no. 11 (November 1991), p. 30.

Chapter 3

The Internal Organization
of Insurance Companies

After reading this chapter, you should be able to

- Describe five factors that are essential in order for a company to operate effectively
- Explain how organizational charts can differ among companies and what a company's organizational chart can tell you about the company's management style
- Describe the kind of authority that exists at each level of an organizational pyramid
- Compare and contrast the duties of a company's board of directors, officers, managers, and supervisors
- Distinguish between line and staff units
- Describe the differences among companies organized by function, product, territory, and profit center
- Explain why committees are important to a company's operations
- Describe the functions performed by the typical departments of a life and health insurance company

All human endeavors—including the operation of an insurance company—require some sort of organization. Various factors are involved in how an insurance company organizes itself. An insurer can choose from a variety of organizational structures, which often reflect the style and perceptions of the company's senior management. The purpose of this chapter is to describe how companies organize their operations and to identify specific functions typically found in insurance companies. In the succeeding chapters of this book, the functions described in this chapter will be discussed in detail.

ESSENTIAL ORGANIZATIONAL FACTORS

Five factors are essential for any company to operate effectively. These five factors are *responsibility, authority, accountability, delegation,* and *coordination.* Each factor is described below.

Responsibility is an employee's obligation to perform assigned duties. A company needs to be organized in such a way that the responsibility of each employee is as clear as possible. All employees must understand what they are expected to do.

Authority is the right of an employee to make decisions, take action, and direct others in order to complete assigned duties. For a company to operate effectively, employees must be given the authority to fulfill their responsibilities. For example, a manager who is responsible for seeing that all policyowner correspondence is answered within four days should be given the authority to hire enough people, rotate workers, assign overtime, or take any other action that is appropriate to meet the assigned deadline.

Accountability means that employees are answerable for how well they use their authority and handle their responsibility for achieving goals. An effective company is organized so that specific accountabilities are clearly assigned to individuals or groups. The term *accountability* often carries a negative connotation, implying that people are punished if work that has been assigned to them is not done properly. However, accountability also has a positive connotation, in that people are rewarded if they handle assigned work especially well.

Delegation means assigning to one employee the authority to make decisions for and act for another employee. An effective company establishes a formal organizational structure and sets clear guidelines for delegating authority. Without such delegation, the resources of a company would not be adequately and efficiently used. Furthermore, a company would not be able to respond to opportunities and problems in a timely manner, because only a limited number of high-level employees would have the authority to take effective action.

Coordination is the orderly arrangement of a company's activities so that the company's goals can be achieved. A well-planned organization provides for smooth coordination so that goals are achieved in the most efficient and effective manner possible.

COMPONENTS OF THE ORGANIZATION AND ORGANIZATIONAL STRUCTURE

The formal internal organization of a company is reflected in its organization chart. An ***organization chart*** visually depicts various jobs performed in a company and the lines of authority and responsibility among company units (see Figure 3-1). Organization charts can vary from simple representations of only major functions to complex drawings of all activities within a company, showing levels of authority and the interrelationships among jobs and people.

In this book, some model organization charts are shown to help explain how the work for specific functions can be organized or to show forms of organization that are fairly common for life and health insurance companies. These charts do not represent the organization of any particular company but are instead intended to show some typical patterns of organization.

An organization chart gives the impression that a company's organization is static and inflexible, but that is rarely true. Management continually revises the organization in order to increase the company's ability to compete. Changes in a company's organization are often small adjustments that make the company run just a little more smoothly than it did before. Sometimes, however, if pressures in the business environment are strong enough, company organization might be completely reordered. These types of changes can be costly and can cause great uneasiness among employees. Generally, because of the risks involved, a company's management attempts a major organizational change only if the continued success of the company is thought to depend on such a reorganization.

As we have seen in previous chapters, today's environment requires insurance companies to make many changes. Many companies find that changing their organizational structure can help them achieve and maintain the flexibility needed to respond to customers' needs.

Pyramidal Structure and Levels of Authority

The classic organization chart resembles a pyramid (see Figure 3-2). The pyramid structure illustrates that the authority and responsibility in a company start at the top with one person or a small group of key people.

Figure 3-1
Sample organizational chart.

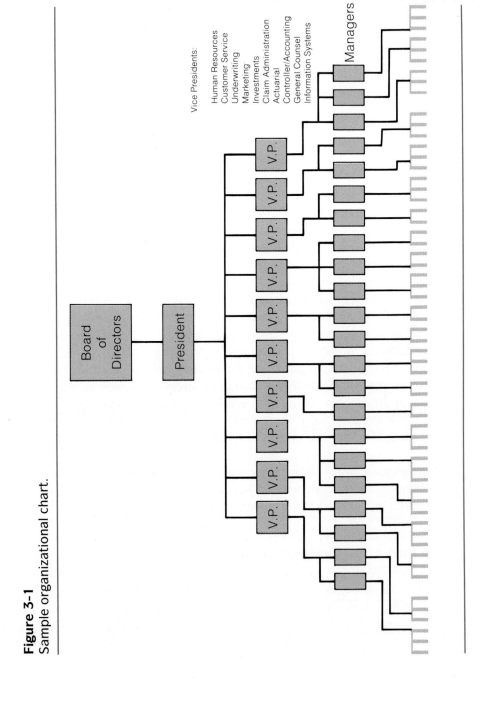

Figure 3-2
Pyramidal structure of an organization.

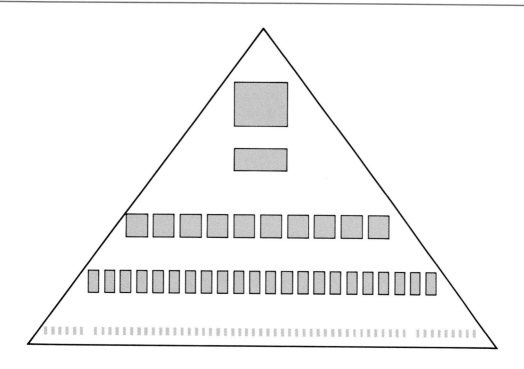

Authority and responsibility are then distributed to ever larger numbers of people throughout the company.

Policyowners or stockholders

Theoretically, the top of a life insurance company's organization chart is occupied by the policyowners (in mutual companies) or stockholders (in stock companies). These groups are the company's owners and the ultimate source of authority. However, the owners do not usually direct the actual operations of the company and, therefore, they are not generally shown on the organization chart. Instead, the owners elect a board of directors to whom this authority is delegated.

Board of directors

The *board of directors,* elected by the owners and shown on the top level of the organization chart, is the primary governing body of a corporation. In representing the owners of the corporation, the board's major responsibility is to assure the continued existence of the firm. To this end, the board periodically reviews the activities and finances of the company and sets company policies accordingly. The board of directors appoints the chief executive officer and other executives of the company and holds these executives responsible for the company's operations.

The minimum number of directors is usually specified by the charter of the corporation and sometimes by state insurance regulations. For example, New York insurance law requires a life and health insurance company to have a minimum of 13 directors. Usually, the chief executive officer of the company and several of its principal executives are members of the board. Board members who hold positions with the company in addition to their positions on the board are known as **inside directors.** Board members who do not hold other positions with the company are known as **outside directors.** Outside directors are usually businesspeople, professionals in academia and health services, and community leaders.

In most companies, meetings of the board of directors are held either monthly or quarterly, although special meetings may be called when necessary. Some of the duties that directors perform during board meetings are as follows:

- setting the major policies for the firm
- evaluating the results of the firm's operations
- authorizing major transactions, such as mergers and acquisitions
- declaring the actual dividends to be paid to stockholders or policyowners based on the recommendations of management
- appointing the officers who actually operate the company
- setting the compensation for the chief executive officer and some of the other company officers

The directors maintain their control over the company by approving or disapproving the actions performed or proposed by the executive officers.

To help the directors maintain close contact with company operations, the board is usually divided into a number of standing committees. These committees, such as the *investment committee* and the *audit committee*, receive reports on the operations of particular functions within the company, and the executives responsible for those operations appear before the committees several times each year. The committee chairpersons report to the full board about committee deliberations and recommendations.

Company management

Employees whose responsibilities are primarily concerned with guiding the work of other people are said to be members of *management*, whether they are officers, managers, or supervisors. Their major functions involve *planning* what should be done, *organizing* the human and technical resources to get the job done, *influencing* and *directing* the people doing the work, and *controlling* the work process so that the work is performed in a satisfactory manner. A short description of one company's planning process and how it involves many different people in management is given in INSIGHT 3-1.

INSIGHT 3-1

Planning at Crown Life

At Crown Life Insurance Company, all managers, and ultimately the people who work for them, have a say in the business plan. The business planning process is top-down/bottom-up with planning for a given year starting two years in advance.

The process starts at the top, when Fred Richardson, Crown's president and CEO, drafts a laundry list of what he sees as the company's objectives, major issues, and major action plans. This list is then sent to senior vice presidents and vice presidents, who review and respond to it on one written piece of paper. Senior management then discusses the plan and its revisions, elaborates upon them, and sends the plan to the profit center heads.

The plan goes through the profit centers and then back to senior management. The process goes through three cycles, taking place from the first of January until the first of April. Once the third overview is written, a fourth organizational level is brought in for review—the directors and technical and professional managers. These people go through the plan, write down problems it creates, what resources they'll need to carry it out, and action plans. If revisions need to be made, and invariably they do, it goes back into the cycle starting at the bottom and working its way back up. By the first of July, a business plan is formalized.

"It may not achieve as much as the original plan, and it may cost more, but it will be real," says Richardson. "Now I've had all the people who have to make the plan work tell me what has to be done so it will work. And it's a better plan because I've gotten everyone's commitment," he continues. "I've seen a lot of business plans that are just wish lists of the CEO or, worse, are very technically worked out by a paid strategist who's done a great job but no one understands it."

The commitment to the business plan doesn't stop after its creation; each business unit holds monthly meetings to discuss plan variances. "We find out problems right away and can come up with solutions." This allows the employees to have an increased understanding of their involvement in the business plan, as well as a sense of direction.

Source: Adapted with permission of the publisher from Jill Conversano, "Crown Life Refocuses for the '90s," *Resource,* July 1990, p. 30.

Beneath the board of directors on the typical organizational chart is the chief executive officer (CEO) or chief operating officer (COO). In most companies, the CEO is also the company's president. (In this textbook we will generally use the term *president* rather than *CEO* or *COO*.) The president is entrusted by the board of directors with broad administrative powers.

Reporting to the president are a number of executives, usually called *vice presidents*. Each person at this management level actively supervises a major *division* of the organization. In addition to coordinating the activities of their respective divisions, vice presidents are also expected to

- keep informed about trends in the industry and the general business operations of the company
- advise the president on company operations
- act as representatives for the company as a whole
- be prepared, if the president's position is vacated, to assume the presidency if necessary

A company's chief executive officer, chief operating officer, president, and vice presidents are considered the company's *officers*.

Lower in authority than vice presidents, and usually reporting to them, are the company's middle-level *managers*. Managers are generally in charge of the organizational units known as departments and are responsible for translating company policy into plans for day-to-day operations. Managers may also administer some specialized phase of the company's activities according to the directives of top management.

Even more restricted in authority than middle managers are people at the supervisory level of management. Such people are generally in charge of subdivisions of departments and are responsible for seeing that the policies formulated by top management and the plans made by middle management are carried out. On an organizational pyramid, supervisors are at the lowest managerial level in the organization. People occupying jobs at this level have less latitude in interpreting the directives of top management and spend more time in the direct supervision of subordinates than do higher-level management personnel.

Many people in *non*management positions—that is, whose primary responsibility is not the supervision of other employees—also have important responsibilities that require a great deal of professional training and a high degree of personal judgment. Such upper-level nonmanagement positions may carry a title such as *senior consultant*.

Variations among companies

Most companies have employees at each of the levels depicted in Figure 3-2. Many large companies also have subdivisions of the categories shown. For example, the category of vice presidents often includes executive vice presidents, senior vice presidents, vice presidents, and assistant vice presidents. Large companies may also have managers, assistant managers, supervisors, and assistant supervisors. Even the terminology used to describe various positions varies from company to company. In one company, a person at the managerial level in charge of the accounting department may hold a title such as *accounting manager*. In another company, the person holding a job with the same duties may be called the *chief accountant, controller,* or *comptroller*.

In some companies, the middle management level includes persons with the title of *director*. As part of a title, such as *director of human resources,* the word *director* usually refers to a position between vice president and manager. However, when used with just the name of the company, without any mention of function—for example, "a director of the ABC Life and Health Insurance Company"—the word *director* usually refers to a member of the board of directors.

Span of Control

The number of people directly supervised by a manager is referred to as the manager's **span of control**. Generally, the more people a manager supervises, the broader the manager's span of control is said to be. The number of subordinates that one manager can effectively supervise is limited, but every work situation is unique, and no formula can state an ideal span of control. Some of the factors that affect whether a manager is given a broad span of control or a narrow span of control are listed below.

- *Repetitiveness or complexity of subordinates' tasks.* The simpler and more repetitive subordinates' tasks are, the broader the manager's span of control can be.
- *Skills of the subordinates.* The more highly skilled and competent subordinates are, the broader the manager's span of control can be.
- *Rate of turnover among the subordinates.* The newer and more untrained subordinates are, the narrower the manager's span of control should be.
- *Physical proximity of subordinates to the manager.* The more widely dispersed subordinates are, the narrower the manager's span of control should be.
- *Supervisory skills of the manager.* The better the manager's skills and the greater the manager's experience are, the broader the manager's span of control can be.

Whether a manager's span of control is broad or narrow, all employees should know for whom they work and to whom they are accountable.

According to the principle of **unity of command,** each employee should receive authority from only one person and be accountable to only that person.

Tall pyramids and flat pyramids

Illustrations of the span-of-control principle and its impact on an organization chart appear in Figures 3-3 and 3-4. If a department needs a staff of 12 people to operate effectively, how many supervisors should there be to oversee the work of those 12 employees? Two possible answers are depicted in Figures 3-3 and 3-4.

Figure 3-3 shows an example of a flat organizational pyramid. A flat organizational pyramid has few supervisory levels, and the span of control is broad. Each worker reports directly to the manager and is directly supervised by the manager. Although this flat organizational structure tends to hold down the total amount spent on supervisory salaries, an individual manager may be paid more because of increased managerial responsibilities. However, a manager in such a company may not have the time to give each worker the attention he or she needs. As a result, decisions may be postponed, and backlogs of work may occur.

In a flat organizational pyramid, there are usually fewer problems with communication. Managers and nonmanagers lower down in the pyramid have more opportunities to make decisions that affect their own jobs. Furthermore, decisions can usually be made more quickly in a flat

Figure 3-3
Span of control and a flat pyramidal structure.

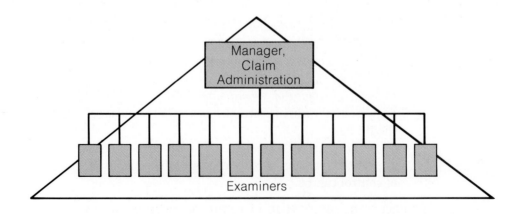

Figure 3-4
Span of control and a tall pyramidal structure.

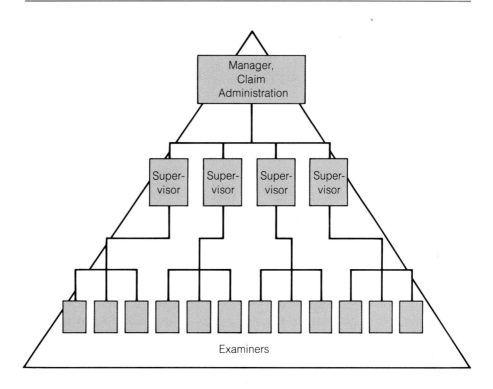

organizational structure than in a tall organizational structure. On the other hand, a flat organizational structure can lead to situations in which supervisors are responsible for more activities than they can reasonably manage. In addition, a flat organizational structure may give employees fewer opportunities for promotion.

Figure 3-4 shows a department in which the span of control is narrow. Each supervisor oversees the work of only three subordinates. As a result, the organizational pyramid tends to be tall. Each supervisor should be able to respond promptly to subordinates' questions and problems. However, this organization adds four supervisors' salaries to the cost of operating the business.

A tall organizational pyramid permits closer control over the work of direct subordinates. Yet because a tall pyramid can have many layers of management between the top and the bottom of the pyramid, communication problems sometimes develop. Information from the bottom of the pyramid may take too long to reach the top of the pyramid, and decisions from the top may take so long to reach the bottom that actions based on those decisions may not be timely.

Traditionally, insurance companies have been known for their tall organizational structures. Many large insurers have had, at one time, as many as 20 levels of authority between the president and the last entry-level employee. Many insurers are now reorganizing their structure by giving more responsibility and authority to employees further down the organizational pyramid, and, in the process, creating flatter organizational structures. One approach to flattening organizational structures is through self-managed teams, which are the focus of INSIGHT 3-2.

INSIGHT 3-2

Self-Managed Teams

Client Resource Services, a division of Indianapolis Life Insurance Company's Information Services Division (ISD), reorganized to form two self-managed teams: the Workstation Support team and the Business Analyst team. Each team has specific responsibilities and the authority to decide how best to meet those responsibilities.

To help define what "self-managed" meant, the division management outlined three phases necessary for migrating from their current structure to the self-managed team structure they envisioned.

- Phase I: Individual Accountability
- Phase II: Team Building
- Phase III: Mature Team

They published a list of specific team responsibilities and defined the level of authority needed by a team member to perform each task. Then, team members attended retreats for orientation and training. During these retreats, the teams defined their teams' rules and goals and identified the support they needed from

management and from each other. Every three months, the teams "revisit" these goals, and identify specific individual tasks that help to accomplish specific goals.

Each team supervises itself through team meetings. During these meetings, team members:

- prioritize work and make job assignments
- discuss training needs
- discuss approaching deadlines and make recommendations
- schedule vacation, personal business time, etc.
- handle conflicts
- formulate individual annual plans
- discuss solutions to production problems
- give input on performance appraisals

The reorganization has freed up two division managers for special assignments. Indianapolis Life has removed three supervisor positions, and the span of control for this division is now twenty-two employees for one division manager. Morale is very high, and the employees are showing pride in their work, because they are now directly accountable. Even though they attend more meetings, employee production has increased.

Each team member has been given the option of returning to the traditional style of management if the member is uncomfortable with any aspect of the team concept. To date, no requests have been received.

Source: Adapted with permission from an Activity Report submitted to LOMA by Vicki S. Lindell, FLMI, ACS, of Indianapolis Life Insurance, November 1990.

Diamond-shaped organizational structures. One step beyond the flattening of the organizational pyramid is the emergence of the *diamond-shaped organizational structure*. The widespread use of computers and the increasing reliance on information technology to stay competitive cause many companies to hire *knowledge workers*. These employees run the systems that do the work previously performed by large staffs of entry-level workers, such as file clerks. Also, because of advances in personal computer technology, technical/professional employees and members of companies' sales forces can perform work that previously was done by secretaries or data processing personnel. Now that so many company employees have access to computers, people who previously would have delegated aspects of their work to someone else may now perform the work themselves.

For example, because word processing technology is so widely available to company employees, members of the legal or marketing staff may process their own documents rather than delegate such work to administrative assistants. Also, agents can access policy information electronically instead of contacting employees at the home office. As a result of such developments, fewer support staff are needed because employees higher up in the traditional pyramid structure can perform certain functions themselves. Because of information technology, eventually fewer technical/professional staff may be required because managers can now retrieve and analyze information on their own. With such developments, the lower levels of the pyramid are narrowed, creating more of a diamond-shaped organizational structure. The actual shape of the diamond varies depending on factors such as the growth of the company and the company's use of technology (see Figure 3-5).

Line and Staff Units

The terms *line units* and *staff units* are frequently used when describing an organization, even though the practical distinctions between the two are

Figure 3-5
Example of a move to a diamond-shaped organizational structure.

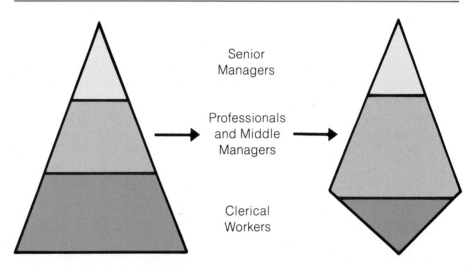

Source: Human Resources: Today and in The Future, LOMA/Arthur D. Little, Inc., 1989.

sometimes unclear. **Line units** are areas of an organization that produce the firm's products or services. **Staff units** support line units by providing advice, information, or the physical materials that the line units need to complete their work. For example, one responsibility of the marketing department is to make sure that insurance products are available for consumers. The marketing department (a line unit) relies on the legal department (a staff unit) for advice on tax laws affecting insurance products.

In a life and health insurance company, the major line units are marketing, actuarial, underwriting, customer service, claim administration, and investments. Staff units include accounting, legal, human resources, and information systems.

Line authority and staff authority

Two important types of authority in an organization are line authority and staff authority. **Line authority** is direct authority over subordinates. For example, the president of a company has line authority over all units within the company. Vice presidents have line authority over the divisions that report to them but no line authority over the other divisions in the company. For example, the vice president of marketing has no line authority over a manager in the claim administration department, who reports to the vice president of claim administration.

Staff authority is indirect authority that staff personnel have over personnel in other departments. In situations where staff authority is minimal, the advice provided by staff personnel may be accepted or rejected by a department. However, line units not only must consult staff units on certain decisions, but the line units must also get the staff unit to concur with or approve the decision before action can be taken.

Managers of staff units exercise both line and staff authority. In managing the work of their own units, they have line authority over their subordinates. In providing advice or services to other units, they exercise staff authority.

Centralized and Decentralized Organizations

The organizational structure of most businesses can be characterized as either centralized or decentralized. In *centralized* organizations, most decisions are made by upper-level management, and lower-level subordinates possess little authority to make decisions. In *decentralized* organizations, general policy is made by upper-level management, and authority for many types of decisions is delegated to lower-level subordinates. (Decentralization can also refer to the fact that a company maintains regional offices.)

Centralized and decentralized organizations each have certain benefits that the other does not. In a centralized organization, policies and actions tend to be consistent because decisions are made by a central authority. Also, certain administrative costs are reduced in a centralized organization because administrative services are usually handled by a single centralized department. In a decentralized organization, managers can respond to situations quickly because they have more authority to make decisions. Having this authority can increase managers' morale and provide them with experience that they can use later in their careers.

TYPICAL ORGANIZATIONAL STRUCTURES

Among life and health insurance companies, the traditional ways to organize activities are by *function*, by *product*, and by *territory*. A particular company may use any one of these systems or, quite likely, a combination of them. For example, a company could organize itself by product and then organize each product unit according to function. However, the use of matrix organizational structures, profit centers, and strategic business units, each of which are described later in this chapter, is also growing.

Organization by Function

If a company is organized by function, its major divisions are differentiated by the work that the divisions perform (see Figure 3-6). The word *function* is generally used to describe a distinct type of work, an essential step in a process, or an aspect of operations or management that requires special technical knowledge. The major functional areas in a life and health insurance company are marketing, actuarial, underwriting, customer service, claim administration, investments, accounting, legal, human resources, and information systems. In a company organized by function, staff in these departments would perform their function for all of the company's products.

Organization by Product

In a life and health insurance company that is organized by product, the work is distributed according to the company's lines of insurance (see Figure 3-7). Each of the lines is administered by a major division of the company. As a result, the group insurance division, for example, takes care of its own marketing, underwriting, and customer service activities. However, investments and other functions are usually handled through centrally administered departments. Organization by product tends to decentralize a company, allowing more decisions to be made by the employees who are most closely involved with a particular type of product.

Organization by Territory

When a company is organized according to territory, its major divisions are determined by the geographical areas in which it operates. A company doing business in the United States and Canada, for example, may have a U.S. division and a Canadian division. A company doing business in only one country may divide its operations according to states, provinces, or even larger regions. Within each of the territorial divisions, companies may further subdivide operations according to product or function. Figure 3-8 shows how a life and health insurance company can organize itself according to geographical areas and then subdivide its territorial divisions according to products.

Figure 3-6
Organization by function.

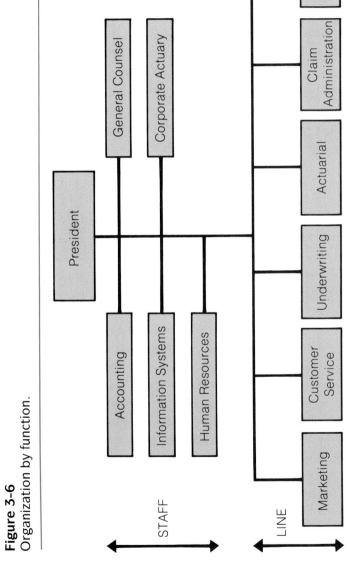

Figure 3-7
Organization by product.

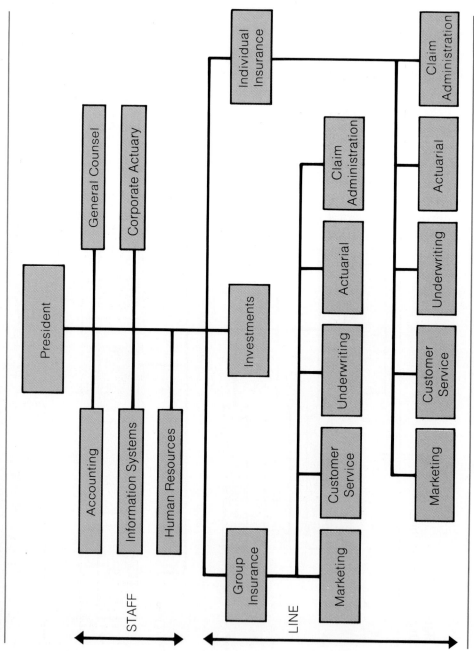

Figure 3-8
Organization by territory.

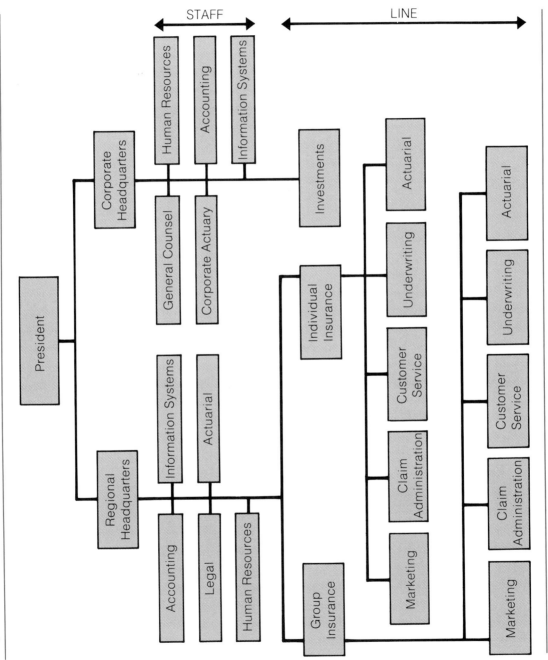

The top executive of a regional office is usually a senior vice president, who reports to the president of the company at the home office. Typically, the operations at regional offices include underwriting, policy issue, premium billing and receipts, customer service, claim administration, and the supervision and support of the marketing activities in the designated region. The regional offices may also have their own human resources units, as well as small legal and actuarial staffs. In some cases, the regional offices might actually be subsidiary companies of a parent company. A ***subsidiary*** is a company that is controlled by another company.

Organization into Profit Centers

Changes in the life and health insurance industry, such as the increased competition described in Chapter 1, have led some companies to restructure their organizations. One relatively new way to organize a company's operations is by profit centers. A ***profit center,*** known in some companies as a *revenue center,* can be described as a segment of an organization that controls its own revenues and expenses and makes its own decisions regarding its operations. In a company organized into profit centers, segments that are not themselves profit centers are known as ***service centers,*** or in some companies *resource centers.* These areas typically provide support services for the profit centers.

One use of the profit center approach is to determine the efficiency of a company's operations. By focusing on efficiency, a company can become more competitive by reducing its operating expenses and controlling the costs of its products.

Life and health insurance companies that use a profit center approach often resemble companies that are organized by product because a company's product lines are typically the main elements of the company that produce revenues. The profit centers could be identified as Individual Life, Individual Health, Annuities and Supplementary Contracts, Group Health, and so on.

In some companies, support functions are incorporated into the different profit centers. Thus, the Individual Life profit center would include its own actuarial, underwriting, human resources, and information systems departments. In such a case, the Individual Life profit center would be considered a strategic business unit. A ***strategic business unit (SBU)*** is an area of a business that is operated as a separate profit center, has its own set of customers and competitors, generally has its own management and support functions, and is capable of having its own plan of operations.

A few companies have established certain service areas, such as information systems, underwriting, or investments, as profit centers. Such companies could market the services of these particular functional areas to outside organizations. In some companies, these service areas charge other departments in the company for their work.

One benefit of the profit center approach is that a company's personnel can become more involved in decision making. Because each profit center is responsible for its own performance, the primary direction provided for each profit center may come from a division's vice president (the profit center leader) rather than from the board of directors or a company's executive offices. As a result, people lower in the organizational chain of command have more input into operations.

However, the profit center/SBU approach may produce a certain amount of duplication of effort, particularly among support personnel. For example, if each of two profit centers—such as Individual Health and Group Health—has its own information systems staff, the company may be spending more money than necessary by maintaining two separate health insurance information systems. Similarly, if each center has its own human resources function, neither center may have the benefit of knowing what the other one is doing. An applicant for a position in the Individual Health profit center may not be hired for the job there, and yet would be qualified for a Group Health position. Because of the separate human resources staffs, though, the applicant's name may never be passed on from one group to the other.

In some cases—whether a company has been using a profit center, matrix, or more traditional organizational structure—a total redesign of business operations might be necessary to respond to environmental changes. INSIGHT 3-3 offers one approach to changing an insurance company's operations.

INSIGHT 3-3

Reengineering Is a Must

"The insurance industry," notes technology expert Michael Hammer, "is probably the industry most actively pursuing and committed to the reengineering enterprise, and the industry most desperately in need of it." Hammer notes that many companies within the industry are operating on procedures developed 30 years ago, procedures that will not suffice in today's business environment.

According to Hammer, when properly done, reengineering entails throwing everything out and starting from scratch, a process he calls "zero-based design." Consequently, reengineering can result in very dramatic reviews of both company and employee performance. However, Hammer admits that reengineering is a painful and uncomfortable experience, because an organization is torn apart by the redesign process.

Hammer describes reengineering as a four-phase process: mobilization, focusing, redesign, and implementation. He defines mobilization as "developing an organizational commitment to reengineering." Focusing means understanding each current process and what needs to be done about it. Redesign is simply "coming up with a new breakthrough idea," and implementation "is making it a reality."

Hammer says that companies have to be prepared to break the rules when getting involved with reengineering. "Reengineering is a cross-functional effort. One reengineers processes, not organizations. Process design is the start, but not the end, of reengineering," Hammer said, adding that reengineering "is not the same as quality improvement. However, reengineering has to be complementary to quality improvement."

It is also important, he states, that reengineering begin at the top of an organization—with its senior management—because nobody wants reengineering. "Because reengineering works top down, it demands real aggressive leadership," Hammer says.

Hammer states that companies that are now actively engaged in reengineering are doing so because they recognize that "in business as usual, doing a little bit better just isn't going to make it."

Source: Adapted with permission of the publisher from Faith Tomei and Tim Kelley, "Use Technology to Reach the Right Customers," *Resource,* May 1991, p. 7.

COMMITTEES

Some aspects of a company's operations do not fall within the jurisdiction of any single department. For this reason, most companies establish special committees to bring together a number of people, each of whom has other responsibilities within the firm, to address these cross-jurisdictional aspects. Committees exist at all levels of an organization and are used when a particular problem or task is best tackled by individuals with different talents and perspectives.

Some committees, called *standing committees*, are permanent and are used by company executives as sources of continuing advice. Other committees—which may be called *ad hoc committees*, *project teams*, *work groups*, or *task forces*—are established for a specific purpose, such as planning a new computer system, establishing a subsidiary company, developing a new product, or revising the company's accounting system. Such committees usually consist of a chairman or project director and several committee members, all of whom are assigned to the committee until the committee's purpose is achieved. During the project, the committee members are responsible to the committee chairman, although all ties with the departments from which the members came are not completely severed. Some committee members may be assigned to the project full-time and others may be assigned only part-time.

The use of ad hoc committees and project teams creates a structure that is parallel to a company's normal organizational structure; the new structure can confuse the normal chain of authority and responsibility. However, the committees themselves can be extremely effective in dealing with unique problems and situations and are usually considered worth any problems they may cause in the chain of command.

Some businesses operate in part by forming ad hoc committees or teams of qualified employees from various disciplines to work on projects. Such a structure, called a ***matrix structure,*** seeks to optimize both the performance of organizational tasks and the use of resources. Some insurance companies are using this structure to a limited extent but few, if any, use it exclusively. The matrix structure typically combines personnel from product areas and functional areas of a company. Among the advantages of operating with a matrix structure are a greater exchange of information, increased flexibility, and in many cases, enhanced commitment to a project from those people involved in the matrix. A disadvantage of this structure is the possibility of power struggles caused by overlapping authority and responsibility. Also, these structures often violate the unity-of-command principle introduced earlier in this chapter—that is, employees may be unsure about to whom they report. The use of the matrix structure in life and health insurance companies is most prevalent for projects in which the input of many different areas of the company is required, such as in new product development.

Committees of the Board of Directors

Several of the most important standing committees of any business are made up of members of a company's board of directors and the company's key executives. In life and health insurance companies, committees of the board commonly include the *executive committee, investment committee, audit committee,* and *tax committee.* Some companies establish additional committees, such as claim committees, as the situation demands. By participating on committees, board members are kept informed of the company's activities during the intervals between board meetings and can report on these activities at regular board meetings.

Executive committee

Sometimes called the *insurance committee,* the *executive committee* is concerned with matters that bear directly on the general business policy of the company. This committee deals with questions of overall company policy, the lines of business that the company sells, the territory in which it operates, policies affecting the company's employees, and items not specifically assigned to other committees of the board of directors. In some cases, this committee, in conjunction with a special project team, will conduct the **strategic planning,** or *long-range planning,* for the company by studying the company's current performance, identifying the company's position in the insurance market, predicting future trends, and creating a plan of development for the company's future.

Investment committee

The *investment committee,* also called the *finance committee,* determines the broad investment policy of the company. The investment committee prescribes the types of investments in which the company's funds are to be placed and decides on the general distribution of assets among different classes of investments—bonds, stocks, mortgages, real estate. Day-to-day investment activities are conducted by the firm's financial officers, who direct the company's investment department and operate within the general policies prescribed by the committee. Major investment actions proposed by the investment department are reported to the investment committee, which then approves or disapproves the proposed transactions. The committee may also select the banks in which the company's funds are to be deposited and designate the amount of money to be maintained in each account.

Audit committee

The *audit committee* supervises the company's accounting operations, oversees internal and external accounting audits, and reviews the company's periodic financial statements. Audits conducted by regulatory bodies and private accounting firms are called **external audits;** audits conducted by the company's own accountants are called **internal audits.** The committee employs an independent accounting firm to perform the periodic external audits. Many insurance companies have established internal audit units that audit every division in the company and report directly to the audit committee. In order to enhance the objectivity of the auditing process, the audit committee normally does not include the president or any other officer of the company. In some states, company employees are prohibited from being members of the audit committee.

Tax committee

The *tax committee* is responsible for analyzing and evaluating the tax implications of company policies, programs, and rules, and for keeping informed about corporate tax legislation.

Interdepartmental Committees

In addition to committees of the board of directors, companies often have interdepartmental committees comprised of executives and upper-level managers from different departments. The functions and types of interdepartmental committees vary from company to company, but common ones include the *marketing committee, budget committee, corporate communications committee, research committee,* and various types of *human resources committees,* such as a *grievance committee* and an *awards committee.*

Marketing committee

The *marketing committee* reviews market research and recommendations from agents, brokers, and various departments to decide whether there is enough consumer demand for the company to develop a new product or revise a current product. If the committee decides that a product is worth considering, it will establish a *product design task force* to plan the product. Critical decisions about the design and use of the product are still usually made by the marketing committee.

Budget committee

A *budget committee* is responsible for preparing an annual budget of the company's estimated operating expenses. In its work, the committee draws on information and assistance from the accounting department. Generally, the managers of the various departments submit information that the committee uses to establish a budget. The budget proposal formulated by this committee is subject to the approval and authorization of the board of directors.

Corporate communications committee

The *corporate communications committee*, also called the *public relations committee*, reviews and coordinates the company's policies on advertising, publicity, charitable contributions, sales promotion, and relationships with the public. The committee establishes guidelines that are followed by the company's marketing department and by any company employee who deals with the public.

Research committee

Many companies make each department responsible for research in its own area, but some companies establish a separate *research committee* or *research and development (R & D) committee*. Generally, a research committee studies a wide variety of subjects. It analyzes product development and structure, underwriting practices, operational procedures, and actuarial problems. It collects data and participates in intercompany studies, appraises the competitive position of the company, and reports on the actions of other companies.

Human resources committees

Some companies have various interdepartmental *human resources committees* that develop rules and regulations pertaining to the hiring, training, dismissal, and welfare of employees. Such committees review compensation plans, recommend changes in salary scales, and administer retirement and pension programs. Their activities are closely coordinated with the work of the human resources department.

FUNCTIONAL AREAS IN A LIFE AND HEALTH INSURANCE COMPANY

As mentioned earlier, the functional areas found in a typical life and health insurance company include *marketing, actuarial, underwriting, customer service, claim administration, investments, accounting, legal, human resources,* and *information systems*. Sometimes these functional areas are organized in separate departments. For example, in some companies all actuarial activities take place in a single actuarial department. However, it is just as common for each of these functions to be performed by individuals or staffs in many different departments. For example, if a company is organized along product lines, each product line may have its own actuaries or underwriters. As we describe the various functions throughout the rest of the book, we will try to indicate some of the different ways that these functions may fit into a company structure, but for ease of reference we will usually describe functional activities as the activities of a single department.

Marketing

The *marketing department* of a life and health insurance company has a number of responsibilities: conducting market research, working with other departments in the company to develop new products and revise current ones to meet the needs of the company's customers, preparing ad campaigns (in conjunction with the company's executive office and corporate communications committee), designing promotional materials, and establishing and maintaining distribution systems for the company's products.

Many of the functions performed in a life and health insurance company's marketing department are determined by the type of distribution system the company uses. The distribution systems commonly used by insurance companies include the following:

- ordinary agency system
- multiple-line agency system
- home service system
- brokerage system
- salaried sales system
- direct response system
- location selling system

In companies that use the agency distribution system, the marketing department is sometimes called the *sales* or *agency department*.

Actuarial

The *actuarial department* is responsible for ensuring that the company's operations are conducted on a mathematically sound basis. In conjunction with other departments, actuaries design and revise a company's life and health insurance products. The actuarial department establishes premium and policy dividend rates, determines what a company's reserve liabilities should be, and establishes nonforfeiture and loan values. It also does the research needed to predict mortality and morbidity rates, establish guidelines for selecting risks, and determine the profitability of the company's products.

In addition, actuaries usually participate in a company's strategic planning and are influential in mergers and acquisitions and in the company's relations with state, provincial, and federal regulators. Finally, an actuary must sign a company's Annual Statement in order for it to become a valid document.

Underwriting

The *underwriting department* is responsible for making sure that the actual mortality or morbidity rates of the company's insureds do not exceed the rates assumed when the premium rates were calculated. To do so, the underwriting department works with the actuarial department and with medical personnel to establish criteria for evaluating applications for insurance. The underwriter considers an applicant's age, weight, physical condition, personal and family history, occupation, financial resources, and other selection factors to determine the degree of risk represented by the proposed insured. This department may also participate in the negotiation and management of reinsurance agreements, through which an insurance company transfers some or all of an insurance risk to another insurance company.

Customer Service

As its name implies, the *customer service department*, also called the *policyowner service department*, the *client service department*, the *service and claim department*, and the *policy administration department*, is charged with providing assistance to the company's customers. A company's customers include agents, brokers, other employees, and beneficiaries, as well as its policyowners. Customer service specialists answer requests for information, help interpret policy language, answer questions about policy coverage, and make changes requested by the policyowner, such as changing an address, beneficiary designation, or mode of premium payment. The customer service department also calculates and processes policy loans, nonforfeiture options, and dividends. In some companies, the customer service department processes commission payments for company agents, sends premium notices, collects premium payments, and handles some claim administration.

Claim Administration

Processing claims is the duty of the *claim administration department*. In this department, claim examiners review claims presented by policyowners or beneficiaries, verify the validity of the claims, and authorize the payment of benefits to the proper person. If a company disputes a customer's claim, the claim examiner may be required to present evidence for the company in court.

Investments

The *investment department* examines the financial marketplace, recommends investment strategies to the company's investment committee, and manages the company's investments according to the policies established by the company's board of directors and investment committee. Authorized members of the investment department buy and sell stocks, bonds, mortgages, and real estate, as well as other assets. They also act as advisers to the president and board of directors when a merger or acquisition is planned.

Accounting

The *accounting department* maintains the records that show the financial results of a company's numerous transactions and whether the company is being operated in a cost-effective manner. The accounting department is responsible for maintaining the company's general accounting records, preparing financial statements, controlling receipts and disbursements, overseeing the company's budgeting process, administering the company's payroll, and working with the legal department to assure that the company is complying with government regulations and tax laws.

Legal

The *legal department* makes sure that the company's operations comply with federal, state, and provincial laws and with insurance department regulations. The legal department studies current and proposed legislation to determine their effects on the company's operations, advises the claim administration department when claims are disputed, works with the accounting department to determine the company's tax liabilities, represents the company or instructs outside counsel in any litigation, and handles investment agreements, policy assignments, and title searches. It also helps develop policy forms and other contracts used by the company.

Human Resources

The *human resources department*, also called the *personnel department*, is responsible for matters relating to the company's employees. This department formulates company policy with respect to hiring, training, and dismissal of employees; determines levels of compensation; and assures company compliance with federal, state, and provincial employment laws. It also administers employee benefit plans, such as group insurance, tuition refund plans, and employee pensions.

Information Systems

The *information systems department* is responsible for developing and maintaining the computer systems used by a life and health insurance company. As computer technology has increased in sophistication and practicality, its importance to the insurance industry has grown enormously. Today, the information systems department of an insurance company affects every part of the company. It helps other departments in the company develop, buy, and use the computer systems and software that are needed to provide information, maintain records, and administer products. The information systems department also maintains company records in computerized files, helps provide data used to prepare financial statements, and conducts analyses of the various procedures and systems used in the company.

RELATIONSHIPS AMONG COMPANY DEPARTMENTS

Throughout the remainder of this book, as we discuss the functions performed in an insurance company, we will also discuss the manner in which the various departments affect one another and how they interact with individuals and institutions outside the company. It is important to remember that every department affects or is affected by other departments and all rely on one another to produce successful results.

KEY TERMS

responsibility
authority
accountability
delegation
coordination
organization chart
board of directors
inside director
outside director
span of control
unity of command
line unit

staff unit
line authority
staff authority
subsidiary
profit center
service center
strategic business unit (SBU)
matrix structure
strategic planning
external audit
internal audit

Chapter 4

Marketing Fundamentals

After reading this chapter, you should be able to

- Describe the purpose of the marketing function in a life and health insurance company
- Contrast market-driven and product-driven organizations
- Explain the importance of a marketing plan and identify the internal and external factors that affect it
- Name three different sources of marketing intelligence
- Compare and contrast market segmentation and target marketing
- Describe the product development process
- Describe the role of the agent in marketing insurance products
- Identify selling practices in which agents may not engage
- Explain the importance of the conservation of business and describe agents' efforts to conserve business

To operate successfully, a business must identify its customers, determine the types of products its customers want, and distribute those products to its customers in a convenient, timely, and economical manner. This process is known as *marketing.*

In this and the following two chapters, we will talk about the various aspects of the marketing function. In this chapter, we will describe some fundamentals of the marketing process and look at typical functions of the marketing department, such as developing a marketing plan, gathering marketing intelligence, identifying target markets, and developing insurance products based on marketing information. This chapter also will look at the agent's role in the marketing process. In Chapters 5 and 6, we will discuss the different distribution systems that life and health insurance companies use and the ways that companies support those systems.

Because marketing operations can be organized in so many different ways, this text indicates only some representative structures. Marketing functions are generally the same in most companies, but organizational structures vary widely. Figure 4-1 illustrates one common organizational structure.

Figure 4-1
Organization chart of a marketing department.

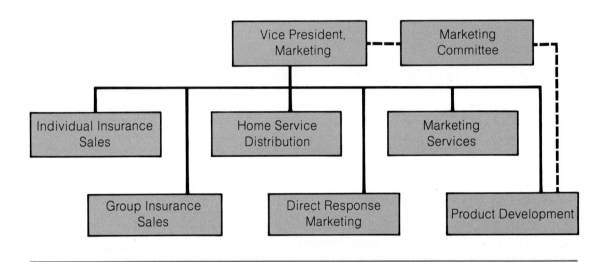

MARKET-DRIVEN VERSUS PRODUCT-DRIVEN ORGANIZATIONS

At one time, life and health insurance companies tended to be largely *product-driven organizations*, which place great emphasis on selling sound products with strong distribution systems and competitive prices. In a product-driven organization, the role of the marketing department is limited to selling the products the company has developed; the marketing department has little input into the design of the products themselves.

More and more companies are now market-driven. A *market-driven organization* responds to the needs of the marketplace and the consumers who make up the marketplace. In a market-driven organization, the role of the marketing department is to determine the needs of its customers and to satisfy those needs. By working with the actuarial and underwriting departments, the marketing department develops and distributes products that customers want, at prices that are both attractive to the consumer and profitable for the company.

A market-driven insurance company is generally more competitive than a product-driven insurance company. Market-driven companies take the lead in developing marketing strategies and products, whereas product-driven organizations react to, and generally lag behind, the marketplace. Because they prevail in the industry, market-driven operations are the focus of the marketing chapters in this text.

MARKETING FUNCTIONS

The marketing department of any firm, regardless of the products or services produced, performs a variety of functions. Each of the following six functions performed by marketing personnel is described in greater detail throughout Chapters 4, 5, and 6.

- *Planning and controlling*—the activities needed to develop a marketing plan, measure and compare marketing results to the marketing plan, and modify marketing activities to meet the plan's objectives.
- *Market identification*—the process of examining and selecting potential markets for the company's products. A **market** is a group of people who, either as individuals or as members of organizations, are the actual or potential buyers of a product. Market identification typically involves a two-step process of market segmentation and target marketing.
- *Product development*—the activities needed to create or revise products to meet the needs of an identified market. The product development process can involve almost every functional department in an insurance company: marketing, underwriting, claim administration, investments, actuarial, information systems, customer service, legal, and accounting.
- *Distribution*—the activities and resources needed to make products available to consumers. In some companies, a separate agency unit manages the distribution function.
- *Promotion*—the activities used to communicate with consumers in order to influence their product purchase decision. Promotion may include anything from one-to-one conversation to television advertising.
- *Gathering market intelligence*—the process of finding and compiling information about the company's environment, including its competition; marketing opportunities or problems; and marketing performance.

Two other aspects of the marketing function should be described. In most cases, these marketing-related functions are performed in cooperation with other departments in the insurance company.

- *Pricing*—the process of determining how much to charge for an insurance product. When pricing products, the marketing department works with the actuarial department to meet a number of different objectives. These objectives include determining (1) how much monetary return the company wants to earn on its products, (2) what level of sales the company expects to achieve, and (3) where the company wants to position its products in relation to the products of its competitors.
- *Customer service*—those activities directed toward keeping a company's customers satisfied so that they want to continue as clients of the insurer. The customers of an insurance company include its poli-cyowners, beneficiaries, insureds, group policyholders, agents, brokers, employee benefit consultants, and others.

In the remainder of this chapter, we will describe planning and controlling, market intelligence, market identification, product development, and the role of the agent. Distribution systems will be described in the next two chapters. Pricing and customer service are discussed in more detail in the actuarial and customer service chapters of this text, respectively.

PLANNING AND CONTROLLING

A company's marketing strategy is outlined in the company's marketing plan. The **marketing plan** specifies a company's marketing objectives, the strategies needed to achieve those objectives, and the particular goals for each critical product or line of products. More specifically, the marketing plan deals with the company's **marketing mix**—the product, pricing, distribution, and promotional strategies a company adopts in order to satisfy its overall objectives. The marketing plan is also used as a control tool, so that the marketing department can analyze the results of its operations and see how well its objectives are being met. Without this control tool, the marketing department would have difficulty judging its progress, identifying trends in performance, or planning corrective actions.

Developing the Marketing Plan

Because the marketing plan is used to coordinate all marketing activities, careful development of this plan is critical to a successful marketing operation. Furthermore, the marketing plan affects many other divisions throughout the company. For these reasons, senior company executives and participants from other divisions and departments are generally involved in creating the marketing plan. Often, key members of the distribution system are also included. For example, insurance companies that use the agency distribution system usually include members of the agency force in this planning process.

Development of the marketing plan begins with a careful review of the company's long-range and short-range business objectives. By considering both types of objectives, the marketing staff assures that the marketing plan agrees with overall corporate goals and helps turn these goals into specific, action-oriented strategies. For example, if a corporate goal is to increase overall company sales by 15 percent, one facet of the marketing plan may include an objective of increasing sales by 20 percent in the southeastern United States. In this case, the plan would describe the steps needed to bring sales up to that level, such as opening two new sales offices in the Southeast and conducting a promotional campaign from June through October.

Typically, a marketing plan covers a period of anywhere from one to five years. In a five-year marketing plan, the first year's goals and objectives and the specific actions needed to meet those objectives are described in detail. The goals for the second year through the fifth year of the plan are discussed in more general terms. The plan is then updated each year so that a five-year plan is always in place.

Factors Affecting the Marketing Plan

A number of internal and external factors affect the type of marketing plan that a life and health insurance company develops. Marketing executives and managers must study these factors and decide which factors can be changed and which ones require the company to change. *Internal factors* arise from the company itself and its business activities. *External factors* come from outside the company. Companies generally have more control over internal factors than external factors.

Internal factors

Among the internal factors that have the greatest effect on an insurance marketing plan are a company's (1) existing products, (2) existing markets, (3) current distribution systems, (4) corporate culture, (5) financial condition, and (6) technological resources (see Figure 4-2). Read INSIGHT 4-1 for a closer look at developing a company's marketing strategy.

Figure 4-2
Internal factors affecting an insurance company's marketing plan.

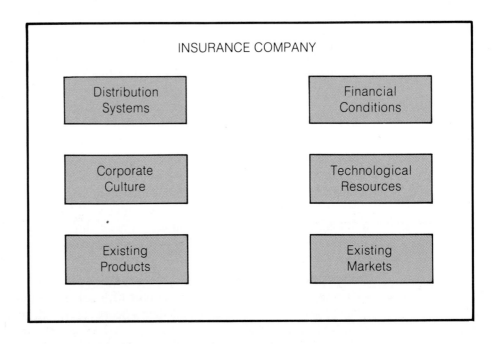

INSIGHT 4-1

Building Blocks to Effective Marketing

Five building blocks are essential to any effective marketing program. Mere awareness of these building blocks, plus a little horse sense, can form the basis for a turnkey marketing program in a small agency. It also can suggest the right questions to ask in the largest and most sophisticated insurance company. The building blocks are customers, needs, distribution outlets, persuasion systems, and products.

Marketing programs must deal with all five building blocks. Moreover, each

relevant marketing component should fit neatly into one of the five blocks. A strong marketing program cannot use small or shaky building blocks. For example, a good product that fills the needs of a well-defined customer base and is backed up by an excellent persuasion system will fail without adequate distribution outlets. The company must work on strengthening the weaker blocks. Each building block is briefly defined, discussed, and highlighted below.

Customers

The lack of customers continues to be the number one cause of business failures. Initially, you must know who your customers are, and then you must grasp what, when, where, and how they buy. During this process, be sure to deal with reality and not fantasies concerning what types of customers the company wants. Be alert for new customers whose underlying characteristics bear similarities to those of your current customers.

Don't commit the cardinal sin of neglecting your current customers. It can cost from 5 to 10 times more to create a new customer than to keep a current one happy. Do you use specific programs to communicate with and help existing customers? If your business spends $1 million to attract new customers, does it spend $100,000 to $200,000 to keep existing ones?

Needs

This building block requires you to understand and appreciate why customers buy. The ability to do this well is what distinguishes successful marketers. One must learn to appreciate that customers buy a drill because they want holes, not because they want pieces of steel.

Understanding customer needs is a vigorous and exacting skill. Major consumer marketers such as Procter and Gamble spend tens of millions of dollars annually on market research to better understand why people buy. How much money and effort does your business spend on this activity? Would it be helpful to spend more time listening to customers? How about some group interviews or simple, well-placed questionnaires? You do not have to spend millions, but a few thousand dollars on do-it-yourself market research can help.

Distribution outlets

Distribution outlets move product titles from producers to consumers. These outlets coordinate the sales process by using the other four building blocks. Outlets can include physical facilities like stores, as well as personnel such as independent sales representatives. Since outlets involve both people and facilities, improving the number and quality of outlets is a long-term, expensive proposition. Although products can sometimes be created overnight, this will not be the case with outlets.

What can a business do beyond finding more outlets and improving training? It can create new processes and techniques. For example, consider group seminars, telemarketing, inbound and outbound 800 numbers, and direct mail as complementary activities for your outlets. Occasionally it makes sense to set up other types of distribution outlets. The danger here is that it is not easy to do. Moreover, managing the inevitable rivalries and jealousies among different types of outlets can be quite challenging.

Persuasion systems

All materials and activities designed to make targeted customers aware of, understand, appreciate, and convinced to buy and rebuy your products are persuasion systems. Emerging markets often find that dollars spent here produce quicker results and more sales per dollar than any other building block.

An ideal persuasion system makes your business visible to your target customers when they are ready to buy and also conveys your product and company advantages. Most persuasion systems simply lack a broad enough base. Is your business making good use of audiovisual materials, conference and meeting exhibits, point-of-sale materials, and contests? How about billboards, speeches, newspaper articles, and talk shows? These avenues can act as low-cost and effective supplements to the usual media advertising and brochures.

Products

In addition to the core product the customer actually uses, tangible features such as name, styling, and packaging require constant review and attention. The total product consists of the core product with these tangible features, plus the intangible features. The intangibles include such things as credit, service, and delivery. Although variable and perishable, these intangibles represent an important, inseparable part of the product. When you review and discuss products, you should perform separate analyses of the core product and its tangible and intangible features.

An attractive product line is essential for marketing success. Consider price an integral part of the product. Do not make the mistake of placing unnecessary emphasis on products and of neglecting the other four building blocks. Rather than chase deceptive mega-product breakthroughs, encourage the everyday fine tuning of products and prices.

Most marketing programs, for one reason or another, tend to be driven by one of the building blocks. For example, Apple Computer in the early 1980s was a product-driven company. Avon Products for many years relied heavily on its distribution outlets—Avon representatives. These driving forces usually evolve over time and are woven into the fabric of a business. The question to ask is whether the total marketing effort can be improved by redirecting some of the focus and resources from the stronger blocks to the smaller and shakier blocks.

Source: Adapted with permission from Paul T. Bourdeau, ''Plod Your Way to Marketing Glory,'' *Best's Review* (Life/Health Insurance Edition), August 1990, pp. 54, 56.

Products.   A company's experience with different types or lines of products has a significant impact on a company's marketing strategy. For example, a company may concentrate more on life insurance products than on health insurance products. Thus, even if that company's researchers uncover a marketing opportunity for health insurance products, the company may not be internally prepared to pursue this market without a significant initial investment in money and personnel. For example, the company may not have the expertise to offer acceptable service to health insurance customers once the products are in place. As a result, the company may choose not to add more health insurance product offerings to its marketing plan.

Markets.   Just as a company's experience in marketing a certain product or a product line can affect the company's marketing plan, a company's experience in serving a particular market can also affect that plan. For example, a company that concentrates on a lower-income market might not have the necessary knowledge or resources to include in its marketing plan an expansion into the single-premium deferred annuity product line, which is directed more toward a higher-income market.

Current distribution systems. A company's distribution system can determine the markets that it plans to enter and the types of products it plans to develop. Insurance companies have several different ways to distribute their products. Most companies use an agency system (described in Chapter 5) in which commissioned insurance agents personally sell insurance to prospective policyowners. Some companies use salaried employees. Some insurers use direct response marketing and advertisements in newspapers and magazines, or on radio and television, to sell their insurance products.

Each distribution system often requires its own sales techniques and, frequently, its own types of products. For example, a complex product such as variable universal life insurance may be easier to sell through an agency system, in which an agent can sit down with a prospective policyowner and explain each aspect of the product. On the other hand, a simple mortgage protection life insurance policy can be sold effectively through a direct response system. As a result, a company's marketing plan must take into account the company's choice of distribution methods to assure a reasonable and successful match of distribution method with the company's products and markets. Companies can, in addition, develop a new distribution system to market a new product that does not fit their current distribution system.

Corporate culture. The attitudes, values, perceptions, and experiences shared by a company's employees and management make up the company's *corporate culture.* Although not as easy to identify or describe as its products or markets, a company's corporate culture can have a significant impact on the marketing plan. For example, if the directors of a company believe that the company should project a conservative image, then the marketing department should plan advertisements that stress a conservative aspect of the company's operations, such as its financial strength. If a company's agents are opposed to selling a certain type of policy, then the marketing plan can take this opposition into account in one of three ways: the company can plan to either (1) not offer the product, (2) make the product more attractive to the agents and try to convince them of its potential value, or (3) investigate an alternative distribution system for the product.

Company finances. A company's financial condition is another important factor in the marketing plan. Generally, a company with more financial resources is better able to enter more markets and provide more products than a company with less financial strength. Also, a company on stable financial ground has a better idea of which resources can be devoted to long-range marketing objectives than a company in a shaky financial position.

Of the internal factors described in this section, company finances is probably the most important factor affecting year-to-year changes in a company's marketing plan, because the other five factors do not generally change as much on a year-to-year basis. A company that has just had an especially profitable year may choose to make more resources available for the next year's marketing efforts.

Technological resources. Many new insurance products require sophisticated computer systems and expensive software programs for support operations such as accounting and customer service. In addition, agents use computers to help sell insurance products. A marketing plan should consider whether a company has or can obtain cost-effective computer support to administer a product. Failure to consider a company's technological resources in this manner may result in the inability to provide proper customer service for a product, which could then have a negative effect on the company's marketing goals.

External factors

Many external factors are also considered when establishing an insurance company's marketing plan. In particular, (1) the economic environment, (2) competition, (3) the regulatory environment, and (4) the societal environment all have a major impact on the formation of a marketing plan (see Figure 4-3).

Economic environment. The economic environment includes such factors as the inflation rate, prevailing and forecasted interest rates, unemployment levels, and other economic conditions that affect the climate in which the company will operate over the time covered by the marketing plan.

Competition. Competition for an insurance company includes other insurance companies as well as other types of financial institutions that are trying to sell similar or replacement products to identical markets. The approach taken by competitors in terms of products offered, markets targeted, prices, and marketing strategies all influence an insurer's marketing plan.

An insurer's marketing plan must also recognize government competi-

Figure 4-3
External factors affecting an insurance company's marketing plan.

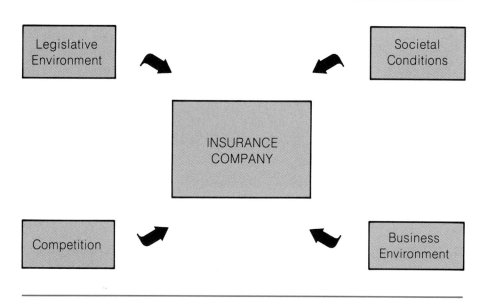

tion in the form of social benefits programs. Some life insurance, health insurance, and pension benefits are provided by government agencies. Any changes in these social benefit programs affect the needs of consumers and, therefore, the marketing objectives of the insurer. This aspect of competition can also be considered a function of an insurer's regulatory environment.

Regulatory environment. New laws and regulations can open or close markets for the company's products, affect distribution plans, and enhance or limit product development opportunities. In the United States, for example, an attractive aspect of permanent life insurance plans is that they build cash values that may not be taxed while the funds are part of the insurance policies. However, if tax regulations change and some of this cash value, also called *inside build-up*, becomes taxable as an investment—as happened in Canada in 1982—then permanent life insurance plans could have one of their most marketable features significantly reduced. A good marketing plan considers such possibilities and makes provisions to adapt to such changes if they occur.

Societal environment. Marketing specialists must study the various groups of consumers who make up a population in order to develop viable marketing plans. Consumer needs are strongly related to **demographics,** which are characteristics of a population such as the numbers of marriages, births, divorces, two-income families, single-parent households, retirements, and the age of the population in general. These factors suggest consumers' needs for insurance products and help to determine effective marketing methods. The education level of the general population is another demographic factor that dictates the types of coverage that appeal to consumers; for example, a well-educated population is better able to understand complex financial products than is a less-well-educated population. Cultural factors, such as a society's values and beliefs, as well as its shared and learned norms of behavior, are also a part of the societal environment a marketing specialist must study to develop appropriate marketing plans.

Allocation of Marketing Resources

One of the most important functions of the marketing plan is the allocation of marketing resources to achieve the company's established goals and objectives. The marketing plan must indicate the amount of money needed for advertising, training, salaries, commissions, and equipment, as well as the number of people needed and their qualifications. Because resources are always limited, this allocation process also helps planners determine whether a specific marketing objective is worth the cost.

MARKETING INTELLIGENCE

In order to have information about the company's current and past performance, as well as the company's current and projected external environment, marketing intelligence must be compiled. This information is then incorporated into the marketing plan. Some insurance companies may devote an entire section of their marketing department to gathering marketing intelligence. In other companies, the intelligence-gathering function may be one of several responsibilities assigned to certain individuals. Still other companies rely primarily on outside research firms for their marketing intelligence. In all cases, though, certain types of information are gathered and made available to the marketing planners.

Sources of Information

Insurance companies use a number of sources for gathering intelligence about current and possible future market conditions (see Figure 4-4).

Figure 4-4
Sources of information for marketing research.

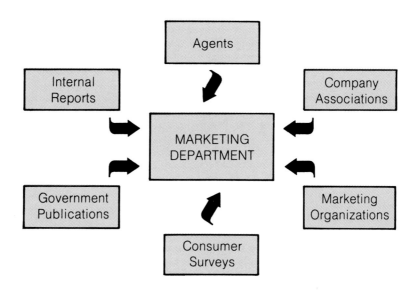

Marketing researchers study their own company's internal reports to determine current sales and profits on various products. Researchers use this information to forecast likely trends within their own company and thus create plans for a variety of situations. Researchers also keep track of their primary competitors' products, commission schedules, and rates.

Marketing researchers survey insurance agents and policyowners to determine their feelings about insurance products. Agents might be asked which products are easiest to sell and which specific markets show an interest in each type of product. Consumers may be asked to provide demographic information about themselves so that the researchers can identify individual market segments, such as professional women, retired couples, families with college-age children, etc. Each of these market segments has its own special insurance needs. Companies that do not distribute their products through agents have become especially adept at using surveys, interviews, and analyses of insurance applications to obtain product development information directly from consumers.

Insurance companies also gather information from a variety of marketing organizations and insurance associations. LIMRA (Life Insurance Marketing and Research Association) conducts a number of marketing studies and makes them available to the insurance industry. Two periodical studies that LIMRA publishes are

- *Life Insurance Sales* reports for the United States and Canada, which
  provide up-to-date information about the types and locations of sales,
  measured by premiums, face amounts, and number of policies
- United States and Canadian *Buyer Studies* reports, which analyze who
  bought ordinary life insurance products in the preceding year and the
  types of insurance bought

LOMA (Life Office Management Association) conducts research on
insurance issues and provides insurance companies with access to a
comprehensive collection of reports on the insurance industry's changing
activities. In 1992, for example, LOMA's Research Division published a
report on the impact of demographics on the insurance market and the
insurance work force.

Material from the Trend Analysis Program (TAP) and the Monitoring
the Attitudes of the Public (MAP) surveys, produced by the American
Council of Life Insurance (ACLI), also provides valuable information about
the changing external environment and the image of insurance companies.
In Canada, the Canadian Life and Health Insurance Association (CLHIA)
produces many reports and surveys, including a major survey on the
attitudes of the public toward life insurers. The Office of the Superintendent
of Insurance also presents more technical and actuarial material.

Government publications, such as census reports and studies of income
distribution, are valuable sources of information about the external
environment. Marketing researchers can also learn about the external
environment from a variety of publications produced specifically for the
insurance industry. Articles about new insurance products, the impact of
various proposed and enacted regulations on the insurance industry, and the
ways other companies respond to challenges in the marketplace all provide
necessary information for insurers as they develop their marketing plans.

Applications of Marketing Intelligence

The results of marketing intelligence-gathering form the basis for many of
the assumptions used in developing the marketing plan. For example, if
research indicates that the economy will probably grow by 3 percent in the
following year, that the size of the labor force at work will probably grow by
5 percent, and that inflation rates will probably stabilize at 6 percent, then
the company's marketing plan should be based on these projections.
Statistical exhibits supporting these projections are often incorporated into
the plan.

After the marketing plan has been in effect for a specified period of time,
marketing specialists study the results of the company's efforts in order to

analyze why the company has or has not met its goals. Marketing research techniques can be used to evaluate the effectiveness of the company's customer service and advertising campaigns as well as the overall success of the company's various products. If sales results do not reach the levels projected in the marketing plan, marketing analysts can try to determine why the sales results are less than expected and can help planners choose the steps necessary to help ensure the future success of the plan. For this reason, marketing intelligence is both a planning tool and a control tool.

MARKET IDENTIFICATION

Even before beginning to develop and market its products, a company typically completes three tasks: (1) identifying and evaluating the total market for the products the company plans to offer, (2) selecting the portion(s) of the market in which the company will offer its products, and (3) evaluating the marketing mix the company will use in designing its products. In order to accomplish these tasks, the marketing department of a life and health insurance company performs two primary activities: market segmentation and target marketing.

Market Segmentation

Market segmentation is the process of dividing large, basically similar markets into smaller markets that share certain characteristics, such as the need for products that fall within a certain price range or that satisfy the same basic consumer desires. These smaller groups of markets are known as *market segments.* The main purpose of market segmentation is to help a company determine which market segments exist among the larger market for insurance products.

Generally, the more narrowly defined the market segment, the more precisely the company can identify the needs of that segment and focus its marketing efforts. The four primary bases used for market segmentation are

- *geographic segmentation*—subdividing a market into homogeneous groups based on the needs and preferences of the populations in different locations, which may be countries, regions, states, provinces, counties, parishes, cities, or even neighborhoods
- *demographic segmentation*—subdividing a market into homogeneous groups based on variables that describe the characteristics of a

population: age, sex, marital status, household composition, income, educational level, occupation, family life cycle, and nationality

- *psychographic (or lifestyle) segmentation*—subdividing a market into homogeneous groups based on personality- or lifestyle-related characteristics: needs, attitudes, motives, and perceptions as affected by social factors in the consumers' environment
- *behavioristic segmentation*—subdividing a market into homogeneous groups based on various types of consumer behavior toward a given product, such as benefits sought, rate of usage, willingness to buy, and the preferred method of purchase

Once a company has defined the various market segments—and as you can see, many different market segments can exist—the company begins the target marketing process.

Target Marketing

Target marketing is the process of evaluating the attractiveness of each market segment and selecting the markets on which the company is going to concentrate. By further narrowing the large market for insurance products, target marketing makes a company's marketing process more efficient and effective.

The groups of individuals or organizations with which a company seeks to do business are known as the company's ***target markets.*** An insurer's choice of target markets helps determine the products developed, the distribution methods used, the type of advertising and promotional techniques employed, the customer service requirements, and the type of image the company needs to project. Depending on the number of segments that a company targets, a firm's target market strategies can be categorized in one of three ways:

- *Undifferentiated (or mass) marketing*. According to an undifferentiated target marketing strategy, a company produces only one product and defines the total market for that product as its target market.
- *Concentrated marketing*. According to a concentrated target marketing strategy, a company focuses all of its marketing resources on satisfying the needs of one segment of the total market for a particular type of product.
- *Differentiated marketing*. According to a differentiated target marketing strategy, a company offers a variety of products designed to appeal to different segments of the total market.

PRODUCT DEVELOPMENT

As the marketing department identifies consumers' needs, the company must develop ideas for new and revised products to meet those needs most effectively. Typically, ideas for insurance products come from the following personnel (see Figure 4-5):

- marketing department personnel, who analyze marketing intelligence and patterns in consumer behavior
- agents, brokers, and other product distributors, who understand the needs of consumers and see other companies' products that are selling successfully
- company executives, through their awareness of general trends and new products in the industry
- claim, underwriting, and customer service personnel, through their awareness of insurance product performance and the technological environment
- company lawyers and compliance analysts, who study laws and regulations and suggest products that take advantage of opportunities presented, such as potential tax savings for customers
- product development actuaries, who conceptualize mathematical models that can be developed into successful products

After ideas for new products are presented in a general fashion, the product ideas deemed to be worthy of additional development eventually reach a stage known as product proposal. Creating a product proposal is basically a five-step process: (1) conducting a market analysis, (2) establishing product design objectives, (3) conducting a feasibility study, (4) developing a marketing strategy for the product, and (5) preparing preliminary sales or financial forecasts. The company must also make sure that the products developed meet long-term corporate objectives.

Technical Design

Once further development of a proposed product has been approved, the next step in product development is technical design. Included in a product's technical design is information about actuarial assumptions, pricing, and underwriting standards. Because of the many different aspects of the technical design of a proposed product, virtually every functional area of an insurance company can become involved at this stage. For example,

Figure 4-5
Product development and the marketing department.

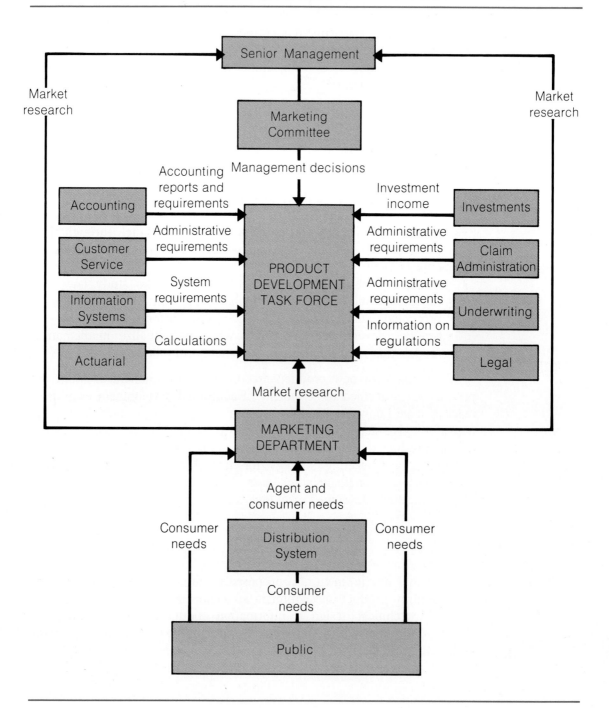

people from the information systems department are asked to identify the kind of computer support that the company needs for the new product. Customer service personnel identify the procedures required to support the product once it is put on the market. Lawyers identify the legal and tax implications of the product. Investment specialists analyze the projected investment income that will help fund the product and the interest assumptions used in determining how the product will perform under different economic scenarios. Underwriters suggest risk appraisal guidelines. Claim personnel help construct benefit specifications and policy language to ensure that the contract is enforceable as intended.

All these different company personnel may be organized into a *product design task force* that works together on the specifications for this particular project. As mentioned in Chapter 2, task force members may perform their task force duties in addition to their regular jobs. When the task force has come up with its working design for the product, the proposed product is then presented to the marketing committee. (As mentioned earlier in the text, the marketing committee is a senior management group whose primary function is to oversee the product development process and to review plans for new or revised products.) The marketing committee may approve the product's technical design or may call for revisions to the design.

Implementation

Once product design is finalized and approved internally, the product enters the *implementation* stage. In this stage, the company (1) obtains as necessary—with the help of the legal department—permission to sell the product from the jurisdictions in which the product will be sold, (2) designs promotional and training materials, and (3) initiates the systems and administrative activities necessary to support the product.

Designing promotional and training materials involves

- selecting a name for the product
- creating sales materials for distributors, customer service personnel, and consumers
- creating advertisements to announce and create interest in the product
- sending advertising and publicity materials about the product to insurance industry publications and general business publications

Companies that rely on direct response marketing or advertisements to reach consumers must place particular stress on their advertising materials, because these companies are marketing or selling directly to the consumer. In such cases, the help of outside advertising agencies is often enlisted.

Companies that use an agency distribution system may design special sales campaigns to encourage agents to sell the new product. Executives may visit agencies and regional offices, conducting seminars to explain and promote the new product, while special prizes or trips may be awarded to agents who sell the new product most successfully.

Proper education of sales agents is a crucial step in introducing a new product. If agents do not understand the product, they cannot sell it effectively, and perhaps may not even try. Frequently, the training section of the marketing department designs sample sales presentations for the new product and may provide visual aids for agents to use. Agents must also be taught how to fill out applications for the product and must be informed of any regulations affecting the sale, such as special disclosure forms or prohibited sales practices. Companies must also keep in mind that to sell equity-based products, such as variable universal life, insurance agents in the United States must have a special license from the SEC.

Test Marketing and Sales Monitoring

Before introducing a new product on a widespread basis, some companies test market the product in certain territories or through certain agencies. *Test marketing* is a kind of experiment: a new product and its marketing program are introduced on a limited scale in the product's target market. Through test marketing, a company can have some indication of how the product is likely to perform before the company commits the full scope of its resources to the product's introduction.

However, because of the intangible, long-term, and often complicated nature of many insurance products, test marketing is more difficult in this field than for other consumer products such as a new tool or a new snack food. For these latter types of products, consumers can give a fairly immediate response as to whether or not they like the product. Because some of the services related to a life insurance product may not take place until an insured dies, gauging total consumer response is often not feasible. Furthermore, even if an insurance product is discontinued as a result of the information obtained through test marketing, the policies already sold—which may be unprofitable because of the costs of administering a small block of policies—may have to be administered for many years. In place of true test marketing, then, an insurer may conduct interviews and surveys with agents, potential policyowners, and other customers.

After a new insurance product has been on the market for a period of time, marketing management must measure the product's success. Success can be measured by identifying the following factors:

- total face amount of insurance sold
- number of policies sold
- amount of premium income generated
- profits realized
- increase in the number of new policyowners
- demographic characteristics of customers who purchased the product
- policy lapse rates, loan rates, and claim experience
- sales success of various distribution systems
- success of various advertising campaigns and sales promotions

By analyzing this marketing information, a company can refine its marketing strategies and improve its likelihood of success.

If the product is unsuccessful, researchers and planners must reassess the product's characteristics to determine why it failed to meet its objectives. A product that did not fulfill its objectives may be redesigned. If failure was for some other reason, such as inadequate promotional effort, then the company can increase its efforts in that area. If the product failed because environmental factors did not behave as anticipated, then the environment needs to be reassessed to determine whether the product should be removed from the market.

If, on the other hand, a product is successful, then the company must continue to monitor that success and build on it. Often success with one product can be used to achieve success with others. Product development personnel must constantly be alert to possible changes in a product's performance, however, because these changes may be a signal that the product needs to be revised to match changes in the environment or the company's overall goals and objectives.

THE ROLE OF THE AGENT

For that large group of life insurance companies that use the agency system of distribution, the success of the company and its marketing function rests, to a considerable degree, on the performance of its soliciting agents. All other company personnel contribute to that success, but the agents are in closest contact with potential purchasers of insurance. Most agents work out of field offices and are referred to collectively as the company's *field force.* Because establishing a field office in every community is impractical, some agents work out of personal offices located in, or close to, their homes. Such agents are sometimes called *detached agents.* However, even detached agents can use the services provided by the field offices.

The functions of an agent fall into three categories: *producing new insurance business, conserving existing business,* and *providing service to policyowners.* In most cases, each individual agent determines the amount of time to spend performing each function and the hours he or she works. New agents, however, are often closely supervised by an agency manager and may be required to work certain hours and devote a certain amount of time per week to specified functions.

Producing New Business

The first step in producing new business is finding potential customers in the company's target markets. Potential customers are called ***prospects,*** and the activity of identifying, contacting, and qualifying potential customers is called ***prospecting.*** Prospecting can be a difficult and discouraging aspect of life insurance marketing, especially for new agents. In fact, the difficulties associated with prospecting, such as rejection by customers and feelings of failure, are among the most common reasons that agents give for leaving the business. Therefore, new agents must receive moral support and must strive to develop strong prospecting skills as early as possible in their careers.

When prospecting, an agent seeks people who need insurance and who are likely to respond positively to a sales presentation. A potential prospect must

- have a need for insurance products
- be able to pay for the products
- be insurable
- be approachable

Agents use several methods of prospecting. Most new agents start by contacting people they know—relatives, friends, and business acquaintances. Established agents sell insurance primarily to their current clients and to referrals from these clients. Agents also find prospects by observing events in the local community. The purchase of a house or the birth of a child usually leads to a reexamination of insurance coverage. Announcements of weddings, promotions, or inheritances can also alert an agent to a potential prospect. Frequently, agents send direct response advertisements to such prospects. Agents can also obtain lists of prospects, either from the home office or from mailing list companies.

When beginning the sales process, an agent must identify a prospect's needs by gathering such information as the prospect's age, income and savings, amounts of any debts or liabilities that may come due, the size and composition of the prospect's family, other policies the prospect owns, and the prospect's average monthly expenses. Having defined the insurance needs, the agent must determine whether the company's insurance products can meet those needs. A prospect can have business insurance needs, personal insurance needs, or both. Business needs for insurance products fall into two main categories: (1) insurance for the protection of the business itself, intended to assure its continuance after the death of the owner or a key member of the firm, and (2) insurance to provide retirement pensions and other benefits to employees of the firm. The next section of this chapter focuses on insurance for personal needs.

Insurance for personal needs

The agent dealing with the personal or family needs of a prospect often engages in any of three distinctive modes of selling: *single-need selling, total-needs programming*, and *estate planning*.

Single-need selling. In ***single-need selling,*** the agent isolates a particular financial need that can be met by insurance. For example, the agent may see the need for life insurance sufficient to cover the outstanding balance on the prospect's home mortgage.

Various studies have identified other typical single financial needs that can be met by insurance, such as:

- funds to pay the prospect's outstanding debts
- funds to pay the funeral and final illness expenses of a family member
- *readjustment funds* to provide temporary income while the survivors adjust financially to the loss of the deceased insured's income
- income to provide the amount necessary, above that provided by government benefit programs, to balance the family budget after the readjustment period
- retirement income to provide funds after an insured's working years
- savings funds to provide a financial cushion against unexpected expenses
- funds for the education of children, whether or not a parent dies before the children complete their education
- funds to replace lost income when a person is unable to work because of a disability
- funds to pay for the medical expenses caused by sickness or injury

In single-need selling, the agent concentrates on meeting one of the prospect's financial needs by finding an insurance policy suited to that purpose. Of course, the fact that a policy is sold in anticipation of a certain need does not necessarily mean that the policy proceeds will be used for that purpose. The proceeds of a policy sold with one need in mind often prove useful or even essential in meeting a completely different need that arises later.

Total-needs programming. In ***total-needs programming,*** the agent brings together all the prospect's life insurance needs, calculates the amount of money required to take care of each of those needs, evaluates the assets that will be available when the prospect dies, and determines the amount of life insurance and types of policies required to cover any shortfall. Thus, total-needs programming considers existing assets; life insurance from all sources, individual and group; and anticipated government benefits.

The following is a simplified example of total-needs programming. A prospect would like to provide the following sums for her family after she dies:

1. $20,000 for immediate expenses and readjustment funds
2. $50,000 to pay off the home mortgage
3. $1,500 monthly income for her family until the youngest child, now aged 3, reaches age 23
4. $900 monthly income thereafter for the remainder of her husband's life

Given this information, the agent must then compute the amount of life insurance needed to provide these amounts. The first of the three desired sums requires an immediate lump-sum death benefit of $20,000. The second requires $50,000. The third requires approximately $200,000, depending upon the assumed interest rate over a 20-year period. The fourth requires perhaps $80,000. These desired sums total $350,000. Note that the insurance required for needs 2, 3, and 4 decreases each month as the benefit period shortens. These calculations must include certain assumptions about the effects of inflation as well as interest.

To determine the amount of new insurance needed for this program, the agent must make allowances for other insurance policies already in force and for anticipated government-provided benefits, thus reducing the amount of insurance needed in a plan like the one described above. Employer-financed benefits, such as those provided by group life insurance policies, are also important but are less certain because coverage may terminate shortly after a person leaves a job. However, group life insurance can usually be converted upon termination of employment.

After calculating the amount of new insurance needed, the agent determines the types of policies that are suitable for the prospect's insurance program. The computations required to set up an insurance program are quite complex, and many life insurance agents use computers to help make these computations. The agent compiles essential data about the prospect and the various needs that are to be met. The computer performs the required calculations and gives the agent one or more solutions regarding the types and amounts of insurance policies that can be recommended to the prospect.

The products available may provide only a death benefit or may also provide a means of accumulating money to meet financial needs during the insured's lifetime. For example, the insurance to pay off the mortgage can be provided through a mortgage redemption insurance policy or rider, and the insurance to provide the monthly income for the child can be provided by a 20-year family income policy or rider. Both of these plans meet decreasing insurance needs through decreasing term insurance. The remaining insurance needed might be provided by a permanent, cash value plan which could also serve as a savings vehicle. Some cash value products provide fixed benefit amounts and fixed cash accumulation features, while others allow the benefit or cash accumulation amounts to vary according to future interest rates or investment earnings. Such adjustable products include universal life and variable life insurance policies and variable annuities. The agent may also offer mutual fund products or insurance products with attractive dividend schedules. In many cases, a creative agent can solve a number of the prospect's needs with one or two products.

In the United States, an agent must be licensed by the SEC to sell either variable insurance policies or mutual fund products. In Canada, agents must be accredited by their provincial securities commission to sell investment funds. These products are called *variable, nonguaranteed,* or *investment-sensitive* because, above any guaranteed minimums, the exact benefit amounts cannot be computed in advance. Certain nonguaranteed products are called *equity-based products,* because the policy benefits rise or fall depending on the value of an underlying portfolio made up primarily of stock investments (equities).

One feature of investment-based products is that they give policyowners an opportunity to offset the decreased value of fixed benefits over time. However, along with that opportunity comes the risk that the investment portfolio may perform poorly and that the value of the policyowner's investment may decline. Consequently, an agent who sells such policies must be thoroughly familiar with their characteristics in order to explain properly the investment risk to the prospective purchaser.

Estate planning. Estate planning is another kind of total-needs programming. However, the objective of ***estate planning*** is not only to provide funds for the prospect's dependents upon his or her death, but also to conserve, as much as possible, the personal assets that the prospect wants to bequeath to heirs. Taxes and expenses that result from a person's death can easily deplete that person's assets. Life insurance can help considerably in protecting against these losses by providing immediate cash to pay taxes and reducing the urgency to convert assets into cash.

Persons whose estates warrant such planning generally possess substantial assets. Thus, estate planning usually involves accountants, lawyers, and trust officers, as well as insurance agents.

Prohibited practices

The agent's conduct during a sales presentation must be above reproach. In fact, the importance of the agent's sales conduct is so great that most states and provinces have specifically prohibited life insurance agents from engaging in certain sales practices. Such prohibited sales practices generally include *misrepresentation, twisting, guaranteeing policy dividends,* and *rebating* (see Figure 4-6). An insurance agent's license can be revoked if the agent engages in prohibited practices.

Misrepresentation is the act of deliberately making false or misleading statements to induce a prospect to purchase insurance. Such statements may involve untrue comparisons between policies, misleading statements about the financial condition or reputation of a competitor company, or false

Figure 4-6
Examples of illegal sales practices.

[NOTE: Although not commonplace, illegal sales practices sometimes do occur, and they can result in serious consequences for the company or agent that engages in them. The purpose of this figure is to help students recognize illegal sales practices when they occur. These examples are fictional.]

Example 1:
Assume George Smith is an agent for the Triple X Insurance Company. Triple X and the Double D Insurance Company have basically the same, strong financial condition and the same reputation for prompt claim payment. Agent Smith is trying to sell Bill Morgan, a prospect, a policy from Triple X.

Agent Smith: "I know you're thinking about buying one of those new Double D policies, but I think you ought to consider this: I've been selling Triple X policies for years, and I know what a strong company it is. Too bad I can't say the same about Double D. They're having real financial troubles over those bad investments they made. They're also having difficulties in making claim payments. Some policyowners are waiting

Figure 4-6 *(continued)*

---

years for their checks. My company would have written you a big claim check even before *investigating* your claim.''

Agent Smith is engaged in the prohibited sales practice of misrepresentation.

Example 2:

Mr. Morgan purchased a whole life insurance policy from Circle C Insurance Company 20 years ago. A considerable cash value has accumulated on the policy. Because of health reasons, Mr. Morgan represents a far greater mortality risk to an insurer now than he did when the Circle C policy was purchased.

Agent Smith: "Bill, that policy you have from Circle C is a real loser. What's that cash value doing for you, just sitting there accumulating interest? You should put that cash value to use in a Triple X policy. It has the same death benefit as your old policy. Plus, Triple X is a much stronger company. Insurability? Don't *worry*. There's the little matter of the medical examination, but you'll pass that, no *problem*. And I think I can guarantee your premium won't even go up from your old policy!''

Agent Smith is engaged in the prohibited sales practice known as twisting.

Example 3:

Agent Smith is telling Mr. Morgan about one of his company's policies.

Agent Smith: ". . . and you wouldn't believe the dividends on this policy! I spoke with the actuaries and the investments people before they brought this policy out. I told them right up front, 'My clients want 20 percent guaranteed!' And now I can give it to them. Yes, we've been averaging a payout of 8 percent for the last 15 years, but that's all in the past. And, Bill, these rates are *guaranteed*.''

Agent Smith is engaged in the prohibited sales practice of guaranteeing policy dividends.

Example 4:

Agent Smith is still trying to convince Mr. Morgan about the benefits of buying a policy from Triple X Life Insurance Company.

Agent Smith: "Now, Bill, a lot of agents wouldn't do this for you, but I feel like we have an *understanding,* you know what I mean? We're almost like *family*. So let me come right to the point. The company gives me 55 percent of your first year's premium to sell you this policy. I'll give 10 percent back to you, no questions asked. Think of buying this policy as an investment in both of our futures.''

Agent Smith is engaged in the generally prohibited sales practice known as rebating. Some states have rescinded their anti-rebating statutes and allow agents to give policyowners a portion of the commissions earned on their policies under certain circumstances.

---

statements about the policy benefits or relationship between an insured and the insurance company.

Twisting is a specific form of misrepresentation. Twisting occurs when an agent induces a policyowner to discontinue an insurance contract with another company and to use the cash value of the original policy to purchase a new policy, without clearly informing the policyowner of the differences between the two policies and of the financial consequences of replacing the original policy. Note that twisting includes a misleading or incomplete comparison of the policies to the disadvantage of the policyowner; replacing one insurance policy with another is not inherently wrong, as long as the agent does not mislead the policyowner.

Most jurisdictions have enacted regulations to protect the public from twisting. Some of these regulations require that a written cost comparison of the two policies be given to the prospect and that the original insurance company be advised of the proposed replacement. Other regulations also require that the insurance department in the jurisdiction where the replacement is taking place be given a copy of all appropriate documents. As long as these regulations are followed, lawful replacements can be made.

Guaranteeing policy dividends is another form of misrepresentation. Statutes generally prohibit agents from giving any estimates of future policy dividends, because the exact amount of future dividends is not known. Agents are permitted to use dividend illustrations based on the dividend scales the company is currently paying. However, such an illustration must include a notation that it is based on the current scale and that no future dividend guarantee or estimate is being made.

Rebating involves offering the prospect a special incentive to purchase a policy. The rebate is usually in the form of a share of the agent's commission. Most jurisdictions have laws prohibiting rebating, but a few states have rescinded their anti-rebating statutes.

Conservation of Business

The second major function of an agent is the conservation of business already in force. The term *conservation* refers to efforts made to prevent a policy from lapsing. Though conservation is an important function of both the agent and the insurer's home or regional office, here we will concentrate mainly on agents' efforts to conserve business. From the viewpoint of the company, the measure of how long a policy or a block of policies remains in force is its *persistency.* The life insurance industry uses persistency to monitor its marketing and service quality. When a company and its agents excel in matching products and services with the needs of insureds, policies stay on the books longer. The longer a policy remains on the books, the greater the likelihood that it will fill the need it was sold to cover. Moreover, persistency directly affects profitability because policies that have been in force for a long time are more profitable for insurers than policies that lapse quickly.

For the agent, the conservation process can be divided into two primary phases: *conservation at the time of sale* and *conservation in anticipation of lapse.* Sometimes, the agent also becomes involved in reinstatement efforts, which are discussed in Chapter 10.

Conservation at the time of sale

Research shows that well-written business is the best form of conservation. *Well-written business* has three characteristics. First, the agent has identified the needs of the policyowner, and the policyowner recognizes that those needs are important. Second, the plan fairly meets those needs. Third, the policyowner is financially capable of paying the premiums. If all three characteristics are present, the policy is well written and probably will remain in force. By selling well-written business, the agent begins the conservation process at the time of sale and helps to ensure that the business will not lapse.

Conservation in anticipation of lapse

In most cases, policyowners indicate their decision to allow their policies to lapse in one of two ways. Policyowners either inform the company that they intend to surrender their policies, or they fail to pay premiums when they are due. Either course constitutes a threatened policy lapse.

A policyowner may choose to surrender a policy for a number of reasons, and the first step in conserving a policy is for the agent or another representative of the company to contact the policyowner to learn the reason for the surrender. Alternatives other than policy surrender can often satisfy the policyowner's needs. For example, the reason for the policy surrender may be that the policyowner has suffered a temporary financial setback, making the policyowner financially unable to meet the current premium payment. The agent, a member of the agency office staff, or a home office employee in customer service could recommend several alternatives to policy lapse, including suggesting that the policyowner

- use the policy's cash value or accumulated dividends to pay the premium due
- convert the contract to a lower-premium plan, such as converting a 20-payment life policy to a continuous-premium whole life policy

- take out a policy loan
- reduce the policy's death benefit

The actual alternative recommended by the agent or company employee would depend on the financial circumstances of the policyowner.

If the policy is being surrendered and replaced with another policy, then, depending on local regulations, the insurance company may receive notice of the replacement from the replacing company. When the insurance company receives such a notice, the home office and the agent take steps to make sure that the replacement is in the policyowner's best interest and, if not, to conserve the business.

Many lapses result from a failure to pay a premium on time. These failures to pay are noticed quickly by the personnel responsible for premium billing and collection at either the home office or the agency. In such a case, the company sends a letter to the policyowner concerning the overdue premium and, usually, notifies the agent that the policy may lapse.

Service to Policyowners

Servicing policyowners' needs is a good way for agents to maintain positive relations with customers. In general, the agent's primary service functions are to remain alert to changes in policyowners' needs, to respond to service requests, to obtain and fill out the proper forms to make requested policy changes, and to send those forms to the company.

Many agents conduct periodic reviews of each client's insurance program. One approach an agent can take is to evaluate the client's existing policies to ensure that they are still adequate and suitable. The agent can then suggest to the client any recommended changes. More commonly, the agent meets with the customer to ask questions that might uncover the need for a change in the customer's insurance program. The agent asks about the current number and age of any dependents, the customer's employment status and income, the funding goals that the customer has for education of children or for retirement, and so on. Such a periodic review can result in new sales as well as in changes in current policy options.

Unfortunately, gaps sometimes exist between the level of service desired by policyowners and that delivered by agents. Policyowners may find that their agents are not always available. One reason for this inaccessibility relates to the agent's compensation schedule. The nature of the commission system under which most agents are paid makes the sale of new insurance policies much more financially rewarding than the service of existing policies.

Another factor leading to agent inaccessibility is the mobility of both the general population and the agency sales force. Years often elapse between the purchase of a policy and the time the policyowner seeks assistance from the agent. During that period, the policyowner or the agent may have relocated, leaving the policyowner without a local contact with the company. Further, each year, a large number of agents retire, leave the company, or die. In such cases, the agent's policyowners are said to become *orphans.* To avoid too much disruption in service, companies frequently assign orphaned policyowners to the home office customer service department until they can be assigned to another agent.

KEY TERMS

marketing	prospect
market	prospecting
marketing plan	single-need selling
marketing mix	total-needs programming
corporate culture	estate planning
demographics	misrepresentation
market segmentation	twisting
market segment	guaranteeing policy dividends
target marketing	rebating
target market	conservation
test marketing	persistency
field force	orphan
detached agent	

Chapter 5

Agency-Building Distribution Systems

After reading this chapter, you should be able to

- Describe the features of a personal selling distribution system
- Distinguish between the branch office system and the general agency system
- Explain several different ways of evaluating the performance of agents and an agency
- Describe some services that the home office marketing department performs to support agency operations
- Describe the different types of compensation paid to agents, general agents, and branch managers
- Describe the multiple-line agency system
- Explain the unique features of the home service distribution system

In an insurance company, the ***distribution system*** is the network of organizations and individuals that perform all the marketing activities required to convey a product from the insurer to its customers. A company's choice of distribution systems affects and is affected by the insurer's target markets and the products designed to meet those markets' needs. The choice of distribution system also affects the organizational structure of the marketing department and the support systems required for effective product distribution. As the marketing environment changes, insurance companies sometimes find it necessary to adjust their distribution systems to remain competitive. The adjustment generally involves adopting some aspects of another distribution system rather than completely switching to that distribution system.

The two distribution systems most commonly used by insurers are personal selling distribution systems and direct response distribution systems. In a ***personal selling distribution system,*** commissioned or salaried sales personnel sell products by making oral presentations to prospective purchasers. Personal selling systems are the main means of distribution for the following types of insurance companies: ordinary life, health, industrial, combination (industrial and ordinary), multiple-line (life, health, and property/casualty), and group companies. In 1990, personal selling systems accounted for virtually all new life insurance premium income in the United States and Canada.

This chapter will focus on the most common type of personal selling system: the agency-building distribution system. We will describe the typical organizational structure used by insurers that adopt agency-building systems, the roles played by agency managers, and the support functions required by agency-building distribution systems. Other personal selling distribution systems and the direct response distribution system are covered in Chapter 6.

Insurance companies use three major types of agency-building distribution systems.

- The *ordinary agency system* uses full-time or part-time agents to sell and deliver insurance policies. The agent's responsibilities include soliciting applications for insurance, collecting initial premiums, and providing certain types of policyowner service. This type of agency system can be divided into two subsystems: the branch office system and the general agency system.
- The *multiple-line agency (MLA) system* uses full-time agents to distribute life, health, and property/casualty products for groups of financially interrelated or commonly managed insurance companies.
- The *home service system* is used to distribute industrial and ordinary insurance products. The distinguishing features of home service agents are that they (1) distribute industrial, or debit, insurance and some ordinary insurance products; (2) collect premiums in the home and perform other policy services; (3) do extensive record keeping; (4) operate within exclusive territories; and (5) are often considered employees of the company and, therefore, exclusive representatives of one company.

THE ORDINARY AGENCY SYSTEM

The ordinary agency system, also called the *career agency system* or the *agency system,* uses career agents to sell and service all types of individual and group insurance and annuity products. A **career agent** is a full-time commissioned salesperson who holds an agent contract with one or more insurance companies. Companies that use the ordinary agency system are often referred to as *career-agent companies* or *ordinary agency companies.* Agents who represent the products of only one company and who are not permitted to sell the products of another company are known as **exclusive agents.**

A company's career agents are collectively referred to as the *field force,* and may work out of *field offices.* A field office has two major areas of responsibility: agency operations and agency services (see Figure 5-1). Agency operations include providing a distribution outlet for the company's products; producing sales, also known as *new business;* conserving existing business; and performing certain customer service functions. The agency services unit supports the sales and service efforts of the field force. Field offices are located throughout a company's **marketing territory,** which is the geographical area in which a company distributes its products. The number of field offices a company establishes depends on the company's size, the size and population density of the marketing territory, and the volume of the company's business.

The person who is the link between the home office and the field office is the manager of agency operations, often called the *superintendent* (or *director) of agencies.* This person, who is a home office employee, works with the home office to

Figure 5-1
Organization chart of an agency distribution system.

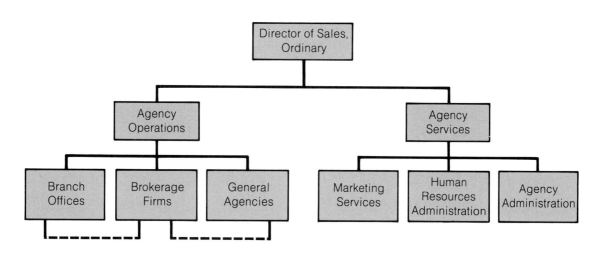

- plan for long-range growth in terms of production goals and number of district offices
- establish an operating budget for each district office
- coordinate district office operations with home office advertising and promotional efforts
- realign territories and districts

The superintendent works with the district managers on such matters as

- developing and training new agents in the district
- processing personnel transfers, promotions, and salary changes
- inspecting and auditing the district offices
- training and developing new assistant managers

Types of Organization under the Ordinary Agency System

The ordinary agency system can be organized in one of two ways: as a branch office system or as a general agency system. Insurance companies may change from one system to the other or add the second system without discontinuing the first. Overall, the U.S. life and health insurance industry has experienced a gradual transition from the general agency system to the branch office system, which is typically associated with large companies. Almost all Canadian companies use the branch office system in their Canadian field offices, although some Canadian companies have added a general agency system in recent years. Canadian companies use both systems for their U.S. operations.

Depending on whether a company uses the branch office system or the general agency system, the individual in charge of a field office is called a **branch manager** or a **general agent (GA),** respectively. (Other terms for branch manager are *agency manager* and *general manager*.) Although the branch office system and the general agency system are similar and insurance companies have modified both systems to meet their own needs, several distinctions can be made between the two systems.

Branch office system

Under the branch office system, field offices are established in key locations throughout the company's marketing territory. These field offices function as extensions of the home office. In large agency offices, the branch manager is assisted by a field office staff, which can include several agent supervisors or assistant managers, one or more office managers, training managers, and clerical and office services personnel. Personnel in the field office are often employees of the insurance company and are subject to the same types of controls normally exercised by an employer. Consequently, these employees may be transferred to another office, and the insurance company can change the field office territory at any time. The agents who work in a branch office are under contract to the insurance company, not to the branch manager, and the agents receive commissions directly from the insurance company.

A branch manager is primarily responsible for the performance of the field office. Most branch managers are permitted to sell insurance products, and many do so when assisting new agents. However, the branch manager is not expected to spend much time on personal sales.

In a branch office system, the insurance company usually provides the funds to pay for all branch office expenses—such as rent, salaries, and equipment costs—but companies are increasingly holding branch managers responsible for the profitability and sound financial management of their offices. The branch manager works within an assigned budget, and any unusual expenses must be approved by the home office. Branch managers are usually paid a base salary and can receive overrides and bonuses based on the performance of the field office.

As compared to the branch manager, who is responsible for the overall performance of the branch office, the *office manager* is more in charge of the day-to-day administrative operations in a branch office. The office manager's duties include maintaining records, managing customer correspondence, supervising clerical staff, and performing a variety of customer service functions.

General agency system

Under the general agency system, the general agent (GA) is an independent contractor who is under contract to the insurance company. Unlike branch managers, general agents are usually active in selling insurance as well as being responsible for the performance of the agency. Each GA is given certain general powers to represent the insurance company and to develop new business within a defined territory.

The general agent's territory may be exclusive, overlapping, or nonexclusive (see Figure 5-2). In an **exclusive territory,** only one GA is authorized to represent the insurer. An **overlapping territory** is one in which some portion of the territory is open to more than one general agent, though some portions of the territory are exclusive to only one general agent. In a **nonexclusive territory,** several GAs may represent the same insurer.

The insurance company's control over its general agents' activities is limited by the terms of the general agents' contracts. Usually, the insurance

Figure 5-2
Exclusive, overlapping, and nonexclusive territories.

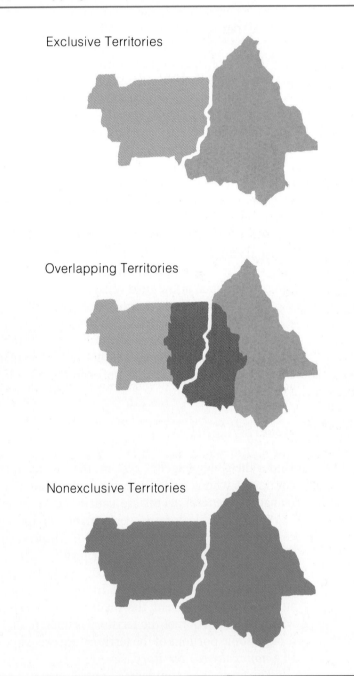

Exclusive Territories

Overlapping Territories

Nonexclusive Territories

company cannot transfer a GA, nor can the company redefine a GA's territory, except as permitted under the original contract. The relationships of the soliciting agents with the insurance company are also governed by the terms of the general agent's contract with the insurance company.

The GA usually does not receive a salary. Instead, the GA receives an *overriding commission*, or *commission override*. Under many older general agency contracts, the insurance company paid all commissions earned in a general agency to the GA, who was then responsible for paying the soliciting agents' commissions. The commission override consisted of the difference between the amount paid by the insurer to the GA and the amount the GA paid to the soliciting agents. Thus, general agents could adjust the amount of their own income by altering the amounts paid to soliciting agents. Today, however, many companies pay commissions directly to soliciting agents, and overriding commissions directly to general agents, thus taking control over the amounts paid to soliciting agents.

In addition to overriding commissions, the GA may receive an expense reimbursement allowance and some income for performing service functions for the insurer. For example, the GA may receive a collection fee for collecting renewal premiums for the insurer. Because few individuals can make the kind of financial commitment necessary to start a general agency, some insurance companies also provide a portion of the initial investment needed. In most cases, the company's investment in a new agency is temporary and may be an advance against the general agent's future earnings. In return for their initial investment, insurance companies can then exercise controls over the general agent's activities that are similar to those exercised over a branch manager's activities. However, as the initial investment is repaid, the GA assumes full control of the agency.

The field office staff in a general agency system is usually employed by the GA. Unlike the branch office system, the general agent—not the insurance company—is responsible for paying all office expenses and salaries.

Comparison of branch office and general agency systems

An insurance company's choice between a branch office system and a general agency system often centers on the question of relative costs. Overall, the two systems fulfill essentially the same functions for essentially the same cost. However, certain conditions can make one system more economical than the other. For example, a new company may be unable to bear the full cost of establishing branch offices. Such a company would probably choose the general agency system, because some or all of the start-up costs are borne by the general agents.

Use of the general agency system may also be more economical for a company because of the close relationship between performance and cost. Under the general agency system, the company pays commissions to the GA based on sales performance. If the GA takes a long time to build up production, then the initial costs to the company are small because commissions are small. However, a company that starts operations with a branch office system is faced immediately with high payroll costs, even though production may be low.

On the other hand, well-established companies often prefer the branch office system because it offers greater control and flexibility. For example, under the branch office system, the company can exercise better control over its marketing plans. If those plans call for an expanded sales effort within a particular territory, then the company can increase its agency personnel accordingly. Conversely, the company can decide to reduce its sales efforts if that seems desirable. Under the general agency system, the general agent has a greater degree of influence on the plans of the life insurance company. For example, a GA can choose not to add to the agency staff, even though the company would like to have more agents in that area.

As mentioned earlier, under the branch office system, personnel can be transferred from one territory to another. This flexibility can benefit the company for two reasons: (1) the company depends less on new personnel to replace departing field office personnel, and (2) the company can reward its personnel by moving them into better positions in other areas. The company's field personnel also benefit from greater promotion opportunities within the company.

Operation of the Ordinary Agency System

The sales activities of soliciting agents and the managerial responsibilities of branch managers and GAs are typically the same regardless of the type of agency system used. Thus, we will describe agent activities and managerial activities without discussing the type of agency system involved. In addition, we will use the term *agency manager* to refer both to branch managers and general agents.

In any company, a manager's responsibilities can be divided into three basic categories: planning, implementing, and controlling. For the agency manager of a life and health insurance company, each of these duties involves the following activities:

- *agency planning*—establishing operational objectives and developing the agency's operating plan

- *implementing the agency's operating plan*—recruiting and selecting prospective agents, training and developing new and established agents, and motivating agents
- *controlling the performance of agents and the agency overall*—supervising and evaluating the methods and results of the agency's operations

Agency planning

Just as the marketing department develops a marketing plan to guide the department's activities, each agency manager develops a plan to guide the agency's operations. The agency manager, particularly the manager of a branch office, must make sure that the field office plans and objectives are consistent with the larger plans and objectives of the insurance company. Thus, the company's overall marketing plan is the most important factor affecting the direction of the field office's yearly operating plan. A number of other factors also affect the plans of individual agency managers. These factors include the marketing territory's

- size
- amount of competition
- population trends
- economic conditions
- income levels

Two important parts of an agency's operating plan are the operating budget and the staffing schedule.

Operating budget. The ***operating budget*** forecasts the levels of new and renewal business that the agency is expected to produce. It also projects the agency's operating expenses. The budget thus provides the agency manager with a standard of performance against which the agency's actual accomplishments can be measured. In addition, the budget indicates to the home office the resources that must be set aside for agency operations, as well as the agency's expected income. By projecting expenses and income from all of its agencies, the home office can estimate the company's overall expected cash flow and possibly adjust the company's operations and investments accordingly.

Staffing schedule. The agency manager uses a ***staffing schedule*** to estimate the number of agents and office personnel needed to produce the projected amount of business, the cost of salaries and training for office personnel, as well as the time and money needed for recruiting, hiring, and training new agents.

Implementing the agency's operating plan

Successful implementation of an agency's operating plan depends upon the achievements of the agents. Although an agency needs qualified and competent personnel to support the agents' actions, the branch office or general agency will falter without sufficient sales activity from the agents. Because the agents' performance is so important, agency managers are continually concerned with recruiting, training, and motivating the agent force.

Recruiting new agents. The first step in bringing new agents into a field office is to locate promising new recruits. Because of the significant investment in money and time that is involved in training new agents and supporting them early in their careers, agency managers must be especially careful to recruit only individuals who appear likely to succeed. In addition, selection of the wrong agents can damage a company's customer relations, adversely affect agency morale, and hamper the achievement of the agency's objectives. The basic steps involved in recruiting are (1) finding sources of prospective agents, (2) selecting qualified prospects, and (3) interviewing the candidates.

Finding sources of prospective agents. Agency managers use a variety of sources for recruiting prospective agents. They advertise in local newspapers, visit college campuses, and contact employment agencies. Generally, however, the best sources are established agents and agency managers, who can contact people in their communities and ask for suggestions for prospective agents. By talking with business and civic leaders, educators, friends, and successful insurance agents, managers can locate job candidates who come highly recommended by people that the managers know and respect. This network of community contact has been the most reliable source for locating high-quality recruits.

Selecting prospective agents. Because not all people are suited to selling insurance, many studies have attempted to determine the characteristics of successful insurance agents. Although selling insurance is not physically demanding, the psychological stress can be quite high, and only certain types of people usually become successful. The majority of people who succeed in insurance sales enter the business between the ages of 25 and 45, are married, possess college degrees, and have previously been involved in sales. Although not all successful agents possess these characteristics, they are present more often than not, and agency managers have found them helpful in screening job candidates.

In addition, agency managers can use a variety of selection tests to help them determine whether a job candidate has the necessary traits to be a successful insurance agent. These selection tests fall into three categories:

- *aptitude tests,* which predict a person's ability to learn a specific job if sufficient training is provided
- *personality tests,* which identify a person's motivational, emotional, interpersonal, and attitudinal characteristics
- *interest tests,* which identify a person's general interests

The test most commonly used by insurance companies in the United States and Canada to select sales personnel is the *Career Profile System* developed by LIMRA. The *Career Profile System* gathers information about a candidate's work history and personal background and uses that information to predict the candidate's likelihood for success as an insurance agent or financial services consultant.

In companies that use the branch manager system, the home office marketing department usually establishes qualifications for candidates and specifies recruiting procedures that the branch manager must follow. In the general agency system, on the other hand, general agents are usually not subject to any insurance company control over agent selection.

Interviewing the candidates. Once an agency manager has decided that an individual meets the basic criteria, the manager conducts a selection interview. During this interview, the manager asks the applicant questions about the applicant's qualifications for the job, answers any questions the applicant has about working conditions, and explains the potential problems and rewards of a career in insurance sales. A successful candidate is then accepted for training.

Agent training. Providing for the training of new agents and the continuing education of experienced agents is an important component of the agency manager's job. However, because the need for agent training is common to all agencies, the home office usually provides training programs as well. These training courses are supplemented by on-the-job training conducted by the agency manager or one of the agency supervisors.

A comprehensive training program for new agents is usually divided into three broad areas:

- *life and health insurance basics*—principles of life and health insurance, types of insurance products, industry terminology, and laws and regulations affecting insurance sales
- *sales and customer service techniques*—target marketing, locating prospective customers, determining customers' needs, making sales

presentations, closing sales, and communicating effectively with customers

- *company procedures*—using a rate book, brochures, or computer illustrations to identify the costs and benefits of various policy coverages; operating the office equipment and computer systems; filling out company forms; and keeping the required records.

Some portions of training programs may be designed for self-study. Other portions may be given in formal classes conducted at the home office, regional locations, or the field office. Training programs use a variety of instructional techniques, from lectures and discussions to role playing. *Role playing* allows the trainee to act out a selling situation. The manager or trainer assumes the role of a prospect and leads the trainee, by guidance and questioning, to the solution of a sales problem that he or she may face in actual circumstances. *On-the-job training (OJT)* is also used extensively. In OJT, an agency manager or an experienced agent accompanies the new agent on a sales call, providing the new agent with advice and moral support.

In most cases, the training of new agents progresses in a series of steps. At first, the agent is taught only the fundamentals of insurance, enough to equip the agent to pass a required licensing examination and sell products to customers with comparatively simple insurance needs. Later, the agent can learn the finer points of insurance sales and the more complex product offerings. In addition, industry programs provide a broader perspective on the insurance industry and company operations.

The agency manager must also provide continuing training opportunities for established agents throughout their careers. If the company introduces a new product or changes operating procedures or underwriting standards, then the established agent must be given additional training. Changes in legislation also require an updating of the agent's knowledge. Moreover, agent licensing requirements in many jurisdictions mandate continuing education.

The agency manager must recognize training needs that are unique to certain agents. Some agents, for example, may need to improve their sales presentation techniques. Other agents may need to improve their letter writing. Thus, the agency manager should be equipped to handle any number of training needs.

Agent motivation. Motivating agents is one of the greatest challenges that agency managers face. The home office staff helps with agent motivation by conducting sales contests and providing timely and adequate support services (see INSIGHT 5-1), but only the agency manager is in a position to detect problems that affect the motivation and, hence, the performance of the agents. The ability to maintain a staff of highly motivated agents is the mark of a successful agency manager.

INSIGHT 5-1

Service to Producers

Pacific Mutual is an insurance company that's not in the business of selling insurance. Rather, the company "is in the business of meeting the needs of producers who sell insurance and bring in profitable premium dollars," said Walt Ridlon, senior vice president and chief marketing officer—Individual Marketing, for Pacific Mutual's Personal Financial Services (PFS) business unit.

To help employees keep in mind just how important producers are to Pacific Mutual, Ridlon created a "Focus on the Producer" service program. This distinctive program allows home office employees to see how their everyday job functions affect the company's producers, as well as the importance of their relationships with those producers. The "Focus on the Producer" program was formulated as a renewal of an existing focus on customer service that has always been part of the company's overall operating philosophy. "We especially wanted a phrase that tried to draw people in, in a very broad sense, to see more clearly how their job relates to the primary mission of the company," Ridlon explains.

Pacific Mutual uses three primary methods of distribution, all of which involve producers of one kind or another: sales offices, which include branch offices and PPGAs; marketing through the M Financial—a premier, select group of producers; and broker/dealers with financial planners.

Activities

"Focusing on producers can involve techniques as simple as using a friendly yet professional tone of voice when answering the phone, or suggesting new methods or procedures that make it easier to send premium dollars to Pacific Mutual," Ridlon says. Activities that Pacific Mutual employs to reinforce the idea of excellent service to producers include monthly employee recognition awards; a newsletter that highlights producers and their activities; wearing "Focus on the Producer" T-shirts on commission closing days; and providing training that emphasizes producers, distribution systems, and markets.

The monthly employee recognition awards, and other periodic special awards, may be the best reinforcer of the program's purpose, notes Louise Romano, assistant vice president, marketing communications, for the PFS business unit. Open to all PFS employees except officers, monthly winners of the "Focus on the Producer" recognition program are nominated by producers or supervisors for outstanding service the employees have given to producers.

Future

"From a bottom-line standpoint," Ridlon says, "this new attitude and relationship has caused the company, within the last year, to add quite a number of really top producers. I think the word has gotten out about the company's attitude toward producers, and recruiting has changed. Producers are being referred to us, having been told by fellow producers that Pacific Mutual is a good company to do business with; that's a pretty favorable situation, from a home office standpoint—to have top producers in the industry approaching us.''

Source: Adapted with permission of the publisher from Tim Kelley, ''Unique Program Spotlights Service to Producers,'' *Resource,* December 1990, pp. 17-19.

The manager attempts to build the confidence of agents, keep up their morale, and offer advice on any problem that adversely affects their performance. By helping an agent to overcome deficiencies, such as poor public speaking skills, the agency manager removes obstacles to the agent's success and boosts the agent's confidence.

Although the commitment to perform well must come from the agent, a manager can create an atmosphere that motivates the agent to increase his or her determination to succeed. Agency managers as well as the home office staff may use achievement awards, social events, newsletters, and regular branch meetings to applaud agents' accomplishments and to foster a positive atmosphere within the agency.

Providing administrative support. Field offices normally include an office support staff to perform the administrative tasks that help agents sell and service insurance products. The office support staff usually is supervised by an office manager, who may also be called the *agency cashier, agency controller,* or, in Canada, the *branch secretary.* In the branch office system, the office manager reports either to the branch manager or directly to the home office. In the general agency system, the office manager always reports to the agency manager. In any case, the office manager is responsible for making sure that the field office support staff is meeting the needs of the agents and their customers. The work of the support staff includes performing routine office tasks, helping agents place new business, and providing customer service. The field office support staff sends and sorts mail, operates the switchboard, purchases office supplies, pays bills, reconciles bank statements, maintains accounting records, and performs a variety of other tasks to keep the field office running smoothly.

The field office support staff also plays a role in helping agents process new business by

- helping agents prepare sales aids
- checking applications for completeness
- submitting applications to the home office
- accepting and depositing initial premiums received with applications
- arranging for any necessary medical examinations and inspection reports

After an agent has submitted an application to the home office underwriting department, the office staff follows its progress through the underwriting process (see Chapter 9). If a delay is encountered, the underwriting department notifies the field office staff, so the agent knows the reason for the delay. When a newly issued policy is received at the field office, a member of the office staff checks the policy for accuracy and completeness and then gives it to the agent for delivery. If the initial premium did not accompany the application, the agent collects the premium when delivering the policy and then gives the premium to the office staff.

The field office staff also helps the agents handle policyowners' requests for changes in their policies. For example, the field office staff routes policy loan requests to the proper department in the home office.

Controlling agency operations

An additional responsibility of agency managers is to evaluate the performance of both the agents and the agency itself. By measuring actual results against results projected in the agency plan, an agency manager can better control the future performance of the agency.

Analyzing agent performance. An agency manager cannot usually observe the activities of all the members of the agency's field force on a daily basis, and thus must rely on production reports, call schedules, sales volume, or other types of quotas to evaluate the ongoing performance of each agent and, thus, the agency as a whole.

For each agent, performance evaluations involve determining (1) whether and how well each agent's sales and other objectives have been met and (2) the strengths and weaknesses in each agent's performance. Most systems for evaluating performance are based on both quantitative factors and qualitative factors. *Quantitative bases for evaluation* measure specific levels of performance in objective terms. *Qualitative bases for evaluation* involve more subjective, more personal judgments about an agent's performance. Examples of these two performance evaluation factors are given below.

Performance appraisal standards used for career agents

Quantitative factors	*Qualitative factors*
dollar sales volume	attitude
total commissions earned	product knowledge
average premium per sale	communication skills
number of new customers contacted or policies sold	time management
persistency of business sold	personal organization

Analyzing agency performance. The level of performance of an agency as a whole is also important to an insurance company. One way of judging performance is determining how an agency succeeds at controlling its expenses. Expenses are an important factor in computing premiums, and in most insurance companies, agency operating costs and agent commissions constitute the largest category of expense. A company with relatively high expenses must charge higher premiums and thus run the risk of losing business to more efficient competitors.

Several standards of comparison have been devised to help the agency manager control and evaluate agency operating expenses. Three common methods are

- ***historical comparison,*** in which the current performance of the agency is measured against its performance or the performance of other agencies in previous years
- ***intracompany comparison,*** in which one agency is compared with other agencies in the same company
- ***intercompany comparison,*** in which an agency is compared with industry averages

Expenses can be too low as well as too high. For example, if the clerical staff is kept small in order to hold expenses down, the agency often incurs higher indirect costs. When an agency office is inadequately staffed, correspondence is slowed, inquiries from prospects or policyowners are subject to delays, and clerical functions are performed by agents whose time could be better spent producing sales. Such indirect costs affect agency operations. The agency manager's responsibility is to maintain a proper level of operating expenses—neither too high nor too low.

The agency manager must also be aware of legal restrictions on the costs of the agency's operations. For example, most agency managers in the

United States need to be familiar with Section 4228 of the New York State Insurance Code. Section 4228 specifies limits on amounts that can be spent in many different areas, including field expenses, overhead expenses, compensation paid to soliciting agents and to general agents, and agents' training allowances.

No other state or Canadian province has followed New York in this matter. Nonetheless, Section 4228 is important because it applies to all business written by companies approved to do business in New York State, regardless of where the business is written. Because most large insurance companies conduct business in New York, that state's regulations affect a large number of agencies. However, many companies have established subsidiaries that operate only in New York, while the parent company operates elsewhere. These companies can conduct the majority of their operations without having to adhere to New York regulations; only the subsidiaries must comply with New York laws.

Expense ratios. Comparisons of operating costs cannot be made solely on the basis of dollar amounts. A large agency naturally incurs more expenses than a small agency. Therefore, agency managers use several ***expense ratios,*** which are mathematical comparisons that show the proportion of expenses to a certain level of production or to the level of a certain marketing-related activity. These ratios frequently require both the premiums generated and the amount spent on expenses to be separated into two categories: first-year business and renewal business. Once the expenses have been allocated into these two categories, the agency manager can use a number of different ratios to analyze the costs of various aspects of agency operations. Among the expense ratios typically calculated and studied are

- expenses per application received
- expenses per $100 of first-year premium income
- expenses per $100 of renewal premium income
- expenses per sales call

The agency manager can use expense ratios with historical comparisons, intracompany comparisons, and intercompany comparisons. Other measures of agency performance include weekly production results, recruiting activity, and production by year of hire.

Functional cost analysis. LIMRA has developed an agency cost control tool known as functional cost analysis, which incorporates data from many life and health insurance agencies. With functional cost analysis, agency managers can compare the costs of such operations as recruiting, staff development, or sales, in their own agencies with the average costs of the same operations in other agencies of the same size.

AGENCY SUPPORT

As we noted earlier, many of the activities involved in the operation of an ordinary agency system are the responsibility of the agency manager. However, the manager usually receives considerable support and guidance from the home office in meeting these responsibilities. A unit of the home office marketing department usually known as the *agency services unit* provides support for the company's agencies. The major activities of the agency services unit concern *training, contracts and licenses, compensation and benefits, technical support, advertising and sales promotion,* and *office services* (see Figure 5-3).

Although the human resources department of the insurance company provides training and compensation for home office employees, the marketing department usually has responsibility for providing such services

Figure 5-3
Organization chart of agency services.

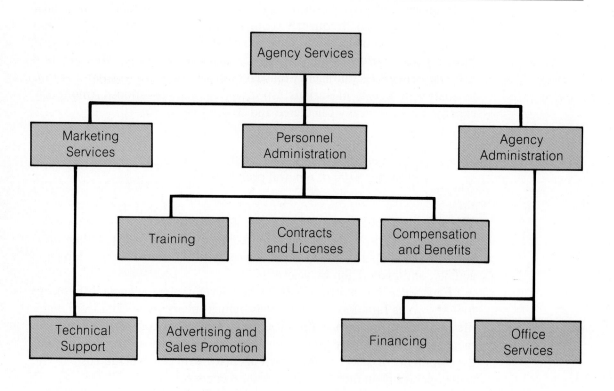

for field personnel. The distinctive characteristics of agency personnel training and compensation differ from those of home office personnel training and compensation. For example, the system of wage and salary administration for home office personnel emphasizes employee skills that are quite different from agent skills. Thus, a company usually needs specialists in agency training, as well as specialists in home office human resources management.

Agent Training

As discussed earlier in this chapter, most agent training is provided through the field offices. Frequently, however, home office sales training specialists locate or develop training materials that are used in the field offices. In addition, many companies conduct some training for field office employees in the home office and also send training specialists to the field in order to conduct seminars and courses. Many companies bring new agents to the home office for extensive training programs that not only reinforce product knowledge and selling skills but also introduce them to the home office environment and instill in them their company's attitudes toward quality and customer service.

Besides providing high-quality instruction, home office involvement in agent training also helps assure that all agents receive a certain minimum level of training. Although training is one of an agency manager's primary responsibilities, not all agency managers are equally gifted trainers. Therefore, agents in one office may receive better training than the agents in another office. The support provided by home office personnel helps to assure some uniformity in agent training.

Home office training assistance also reduces training costs. Because some types of training are needed by all of a company's agents, such training can be developed more economically by the home office training staff than by each agency manager individually. Some companies videotape training programs and send the videotapes to their field offices. Companies may also train agents using business television, also known as *videoconferencing*, a training medium by which the company broadcasts live or pretaped training programs over a private satellite network to field offices or central meeting places, such as hotel conference rooms. In some cases, telephones are used in conjunction with the satellite transmission so that trainees in remote locations can phone in their questions to the trainer.

In addition to developing its own training programs, the home office often promotes the use of programs provided by industry sources and associations, which will be described more in Chapter 18.

Agent Contracts and Licenses

An agent begins a career in insurance sales by signing a contract with either the insurance company or the general agent and by obtaining a license from state or provincial authorities. If the agent's contract is with the general agent rather than the insurance company, then the general agent develops the contract and sets the contract's terms. Otherwise, the insurance company's marketing department, in conjunction with the company's legal department, develops the agent's contract.

Contracts

The contract between a soliciting agent and an insurance company usually contains the following provisions:

- statement of the existence of the contract
- authority of the agent to represent the company, solicit applications, collect initial premiums, and issue receipts
- performance requirements, particularly with respect to adherence to company rules and the prompt remittance of premiums
- production level required to earn minimum compensation and continue in the company's employment
- termination provisions, including the causes for justifiable termination and the length of time required for notice of termination by either the agent or the company
- compensation schedule, stating the rate of commissions, service fees, and bonuses
- reservation of the company's right to revise the commission schedule or reduce commission rates on policies that replace existing insurance
- vesting provisions, stating the circumstances (if any) under which the agent is entitled to receive renewal commissions after the agent's contract has been terminated
- circumstances (if any) under which the agent may submit insurance applications to another company

General agents and branch managers also work under contract to an insurance company. Their contracts are similar to those of soliciting agents in that they contain such information as a statement of appointment, a statement of powers and duties, the authorization to submit applications, and a compensation provision. However, the contracts of general agents usually contain a provision specifying the allowances the company will provide to defray the general agent's operating expenses. Traditionally, the insurance company has paid all the operating expenses of a branch office. However, as we mentioned earlier, today more companies are elevating the importance of branch managers in controlling expenses and have included expense management as part of the manager's contract.

Licenses

All agents in the United States and Canada must be licensed by each state or province in which they sell life insurance and health insurance. An agent in the United States who sells mutual funds or equity-based variable products must also be accredited under the rules of the Securities and Exchange Commission (SEC). In Canada, agents do not need a special license to sell variable insurance products. However, they must be accredited by provincial securities commissions in the provinces in which they plan to sell mutual funds.

In the United States, an agent can be licensed to sell life insurance only, health insurance only, or both. In Canada, some provinces issue one license for both life and health insurance sales. Most of the states in the United States and all the Canadian provinces require an agent to pass a written examination in order to obtain a license.

Some jurisdictions also require that an agent complete a formal course of instruction approved by that jurisdiction's insurance department before a license is granted. Because a person entering the insurance business is generally not able at first to meet these educational requirements, these jurisdictions provide that a person can receive a temporary license immediately after an application is made by the agent's branch manager or general agent. The temporary licensee must meet all the other requirements for a license within a certain period of time, such as 90 days, after receiving the temporary license. Temporary licenses are not issued in Canada.

Home office licensing staff. The home office agent licensing staff ensures that all licensing requirements are met. The responsibilities of this staff generally include ensuring that the correct forms, licensing fees, and applications are filed in each jurisdiction, and monitoring the license renewal requirements, if any, for each agent. Either the agents or the home office may be responsible for paying the actual licensing fees.

The licensing staff must also remain alert to potential violations that could result in the revocation or suspension of an agent's license. As we noted earlier, an agent's license can be revoked for engaging in specified prohibited practices, such as twisting and misrepresentation. In addition, an insurance commissioner can suspend or revoke an agent's license, refuse to issue a license, or impose a fine if the agent has

- violated the laws of that jurisdiction
- acted without a license
- represented or advertised himself or herself as an agent of an unauthorized company
- wrongfully appropriated or used any premiums collected

To keep agents' licenses current, some jurisdictions require continuing education for agents. The home office licensing staff can help keep agents informed about their continuing education status.

Compensation and Benefits

Another function of the agency services unit is setting compensation and benefit levels for agents and agency managers.

Agent compensation

Most agents are paid according to a commission system, because such a system is believed to give the agent a greater incentive to produce more business. Further, such a system makes the cost of acquiring new business a definite percentage of premium income, which in turn makes it easier for the company's actuaries to calculate the amount of the gross premiums that must be charged for each policy.

Commissions. Commissions are classified as either first-year commissions or renewal commissions. A *first-year commission* is based on a policy's first annual premium amount. Therefore, if the first-year premium on a policy is $500, and the commission rate is 55 percent, then the first-year commission will be $275. *Renewal commissions* are those paid for a specified number of years after the first policy year. The renewal commission rate is generally much lower than the first-year commission rate. Renewal commissions are paid only on policies that remain in force. By paying renewal commissions, companies encourage the agent to sell quality business and provide service to policyowners after the agent sells a policy.

In recent years, some companies have established level commission schedules for certain products, especially term insurance. Level commission schedules generally provide for first-year commissions and renewal commissions of equal amounts, thereby encouraging agents not only to make the initial sale but also to conserve business.

The company tries to set commission rates that are both competitive with those offered by other companies and, where necessary, within the

Figure 5-4
Examples of two possible commission schedules.

Company A	First year	55% of premium
	Second through tenth years	5% of premium
	Eleventh and subsequent years	2% of premium
Company B	First year	50% of premium
	Second and third years	12% of premium
	Fourth through seventh years	7% of premium
	Eighth and subsequent years	2% of premium

limits set by law. For example, New York law limits first-year commissions on whole life policies to 55 percent of the first-year premium. The New York law applies not only to all companies operating in that state but also to all insurance sold outside New York by companies that conduct business in that state. In addition to a top limit on first-year commissions, New York law limits the amount and number of renewal commissions, although it permits the payment of a small service fee for a period after renewal commissions cease. Figure 5-4 gives examples of two possible commission schedules offered for sales of individual whole life insurance.

Service fees. An agent's compensation may include *service fees,* sometimes called *persistency fees,* which are usually a small percentage, such as 2 percent, of the premiums payable after the renewal commissions have ceased. In some cases, the service fee is a flat amount for each thousand dollars of coverage sold by the agent. For example, the service fee might be $0.18 per $1,000 of face amount. If service fees are paid by a company, the agent may be required to contact the policyowner at least once a year.

Although service fees are a form of renewal compensation, they differ from renewal commissions in two ways. Renewal commissions are generally paid to the agent who sold the policy; service fees are paid to the agent who is currently providing service to the policyowner, even if he or she is not the agent who originally sold the policy. Renewal commissions are often *vested,* which means they are guaranteed to be paid to the soliciting agent, even after the agent's contract is terminated; service fees are rarely vested.

Bonuses and benefits. Many companies also pay bonuses either to attract agents or to motivate and reward successful agents. Bonuses, such as trips, merchandise, or cash prizes, may be designed to reward production or persistency or both. Many companies also include benefits as part of their agents' compensation. Common examples of benefits are group life insurance, health insurance, and retirement plans. Any bonuses and company contributions made to the various group insurance and retirement plans must, of course, be taken into account in determining the total value of the agent's compensation for comparison with any applicable statutory limitations on agents' compensation; this total value must remain within the legal limits applicable to agents' compensation in the particular jurisdiction.

New-agent compensation. During their first years in the insurance business, new agents often have difficulty earning enough income from commissions to maintain an adequate standard of living. To help new agents through this difficult period, many companies provide financing to new agents during their early years. In some cases, this financing is an advance against future earnings. In other cases, the company pays a higher commission to new agents or pays them an additional monthly amount to supplement their commissions. In most cases, new agent financing is highest in the agent's first year and ends by the time the agent reaches the third or fourth year in the business. A new agent who receives financing may be required to attend training classes or other business meetings or to make at least a minimum number of sales.

Compensation for general agents and branch managers

As discussed earlier, one of the distinctions between a general agent and a branch manager is in the form of compensation. A GA receives compensation in three primary forms:

- commissions on sales made personally
- overriding commissions
- expense allowances

In addition to these forms of compensation, many companies offer their general agents service fees and such benefits as group life insurance, group health insurance, and retirement benefits. Usually, the GA and the company share the cost of these benefits, although some companies pay the entire cost.

In contrast to the general agent, the branch manager receives a portion of his or her compensation in the form of a monthly salary from the company. This salary is usually supplemented by overriding commissions and incentive pay that varies according to the agency's performance. An agency's performance is usually measured in terms of its production, persistency, operating efficiency, and recruiting activity.

Branch managers are expected to devote more time to agency building than to personal life insurance sales. However, when branch managers are allowed to make sales, the manager usually receives the same commission rate as do the company's regular soliciting agents.

Technical Support

The agency services unit generally includes a number of technical specialists to support the agents who are selling in the advanced markets, such as the markets involving complex estate planning and business insurance situations. This unit is often called the *advanced underwriting* unit.

Specialists in this area help the agent design proposals, research tax implications, and, if necessary, make the sales presentation. In addition, members of the advanced underwriting unit write articles for field publications and conduct seminars to teach agents about recent tax law changes and applications of various new products.

Advertising and Sales Promotion

Although advertising is not strictly an agency support function, many insurance companies use advertising to tell others about the quality of their agents. Although the advertising function may be handled by a separate area of the marketing department or by another department, this function is often considered an agency support function.

Insurance companies place advertisements in a wide variety of media—newspapers, television, radio, and magazines. Much of this advertising is known as **institutional advertising,** because it promotes an image of the company rather than a specific insurance product.

The reasons for using institutional advertising, rather than advertisements that describe the features of a specific policy, lie in the nature of insurance products and the regulations in most jurisdictions governing insurance advertising. These regulations typically require that, if a description of a policy is included in an advertisement, the description must be complete in order to avoid possible misrepresentation. A great many words would be needed to completely describe most insurance policies. Therefore, most companies that use the agency system seldom promote a specific product to consumers through their advertisements. Instead, they design their advertisements to build an awareness of the company's name so that, when an agent calls on a prospect, that prospect is more receptive to the agent.

Marketing management generally establishes the advertising budget and determines the selection of media, the timing of the advertising, and the content and design of the advertisements, sometimes with the assistance of an advertising agency. Depending upon the subject, the company's legal counsel might review the advertisement before it appears publicly to ensure that it complies with applicable regulations.

The sales promotion unit designs various sales aids and literature to help agents explain and promote specific products. In addition, this unit develops promotional items, such as calendars and books, for agents to give to policyowners to promote goodwill and company name recognition.

The sales promotion unit also conducts contests to stimulate sales. Such campaigns usually award prizes to the agents or field offices that achieve the highest sales of specified products. For example, such a prize might be an expense-paid trip to the next agent convention.

Office Services

The insurance company provides office services both to its agents and its agency managers. These services typically include

- supplying company forms, stationery, rate books, and manuals of company regulations and procedures
- helping agencies lease office space and acquire office equipment
- providing assistance in office management—floor layout, filing methods, work flow, organization, and scheduling

The increased use of computers in field offices has increased the assistance offered by office services staff. Such computers, which are often linked by telephone lines to a computer in the home office, often require a high degree of standardization in forms and procedures. As a result, the home office staff must assume a larger role in the design of the agency's internal operations, so that uniformity exists among the offices. Computer terminals provide the field offices with rapid access to company data files and to the processing facilities of the company's computer system.

THE MULTIPLE-LINE AGENCY (MLA) SYSTEM

The second type of agency-building distribution system is the multiple-line agency system, also called the *multiple-line exclusive agency system*, and the *all-lines exclusive agency system*. The multiple-line agency (MLA) system, as defined earlier, uses career agents to distribute the life, health, and property/casualty products of a group of affiliated insurance companies. Even though it may appear to a prospect that a multiple-line career agent is representing only one insurer, this agent is actually representing two or more companies that are either financially interrelated or are under some form of common management control. Some MLA companies allow their agents to place business with other companies; other MLA companies do not.

The concept for the MLA system began among property/casualty companies and was based on three factors:

1. The idea that existing property/casualty policyowners constitute a "natural" market for other types of insurance coverage, such as life and health insurance products
2. The desire to provide property/casualty agents with additional sources of income
3. The idea that underwriting profits and losses in the property/casualty business fluctuate unpredictably, but underwriting profits and losses in the life and health insurance business are generally more predictable. Many property/casualty companies have tried to smooth their profit and loss cycles by offering life and health insurance products, which tend to have more stable earnings patterns.

The sale of property/casualty insurance products, life and health insurance products, and other financial services products to the same customer is known as *cross-selling.* This approach reflects the industry's movement from a product-centered orientation to a more customer-centered, market-driven approach to conducting business. A number of benefits result from the cross-selling of insurance products that is made possible by the MLA system.

One of the benefits of cross-selling is that it helps reduce the amount of prospecting necessary to generate new business. Consumers must buy certain property/casualty products—such as auto or homeowners' insurance—so agents who have a property/casualty prospect can also try to sell life and health products to that prospect, knowing that the prospect is already in the market for some type of insurance. Also, because a policyowner may have several different policies in force, agents maintain more frequent contact with the policyowner and can therefore develop more opportunities to seek out additional customer needs for life and health insurance products.

Cross-selling is also believed to improve persistency. The more business a customer generates, and the more satisfied the customer is with the products and service, the more likely the customer is to keep the insurance in force. However, a multiple-line agent with a customer who is dissatisfied with one product risks losing that customer's business on other products as well.

The MLA system also allows companies to benefit from economies of scale by reducing some of the marginal costs associated with distribution, data processing, accounting, and other operations and systems. The agent also benefits from economies of scale in that the average total premium per customer is generally higher, resulting in more efficient use of time and travel expenses.

Multiple-line career agents are considered independent contractors rather than employees of the insurance company. The MLA system is quite similar to the ordinary agency system, with certain exceptions.

One difference between the MLA system and the ordinary agency system is that most career agents within the MLA system establish and maintain their own detached offices and personally hire all necessary clerical staff. In contrast, most career ordinary agents work out of large field offices that are established and maintained by an insurance company or general agent. Usually, MLA career agents must pay for their own office expenses with little or no expense allowance from the company. Moreover, most MLA claim and customer service functions are handled at centralized locations because of the nature and frequency of property/casualty claims.

HOME SERVICE DISTRIBUTION SYSTEM

A third type of agency-building distribution system is the home service distribution system. The home service distribution system, as defined earlier, uses full-time employee-agents to sell products and provide customer service to a block of policyowners in an assigned geographical territory. This territory is sometimes referred to as a *debit,* and the home service agent is often called a *debit agent.* This text will use the term *home service agent* because it more fully describes the agent's role and functions. The term *debit* comes from the insurance company accounting practice of **debiting,** or charging, the agent with the amount of premiums to be collected in the agent's territory.

The home service distribution system was originally created to distribute industrial life insurance. **Industrial life insurance,** sometimes called *debit insurance,* was traditionally characterized by (1) death benefits of $2,000 or less; (2) a weekly, biweekly, or monthly premium payment schedule; (3) minimum underwriting requirements; and (4) the collection of premiums at the policyowner's home by an agent. From 1886 to the early 1950s, industrial insurance constituted a significant percentage of the total sales of life insurance companies. The percentage was as high as 44 percent in 1894, but more often it ranged from 20 to 30 percent. Since the 1950s, the percentage has dropped sharply. In 1990, industrial policies accounted for only 0.2 percent of all life insurance in force in the United States, but this small percentage still represented $25.7 billion of life insurance. Industrial insurance sales have almost disappeared in Canada.

As the proportion of industrial insurance sales has declined, the home service system has turned to sales of ordinary products—such as *monthly debit ordinary (MDO)*, regular ordinary, and universal life products—to meet the needs of their customers. These products function much like other ordinary insurance products. The only distinguishing features are that they are marketed through the home service distribution system and that policyowners are given the option of premium collection and other customer services—such as policy loans and policy changes—at home. Home service agents can sell any type of policy offered by their companies, not just industrial insurance policies. Depending on the type of policy, premiums can be collected by the agent or sent by the policyowner directly to the company. Companies that market both industrial and ordinary insurance products are referred to as ***combination companies***.

Field Office Organization

Most companies that use the home service system divide their marketing area into *districts*, each of which is managed by a *district manager*. The role of the district manager is essentially the same as the role of a branch manager in the ordinary agency system. In most companies, however, the district manager is provided with a staff of several *assistant managers* or *staff managers*. These assistant managers supervise the individual home service agents. In addition, a *cashier* also reports to the district manager. The cashier, also called the *office supervisor*, is responsible for supervising the clerical staff and checking premium accounting and deposit reports.

The size of the area served by each district office depends on geographical characteristics. A large city may be divided into several districts; in rural areas, a single district may encompass several towns. The area served by each district office is subdivided into individual ***territories,*** or *accounts*, and each territory is assigned to an agent. The size of an agent's territory varies with the density of the population in the area. Figure 5-5 illustrates the division of a marketing region into districts and territories. Figure 5-6 shows a typical organizational structure for a home service agency operation.

Figure 5-5
Home service regions, districts, and territories.

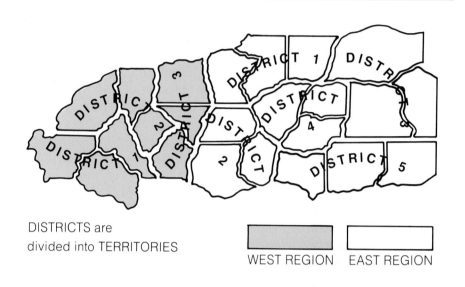

DISTRICTS are
divided into TERRITORIES

WEST REGION   EAST REGION

Comparison of the Home Service System and the Ordinary Agency System

The ordinary agency system and the home service system have many similarities; for example, both rely on agents working in the field to produce new business. Consequently, these two distribution systems are very similar in their functions and organization. Under both types of distribution systems, companies

- recruit, train, and license new agents
- offer agents compensation and benefit plans
- provide administrative and home office support for agents

However, these two distribution systems differ in the areas of collecting and recording premiums, transferring records, and compensating agents.

Collecting and recording premiums

A home service agent is responsible for collecting renewal premiums on all industrial policies and debit ordinary policies in force in his or her territory. This responsibility is the major difference between the duties of a home service agent and the duties of an ordinary insurance agent. Indeed, many companies do not authorize their ordinary agents to collect renewal

Figure 5-6
Organizational structure of a home service distribution system.

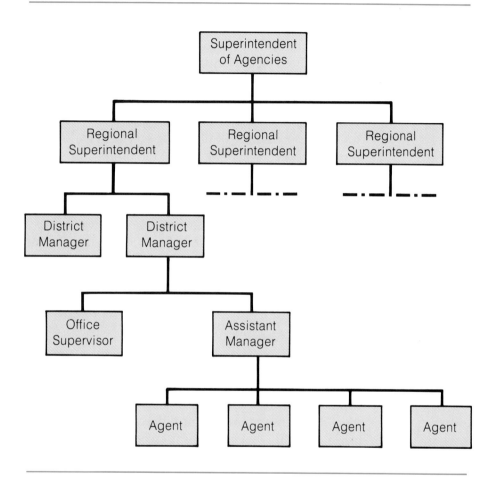

premiums. Because of this premium collection duty, a home service agent must devote more time to recordkeeping than an ordinary agent. The home service agent usually maintains two basic sets of records for industrial policies and debit ordinary policies: the premium receipt book and the collection report.

The ***premium receipt book*** is given to the policyowner when the agent makes the policy sale. This book contains prenumbered receipts. When the agent collects a premium, he or she signs one of the receipt forms in the receipt book, and the policyowner keeps the receipt. Because such payments are often made in cash, the premium receipt is usually the only record of payment the policyowner has.

At the end of each day, the agent deposits the premium collections with the cashier at the district office and receives a receipt. Once a week or once a month, a **collection report** is prepared. This report shows the total premiums collected, the premiums paid in advance, and the premiums overdue. The data for the collection report is prepared by computer and may be kept at both the agency office and the home office.

Transferring records

Another responsibility of the home service agent involves transferring the records of policyowners who move out of the area. If a policyowner moves out of the agent's territory, then the policy records and responsibility for collecting any premiums and servicing the policy are transferred to an agent in the new territory. In areas where the population is very mobile, the transfer of records occupies a significant portion of the agent's time. One insurance company estimated that such transfers constituted about 40 percent of all industrial policy transactions in a single year. Because ordinary agents are not responsible for collecting renewal premiums, such agents are not responsible for transferring records when a policyowner moves.

Compensating agents

Home service agents receive commissions on regular ordinary insurance sales on the same basis as ordinary agents. However, when selling industrial insurance or debit ordinary insurance, home service agents generally work under a compensation system different from that provided for ordinary agents. The different system is used because (1) the industrial policies and debit ordinary policies sold by home service agents are smaller and, therefore, generate lower total commissions per policy than do policies sold by ordinary agents, and (2) home service agents spend a relatively large portion of their time collecting premiums and providing policyowner service. Compensation plans for home service agents usually include the following features:

- *first-year commissions* on new sales of industrial and debit ordinary policies, sometimes with the restriction that the policy must remain in force for six months or a year
- *conservation awards,* based on the agent's lapse ratio, as compared to a predefined standard
- *collection or service fees,* usually a fixed percentage of the amount of premiums actually collected by the agent

- *expense allowances* of a fixed amount per week, often depending on the amount of travel required to service the territory
- *minimum total servicing fees* paid to agents who must serve comparatively small territories

The district manager and all other district office personnel are employees of the company. The manager's basic compensation is in the form of a salary, which is frequently supplemented by bonuses based on persistency of business and staff development efforts. If the insurance company permits the manager to engage in personal sales, then the manager receives commissions on such sales.

KEY TERMS

distribution system
personal selling distribution system
ordinary agency system
multiple-line agency system (MLA)
home service distribution system
career agent
exclusive agent
marketing territory
branch manager
general agent
exclusive territory
overlapping territory
nonexclusive territory
operating budget
staffing schedule
aptitude test
personality test

interest test
historical comparison
intracompany comparison
intercompany comparison
expense ratio
first-year commission
renewal commission
service fee
vested renewal commission
institutional advertising
cross-selling
debiting
industrial life insurance
combination company
territory
premium receipt book
collection report

Chapter 6

Additional Distribution Systems

After reading this chapter, you should be able to

- Describe the features of distribution systems other than agency-building distribution systems
- Distinguish between an agent-broker, a career agent, and a personal producing general agent
- Explain why group insurance requires a method of distribution different from those used for individual products
- Describe the primary responsibilities of group representatives
- Name the types of products distributed through salaried sales personnel
- Describe the features of a direct response marketing campaign
- Explain how advertising effectiveness is tested
- Describe the features of a location selling distribution system

Although agency-building distribution systems account for a significant portion of life and health insurance sales, insurance companies also use several other systems to distribute their products. These distribution systems may be used by a company in place of or in addition to an agency-building system. In this chapter, we will describe the *brokerage, personal producing general agency (PPGA), salaried sales, direct response,* and *location selling* distribution systems.

- The **brokerage system** relies on commissioned agents, called **brokers,** who sell the products of more than one company. Some brokers are agents who are under contract to only one company but occasionally sell the policies of other companies; other brokers, however, work with several companies and regularly sell the policies of those companies.
- The **personal producing general agency system** uses personal producing general agents (PPGAs), who hold agency contracts with

several insurance companies and who spend most of their time selling insurance rather than managing an agency.

- The *salaried sales distribution system* uses salaried employees of the insurance company to sell and service policies. Salaried sales personnel may work either with agents or independently and are often used to distribute group insurance products.
- The *direct response distribution system* relies on advertisements, telephone solicitations, and mailings to generate sales. No agents visit customers to induce sales; the consumer purchases products directly from the company by responding to the company's advertisements and mailings.
- The *location selling distribution system* distributes insurance products by placing insurance offices and agents where consumers generally shop, such as department stores and grocery stores. In such cases, the insurance company is usually affiliated with the retail outlet in some manner.

Some companies, as you'll read in INSIGHT 6-1, use a variety of the distribution systems that are the focus of this chapter.

INSIGHT 6-1

Distribution Systems — Changes for the '90s

Can adding distribution channels improve the bottom line? This critical question was addressed by Life of Virginia's Senior Vice President of Marketing and Executive Director David O'Maley at LOMA's 1989 Expense Management Program (EMaP). With ever-rising expenses, antiquated systems and technology, and low productivity characterized by flat or declining sales as well as matured life policies, insurance companies could get "behind the power curve." In O'Maley's aeronautical terminology, this means that if you don't react fairly quickly, you'll soon be looking at the ground approaching you from an uncomfortable angle and fast.

Between 1980 and 1988, Life of Virginia was transformed from a relatively small regional career agency company into an enviably profitable and effective multi-company business spread over several states. Life of Virginia's compound growth rate in new premium sales was 48 percent for 1980-88. But success is not hinged totally on growth in premium sales. High costs and poor quality can easily negate big sales.

Life of Virginia realized that, in order to become competitive, it had to price to the marketplace and drive costs down to pricing. The company went from being virtually the highest field expense company in 1982-83 to being the absolute lowest in 1986. "We did that," O'Maley stated, "by driving down field overhead expenses. We actually had the same level of expense in 1988 that we had in 1982, and this includes expenses associated with the addition of three new distribution systems in addition to our existing career system," but the same level of expenses were incurred in generating a greater amount of premium income.

Life of Virginia's eventual success was not without its costs. O'Maley believes that even though acquisition of the brokerage business—the company's first additional system—was the quickest way to achieve growth, it was not necessarily the cheapest alternative, at least in terms of the people aspect of the business. "The mistake we made was prohibiting our career shops from doing any brokerage business and, worse yet, we transferred all of their existing brokers to our new MGAs (managing general agents)," he added. Now each of the products the company sells is available to all its distribution systems on an equal basis.

"The key to gaining acceptance from an existing distribution channel—in our case the career system which immediately believed that their days were numbered—is communication," O'Maley said. It took about four years for the career system to gain an element of comfort with the brokerage system. "What made it eventually work was [that] we met with them continually, reassuring them of their place in our plan," commented O'Maley.

New Ventures

The company made valuable use of this lesson with its subsequent new ventures. "We relied on communication, relationships, and trust to overcome the feelings of field uncertainty, and the acceptance period was greatly shortened," O'Maley remarked. Also, information from several company comparison studies was useful in convincing the field and the marketing organization to be responsive in keeping costs down.

Life of Virginia's third distribution system, a franchising operation known as Fourth Financial Network, has the best ratio of expense to commission. The company had learned from its mistakes and disciplined itself for a slower, more painful, growth posture which was more rewarding in the long run "because we didn't have to back up," O'Maley explained.

Life of Virginia's experience has shown that a company can reduce expenses and increase sales. Additional distribution systems can be added to a company's career agency system—in this case, brokerage and franchising—without having proportional rises in expenses.

Source: Adapted with permission of the publisher from Lucy Barnes McDowell, "Looking Ahead: Distribution Strategies for the 1990s," *Resource,* November/December 1989, pp. 13-14, 16.

BROKERAGE DISTRIBUTION SYSTEM

Many insurance companies distribute their products through brokers. The term *broker* has several meanings in the insurance industry. In a legal sense, a broker is an insurance salesperson who (1) operates independently of any life and health insurance company and (2) is considered to be the agent of his

Figure 6-1
Relationships of agent-brokers to insurance companies and consumers.

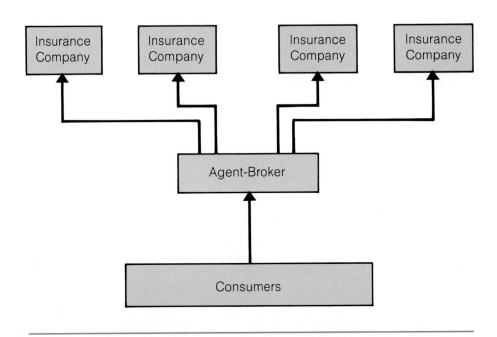

or her clients, rather than the agent of any insurance company. However, few such individuals exist, and in several states and all Canadian provinces, such an individual cannot legally sell insurance products unless that individual is under contract with an insurance company. The more commonly accepted meaning of **broker** is an agent who sells insurance products for more than one insurance company. This text uses the term *agent-broker* to describe this type of individual. The relationship of agent-brokers to other parties in the insurance transaction is shown in Figure 6-1.

The use of the brokerage distribution system by life and health insurance companies varies. Comparatively few companies distribute their products exclusively through agent-brokers. Some companies actively seek brokerage business; others accept, but do not encourage, brokerage business. In most companies that accept brokerage business, a part of the marketing department is devoted exclusively to developing and maintaining contacts with agent-brokers.

In most cases, insurance companies allow their own full-time agents to **broker** business, that is, to submit insurance applications to companies other than the agent's own company. The ability of an agent to submit an application to an insurer other than the agent's primary company is determined by the terms of the agent's contract. The contract of a full-time agent naturally supposes that the bulk of the agent's applications will be submitted to his or her primary company. Nonetheless, the agent sometimes needs to be able to submit applications elsewhere. One common reason that an agent brokers business is that clients want products that the agent's primary company does not offer. Another reason might be that the primary company's underwriting department has declined the application or accepted it as a substandard risk, thereby requiring the policyowner to pay higher-than-standard premium rates.

Essentially, the agent-broker functions in the same manner as an ordinary agent. The agent-broker must find prospects, identify their needs, design insurance programs to fit those needs, make sales presentations, and provide service to clients. The client may not know whether the person selling the insurance is acting as a broker or an agent. Competition between companies that use brokerage distribution systems is intense, because the broker is able to sell for any number of companies. Products, underwriting, customer service, and commission levels must be consistently competitive to attract brokerage business.

Soliciting Brokerage Business

Companies use several methods to attract brokerage business. One common method is through brokerage managers. A **brokerage manager** is a salaried insurance company employee or an independent agent charged with encouraging agent-brokers to sell the company's products. Brokerage managers may establish their own offices, may be located in the home office, or may be located in field offices. Those located in field offices spend only a small part of their time attracting brokerage business; the rest of their time is spent selling insurance products. Brokerage managers are compensated with salaries, bonuses, and overriding commissions on sales that agent-brokers place through them. Those brokerage managers that sell insurance products also receive commissions on personal sales.

Insurers also use brokerage shops to solicit brokerage business. A **brokerage shop** is a field office operated by a general agent who is under contract to a number of insurance companies. In some cases, the brokerage shop specializes in substandard business, and the general agent helps other agents or agent-brokers place applications that their primary company has declined or rated as substandard. General agents receive overriding commissions on business that other agent-brokers place through them. An insurer that relies on brokerage shops often underwrites more substandard business than the average company.

Compensation

Agent-brokers are compensated on a commission system. First-year commissions and renewal commissions are generally offered to agent-brokers in much the same way that they are offered to agents. However, because agent-brokers are not located in company branch offices and, therefore, do not cost the company overhead expenses, agent-brokers' commissions can be somewhat higher than those paid to agents. On the other hand, most agent-brokers receive no service fees, and by placing business through several companies, they fail to generate the maximum benefits and bonuses from a single company. Those agent-brokers who do frequently place business with a specific insurer may receive expense reimbursement, group insurance benefits, and bonuses.

Home Office Support Services

The primary difference between the agency-building distribution system and the brokerage distribution system is found in the functions of the home office support services unit. The support services that an insurance company provides for agent-brokers are vastly different from the services provided to agents. Usually, insurers provide little or no career training for agent-brokers; most have worked as agents for other insurance companies and, thus, have already been trained in sales techniques and insurance principles. On the other hand, insurance companies do provide product training for agent-brokers as required.

PERSONAL PRODUCING GENERAL AGENCY (PPGA) DISTRIBUTION SYSTEM

The personal producing general agency distribution system uses personal producing general agents to distribute products. A personal producing general agent (PPGA) typically works alone and engages primarily in prospecting and sales. The PPGA does not operate out of a company field office, which is one of the PPGA system's primary benefits for a company. Because no money is spent recruiting and training agents and nothing is paid to a PPGA salesperson until a sale is made, a company using the PPGA system incurs few up-front expenses or development costs.

The PPGA distribution system was once considered a subdivision of the agency system, but has now evolved into a system more closely aligned with the brokerage distribution system. The PPGA system originated where the populations were too small to justify the expense of maintaining a field office. Today, most PPGAs are under contract to several insurance companies, and such agents operate in much the same fashion as career agents. However, instead of working through a branch office or general agency, the PPGA usually works with a regional office or directly with the home office. Because PPGAs are usually experienced agents, the only training a company generally provides to PPGAs concerns the company's products and procedures.

Compensation

PPGA compensation schedules resemble those of general agents. First-year and renewal commissions and overrides are generally fully vested. A PPGA receives an overriding commission on business sold by subagents who work for the PPGA. Although some overhead expense allowance is usually provided as part of a PPGA contract, the responsibility for managing and controlling the agency's insurance operations rests solely with the PPGA. Many companies provide benefits, such as group life and health insurance, to PPGAs who meet specified production or persistency requirements. Some companies also offer PPGAs additional noncash compensation, such as access to communications links with the home office, assistance in obtaining computer hardware and software, assistance with attaining professional designations, and trips to business conventions. INSIGHT 6-2 describes one company's efforts to shorten the time it takes to send PPGAs their commission checks.

INSIGHT 6-2

Accelerating PPGA Commission Payments

One major life insurance company has developed a program designed to accelerate the issue and commission payment on certain universal life insurance products to its personal producing general agents.

The basic procedures involved in the instant issue and instant commission program are

1. An eligible PPGA takes a completed nonmedical application to any regional office. The qualified appli-

cation is immediately faxed to the home office.

2. A specially qualified underwriter reviews the application within minutes after it arrives in the home office. If the application is approved at this review, the policy is issued that night. If the application does not qualify for instant issue, it is sent through the regular underwriting channels and processed at the earliest possible date.

3. Approved policies are produced and checked for accuracy. If the business qualifies for instant commissions, the commission checks are drawn immediately.

4. Policies and qualified commission checks are sent twice per week via an overnight delivery service to the regional office where the applications originated. In many instances, a policy and commission check are in the PPGA's hands within 48 hours after the application has been submitted to the home office.

Source: Adapted with permission from an Activity Report submitted to LOMA, September 1988.

Differences between the PPGA System and the Brokerage System

A number of differences exist between the PPGA system and the brokerage system. Most agents' contracts used under the brokerage system resemble a soliciting agent's contract, but contracts used for PPGAs resemble those for a general agent. In addition, most companies have no minimum production requirements for brokers, but companies that use PPGAs generally establish such requirements that the PPGAs must meet to maintain their contracts. Further, insurance benefits and other types of noncash compensation are usually not provided under the brokerage system, except in the case of agent-brokers who frequently place business with a specific insurer, as we mentioned earlier. By contrast, such benefits and other noncash compensation are used in compensating PPGAs.

SALARIED SALES—GROUP INSURANCE

Until now, this text has discussed life and health insurance distribution systems in which people are paid commissions for the products they sell. However, because of the nature of group insurance and the distinctive characteristics of its market, the distribution of group products is quite different from the traditional commission-based systems used to distribute individual products. The characteristics of group insurance that affect its method of distribution are as follows:

- *The prospect is not an individual but is an organization, usually an employer.* Because the prospect's ultimate decision is often subject to the approval of the company's directors, the prospect must be prepared to justify the selection of a particular insurer and a particular contract. Therefore, the prospect is likely to be better informed about insurance products than is a prospect for individual insurance. To select the best possible contract at the best possible price, the prospect is likely to seek competitive proposals from several insurance companies.
- *In many companies, the total amount of coverage provided by a group contract is usually much larger than that provided by an individual policy.*
- *The specific provisions of a group life or health insurance contract are subject to negotiation between the insurer and the prospect.* In a competitive situation, the life insurance company tries to structure a contract that is designed specifically to meet one prospective group's needs. Individual life insurance contracts are much more standardized, although the policyowner may have choices regarding some optional features.

Most insurance companies employ group representatives to provide group insurance prospects with proper service. A ***group representative*** finds group insurance prospects, designs proposals, installs the group product, and renegotiates the policy at renewal. Group representatives are salaried employees of the insurance company, although many companies also pay their group representatives bonuses or commissions based on sales.

Prospecting

In some cases, the group representative is the only contact between the prospect and the insurer. In such cases, he or she must find prospects in much the same way that agents find prospects for individual insurance. The group representative generally calls on local businesses, reads the business section of the newspaper to identify companies in the area, and gathers referrals from satisfied clients.

Group representatives generally rely to a great degree on leads furnished by agent-brokers and ordinary agents. Agent-brokers, in particular, are valuable resources because many specialize in placing group business and have developed numerous connections in that market. In most cases, the agent or agent-broker who initiates the contact with a prospect calls on the group representative for assistance. Most companies provide the services of a group representative to agents and agent-brokers at no charge; that is, the use of the group representative does not affect the commission that is payable to the agent or agent-broker.

Preparing the Proposal

The group representative must acquire background information about the prospect's needs and specific objectives. The objectives of the group insurance purchase may be to match the benefits offered by other local firms, to respond to union requests, or to increase employees' compensation without giving them a salary increase. The representative must also determine the premium the prospect can afford for the group coverage and must obtain specific data about the group's members. This information includes the age, sex, and occupation of each member, as well as information about any special hazards that group members share as part of their jobs. The group representative also gathers information about the group's previous claim experience.

With this information, the group representative and the insurer's group underwriters can prepare a proposal to submit to the prospect. Preparing the proposal may require the additional services of group actuaries if the policy offered has unique benefits and features that require special computations. On occasion, the representative adds a feature to satisfy the prospect or to match a proposal made by a competing insurance company. Each such modification is likely to require recalculation of the policy's premium rate. Many group representatives use computers connected to the home office in order to expedite proposal design and enable the group representative to respond quickly to requests from the prospect.

Installing the Product

Installation is the term used to include all the activities from the time the prospect decides to purchase the group insurance policy to the time the master group policy and its individual certificates are issued and delivered. For the purposes of this discussion, we will assume that the group is an employer-employee group.

One of the first steps in the installation process is informing the group members of (1) the policy's purchase, (2) the plan's eligibility requirements, (3) the benefits provided by the policy, (4) the policy provisions, and (5) the amount of the premium that employees must pay, if any. Experience has shown that employee acceptance of the plan is greater if it is viewed as the employer's program rather than as the insurance company's program. For this reason, the announcement of the policy's purchase is usually made by the employer through letters and employee meetings. To assure completeness and accuracy of the employer's announcements, the group representative usually reviews any material that the employer uses to describe the plan to employees. In addition, the group representative usually attends all employee meetings concerning the plan.

Enrollment of group members

If the group plan is *noncontributory,* which means that the premium is paid entirely by the employer, then the enrollment of group members is automatic; all eligible group members are covered. In such cases, each group member fills out an enrollment form designating the beneficiary for any life insurance benefits. If the plan is *contributory,* which means that group members pay a portion of the insurance premium, then group member enrollment is voluntary. Employees who do not want to be covered under a contributory plan are usually asked to sign waivers of coverage. An eligible employee who elects to receive coverage signs an enrollment form and indicates the beneficiary of any life insurance benefits. The enrollment form shows that the employee accepts the coverage provided under the plan and authorizes the deduction of the applicable premium from his or her paycheck.

Negotiating Policy Renewals

Most group insurance policies are renewable on a yearly basis. When the time arrives for the policy to be renewed, the group representative generally reevaluates the policyholder's needs to determine whether changes should be made in the plan. If so, new information is collected and the group representative designs a new proposal. At this time, the group representative also describes any applicable premium rate changes.

Home Office Support Services

In some insurance companies, the marketing of group insurance is directed by a subdivision of the marketing department. In many large companies offering group insurance, all group functions are organized in a single group department because of the many differences between group and individual insurance. These differences are reflected in such functions as actuarial operations, underwriting, and customer service. Regardless of the organizational system used, certain support services are provided to the company's group representatives. Many of these support functions are similar to those provided to a company's agents—for example, training, sales promotion materials, and administrative support.

As company employees, group representatives may work in either regional offices or in the company's home office, and enjoy the same basic support services as other company employees. Group representatives who work for small insurance companies doing business in a limited geographic area often work from the home office. Large insurance companies divide their marketing territory into regions, each with several local group offices that house group insurance representatives.

SALARIED SALES – OTHER PRODUCTS

Salaried sales personnel are used to distribute other types of insurance besides group insurance. Those companies marketing *pension products, savings bank life insurance (SBLI)*, and *fraternal life insurance* also use salaried sales personnel to distribute their products.

Pension Products

An insurance company's pension products, like its group life and health insurance products, are often distributed by salaried sales personnel as well as by agents and agent-brokers. The pension products' distributors must be well versed in the types of investment contracts available and how these contracts function. Most pension product representatives work on a salary and bonus arrangement and are considered employees of the insurer. These pension representatives may also work with agents and agent-brokers in much the same way that group insurance representatives do.

Savings Bank Life Insurance (SBLI)

As mentioned in Chapter 2, savings bank life insurance (SBLI) is life insurance that is sold through savings banks in a few states in the United States. SBLI is distributed (1) through over-the-counter sales in participating banks and (2) through the mail. In a small bank that offers SBLI primarily as a convenience to its customers, the sale of SBLI is generally handled by one bank employee. In larger banks, the sale of SBLI is handled by a staff of bank employees trained to help prospective purchasers choose

666

the type and amount of coverage that meets their needs. Sales personnel receive salaries and, frequently, bonuses based on sales. Direct commissions are not paid.

Fraternal Life Insurance

Also discussed in Chapter 2, fraternal life insurance is life insurance that fraternal benefit societies issue to their members. Fraternal benefit societies are nonprofit social organizations established and operated solely for the benefit of members, and fraternal life insurance benefits are available only to fraternal society members. Fraternal life insurance can be distributed through the officers and salaried employees of the fraternal benefit society as well as through the agency-building system and the direct response system.

DIRECT RESPONSE MARKETING

The distribution system that permits the supplier and the consumer to make transactions directly with each other is known as *direct response marketing* (see Figure 6-2). In direct response marketing, sales offers are made directly to consumers, usually through the mail or by advertisements in newspapers, magazines, television, or radio (see Figure 6-3). In turn, consumers must contact the insurance company directly, usually by telephone or mail, rather than through commissioned agent-brokers or agents. Some direct response marketing is also done over the phone, which is known as *telemarketing.*

The use of direct response marketing within the life and health insurance industry is widespread. Some insurance companies rely completely on the direct response system to distribute their products. Others use direct response marketing in conjunction with other distribution systems. Insurance agents also use direct response techniques to locate prospects. Our discussion, however, will center on the use of direct response marketing by insurance companies to distribute products without the use of an agent or agent-broker.

Direct response marketing is generally used to distribute relatively simple insurance products that can be easily explained and understood, because the entire description of the product and sales presentation is contained in the advertising copy. Also, because the entire product is described in detail, the legal department is often involved in approving the text of direct response promotional literature. In most cases, the products marketed through direct response marketing are intended to be supplemen-

Figure 6-2
Direct-response marketing and consumers.

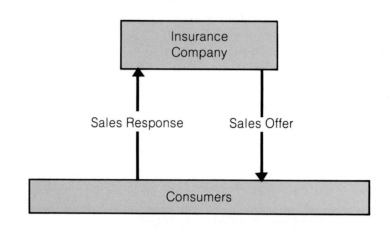

Figure 6-3
Media used for direct-response marketing.

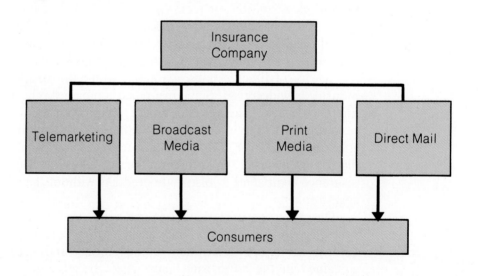

tary in nature. For example, a hospital confinement policy, which provides a specified dollar amount for each day the insured is hospitalized, is often used to supplement other hospital expense coverage. Underwriting requirements for direct response products are typically simple. Medical examinations and detailed medical histories are usually not required. In fact, many direct response products are designed to be offered on a *guaranteed-issue* basis, meaning that an applicant for insurance cannot be turned down for reasons related to health status.

In order to distribute insurance products successfully through the direct response marketing system, insurers must (1) select specific target markets identified through the use of market segmentation; (2) conduct extensive market research; and (3) design and test product features, sales promotion materials, and various advertising media. Although some aspects of these marketing functions were described in Chapter 4, they take on a special importance for companies that use the direct response distribution system, and they are described more fully here.

Marketing Intelligence and Direct Response Distribution

An insurance company that uses direct response marketing has a number of uses for marketing intelligence. Among these uses are

- defining and locating prospective purchasers of its products
- designing products
- planning advertising copy
- anticipating underwriting problems

Marketing studies help insurers identify various market segments and narrow those segments into target markets that are likely to purchase the company's products. Companies that sell insurance through direct response methods also use marketing intelligence to measure items such as

- consumers' purchasing frequency
- time of last direct response purchase of any type of product
- monetary value of purchases from direct response media

Research has shown that people who have already purchased goods or services through direct response are likely to continue to make such purchases. These people are prime prospects for direct response insurers.

Properly focusing promotional materials for the desired target market is one important step in direct response distribution of insurance products. Sales promotion materials developed to appeal to young families, for example, would not be effective if sent to a retirement community. Thus, direct response insurance companies need to learn not only about the needs of their target markets, but also about certain personal characteristics and behaviors, such as where the customers live, the types of magazines they read, and the television programs they watch. Consumer behavior research is thus essential in reaching potential customers.

Target markets

Two groups commonly targeted by direct response companies are credit card holders and senior citizens. One of the main benefits of directing sales campaigns to credit card holders is that insurance companies can buy current mailing lists of credit card holders and use these lists to market their products. In addition, direct response marketing insurance companies can make agreements with department stores and banks that issue credit cards. In these agreements, the stores and banks endorse—for a fee—the insurance company's products, announcing that card holders can charge the insurance premiums to their credit card accounts. Through such arrangements, insurers can increase consumer response, improve persistency, and reduce administrative costs.

Senior citizens typically share a common need for small amounts of life insurance and supplemental health insurance products. Because these products are ideally suited to direct response distribution, insurers often target direct response marketing efforts to senior citizens. In addition, senior citizens can often be reached through a variety of associations that can endorse the insurer's products.

Designing Sales Promotion Materials

Once the company has determined which product to offer to a specific target market, advertising copy must be designed and tested. The advertising copy must explain the product to the consumer and induce the consumer to buy the product. Unlike other insurance advertising, direct response advertisements always attempt to elicit an immediate response from consumers. As we noted in Chapter 5, most other forms of insurance industry advertising seek only to build an awareness and positive image of an insurance company.

Direct response insurers use a variety of advertising media. The most important of these media are *direct mail, print, broadcast,* and *telemarketing.* One way to measure the effectiveness of the various types of advertising media is to calculate advertising costs per policy sold and compare these costs to the company's projected costs.

Direct mail

Direct mail uses printed solicitations that are addressed directly to prospective purchasers. Such printed materials generally consist of an *introduction letter*, or *mother letter*, a brochure that describes a particular product, an insurance application or an inquiry form to request further information, and a return envelope. Direct mail sales literature is referred to as a ***mail kit,*** because it includes all the information and forms that a customer needs to make a purchase decision and apply for the policy. As mentioned earlier, the mail kit must be designed to have an appearance and tone that appeal to the prospect.

The mail kit is sent to people whose names appear on a list compiled according to criteria established by the company's market researchers. Mailing lists are available from a number of sources, including brokerage houses, other direct response companies, banks, and credit card companies. Insurance companies also use their own lists of customers, ex-customers, and leads furnished by other customers. Because mailing lists can be segmented in a number of ways, such as by income level or profession, direct mail allows the greatest degree of market specification of any of the direct response media. Most insurers send an initial mail kit to selected names on the list and may send several follow-up kits to some or all of the people who have not responded. List maintenance—to avoid duplications or mailings to poor prospects—is important; a bad list can negatively affect an otherwise effective mailing.

Print media

Print media advertising refers to all advertising placed in newspapers and magazines, whether actually printed on the pages or in ***free-fall advertisements,*** which are preprinted ads that are stuffed in, but not bound to, newspapers or magazines. To print an advertisement in a newspaper or magazine, the insurer buys space in the publication and designs an ad to fit that space. To be successful, the direct response advertisement must capture the reader's attention, describe the essentials of the product, and, ideally, induce the reader to buy, or at least inquire about, the product. The advertisement also includes either an application for the product or a coupon that the consumer fills out and sends to the insurer to receive more information.

Print media reaches a more general audience than direct mail. However, by advertising in special-interest publications, insurers can target specific groups of readers. The response rate is usually much higher for direct mail than it is for print advertising, although the cost per person exposed to print advertising is far lower than the cost of direct mail.

Broadcast media

Radio and television—known together as the **broadcast media**—are used to support print advertisements and to make direct sales offers. Direct response radio and television advertisements generally last for 30 to 120 seconds. The last 15 to 20 seconds are spent describing ways the consumer can buy or obtain more information about the product. Generally, the consumer is asked to call a toll-free telephone number or write to a specific address. In direct response broadcast media advertising, insurers frequently hire a celebrity to serve as a spokesperson for the product.

Telemarketing

With *telemarketing,* the telephone helps produce sales. Although some insurers use telemarketing to initiate contact with prospects, telemarketing also supports other direct response media. For example, an advertisement or mailing may urge the consumer to call a toll-free number for information. The caller tells the operator which product he or she is calling about, and the operator asks the caller a series of questions. Operators may ask for information such as the person's name, address, phone number, and age. Operators may not, however, accept an order for an insurance product, because only individuals who are licensed agents may make sales. Instead, the operator usually sends the caller a **fulfillment kit,** which consists of an application and, usually, more information about the product.

Telemarketing is a high-cost medium. However, the high response rate from callers generally justifies the expense. In addition, telemarketing allows two-way communication and an opportunity to personalize the direct marketing process.

Testing Advertising Effectiveness

Testing the effectiveness of direct response advertising is fairly simple because of the immediate-response nature of the media. Institutional advertising is much more difficult to test because such advertisements do not call for a discernible response from consumers. Most direct mail pieces and print advertisements are coded, so that each response can be traced to its source advertisement. Telemarketing operators maintain records of calls so that the information can be analyzed to determine the source of the consumer's interest.

Direct response advertisers test advertising both before and after a sales campaign is conducted. Before advertisements are released to a large market, they are generally tested on a small sample of the target market. Based on the results of that sampling, the advertising copy or the design of the kit can be modified to produce more favorable results. In this way, the company can avoid wasting a large amount of money conducting a full-scale campaign with an ineffective advertisement. In broad market mailings, a response rate of 0.5 percent usually allows an insurer to meet its marketing goals. Actual sales are typically less than this 0.5 percent.

LOCATION SELLING DISTRIBUTION SYSTEM

The *location selling distribution system* relies on consumers to initiate insurance purchases by visiting an insurance company office that is located in a store or other business where consumers shop for other items. In most cases, the insurer is in some manner affiliated with the store.

For location selling to be successful, the insurance office should be located in a place where a large number of consumers regularly shop. Alternatively, the insurer must use advertising to attract consumers to the office. These offices are staffed by licensed insurance agents who may sell property and casualty insurance products as well as life and health insurance products. Because sales presentations are generally initiated by prospects, location-selling agents are not as concerned with prospecting as are other ordinary agents. However, agents in retail locations do prospect over the telephone, and they may have schedules that allow in-home sales.

Location selling distribution does not yet account for a large percentage of life and health insurance sales, although the system has been used for a number of years to sell a fairly large volume of property and casualty insurance.

KEY TERMS

brokerage system	salaried sales distribution system
broker	direct response distribution system
personal producing general agency (PPGA) system	location selling distribution system
	brokerage manager

brokerage shop
group representative
installation
noncontributory plan
contributory plan
direct response marketing
telemarketing

guaranteed-issue
direct mail
mail kit
print media advertising
free-fall advertisement
broadcast media
fulfillment kit

Chapter 7

Actuarial Functions for Individual Life Insurance

After reading this chapter, you should be able to

- Describe the functions that actuaries perform
- List the responsibilities of the corporate actuarial unit
- Describe the factors that insurers consider when setting premium rates
- Give an example of the law of large numbers
- State the purpose of safety margins
- Distinguish between a select group and the general population
- Compare the effects of compound and simple interest
- Distinguish between net and gross premiums and explain how these premiums are calculated
- Describe the purpose of an asset share calculation

Life and health insurance products are based on mathematical principles. By applying these principles soundly, insurance companies can guarantee that they will have enough money to pay the benefits that they have promised to pay. The job of *actuaries* is to apply mathematical principles to life and health insurance. Actuaries calculate and predict the rates of death, illness, and injury among insureds. Actuaries also calculate their companies' legal reserve liabilities and the premium rates of insurance products. They conduct basic research on long- and short-term trends in interest rates, mortality and morbidity rates, expenses, policy lapses, and policy loans. They assist in strategic planning, and they frequently represent the company in discussions with industry regulators and government representatives.

Actuarial work is highly specialized and requires many years of training. Because of their extensive training and broad knowledge of insurance matters, actuaries frequently hold positions of great responsibility in insurance companies. Many executive and managerial positions in insurance companies are entrusted to actuaries, even when those positions do not involve traditional actuarial functions. For example, people with actuarial backgrounds sometimes manage operations such as customer service or underwriting.

We will begin this chapter with a brief discussion of actuarial duties in a life and health insurance company. After that, we will discuss actuarial functions as they affect individual insurance. We will discuss mortality rates and mortality tables, interest rates, net premiums, gross premiums, reserves, surplus, cash values, and dividends. In Chapter 8, we will describe actuarial functions as they relate to group and health insurance.

WHAT IS AN ACTUARY?

The executive in a life insurance company who has overall responsibility for the actuarial function is the company actuary, often called the *chief actuary* or *senior actuary*. The chief actuary is responsible for making sure that the company's insurance operations are conducted on a sound financial basis. To fulfill this responsibility, the chief actuary works with people from various functional areas, such as accounting and investments, to analyze premium rates, reserve levels, dividend schedules (if the company markets participating policies), investments, and cash inflow and outflow. Other employees working under the chief actuary may also be accredited actuaries, and they often have titles such as *associate actuary* and *assistant actuary*, or simply *actuary*. In addition, many insurance companies employ actuarial trainees who are taking the courses required to become accredited actuaries. These trainees are usually called *actuarial assistants* or *actuarial students*.

The largest life and health insurance companies may employ dozens of full-time actuaries and actuarial assistants; small companies may have just one professional actuary or no actuary at all. However, because actuarial functions are vital to sound insurance operations, an insurance company without an actuary hires consulting actuaries, who provide actuarial services for a fee. Even companies with a large actuarial staff may occasionally need consulting actuaries for special projects or analyses.

Associations, such as the Society of Actuaries and the American Academy of Actuaries in the United States and the Canadian Institute of Actuaries in Canada, establish and maintain standards of competence and performance for actuaries. These associations also promote the advancement of actuarial science by conducting research and providing an education and certification program for actuarial trainees (discussed in Chapter 18).

ACTUARIAL FUNCTIONS IN AN INSURANCE COMPANY

Specific actuarial functions are usually distributed throughout a company according to the types of products that an insurance company sells. As an example, Figure 7-1 illustrates the various actuarial functions in a large company that sells individual life insurance, individual and group health insurance, individual annuities, and pensions. Actuaries trained to deal with

Figure 7-1
Organizational chart of actuarial functions.

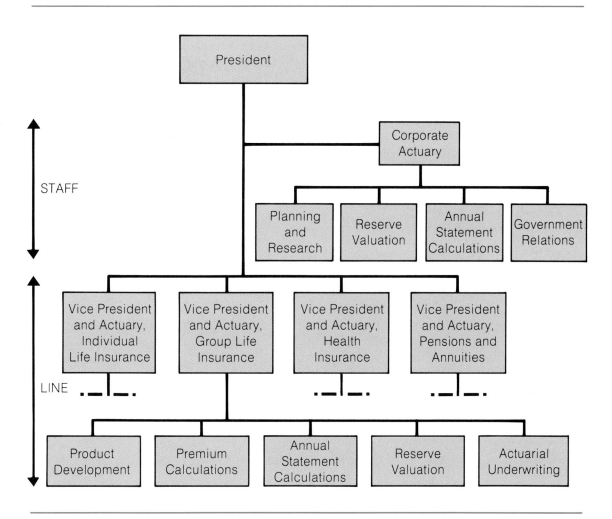

each of these products frequently work with the vice presidents in charge of these products.

Some companies establish a corporate actuarial unit to support upper-level management. The corporate actuarial unit is not affiliated or associated with any particular product. The functions of a corporate actuarial unit are to

- conduct long-range statistical and financial studies
- help represent the company in discussions with state, provincial, and federal agencies
- calculate the value of the company's reserve liabilities
- advise the president and board of directors on future courses of action for the company

Finally, state laws in the United States require that, in order for a company's Annual Statement to be certified, the statement must be signed by an actuary who is a Member of the American Academy of Actuaries (MAAA). In Canada, a company's Annual Statement must be signed by a Fellow of the Canadian Institute of Actuaries (FCIA).

Actuarial Research

Actuaries conduct a great deal of research for life and health insurance companies. Actuarial researchers use statistics gathered from throughout the company to project future strategies or recommend new products that can help the company maintain or improve its share of the insurance market. For example, actuarial researchers may prepare reports for the executive office suggesting ways to modify dividend allocations or reserve valuations. Actuaries can also project profits by product line, evaluate future capital and surplus requirements, and provide the mortality and morbidity statistics that are used to set underwriting standards for the company.

Professional actuarial societies, such as the Society of Actuaries or the Canadian Institute of Actuaries, conduct statistical studies using data collected from a large number of insurance companies. For example, the Society of Actuaries has a standing committee on life insurance and annuities that prepares yearly reports on the mortality rates that various insurance companies have experienced on their standard ordinary policies. By pooling data from a large number of companies, actuaries can develop reliable statistical tables that reflect overall mortality rates and morbidity rates for insured people.

Interest rates and income taxes

Fluctuating interest rates and changing income tax regulations have had an important impact on actuarial work. As interest rates move, insurance companies modify their products in order to keep them competitive with other financial products. The job of insurance company actuaries, assisted by investment specialists, includes new product development and the revision of current products either to take advantage of higher interest rates or to maximize returns when interest rates fall. Actuaries responsible for investment-based products must consider shifts in interest rates when calculating changes in premium amounts, projected death benefits, and other policy values.

Income tax laws also affect the work of actuaries. Changes in income tax laws have meant that actuaries must

- develop and revise products to help policyowners take advantage of tax savings and tax deferrals
- change premium rates and dividend scales, as necessary, to meet the requirements of income tax laws

Government Liaison

Communication between the government and a life and health insurance company often involves actuaries. Frequently, an actuary, in consultation with a member of the company's legal staff, represents the company's position on proposed laws and rules in front of regulatory and legislative bodies. The actuary must, therefore, remain up-to-date on legislative and regulatory changes, assess their impact, and report their effect to company management. Furthermore, actuaries are often involved in drafting insurance contracts and presenting these contracts for approval by state and provincial insurance departments.

Financial Statements and Reports

Actuaries are closely involved in the preparation of various reports that describe the condition and operations of their company. Some reports, such as studies of the company's mortality experience, are prepared solely by actuarial personnel. The preparation of financial reports, however, requires actuaries to work closely with people in other areas, such as accounting.

One of the key reports of an insurance company is its Annual Statement. Some of the information appearing in the Annual Statement, such as the amount of policy reserves, is actuarial by nature, and data pertaining to such information is prepared under the direction of actuaries. Most of the data is of a nonactuarial nature and is often prepared by the company's accountants. However, in some companies an actuary has overall responsibility for preparing the Annual Statement.

In addition to the Annual Statement, the company usually prepares an annual report for distribution to its policyowners or stockholders. The *annual report* includes financial statements that are generally prepared in a fashion different from those that appear in the Annual Statement. Actuaries do not usually produce the annual report, but they provide some of the information used in it. The annual report and the Annual Statement are both discussed further in Chapter 13.

Actuaries also prepare the actuarial sections of other reports required of the company, such as income tax returns, corporate financial statements, and periodic reports required by state, provincial, and federal insurance departments. Actuaries are involved in audits of the company by public accountants and by state, provincial, and federal insurance examiners.

In addition to the reports for outside agencies, many reports prepared for the use of company management have actuarial aspects. For example, analyses of operating expenses often involve the allocation of expenses to different lines of business. Although recording expenses is part of the accounting function, the allocation of these expenses to various products and product lines often requires the participation of an actuary.

INDIVIDUAL LIFE INSURANCE CALCULATIONS

One of an actuary's most important duties is rate making. **Rate making** is the establishing of premium rates for an insurance company's products. A company must have enough income to pay its claims and operating expenses, and part of its income comes from premiums. If premium rates are set too low, the survival of the company may be jeopardized. If rates are set too high, the company can lose business to its competitors. Therefore, life and health insurance companies depend on the rate-making skills of their actuaries. Some companies have actuaries that specialize in rate making and product development.

Actuaries consider several factors when they establish life insurance premium rates. The most important factors are

- mortality rates
- expenses
- interest rates
- lapse rates

MORTALITY RATES

In order to produce sound life insurance products, actuaries must be able to predict, as accurately as possible, the mortality rate of the people that their companies will insure. As defined in Chapter 1, the *mortality rate* is the frequency with which death occurs among a defined number of people.

Probability and the Law of Large Numbers

Actuaries use the *theory of probability* to predict the mortality rate of a given group of people. **Probability** is the likelihood of an event's occurring. In a mathematical sense, probability refers to the number of times that an event is likely to occur out of a number of possible occurrences. Consider the probability of drawing an ace from a standard deck of cards. The probability is calculated as

$$\frac{\text{number of possible successes}}{\text{number of possible occurrences}} = \frac{4}{52}$$

The number of possible successes is 4, because a standard deck of playing cards has 4 aces. The number of possible occurrences is 52, because a standard deck of playing cards has 52 cards. Therefore, the probability of drawing an ace is 4/52, which can be reduced mathematically to 1/13. Theoretically, the 1/13 probability means that if you take a well-shuffled deck of cards, draw a card, *replace the card in the deck,* reshuffle the deck, and draw again, then out of every 13 times you draw a card from the deck, you should draw one ace. However, anyone who has drawn cards from a deck knows that, under these circumstances, it is quite possible to draw aces on the first two draws or even draw no aces in fifty-two draws.

The reason that the actual results and the results predicted by probability differ is that the accuracy of a prediction depends on the statistical concept called the law of large numbers. The **law of large numbers** states the greater the number of observations, the more likely it is that the results will be the same as the actual underlying probability. In other words, actual results and predicted results are more likely to be the same if a person draws from a deck of cards four million times rather than four times.

Actuaries use probability theory and the law of large numbers to predict the number of people in a given population who are likely to die in a given period of time. Actuaries cannot predict *who* will die in a given period of time, but they can predict fairly accurately *how many* people in a given population will die during a certain period.

Calculating Mortality Rates

Actuaries in most insurance companies record their company's *mortality experience;* that is, they keep records of the number of their insureds who die each year. However, the most extensive mortality statistics are gathered by the Society of Actuaries and the Canadian Institute of Actuaries. These organizations collect data from government agencies and insurance companies to calculate the mortality rates of people in the United States and Canada.

Generally, the mortality rate increases as people grow older, although this progression can fluctuate. A good visual representation of the mortality rate is a *mortality curve,* which is a line graph that represents the mortality rate as it changes from age to age. Figure 7-2 presents the mortality curves that show the predicted mortality rates for men and women in the most recent valuation mortality table, called the Commissioners 1980 Standard Ordinary (1980 CSO) mortality table. Note that before age 40, mortality rates increase fairly slowly, but after age 40, mortality rates rise sharply.

Developing Mortality Tables

Once mortality rates are calculated, they are presented in the form of mortality tables. *Mortality tables* present the probabilities of living and dying for a large group of people. Most life insurance mortality tables begin at age 0 and end at age 99 or 100, even though some insureds live past this age. Life insurance companies usually pay the full death benefit of the insurance policy to those insureds who live to the final age listed on the companies' mortality tables.

A typical mortality table

Figure 7-3 displays the 1980 CSO mortality table, which is actually two tables, one for women and one for men. The Society of Actuaries also develops unisex mortality tables, because some policies now base premiums on the combined mortality rates of men and women. The right-hand column of each table shows how many of a group of 1,000 people—all the same age and same sex—are expected to die in a given year. For example, the mortality rate for 40-year-old females is 2.42, meaning that, on average, 2.42 out of 1,000 40-year-old women can be expected to die in a given year. Another way of looking at the same number would be to say that 242 out of 100,000 40-year-old women can be expected to die in a given year.

Adding safety margins

Once mortality rates are determined, actuaries may add a safety margin to the data. The safety margin is often expressed as some designated percentage

Figure 7-2
Mortality curves based on the Commissioners 1980 Standard Ordinary mortality table, ages 0-60.

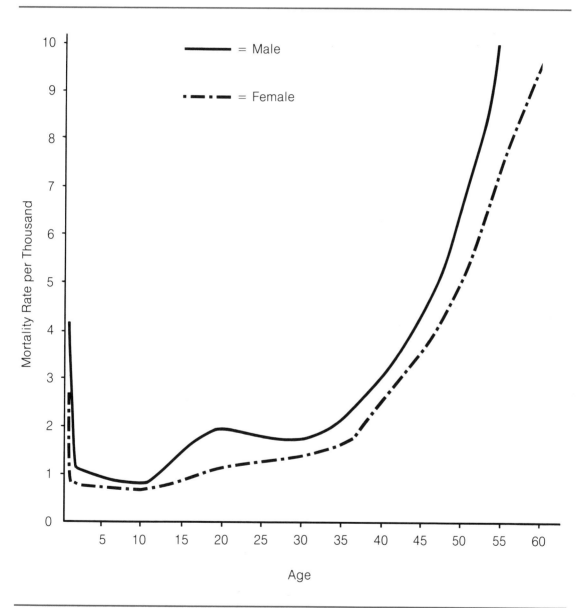

Figure 7-3
Commissioners 1980 Standard Ordinary mortality table.

	MALE			FEMALE			
AGE	Number Living	Number Dying	Mortality Rate per 1,000	Number Living	Number Dying	Mortality Rate per 1,000	AGE
0	10 000 000	41 800	4.18	10 000 000	28 900	2.89	0
1	9 958 200	10 655	1.07	9 971 100	8 675	.87	1
2	9 947 545	9 848	.99	9 962 425	8 070	.81	2
3	9 937 697	9 739	.98	9 954 355	7 864	.79	3
4	9 927 958	9 432	.95	9 946 491	7 659	.77	4
5	9 918 526	8 927	.90	9 938 832	7 554	.76	5
6	9 909 599	8 522	.86	9 931 278	7 250	.73	6
7	9 901 077	7 921	.80	9 924 028	7 145	.72	7
8	9 893 156	7 519	.76	9 916 883	6 942	.70	8
9	9 885 637	7 315	.74	9 909 941	6 838	.69	9
10	9 878 322	7 211	.73	9 903 103	6 734	.68	10
11	9 871 111	7 601	.77	9 896 369	6 828	.69	11
12	9 863 510	8 384	.85	9 889 541	7 120	.72	12
13	9 855 126	9 757	.99	9 882 421	7 412	.75	13
14	9 845 369	11 322	1.15	9 875 009	7 900	.80	14
15	9 834 047	13 079	1.33	9 867 109	8 387	.85	15
16	9 820 968	14 830	1.51	9 858 722	8 873	.90	16
17	9 806 138	16 376	1.67	9 849 849	9 357	.95	17
18	9 789 762	17 426	1.78	9 840 492	9 644	.98	18
19	9 772 336	18 177	1.86	9 830 848	10 027	1.02	19
20	9 754 159	18 533	1.90	9 820 821	10 312	1.05	20
21	9 735 626	18 595	1.91	9 810 509	10 497	1.07	21
22	9 717 031	18 365	1.89	9 800 012	10 682	1.09	22
23	9 698 666	18 040	1.86	9 789 330	10 866	1.11	23
24	9 680 626	17 619	1.82	9 778 464	11 147	1.14	24
25	9 663 007	17 104	1.77	9 767 317	11 330	1.16	25
26	9 645 903	16 687	1.73	9 755 987	11 610	1.19	26
27	9 629 216	16 466	1.71	9 744 377	11 888	1.22	27
28	9 612 750	16 342	1.70	9 732 489	12 263	1.26	28
29	9 596 408	16 410	1.71	9 720 226	12 636	1.30	29
30	9 579 998	16 573	1.73	9 707 590	13 105	1.35	30
31	9 563 425	17 023	1.78	9 694 485	13 572	1.40	31
32	9 546 402	17 470	1.83	9 680 913	14 037	1.45	32
33	9 528 932	18 200	1.91	9 666 876	14 500	1.50	33
34	9 510 732	19 021	2.00	9 652 376	15 251	1.58	34
35	9 491 711	20 028	2.11	9 637 125	15 901	1.65	35
36	9 471 683	21 217	2.24	9 621 224	16 833	1.76	36
37	9 450 466	22 681	2.40	9 604 291	18 152	1.89	37
38	9 427 785	24 324	2.58	9 586 139	19 556	2.04	38
39	9 403 461	26 236	2.79	9 566 583	21 238	2.22	39
40	9 377 225	28 319	3.02	9 545 345	23 100	2.42	40
41	9 348 906	30 758	3.29	9 522 245	25 139	2.64	41
42	9 318 148	33 173	3.56	9 497 106	27 257	2.87	42
43	9 284 975	35 933	3.87	9 469 849	29 262	3.09	43
44	9 249 042	38 753	4.19	9 440 587	31 343	3.32	44
45	9 210 289	41 907	4.55	9 409 244	33 497	3.56	45
46	9 168 382	45 108	4.92	9 375 747	35 628	3.80	46
47	9 123 274	48 536	5.32	9 340 119	37 827	4.05	47
48	9 074 738	52 089	5.74	9 302 292	40 279	4.33	48
49	9 022 649	56 031	6.21	9 262 013	42 883	4.63	49
50	8 966 618	60 166	6.71	9 219 130	45 727	4.96	50
51	8 906 452	65 017	7.30	9 173 403	48 711	5.31	51
52	8 841 435	70 378	7.96	9 124 692	52 011	5.70	52
53	8 771 057	76 396	8.71	9 072 681	55 797	6.15	53
54	8 694 661	83 121	9.56	9 016 884	59 602	6.61	54
55	8 611 540	90 163	10.47	8 957 282	63 507	7.09	55
56	8 521 377	97 655	11.46	8 893 775	67 326	7.57	56
57	8 423 722	105 212	12.49	8 826 449	70 876	8.03	57
58	8 318 510	113 049	13.59	8 755 573	74 180	8.47	58
59	8 205 461	121 195	14.77	8 681 413	77 612	8.94	59
60	8 084 266	129 995	16.08	8 603 801	81 478	9.47	60
61	7 954 271	139 518	17.54	8 522 323	86 331	10.13	61
62	7 814 753	149 965	19.19	8 435 992	92 458	10.96	62
63	7 664 788	161 420	21.06	8 343 534	100 289	12.02	63
64	7 503 368	173 628	23.14	8 243 245	109 223	13.25	64
65	7 329 740	186 322	25.42	8 134 022	118 675	14.59	65
66	7 143 418	198 944	27.85	8 015 347	128 246	16.00	66
67	6 944 474	211 390	30.44	7 887 101	137 472	17.43	67
68	6 733 084	223 471	33.19	7 749 629	146 003	18.84	68
69	6 509 613	235 453	36.17	7 603 626	154 810	20.36	69
70	6 274 160	247 892	39.51	7 448 816	164 693	22.11	70
71	6 026 268	260 937	43.30	7 284 123	176 494	24.23	71
72	5 765 331	274 718	47.65	7 107 629	190 982	26.87	72
73	5 490 613	289 026	52.64	6 916 647	208 260	30.11	73
74	5 201 587	302 680	58.19	6 708 387	227 616	33.93	74
75	4 898 907	314 461	64.19	6 480 771	247 825	38.24	75
76	4 584 446	323 341	70.53	6 232 946	267 830	42.97	76
77	4 261 105	328 616	77.12	5 965 116	286 564	48.04	77
78	3 932 489	329 936	83.90	5 678 552	303 519	53.45	78
79	3 602 553	328 012	91.05	5 375 033	318 008	59.35	79
80	3 274 541	323 656	98.84	5 056 025	333 647	65.99	80
81	2 950 885	317 161	107.48	4 722 378	347 567	73.60	81
82	2 633 724	308 804	117.25	4 374 811	360 484	82.40	82
83	2 324 920	298 194	128.26	4 014 327	371 446	92.53	83
84	2 026 726	284 248	140.25	3 642 881	378 167	103.81	84
85	1 742 478	266 512	152.95	3 264 714	379 033	116.10	85
86	1 475 966	245 143	166.09	2 885 681	373 090	129.29	86
87	1 230 823	220 894	179.55	2 512 591	360 105	143.32	87
88	1 009 929	195 170	193.27	2 152 486	340 480	158.18	88
89	814 659	168 871	207.29	1 812 006	315 180	173.94	89
90	645 788	143 216	221.77	1 496 826	285 520	190.75	90
91	502 572	119 100	236.98	1 211 306	253 005	208.87	91
92	383 472	97 191	253.45	958 301	219 269	228.81	92
93	286 281	77 900	272.11	739 032	185 874	251.51	93
94	208 381	61 860	295.90	553 158	154 503	279.31	94
95	146 721	48 412	329.96	398 655	126 501	317.32	95
96	98 309	37 805	384.55	272 154	102 259	375.74	96
97	60 504	29 054	480.20	169 895	80 695	474.97	97
98	31 450	20 693	657.98	89 200	58 502	655.85	98
99	10 757	10 757	1000.00	30 698	30 698	1000.00	99

of the mortality rate. For example, a safety margin of 20 percent would result in the final mortality rates in a life insurance mortality table being set at 120 percent of the calculated mortality rates. By incorporating such margins into mortality tables, a life insurance company protects itself against *adverse experience* caused by unforeseen events, such as natural catastrophes, wars, epidemics (such as AIDS), statistical fluctuations, and unfavorable mortality trends among its insureds. By assuming that a greater number of deaths will occur than the mortality rates originally indicated, the company is prepared to pay more in death benefits than it will probably have to pay.

To calculate mortality rates for annuity contracts, a safety margin is provided by *decreasing* rather than increasing the mortality rates. Because annuity benefits are payable during the lifetime of the insured person, called the *annuitant,* the company's risk of loss on an annuity is measured by the probability of living, not dying. The longer an annuitant lives, the longer the company makes payments to the annuitant. Therefore, the company prepares for adverse experience by adjusting annuity mortality rates to show fewer people dying at each age than are actually expected to die. Again, a simple percentage can be used. For example, the margin may provide for the final mortality rates on an annuity table to be set at 90 percent of the calculated rates.

Not all mortality tables have safety margins. Tables without margins are called **basic mortality tables,** or *basic experience tables.* For more than 50 years, a group of major insurers has collected data on the mortality experience among their own insureds and made the data available to the Society of Actuaries to develop basic mortality tables. Actuaries use these basic tables to study mortality trends and to compare the experience of other companies with their own.

Factors in developing mortality tables

Mortality tables such as that shown on page 190 represent the mortality rates of specific groups of people. Any predictions based on a mortality table are only as accurate as that table and represent only the mortality experience of the groups included in the table. For example, mortality rates developed for the population as a whole would not accurately predict death rates in a hospital's intensive care unit. Nor would mortality tables developed from experience in Canada or the United States properly depict mortality experience in poorer, less-developed nations. Some of the factors that affect mortality—other than age—are health, sex, socioeconomic status, occupation, smoking status, and geographical region within a country. These differences must be recognized if mortality projections are to be valid. Many mortality tables, such as the United States Life Tables prepared by the

National Office of Vital Statistics, are based on the experience of the general population. However, life insurance companies do not use these tables. Insurers are selective when they evaluate possible insureds and do not issue coverage to every person who applies for a policy. A small percentage of applicants who are not in good health are declined for insurance coverage, and most others who are not in good health are offered coverage at higher-than-standard premium rates.

The selection process

As part of the life insurance underwriting process, insurance companies try to assure that only persons in good health are offered insurance coverage at standard premium rates. The underwriting process, discussed in greater detail in Chapter 9, is also called *selection of risks*. Applicants who are accepted for insurance at standard rates become a part of the **select group.** The mortality rate of a select group is better than the mortality rate of the general population. Furthermore, the mortality rate of a select group that has recently undergone the selection process is better than the mortality rate of a group selected several years previously.

To illustrate the effects of selection, consider four large groups of people, in which each person is now 40 years old.

Group	Status
A	Recently insured at standard insurance rates.
B	Insured at standard rates 2 years ago.
C	Insured at standard rates 20 years ago.
D	Insured at standard rates 25 years ago.

The lowest mortality rate among the four groups is in Group A. People in Group A have passed tests of insurability and good health more recently than people in the other three groups. Those people in Group B, who were evaluated two years ago, have a mortality rate higher than that of Group A but lower than that of Groups C and D. The rates for Groups C and D are the highest of the four groups, although they are probably not very different. These differences in mortality rates among people who are the same age reflect the length of time since they were selected for insurance coverage. As years pass, differences between the mortality rates of different select groups gradually disappear. For example, although Groups C and D were selected for insurance five years apart, the date of selection was so long ago that their mortality rates are probably not very different. The length of time during which the effects of selection are assumed to be observable and significant is called the *select period* and normally lasts 5 to 15 years.

The effects of selection must be considered when a mortality table is being constructed for life insurance use. Insurance companies frequently pool the experience of their select groups to create mortality tables that apply to the companies' circumstances more so than general population mortality tables.

Individual Valuation Mortality Tables

An insurer frequently uses one mortality table to calculate its policy reserves and another to calculate its premium rates. The tables described in the next few pages are called *valuation mortality tables,* because they were developed and published as industrywide standards for computing the value of policy reserves. These tables usually have wide margins of safety, indicating much higher rates of mortality than the tables used for calculating premiums. State regulations require insurance companies in the United States to use certain valuation tables to calculate minimum policy reserves. In Canada, insurance companies are required only to choose valuation tables that are appropriate to the circumstances of the company and the policies in force.

Insurance regulators do not specify the tables that insurance companies must use for premium calculation. Insurance companies depend on their actuaries to locate or develop tables that allow for competitive premium rates and accurately forecast the mortality experience of the company's insureds.

Ordinary life insurance valuation tables

The valuation table insurance companies use to calculate minimum ordinary life insurance policy reserves in the United States is the 1980 CSO table discussed earlier. The 1980 CSO table, which is based on mortality experience from 1970 to 1975, supersedes the 1958 CSO table. Companies may use another mortality table if they wish. However, the total reserves may not be less than those produced by the 1980 CSO table. The task of implementing the 1980 CSO table is the focus of INSIGHT 7-1.

INSIGHT 7-1

CSO Conversion

January 1, 1989, was the deadline for insurance companies to update the policies in their product portfolio to bring them into compliance with the 1980 Commissioners' Standard Ordinary (CSO) Mortality Table. Although the industry had at least eight years to meet this requirement, "it has always been recognized that the process of switching to a new mortality table for your entire portfolio is a complicated one," said Alan Lauer, vice president of Huggins Financial Services. Lauer pointed out that, in addition to updating policy forms and filing with every state in which it is licensed to do business, the company had to adjust its computer systems and software to accommodate the new table.

According to John Montgomery, chief actuary and deputy insurance commissioner for the California Department of Insurance and chairman of the National Association of Insurance Commissioners (NAIC) Life and Health Actuarial Task Force, normally it takes five years for all the states to adopt an NAIC model table. The 1980 CSO Mortality Table was adopted by all states within three years. This was due in part to rapidly changing interest rates at the time, and the fact that the NAIC resolved many potential problems before drafting and adopting the model.

What typically happens when mortality tables become outdated, explained William Carroll, actuary for the American Council of Life Insurance, is that actual mortality is so much better than projected mortality that insurance companies find the state-mandated reserve requirements too high.

Thus, because of the outdated tables, insurance companies have to charge more for policies than they need to charge. The Society of Actuaries tracks mortality experience and compares it with the basic experience that underlies the mortality table already in use. When mortality "strays too far" in either direction, revisions to the table are suggested.

For competitive reasons, companies are developing new products every 12 to 24 months, rather than every three to five years, so the companies have simply been electing to use the new table as their basis. Although it is true in general that the new table allows companies to set up lower reserves, Carroll said, the type of product offered makes a difference. For an interest-sensitive product, the statutory reserves are basically equal to the policy's cash value. This is similar to the reserve required under the 1958 CSO Mortality Table. The lower reserve requirement under the 1980 CSO Mortality Table primarily applies to traditional products such as whole life and term life insurance, Mr. Carroll remarked.

The NAIC is talking about drafting a new model law that will include flexibility features, according to Montgomery. This standard valuation law may "require statements from actuaries that involve projections of cash flow and introduce the whole concept of variability into the matter of valuation." If this law comes into being, companies would have to set up additional reserves under the new model if the amount indicated were greater than the amount that would be required under the current law.

Source: Adapted with permission from Anne Gilmore Clarke, "CSO Conversion—the Eleventh Hour," *Best's Review,* June 1988, p. 60.

Canadian valuation actuaries sometimes use the 1980 CSO table, the 1958 CSO table, or, with modifications, the 1969-1975 Canadian Institute of Actuaries (1969-1975 CIA) mortality table.

Individual annuity valuation mortality tables

The most common individual annuity mortality table is the 1983 Table *a*. A committee of the Society of Actuaries developed the 1983 Table *a* using mortality experience from 1971 to 1976. This table shows lower mortality rates than comparable life insurance mortality tables. The lower mortality rates are indicative of the type of margin that is built into annuity tables and the lower mortality actually experienced by annuitants.

Actuaries update annuity tables using the projection method. In the **projection method,** the mortality rate at any given age is assumed to decrease—that is, the rate improves—by a constant percentage each calendar year. For example, people who were 60 years old in 1990 had a better chance of living to age 61 than people who were 60 in 1975, because of such factors as advances in medical care. By projecting improved mortality rates by set percentages each year, actuaries maintain the proper margins for annuity tables and avoid the cost of developing new tables. However, the projection method cannot maintain a table's proper margins indefinitely, and a new table with new projection percentages must be developed periodically.

INTEREST AND INTEREST RATES

The second factor involved in premium rate calculation is interest. *Interest* was defined earlier in this book as the money paid for the use of money. Interest is important not only in determining insurance premiums but also in calculating policy reserves, dividends, and nonforfeiture values, such as cash values.

Although some of the premium money that insurance companies receive is used immediately to pay insurance claims, much of the money is invested to provide for the payment of claims in future years. The amount by which invested money grows is measured by the *interest rate*. The interest rate is often identified as a percentage, such as 10 percent (10%). Interest can be classified as either simple interest or compound interest. **Simple interest** is interest payable on the amount of money originally borrowed or invested. **Compound interest** is interest earned on the amount originally borrowed or invested *and* on the interest previously earned. The amount of money that is originally borrowed or invested is called the ***principal.*** To calculate simple interest, multiply the principal by the interest rate:

$$\text{Simple Interest} = (\text{Principal}) \times (\text{Interest Rate})$$

For example, assume that an insurance company invests $100,000 for one year at an annual interest rate of 10 percent. The amount of simple interest is determined as follows:

$$\text{Simple Interest} = \$100,000 \times 10 \text{ percent}$$
$$\text{or}$$
$$= \$100,000 \times \frac{10}{100}$$
$$= \$100,000 \times .10$$
$$= \$10,000$$

In two years of earning simple interest, the insurance company will earn $20,000 in interest ($10,000 + $10,000 = $20,000).

If the insurance company decides to add the $10,000 interest to the $100,000 principal and reinvest the total amount for a second year at an annual interest rate of 10 percent, the insurance company is compounding its money.

$$\text{Compound Interest} = (\text{Principal} + \text{Interest}) \times (\text{Interest Rate})$$
$$= (\$100,000 + \$10,000) \times .10$$
$$= \$110,000 \times .10$$
$$= \$11,000 \text{ earned in the second year}$$

In two years, the insurance company earns $21,000 in compound interest ($10,000 + $11,000 = $21,000), instead of the $20,000 earned using simple interest.

The difference between compound interest and simple interest can be sizable, particularly over long periods of time. For example, at 4 percent simple interest, money doubles in 25 years, whereas at 4 percent compound interest, money doubles in less than 18 years. Financial institutions, such as life and health insurance companies, deal almost solely with compound interest.

Note also that interest need not be computed only on an annual basis. It may be computed and compounded more frequently: semiannually, monthly, weekly, or even daily. The shorter the compounding period, the larger the total amount of interest will be. However, for the purposes of this book, we will assume that all interest is compounded annually.

Present Value of Money

When actuaries calculate premium rates, they assume that the insurance company will earn a certain interest rate on its investments. The actuaries make this assumption by studying the interest rates that the company has earned in the past and asking investment personnel what the company expects to earn in the future. The interest-rate assumption affects the amount of premium that policyowners pay. For example, assume that an insurance company needs to pay $1,000,000 in claims one year from today. The actuaries calculate the amount of money the company needs to invest today at a certain interest rate in order to have $1,000,000 one year from today. This process of calculating the amount of money needed today to accumulate a specific amount of money in the future is called calculating the present value of money, also known as **discounting.** The **present value** of a sum of money is defined as the amount of money that must be invested at the beginning of a period in order to increase to a predetermined amount at a specified later date.

NET PREMIUMS

In order to calculate premiums, actuaries must use information about mortality rates and interest rates. The premiums derived from combining just these two factors are called **net premiums.** Actuaries use the amount of a product's net premium to establish the minimum premium rates and calculate policy reserves. The **policy reserve** is the fund made up of assets and future premiums to be received from in-force policies that should total enough to pay future claims on those in-force policies.

The amount of the net premium for any given policy is determined by the mortality table and the interest rate that the actuaries decide to use. A conservative table, such as the 1980 CSO table, shows higher mortality rates than some other tables and, therefore, results in higher net premiums. A mortality table with lower mortality rates results in lower net premiums. Varying interest rates can also change the level of net premiums. High interest rates lower net premiums; low interest rates raise net premiums.

The net premiums used to calculate policy reserves are based on conservative assumptions—high mortality rates and low interest rates—because reserves must be high enough to allow for possible fluctuations in both interest rates and mortality rates. On the other hand, the premium rate that is charged to the policyowner is usually based on less conservative assumptions that more closely reflect expected mortality experience and available investment earnings. Using less conservative assumptions for calculating premium rates charged to policyowners allows companies to offer lower premiums.

With certain investment-based products such as universal life insurance, the amount of premium that is applied toward insurance coverage depends on the mortality rate and interest rate experience during the life of that block of policies. Consequently, actuaries price such policies retrospectively—that is, looking back on the experience of the policy. In contrast, actuaries price more traditional ordinary policies prospectively—at the outset—and do not alter the rates later based on experience.

Net Single Premiums

The *net single premium* for a block of insurance policies at the time that the policies are issued can be defined as the *actuarial present value* of the benefits that are expected to be paid on that block of policies. The net single premium is the amount of money that must be collected at the time the policies are issued to assure the accumulation of enough money to pay the death benefits on the policies, assuming that interest is earned at the expected rate and that claims occur at the expected rate.

For example, assume that the actuaries of an insurance company are calculating the net single premium per insured for a block of one-year term life insurance policies issued to 35-year-old women. The block includes 100,000 policies, and each policy has a death benefit of $50,000. To calculate the net single premium for this block of policies, the actuaries must choose a mortality table and an interest rate. If they choose the 1980 CSO table, the assumed mortality rate for 35-year-old women is 1.70 per 1,000 (see Figure 7-3). After consulting with the company's investment specialists, who project the level of interest that the company expects to earn on its investments in the coming year, the actuaries choose an interest rate of 8 percent. Once the mortality table and interest rate are chosen, actuaries can use a mathematical formula to determine the net single premium.

To be more conservative in calculating the net single premium, the actuaries could use an older mortality table that shows a higher mortality rate, such as the 1958 CSO, or they could use a lower interest rate. For a less conservative calculation, the actuaries could use a higher interest rate or a lower mortality rate. However, when calculating reserves, the freedom to choose the assumptions is limited by minimum reserve standards and the requirements of sound actuarial procedures.

Net Level Annual Premiums

Some types of life insurance policies, particularly whole life policies, require policyowners to pay premiums of equal size annually or at other intervals during the policy period. These premium amounts are known as *level premiums* because the amount of each premium paid by the policyowner remains the same during the premium payment period. To calculate the amount of the net level annual premium for a block of policies, actuaries determine the amount of money that the company needs to collect from living policyowners at the beginning of each policy year so that all expected claims can be paid. For example, in the case of a whole life policy being sold to provide coverage to 35-year-old women, the actuaries must calculate the following amounts:

- the number who will die each year until the last year of the mortality table
- the number who will be alive each year to pay for benefits
- the amount that will be payable in benefits each year
- the amount that will be paid in premiums each year
- the present value of benefits as they are affected by the insurance company's interest earnings
- the present value of premiums as they are affected by the insurance company's interest earnings

With net level annual premiums, policyowners actually pay more in premiums during the early years of the contract than is necessary to pay for death benefits during those years. The money that is not used to pay death benefits is invested by the insurance company to accumulate in value. Then, during the later years of the contract, when mortality rates increase and premiums are too small to pay for death benefits, the money that the insurance company had invested will be available, with interest, to make up the difference between premium income at that point and the cost of death benefits.

GROSS PREMIUMS

If an insurance company charges only the net premium for its insurance, the company will receive just enough money to pay insurance benefits, but not enough money to pay operating expenses. Therefore, the company places an additional charge, called the ***loading,*** on the net premium. The company adds on the loading to

- pay for the company's operating expenses
- compensate for the loss of income when policies lapse
- provide money for contingency funds in case unexpected events, such as natural disasters, increase the mortality rate
- provide margins for profit and contributions to surplus

The net premium plus the loading equals the ***gross premium,*** which is the amount that policyowners actually pay for their insurance.

Operating Expenses

The expense factors included in calculating the gross premium of an insurance policy can usually be divided into several general categories: development expenses, acquisition expenses, distribution expenses, maintenance expenses, termination expenses, general administrative expenses, and taxes.

Development expenses include the costs of planning and creating insurance products. These costs might include the salaries of the employees who helped develop the product, the computer time used, and any research done during the planning of the product.

Acquisition expenses include the costs of processing the application for insurance and issuing the policy to the policyowner—for example, underwriters' salaries, the costs of medical examinations, and printing costs.

Distribution expenses can be one of the largest and most direct expenses involved in providing insurance. Depending on the distribution system in place in an insurance company, this category can include (1) agent compensation, usually in the form of commissions; (2) postal, printing, telecommunications, and salary expenses for those companies that use direct response marketing; and (3) group sales representatives' salaries. Most marketing expenses, such as advertising and promotion, are counted as either acquisition or distribution expenses.

Maintenance expenses represent the costs of keeping the policy in force. Maintenance expenses include the time that agents and customer service personnel spend conserving policies that are in force and the cost of processing annual premium and policy dividend payments.

Termination expenses are the costs of processing death benefit claims and cash surrenders. *General administrative expenses* include the home office and field office costs of supplies, building maintenance, rent, and salaries. *Taxes* would include the basic premium taxes that all state and most provincial governments charge on insurance policies and the corporate income taxes that state, provincial, and federal governments charge on corporate income, including the income of insurance companies.

Allocation of expenses

A company's various operating expenses are allocated to the company's respective products. This allocation attributes to each product the expenses that are incurred in developing, selling, and servicing that product. This information is used to control operations, prepare financial reports, and calculate premium rates. Expenses are usually classified according to

- *type of expense,* such as rent, salaries, postage, and supplies
- *function,* such as marketing, actuarial, underwriting, and customer service
- *activity,* such as premium collection, claims payment, and policy issue

Allocating expenses is not easy. Some expenses, such as commissions, vary with the amount of the premium, because commissions are calculated as a percentage of the premium amount. Other expenses, such as those incurred in preparing and mailing premium notices, are related to the number of policies. For example, the cost of sending premium notices is usually a set amount per policy per year, depending on the number of premium notices sent. Usually, the more premium notices there are for a certain block of policies, the less it costs to send each notice. Some expenses associated with an insurance policy are greater in the first policy year. For ordinary insurance, agents' commission schedules often allow for first-year commissions that are higher than those in subsequent years. Other first-year expenses can include the costs of underwriting the policy, conducting a medical examination, and issuing the policy. See Figure 7-4 for an illustration of expenses as they are allocated to an ordinary life insurance policy.

As you look at Figure 7-4, notice that the expenses that the insurance company incurs during a policy's first year can exceed the premium that the company collects. An insurance company expects to recover these expenses during the succeeding years of the policy. Therefore, insurance companies like to see policies remain in force at least until the policies pay for their start-up costs.

Lapses

A policy *lapse* occurs when a policy is terminated because of nonpayment of renewal premiums. When policies lapse before enough premiums are paid to

Figure 7-4
Example of an expense analysis for an ordinary life insurance policy.

Policy Year 1

Distribution Expenses	23% of premium	
Commission	60% of premium	85% of premium
Premium Tax	2% of premium	
Underwriting	$20.00 per policy	
Acquisition Expenses	21.81 per policy	$47.70 per policy
Maintenance	5.89 per policy	
Production Bonus	$ .50 per $1,000	$ .50 per $1,000

Policy Year 2

Commission	10% of premium	
Premium Tax	2% of premium	12% of premium
Maintenance	$5.89 per policy	$5.89 per policy

Policy Years 3 through 10

Commission	5% of premium	
Premium Tax	2% of premium	7% of premium
Maintenance	$5.89 per policy	$5.89 per policy

Policy Years 11 on

Commission	2% of premium	
Premium Tax	2% of premium	4% of premium
Maintenance	$5.89 per policy	$5.89 per policy

Event Expenses

Death Claim	$51.47 per policy
Premium Collection and Commission Processing	$ .35 per collection

compensate for expenses, insurance companies lose money. One actuarial function is to predict the number of lapses that a company can expect each policy year and increase the gross premium to compensate for the lost income caused by lapses. The number of lapses that a company experiences can have a significant effect on the company's gross premiums. A company with a lapse rate of 5 percent in the first policy year is in a position to charge lower gross premiums than a company with a lapse rate of 25 percent.

The **lapse rate** is determined by dividing the number of policies that lapse during a given policy year by the number of policies in force at the beginning of that policy year. The lapse rate is also referred to as a *withdrawal rate* or a *voluntary termination rate*. Lapse rates are usually expressed as percentages. A first-year lapse rate of 20 percent means that 20 percent of newly issued policies lapsed by the end of the first policy year or by the end of the first premium payment period of the next policy year. The complement of the lapse rate is called the *persistency rate*. For a block of policies, the **persistency rate** is the ratio of the policies in force for which renewal premiums were paid during a given period to the policies for which premiums were due during that period. Another way to calculate the persistency rate is to subtract the lapse rate from one $(1 - \text{lapse rate})$. Thus, if the lapse rate is 20 percent, or .20, then the persistency rate is 80 percent, or .80. The lapse rate and the persistency rate added together always equal 100 percent. When analyzing lapse rates, the actuary often constructs a *lapse table* by dividing the number of lapses during a year by the number of policies in force at the start of that year. A typical lapse table is shown in Figure 7-5.

Figure 7-5
Lapse rates by policy year.

Policy Year	Number of Policies in Force at Beginning of Year	Number of Policies Lapsing	Lapse Rate (%)
1	1,000	200	20.0
2	800	96	12.0
3	704	53	7.5
4	651	39	6.0
5	612	34	5.6
6	578	29	5.0
7	549	25	4.6
8	524	21	4.0
9	503	18	3.6
10	485	15	3.1

For the purposes of this illustration, it is assumed that no claims have been incurred on these policies.

Many factors affect lapse rates. One of the most important factors is the policy's frequency of premium payment. Policies with monthly premium payments typically lapse at a greater rate than do policies with annual premium payments. Another factor affecting lapse rates is the method of premium payment. Policies that have monthly premiums paid through an Electronic Funds Transfer (EFT) or a preauthorized check (PAC) system tend to have far better persistency than policies for which payments are mailed on a monthly basis. Another major factor affecting lapse rates is the insured's age. Studies show that lapse rates are highest for insureds in their twenties. Thereafter, the lapse rate decreases.

Lapse rates also vary by policy size, the insured's income level or occupation, ownership of other policies, distribution method, and general economic conditions. For example, lapse rates tend to be low among policyowners with high income levels. During depressed economic times, lapse rates tend to be high.

Lapse rates vary greatly from one insurance company to another. The rates of one company may consistently be twice as high as those of another company. The difference may be attributable to the above factors, or to other factors such as the types of products sold, the quality of the sales force, or the attention that companies pay to conserving existing policies. Most companies conduct studies of lapse rates among their own policyowners. The Life Insurance Marketing and Research Association (LIMRA) conducts intercompany lapse studies so companies can compare their lapse rates to those of other companies. Figure 7-6 contains a table from a 1989 LIMRA study showing persistency rates for different distribution systems. In looking at the figure we can see, for example, that 59 percent of policies sold through the multiple-line exclusive agency system were still in force after 25 months. This 59 percent represented 61 percent of the original premiums collected and 58 percent of the original face amount of the policies in force at the outset of the 25-month period.

Contingency Funds

Unexpected events can cause mortality rates, interest rates, operating expenses, and lapse rates to vary significantly from company estimates. These unexpected events may result in higher costs for the company. To make sure that their companies have enough money to pay the expenses associated with such unexpected events, called *contingencies,* actuaries increase the loading to create *contingency funds.* The loading used to establish contingency funds varies with the type of policy issued and the amount of insurance involved.

Figure 7-6
25-month persistency rates by distribution system structure.

Distribution System	Percent of original policies in force after 25 months	Percent of original premiums still being collected after 25 months	Percent of original face amount remaining in force after 25 months
Career			
General agency	72%	76%	74%
Managerial	71	77	72
PPGA/broker	65	70	64
Multiple-line exclusive agent	59	61	58
Home service	59	59	54

Source: Life Insurance Marketing and Research Association, *U.S. 25-Month Persistency,* Paul Ganette Powell (project director), 1989.

Profits and Contributions to Surplus

All insurance companies plan to make more money than is needed to pay for the cost of providing insurance. This extra income is called ***profit*** in stock companies and ***contribution to surplus*** (also called *earned surplus* and *additions to surplus*) in mutual companies. Profits or contributions to surplus ensure that insurers have enough money to grow and remain competitive. A portion of these profits and contributions to surplus are distributed to stockholders and policyowners through dividends.

Setting the Gross Premium

Having chosen the assumptions for mortality rates, interest, and loading, actuaries can then develop tentative gross premiums for various key ages, such as 15, 25, 35, 45, and 55. The gross premiums at these ages are then tested using *asset share* calculations, which will be discussed later in this chapter in relation to product development. If the actuary is satisfied with the gross premium scale developed for the key ages, then the scale is extended to a full range of ages.

POLICY RESERVES, CASH VALUES, AND POLICY DIVIDENDS

In the following sections, we will discuss two essential components of many life insurance products: policy reserves and cash values. In addition, we will describe the policy dividends that may be paid to owners of participating policies.

Policy Reserves

As mentioned earlier in this chapter, the level-premium system leads to a situation in the later years of a policy's life in which the total of net premiums collected is less than the future amount of expected claims. To account for the excess premiums received under the level premium system, an insurance company establishes a ***policy reserve*** account, which identifies the money that the insurance company must pay in future claims. Policy reserves are thus treated as *liabilities*, which are discussed more in Chapter 13. Policy reserves are also called *legal* or *statutory* reserves because they are required by statute. Insurance companies in Canada and the United States are required by law to maintain assets in an amount sufficient to cover the policy reserve. A company that does not have enough assets to cover its reserves and other liabilities is considered insolvent and can no longer operate as an insurance company. For most companies, the policy reserve is by far the largest liability item on their balance sheet.

Actuaries calculate reserves for all policies that their company has in force. Many companies have actuaries who are responsible for calculating the reserves for a specific product line. The reserve valuations for the entire company are included in every company's Annual Statement and must, in the United States, be certified by an actuary who is a Member of the American Academy of Actuaries (MAAA). In Canada, reserve valuations must be certified by an actuary who is a Fellow of the Canadian Institute of Actuaries (FCIA).

Cash Values

The ***cash value*** of a policy is the amount of money that the insurance company guarantees to pay to the policyowner if the policyowner cancels the insurance coverage and surrenders the policy to the company. As mentioned, under the level-premium system, premiums paid during early policy years provide more money than is needed to pay death benefits. The money that is not needed to pay death benefits or loading costs is invested and is the source of the policyowners' cash value in their own policies. A policy's cash value is often called the policyowner's *equity*, or ownership, in the policy.

Actuaries must calculate the cash values for all of a company's in-force policies. When a company develops a new type of level-premium whole life policy, the actuary must calculate the cash values that will accumulate between the day the policies are issued and the day they mature. The Standard Nonforfeiture Law in the United States requires that cash values be calculated before a policy is issued and that a table showing the cash values at the end of certain policy years be printed in the policy contract.

Policy Dividends

The premium scale for a participating policy is usually set at a higher level than that for an otherwise identical nonparticipating policy. As a result, people who purchase participating policies generally pay higher gross premiums than they would if they had purchased similar nonparticipating policies. One of an actuary's responsibilities is to determine how much premium to return in the form of dividends for each type of policy and to make recommendations regarding these dividend amounts to the company's board of directors.

Policy dividends are paid from a company's surplus. A life and health insurance company's **surplus** is the amount by which its assets exceed its liabilities and capital. Actuaries must calculate the company's surplus every year and then decide (1) the portion of the company's surplus that should be considered **divisible surplus,** which is the amount available to be distributed as dividends to participating policyowners, and (2) the manner in which the divisible surplus should be apportioned as dividends among the different policies in force.

Sources of surplus

As you have learned, in setting the gross premium scale for a life insurance policy, an actuary makes certain assumptions about mortality rates, interest rates, and expenses. If fewer insured people die in a given year than the actuaries assumed would die, then the company realizes a gain because fewer dollars than projected were paid out in claims. Similarly, if a company earns more interest on its investments or spends less on expenses than had been anticipated, the company realizes gains and adds to surplus. On the other hand, if the company experiences higher mortality rates, lower interest rates, or more expenses than anticipated, the company's surplus may be reduced. Thus, surplus is affected by the difference between

- actual and assumed mortality experience
- actual and assumed interest income
- actual and assumed expenses

Dividend distribution

Each year, actuaries review the company's surplus position and recommend to the company's board of directors the portion of the company's surplus that should be distributed as dividends. Many factors must be considered in arriving at the amount of the divisible surplus. If the actuaries' calculations indicate that the company has conservative policy reserves, then the company's board of directors might follow a liberal surplus distribution policy. If, on the other hand, a company has only the minimum statutory policy reserves, then the directors may wish to retain a higher proportion of the company's surplus as an added safety factor.

Other factors influencing a company's surplus distribution practices include the stability of the national economy, trends in mortality, forecasted changes in interest rates and operating expenses, and the type and quality of investments held by the company. Government regulations also affect divisible surplus. Such regulations are intended to assure that companies neither pay more dividends than they can safely afford nor keep more surplus than they actually need.

Although many factors influence dividend distribution, the overriding consideration is the solvency of the company: the company must *always* be able to meet its future obligations. This requirement must be satisfied before any dividends are paid.

The dividend scale constructed by the actuaries should be both fair and practical. It is considered fair if it does not favor any class of policies at the expense of any other class. The dividends should be apportioned so that they reflect their sources. Therefore, the actuary analyzes earnings in terms of such policy characteristics as type of plan, sex of insureds, age at issue, year of issue, and premium payment plan. The dividend scale should be practical in terms of its administration. Generally, a simple scale, which is easier to administer, is preferred to a complex scale. However, the simplicity of the dividend scale should not undermine fairness.

PRODUCT DEVELOPMENT

Many insurance companies have at least one actuary concerned solely with developing or revising insurance products. Although smaller companies might have one product development division, larger companies might have a product development division for every type of product sold. For example, a large company would probably have a product development division for (1) ordinary guaranteed level-premium life insurance products, such as level-premium whole life; (2) ordinary investment-based products, such as universal life; (3) group life insurance; (4) individual and group health insurance; (5) individual annuities; and (6) pensions, also called group annuities.

In the next few pages, we will discuss the actuary's role in product development. Figure 7-7 illustrates some of the activities required of actuaries during product development.

Asset Share Calculations

As mentioned in Chapter 4, once the design objectives of a product have been planned and a working outline of the product developed, actuaries perform mathematical calculations to help provide assurance that the product will be financially sound. A common type of calculation performed at this time is an asset share calculation.

An *asset share* can be defined as the amount of assets that any block of policies will accumulate at any given time. An *asset share calculation* simulates the way in which the assets of a block of policies should grow, depending on various assumptions about future interest rates, mortality, expenses, lapses, etc. By observing the simulated results in the asset share calculation, actuaries can determine whether the product will be sound, fair, and competitive over time.

One of the first steps in policy development is the analysis of the competitive position of the product. Company actuaries frequently consider the premium rates that other companies charge for similar products. For example, suppose that the Alabaster Life and Health Insurance Company wants to sell a product that would compete with a similar whole life insurance product sold by the Greystone Life Insurance Company. The gross premium for Greystone's product per $1,000 of insurance for men age 35 is $12.36, so Alabaster's product design task force decides to develop a similar product that sells for $12.00 per $1,000 of insurance. The product

Figure 7-7
Product development and the actuarial department.

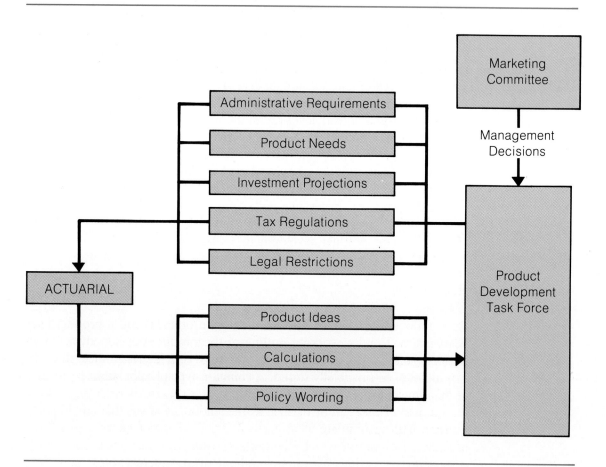

actuaries then develop an asset share calculation with a $12.00 gross premium. From this starting point, Alabaster's actuaries try to create a sound and competitive insurance product.

Normally, actuaries select a conservative mortality table and interest rate to calculate the product's reserves. Then they usually choose a more liberal mortality table and a higher interest rate to determine the premium. Next, they set a policy dividend assumption (if the policy is a participating policy), an expense rate, and lapse rates for the first policy year and all succeeding years. Almost always, actuaries use a computer to perform asset share calculations.

Based on different assumptions—about mortality, interest rates, expenses, lapse rates, and policy dividends—a properly constructed asset share calculation shows the amount of money that the company will receive each year in premiums and interest as well as the amount of money that will be paid out in claims, cash surrenders, policy dividends, and expenses. An asset share calculation also shows how the reserves and asset shares increase each policy year. By comparing reserves to asset shares, the actuaries can see how the product under development would add to the company's liabilities and assets. The comparison of reserves to asset shares is probably the key comparison in the asset share simulation, because an insurance product does not make a profit for the company or add to surplus until the asset share is larger than the reserve. The amount of time that it takes for a product to become profitable or begin adding to surplus is called the *validation period,* also called the *break-even period.* A product that makes a profit or adds to surplus is said to have reached and passed the *validation point,* or *break-even point.*

If the validation period is considered to be too long, the actuaries can change some of the factors in the calculation as long as the changes are actuarially sound. Product design actuaries can increase the gross premium or decrease cash values or dividends. They can recommend product design changes to their company's management that would improve the mortality experience, lapse experience, expense levels (such as reducing the planned commissions), and interest rates. If these recommendations are adopted, actuaries can then incorporate these changes into the asset share. This revision process continues until the actuaries have developed a product that they believe will be financially competitive and actuarially sound.

Every change that the actuaries make requires a new asset share calculation. If the actuaries raise interest assumptions by 0.5 percent or decrease expense assumptions by $0.25 per $1,000 of insurance, then the asset share will change. Using computers, actuaries can conduct hundreds of asset share calculations, simulating every practical contingency that could affect an insurance product.

Asset share calculations for products such as universal life, adjustable life, and variable life pose particular challenges for actuaries. Because of the flexibility granted to the policyowner by each of these products, the actuary must determine the outcome of a much wider variety of scenarios in order to assure a particular policy's success over time. Asset share calculations become much more important with such products, because the death benefit, premium amount, and cash value can change as many other factors change.

Besides performing asset share calculations, product development actuaries—through the product design task force—must also work with other functional areas of the company to consider a product's tax implications, policy wording, systems requirements, and administrative aspects. After incorporating all relevant considerations, the product development actuaries present the new product to the product design task force, which may approve the product or call for further revisions and new asset share calculations.

Once the product is approved, the actuaries and other members of the product design task force may meet with a select group of agents to present the product and listen to the agents' reactions. The product actuaries may show the agents some of the asset share calculations that were used to develop the product. Following this meeting and approval of the policy by regulatory authorities, the actuaries make final adjustments in the product and help the company's marketing personnel prepare it for presentation to the company's entire field force.

KEY TERMS

actuary	policy reserve
rate making	net single premium
probability	level premium
law of large numbers	loading
mortality curve	gross premium
mortality table	lapse
basic mortality table	lapse rate
select group	persistency rate
select period	profit
valuation mortality table	contribution to surplus
projection method	cash value
simple interest	surplus
compound interest	divisible surplus
principal	asset share
discounting	asset share calculation
present value	validation period
net premium	validation point

Chapter 8

Actuarial Functions for Group and Health Insurance

After reading this chapter, you should be able to

- Describe the role of experience rating in group insurance
- Distinguish between manual rates and blended rates
- Show how gross premiums are computed and how the monthly gross premium for a group is calculated
- Describe the factors that determine a group's experience rating refund
- Distinguish between morbidity tables and mortality tables
- Recognize the basic formula for calculating annual claim costs for individual health insurance

In the preceding chapter, we described the role of actuaries in individual life insurance. In this chapter, we will describe how actuarial principles apply to group life insurance and health insurance.

FUNCTIONS OF A GROUP INSURANCE ACTUARY[1]

The functions performed by an actuary in the design, marketing, and delivery of group insurance programs are essentially the same as those performed for any type of insurance product sold by an insurance company. These functions include developing the benefit structure, pricing the product, and determining the financial outcome of each experience period. A group insurance actuary is also concerned with the allocation of interest earnings, solvency, cash flow management, reserve adequacy (if necessary), risk capacity, and earning objectives. These functions can be performed either for a single policy involving a large number of employees of a single employer or for a collection of smaller policies.

The actuary develops sound group insurance plans through five main areas of activity. The first activity is the design of the product or its benefits. Second, the actuary is involved in selecting the types of risks the insurer will underwrite. The third and perhaps most important activity is pricing the product. Experience rating, the fourth major actuarial activity, is the process of adjusting the gross premium paid by a policyholder after the end of a policy period (generally one year) to reflect more closely that policyholder's actual claim experience. Portfolio management is the fifth major activity of a group insurance actuary.

Each of an actuary's functions is a counterpart to a comparable function performed in any business. The actuary's specific role in group insurance is to lend technical expertise to the financial and contractual aspects of these plans. Generally, group insurance is marketed on the basis of two criteria: service, usually in the form of prompt and efficient claim payment, and cost. The actuary must address each aspect of a product's cost, so the actuary's role is similar to that of a treasurer or controller in other industries. Sometimes it is difficult to draw a clear line between the actuary's purely technical functions and the general management function involved in operating the group line of business. Demands of recent legislative changes have also complicated the task of actuaries. INSIGHT 8-1 reports on one company's response to an environment of change in the small group health insurance business.

INSIGHT 8-1

Rating Management in the 1990s

Gone are the days when differences among states were minor and insurers could market one basic health insurance policy across the country. Today, as many as 30 percent of a policy's coverages may be state-specific. Health insurers also face new demands from state regulators and consumers to justify on an actuarial basis the rates they charge. Steven Stichweh, applications system manager for Mutual of Omaha, estimates that his staff has made more than 10 rating changes to the company's small group products during the past three years.

"Products and rates are in a state of constant flux. This is particularly true for small group health insurance, an extremely competitive business with dynamic rates that are continuously fine-tuned," he said.

Pricing flexibility gives Mutual of Omaha a competitive advantage, he noted. Because medical care costs inflate so rapidly, the company builds trend factors into its rates. When a rate is quoted, Mutual of Omaha guarantees it until the end of the quarter. A prospect may not accept a proposal, however, until one month after it was quoted, early into the next quarter. The rates for that quarter may have risen by 4 percent. However, Mutual of Omaha can easily break out trend factors by month. To the prospect, this may mean the rates have increased by only 1 percent, making the company's bid more competitive.

The marketing and actuarial demands for more flexible pricing structures have exceeded most information systems' rating capabilities. Companies that cling to traditional programming development and systems maintenance methods find themselves at a competitive disadvantage — unable to respond quickly when new marketing opportunities demand rapid adjustments to existing rates, and unable to automate entirely new rating structures to support potentially profitable new products.

Source: Adapted with permission of the publisher from F. Reilly Cobb, "Rating Management in the 1990s," *Resource,* April 1990, pp. 40-43.

GROUP LIFE INSURANCE

A group life insurance policy insures a number of people under a single contract, called a ***master contract,*** which is a contract between the insurance company and the group policyholder. The individuals insured under the group life insurance policy are not parties to the contract, although they do have certain rights under the policy. Approximately 90 percent of the groups insured under group life insurance policies are employer-employee groups. In this type of insured group, the employer is the group insurance policyholder and the employees are the persons insured.

Approximately 99 percent of group life insurance policies are issued as one-year renewable term insurance, and the premiums are intended to cover expected benefits and expenses for only the current policy year. Thus, from an actuarial standpoint, the vast majority of group life insurance products are much simpler than individual life insurance products. Like individual life insurance premium rates, group life insurance premium rates consider the factors of mortality, interest, and expenses. However, because of the short-term nature of this group coverage, the interest factor is not as important in premium rate calculation as it is in the calculation of premium rates for longer-term insurance contracts. In addition, the group actuary is not generally required to determine policy reserves or establish a policy reserve liability for a one-year term group life policy. Cash values need not be established, because one-year term insurance has no cash value.

Although one-year term insurance is the predominant form of group life insurance, some life insurance companies offer other types of group policies, such as *level-premium permanent group insurance* and *group paid-up life insurance*. Some employers also offer group coverage through products such as group universal life insurance. The actuarial work needed to determine the premium rates for such nonterm policies is necessarily more involved than the work needed to calculate premiums for group term policies. Furthermore, for level-premium permanent group insurance, the calculation of policy reserves is essentially the same as that used for individual life insurance. In the following discussion of group insurance, though, we will consider only group term insurance.

Mortality Tables

The first mortality table developed for group insurance was the Commissioners 1960 Standard Group (1960 CSG) mortality table (see Figure 8-1). The rates in this table were based on the group experience of 10 insurance companies from 1950 through 1958. Only employer-employee groups with more than 25 members were included in the study. The study also excluded groups from industries that by their nature involved special occupational hazards. The basic mortality rates determined by the study were increased by adding margins. Although the 1960 CSG is still in use, some companies also consult more recently published mortality experience tables—such as that presented in the 1975-1979 study of the Society of Actuaries—to investigate how reserves would accumulate under different experience

Figure 8-1
Comparison of mortality rates in commonly used group and ordinary mortality tables.

	Deaths per 1,000 at age									
	0	10	20	30	40	50	60	70	80	90
1960 CSG (group insurance)										
Unisex rates	8.32	1.42	2.09	2.40	4.02	9.52	22.62	52.33	115.48	239.55
1980 CSO (ordinary insurance)										
Rates for men	4.18	.73	1.90	1.73	3.02	6.71	16.08	37.51	98.84	221.77
Rates for women	2.89	.68	1.05	1.35	2.42	4.96	9.47	22.11	65.99	190.75

scenarios. Many companies maintain their own experience tables for group insurance as well.

Premiums

Rate making for group life insurance depends to a large extent on the previous claim experience of the group that is seeking insurance. If a group has been covered by another group policy, then the actuary can use that group's prior claim experience to help determine the group's initial premium rate. The process of using a group's own experience to develop premium rates is called *experience rating.*

The size of the group is important in determining the degree to which experience rating is used. If the group is large, with 1,000 members or more, then the group's own past experience is given a great deal of credibility when setting premium rates. If the group is small, then the group's previous claim experience is not usually a major factor in calculating premium rates. Instead, standard mortality experience would be used for rate making. These standard rates, usually called *manual rates,* are developed independently of the mortality experience of any particular group and are based on the experience of an average group. However, the rates are usually adjusted according to the experience of the insurance company's insureds and according to factors—such as age, sex, income, and geographical location—that affect the group currently seeking insurance. For an intermediate-size group, the actuary may use *blended rates,* which are based partly on manually rated data and partly on the company's experience-rated data.

Minimum initial gross premiums

Several states specify the minimum first-year premium amount that an insurer can charge a group that has not been covered by another group life insurance policy. In these states, the minimum gross premium rates required for group insurance policies are determined by factoring into the net premiums (1) an amount to allow for basic operating expenses, (2) an amount to allow for the higher expenses involved in administering small groups, and (3) an adjustment to reflect the proportionately lower costs of administering large group policies.

The minimum premium rates apply only to the first policy year. After the first policy year, the insurance company can charge whatever rates are competitive, fair, and adequate. The minimum rates apply only to group term insurance and not to any other type of group life insurance.

Calculating group premiums

Almost all premiums for group life insurance are paid on a monthly basis. The first step in setting the initial monthly premium for a group to be covered under a group life insurance policy is to determine the amount of insurance coverage that each person will receive. Under some plans, all insureds receive the same amount of coverage. Under other plans, each person's coverage is a multiple of that person's salary, or the amount is related to the individual's position in the organization.

The next step in establishing a group's premium is to calculate a net premium rate for each person's attained age. This net premium is based primarily on group mortality rates. As mentioned earlier, the interest factor is of little consequence in calculating yearly renewable term rates. If the group is large, the mortality rates used to calculate the net premium are usually based, at least in part, on the group's previous claim experience. The insurer then adds a loading amount to the net premium to cover the insurer's expenses, contingencies, and other costs. The total of the net premiums plus the loading is the premium for the group. If the plan includes extra coverages, such as disability benefits, then an appropriate amount is added to the life premium. Large groups sometimes receive a discount on their premiums.

The average monthly premium rate per $1,000 of insurance is then computed by dividing the total monthly premium for the group by the total death benefit provided by the insurance. This premium rate per $1,000 of insurance is used each month throughout the policy year and is applied to the total amount of insurance for the group. The average monthly premium rate per $1,000 of insurance is usually guaranteed for one policy year. Each month this average monthly premium rate per $1,000 is multiplied by the total amount of insurance in force during that month to determine the total monthly gross premium.

For example, assume that a business buys a group policy that provides $10,000 of insurance for each of its employees. The monthly premium rate per $1,000 is $0.33. One month, the business has 10 covered employees, which means that the group policy will provide $100,000 of insurance. For that month, the premium amount due is 100 (number of thousands of dollars of insurance) × $0.33 (rate per thousand) = $33.00. In the following month, however, one employee retires, and the business has only 9 covered employees, which means that the group policy is providing $90,000 of insurance. For that month, the premium due is 90 x $0.33 = $29.70. Thus, the total premium amount can vary from month to month even though the premium rate per $1,000 remains the same. Factors affecting the total monthly premium amount include the following:

- the number of insured individuals in the group
- changes in policy benefits
- changes, such as salary increases and promotions, that increase the amount of coverage provided

At the end of the policy year, a new premium rate is established for the next year. This new premium rate reflects changes in the amounts of coverage and in the age distribution of the group. Further, the renewal premium rate may reflect the group's mortality and expense experience of the previous year. As with establishing initial premium rates, a larger group provides more reliable experience by which to set renewal premium rates. The renewal premium rate is also generally guaranteed for one year.

Experience rating refunds

Group insurance policies are either participating or nonparticipating. However, the holder of either type of policy can receive a premium refund if the group's experience was better than anticipated when the premium rate was established and if the policy contract includes refund provisions. If the policy is participating, this refund is called a *dividend.* If the policy is nonparticipating, the refund is generally called an *experience rating refund,* an *experience refund*, or a *retroactive rate reduction.*

To determine how much, if anything, a policyholder receives as an experience rating refund or dividend, the actuary considers three main factors:

- the claim experience of the group during the previous year
- the size of the group
- the insurance company's expenses for administering the group policy

Claim experience. To analyze a group's claim experience, actuaries compare the amount of incurred claims with the amount of the claims that were expected during the same policy year. If the actual claims are less than those expected, then the group policyholder may receive a refund of part of the premium paid.

Group size. The credibility of a group's actual experience increases as the size of the group increases. The larger the group, the more confident the actuary can be that a year of favorable claim experience—that is, a year in which fewer claims occurred than the actuary expected—properly represents a situation that calls for returning a part of the premium to the policyholder. By contrast, the smaller the group, the greater the possibility that a favorable year of claim experience was a one-time occurrence and that the experience of the following policy year may be quite different. This concept makes use of the law of large numbers introduced in the last chapter. With a larger group, the actuary can be more confident that a year of favorable claim experience represents experience that can be expected to continue in the future.

Because actuaries often feel that the actual claim experience of a small group is not credible, they may use some type of average between the expected claims and the actual claims, or they may average the group's claim experience over a given period, such as the previous five years. Alternatively, the claim experience of several small groups may be pooled to determine the average experience of the combined small groups.

Expenses incurred. The third major factor in determining the experience rating refund for group contracts is the insurer's expense of administering the contract. Just as mortality rates vary from one group to another and from year to year for the same group, so do operating expenses.

Some expenses, such as commissions and premium taxes, can be related directly to specific group policies. Other expenses, such as correspondence and general office expenses, may not be allocated to specific policies because the cost of keeping such detailed records would be too high. For these unallocated expenses, the insurance company may divide the costs into a flat charge per group policy, a charge per individual life insured, a charge per transaction, a charge computed as a percentage of premiums, or a combination of some or all of these. If the actuary has determined that the administrative expenses attributable to a group were lower than anticipated, then part of the savings can be added to the amount of the experience rating refund or dividend.

Claim Fluctuation Reserve

After analyzing the claims, group size, and expenses of the previous policy year, the actuary must determine the disposition of any excess premiums paid by the policyholder. The exact formula for determining how much of the premium is to be returned in the form of an experience rating refund or dividend varies from one insurance company to another. Theoretically, the entire amount of the premium that is in excess of the amount needed for claims and expenses could be returned to the policyholder. In the case of a large group, the full amount is frequently refunded. In the case of a small group, however, the actuary may decide that part or all of the excess should be added to a special reserve, called a *claim fluctuation reserve,* instead of being returned to the policyholder.

The purpose of a ***claim fluctuation reserve*** is to provide for possible unfavorable claim experience in future years. By setting aside funds in such a reserve, the insurance company can offer the small group stable premium rates in future years. Once such a reserve has reached an acceptable level, as determined by the actuary, further contributions to this reserve will not be necessary.

HEALTH INSURANCE

Health insurance can be divided into two broad categories: disability income insurance and medical expense insurance. ***Disability income insurance*** provides for benefits to be paid in regular installments to an insured person in order to replace some of the insured's income when he or she is disabled by sickness or accident. Group disability income insurance is classified as *long-term disability (LTD) insurance* if the disability period is over five years.

The purpose of ***medical expense insurance*** is to pay for part or all of an insured's health care expenses, such as hospital room and board, surgeons' fees, visits to doctors' offices, prescribed drugs, treatments, and nursing care. Insurers offer several types of medical expense insurance:

- hospital insurance
- surgical insurance
- major medical insurance
- hospital confinement insurance
- limited coverage (or dread disease) insurance
- dental insurance

In 1990, life and health insurance companies in the United States received approximately 22 percent of their premium income from sales of health insurance. This percentage is much smaller in Canada, where many health benefits are provided through government-sponsored health insurance plans. Canadian insurers normally sell only disability income insurance and supplemental medical expense plans that provide benefits in addition to those provided through government-sponsored programs.

Morbidity Statistics

The statistics needed to develop health insurance products are generally more complicated than those used to develop life insurance products. Although the calculation of premium rates for health insurance follows the same general pattern as that for life insurance, there are differences, such as the following:

- Morbidity rates, not mortality rates, are used to calculate expected claims. The *morbidity rate* indicates the likelihood that a person of a given age will suffer an illness or a disability.
- The aggregate claims expected under the terms of a health insurance contract are a primary element in calculating health insurance premium rates. The amount of *aggregate claims* is arrived at by multiplying the claim frequency rate per insured by the average dollar amount per claim by the number of insured lives. The *claim frequency rate* is the expected percentage of insured people who will file claims. In order to determine the average claim cost, actuaries must forecast not only the number of insured people who will become sick or disabled but also the length of individuals' illnesses and disabilities, the cost of hospital expenses and physicians' fees, and the differences in such costs from one geographical region to another and from one economic cycle to another. Premium rates must reflect all of this information.

Actuaries gather morbidity data from the experience of their own company, intercompany studies conducted by the Society of Actuaries, and statistics provided by government agencies. INSIGHT 8-2 describes the work of a Society of Actuaries Task Force created to gather data on long-term-care insurance.

INSIGHT 8-2

Actuarial Considerations for Long-Term-Care Products

In the early years of long-term-care (LTC) insurance development, many companies had a fear of bringing products to the market because of a lack of actuarial data. There was—and still is—a lack of extensive numbers indicating the frequency and severity of claims or claim continuation information for LTC on either an insured or uninsured basis.

Very early programs used data from Medicare and private insurance coverages.

Later entrants into the marketplace were able to benefit somewhat from the results of the 1977 and 1985 National Nursing Home Studies prepared by the Department of Health and Human Services. These and other reports have helped with data relative to nursing home stay experience, yet they are not conclusive in pricing insureds for nursing home coverage. Neither have they been helpful in pricing most community benefits such as home health care, home care, personal care, respite care, and adult day care.

The Society of Actuaries "Task Force on Long Term Care Insurance" is working diligently to secure data on insured lives. The task force has designed a basis for gathering, compiling, and reporting in-force and claim results in a first-ever morbidity study. Eight companies will initially provide data based on their 1984-88 claims experience.

Because so many companies have entered the LTC marketplace, it may be assumed that there are sufficient data to price LTC policies. Not so. The only issue that has been resolved has been the "fear" of using limited data for theoretical pricing. Companies that were early entrants into the LTC marketplace are now offering policies with different benefits, so historical claims experience is not as useful for newer policies.

In addition, there are differences between claims experience on insured and uninsured lives, between theoretical and practical pricing, and between profitability results from one insurance company to another. For example, some companies have discovered that the relationship between uninsured male and female experience is wider than expected, that spousal impact is stronger than expected, that shorter elimination periods and longer benefit periods have worse experience than less-rich benefit packages, and that successful underwriting of substandard applicants has a long way to go.

Source: Adapted with permission of the publisher from Gary L. Corliss, "The Evolution of Long Term Care Insurance," *Resource,* February 1991, pp. 18-20.

Continuance tables

Continuance tables contain morbidity statistics that indicate the distribution of claims according to the duration of the illness or amount of expense involved in the claims. For example, a hospital continuance table predicts the number of 40-year-old hospital patients who will remain confined for a given number of days (for example, 5 days, 10 days, 18 days, etc.). Similarly, disability continuance tables predict the number of days that people of a certain age who have certain disabilities will remain disabled. Continuance tables also allow for the termination of illness through recovery or death.

Premiums

Individual health insurance

The premiums for individual health insurance are developed in a manner similar to those for individual life insurance. Individual health insurance premiums are frequently based on level annual premiums.

Once the health actuaries have found or developed the morbidity statistics that they need for a certain type of health plan, they calculate the **annual claim costs,** which are equal to the expected number of claims for one year multiplied by the average amount payable for each claim. Annual claim costs are calculated for each age and sex and, if appropriate, for each occupational class and geographical region. For example, assume that actuaries are calculating the annual claim costs for a block of one-year surgical expense policies for 1,000 women who are 45 years old. The actuaries predict 50 claims averaging $600 each. Therefore, the annual claim costs for this block of policies will be $30,000 (50 claims × $600 per claim = $30,000). The net one-year term premium is then $30 ($30,000 ÷ 1,000 insureds).

As with all other types of insurance, the actuaries add a loading to this net premium in order to determine the gross annual premium that the policyowners actually pay. If the premium for the individual health insurance policy is calculated for more than one year, then the actuaries must also calculate the number of policyowners who will die or withdraw from coverage in the succeeding years and then reduce the succeeding annual claim costs and the number of persons paying premiums accordingly.

Interest can also be an important factor in determining the structure of health insurance premiums, particularly in disability insurance, where the benefits are expected to be paid over a long period. Interest would be a less important consideration in the calculation of medical expense insurance.

Group health insurance

As with group life insurance, group health insurance premium rates are normally calculated using experience rating, manual rating, or blended rating, depending on the size and previous claim experience of the insured group. Premium rates are normally calculated and guaranteed for one year, with premiums being paid on a monthly basis.

Reserves

Individual health insurance

The reserve calculations for individual health insurance are much like the reserve calculations for life insurance. To calculate reserve liabilities for medical expense insurance, many companies rely on morbidity tables that reflect the experience of their own insureds. To calculate reserves for disability income coverage, one table commonly used is the 1985 Commissioners Individual Disability (CID) Table, which is based on experience from the 1970s. Two versions of the 1985 CID table are available. Table A, which is used for large cases, is based on highly detailed statistics such as severity, duration, and frequency of various types of disabilities. Table B is used for small groups that do not have sufficient size to determine or predict these characteristics. Another table available to insurers is the 1964 Commissioners Disability Table, which is based on the experience of 17 insurance companies from 1958 to 1961.

Group health insurance

Claim reserves are established for each of the different types of group health insurance sold, such as disability income insurance, major medical insurance, surgical expense insurance, and dental insurance. Some companies establish contingency reserves to protect themselves against unexpected upward trends in claim costs.

KEY TERMS

master contract	disability income insurance
experience rating	medical expense insurance
manual rates	morbidity rate
blended rates	aggregate claims
dividend	claim frequency rate
experience rating refund	continuance table
claim fluctuation reserve	annual claim costs

NOTE

1. The following section of this chapter is adapted from *Group Insurance Course Manual*, compiled by Harriett E. Jones, J.D., FLMI (Atlanta: LOMA, 1988).

Chapter 9

The Underwriting Function

After reading this chapter, you should be able to

- Describe the underwriting process and its purpose
- List and explain the major objectives of the underwriter
- Explain the role of agents in risk selection
- Identify a variety of sources of underwriting information
- Discuss risk factors that influence the underwriting decision
- Describe the risk classes used by life insurance underwriters
- Explain how the numerical rating system is used
- Explain the different risk factors used in health insurance underwriting and life insurance underwriting
- Contrast the underwriting of group insurance with the underwriting of individual insurance
- Explain the purpose of reinsurance and describe different reinsurance treaties and plans

Some insurance policies are sold on a guaranteed-issue basis—that is, without evaluating the risk each policy presents to the company. However, most applications for insurance are evaluated to determine the degree of risk presented by the proposed insured. The job of evaluating applications for insurance and assessing the risk they present is performed by *underwriters*. Once a proposed insured's degree of risk has been determined, the underwriter can determine whether the proposed insured is an acceptable risk and, if so, what premium amount to charge the applicant. In this chapter, we will discuss the process of underwriting life and health insurance: the risk factors that are involved, the sources of underwriting information, the manner in which risks are classified, the use of reinsurance by insurance companies, and the relationships between underwriters and other company personnel.

WHAT IS UNDERWRITING?

Underwriting, also called *risk selection* or *selection of risks*, is the process of assessing and classifying the degree of risk that a proposed insured represents. Based on the degree of risk, the company decides whether to accept or decline an application for insurance. The employees responsible for accepting or declining the application based on this risk assessment are called *home office underwriters*. In some companies, underwriters may work in regional offices as well.

The term *underwriter* can also be used to describe an individual or organization that sells insurance. For example, insurance agents are often called *field underwriters*. In this text, the term *underwriter* means a home office or regional office underwriter unless otherwise noted.

THE UNDERWRITING DECISION[1]

In assessing risk and assigning proposed insureds to the appropriate risk classes, the home office underwriter's objectives are to approve and issue a policy that is (1) equitable to the client, (2) deliverable by the agent, and (3) profitable to the company.

Equitable to the Client

One of the basic principles of insurance is that each individual insured should pay a premium proportionate to the amount of risk that the company assumes for the person. As each application for insurance is received, the insurance company must determine the degree of risk and must charge a fair premium for this risk.

An understanding of how various factors influence mortality enables the underwriter to identify applicants who present comparable mortality risks and to classify these applicants accordingly. Classifying insureds in this way enables the insurance company to charge each individual policyowner an equitable premium proportionate to the degree of mortality risk he or she presents to the company.

Deliverable by the Agent

The consumer makes the ultimate decision as to whether a particular insurance policy is acceptable. If the consumer chooses not to accept the policy when the agent attempts to deliver it, that policy is said to be *undeliverable*, or *not taken*. One of the many reasons a policy may be considered not taken is because of an unfavorable underwriting decision that results in a higher-than-anticipated premium charge.

For a policy to be acceptable to the buyer, it must satisfy three basic requirements:

1. The policy must provide benefits that meet the consumer's needs.
2. The cost of the coverage provided by the policy must be within the consumer's financial means.
3. The premium to be charged for the coverage must be competitive in the marketplace.

The third requirement listed above is particularly important because of competition in the life insurance industry, especially in the area of pricing. The price that agents quote to their clients is generally based on the company's standard premium rates. Agents may have difficulty delivering the issued policy to a client if the underwriter's decision has made the policy more expensive than the premium rate that the agent originally quoted to the buyer. When such is the case, agents may exert pressure on the underwriter or on company management to lower the price. If the company does not yield, the agents may take their business to a competitor that offers a more deliverable product. When agents attempt to put pressure on an underwriter and no change in the decision is possible, underwriters must be able to explain the reasons for their adverse decisions with enough credibility that the agents will continue to sell insurance for the company.

Profitable to the Company

Finally, an underwriter must make decisions that will be profitable to the company. All insurance companies, whether stock, mutual, or fraternal benefit societies, require sound underwriting to assure favorable financial results. Stock companies pay dividends to stockholders and, in some cases, policyowners, while mutuals and fraternals pay dividends only to policyowners. Surplus should grow in all companies if they are to continue to fulfill their economic role. The profitability of an insurer is, to a large extent, built into the rate structure established by its actuaries. Although underwriters are not directly involved in establishing a company's premium structure, underwriters' decisions are crucial in producing actual mortality results that coincide with the actuaries' mortality projections.

THE UNDERWRITING FUNCTION

The underwriting function can be organized in a variety of ways. An organizational chart for one typical underwriting department structure is shown in Figure 9-1. Team underwriting in various forms has also been used for many years. An underwriting team organized along geographic or product lines (or both) works with a given group of agents and develops a relationship with the agents it serves. INSIGHT 9-1 illustrates one company's approach to underwriting teams.

Figure 9-1
Organization chart of an underwriting department.

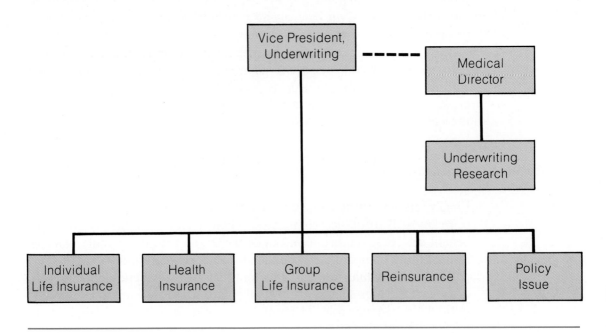

INSIGHT 9-1

The Team Approach to Life Insurance Underwriting

North Carolina Mutual began using the team approach to underwriting in November 1988, when it organized its underwriting division into three separate underwriting teams—Zones A, B, and C—which correspond to the company's three Agency Zones. Each team is headed by a lead underwriter and includes one additional underwriter and two or more trained technicians known as underwriting service representatives (USRs). Rather than divide the work by the kind of transaction required, work is assigned so that all USRs perform all functions and transactions.

North Carolina Mutual's style of team underwriting makes each team leader a manager. In addition to risk selection responsibilities, the team leader is responsible for directing the activities of the team's USRs. This places the underwriter in a po-

sition of having the ability to control service. Each team maintains its own file of applications pending for underwriting requirements or delivery requirements. The only time an application leaves a team is for referral to the medical director, division supervisor, or chief underwriter. The file is logged out when it leaves the unit. Each team has a considerable degree of autonomy. This is a real plus when it comes to fostering team pride in the quality and timeliness of the service the team provides.

Team autonomy also creates the need for constant, free-flowing communication. The underwriting division has a semimonthly underwriters' meeting and requires weekly progress reports from each team leader. A weekly management report is also made available to its agency management.

Source: Adapted with permission from an Activity Report prepared by Milton Taylor, FLMI, CLU, ChFC, and submitted to LOMA by Charles Blackmon of North Carolina Mutual Life Insurance Company, April 1990.

Underwriters have various levels of authority, as indicated by some representative underwriting job titles (the titles may change from company to company):

- underwriting officer
- underwriting manager
- chief underwriter
- senior underwriter
- underwriter
- junior underwriter
- jet underwriter
- underwriter trainee

The different job titles reflect the experience and professional training of the underwriters as well as their levels of authority. The higher the authority level of the underwriter, the greater the amount of coverage the underwriter can approve on a standard basis for any single proposed insured without review by a more experienced underwriter. In addition, an underwriter's authorization to decline or rate an application without approval or review usually increases with the underwriter's experience level (see Figure 9-2). To *rate an application* means to approve the application but, because the proposed insured presents a greater-than-average risk, to charge a higher-than-normal premium for the policy.

The first underwriters had little data on which to base their risk assessments. They depended entirely on their own experience and judgment to determine which risks were acceptable. Gradually, their task was made

Figure 9-2
Sample guidelines for life underwriting approval authority.

Approval Authority for Standard Issue

Applied for	In Force not in Excess of	Single Approval by
0–$ 50,000	$150,000	Junior Underwriter
$ 50,001–$100,000	$250,000	Underwriter
$100,001–$200,000	$500,000	Senior Underwriter
$200,001–$350,000	No limit	Chief Underwriter
$350,001–Up	No limit	Underwriting Officer

All rejections must have the review of the chief underwriter or the underwriting officer. The right to approve for any stated amount implies the right to overrule an approver whose limit is lower. The right to approve for any stated face amount of insurance implies the right to approve special benefits for a similar amount.

Rated or Modified Issue
(Amounts as with Standard Approval Authority)

Junior Underwriter	Must get a second review by chief underwriter.
Underwriter	Must get a second review by underwriting officer.
Senior Underwriter	May act independently through extra premium of $7.50 per thousand for physical reasons. Beyond this point, for physical and all other reasons, a second review by the underwriting officer is required

easier by the gathering of statistics relating to different risks, particularly mortality statistics. As this data became more dependable, company actuaries, physicians, underwriters, and claim examiners were able to identify certain factors, such as medical conditions or occupations, that might increase the rate of mortality or morbidity. With this knowledge, companies were able to establish underwriting guidelines for life and health insurance. By using these guidelines, employees without underwriting backgrounds can be trained to assess mortality and morbidity risk.

Most insurance companies employ physicians as medical experts or medical directors, either on a part-time or full-time basis. A large company may have a staff of several physicians and nurses. The medical director's staff prepares and updates the company's medical underwriting standards, consults with underwriters on applications that have unusual or difficult medical histories, and, on rare occasions, performs physical examinations on proposed insureds. Medical directors from many companies may pool company data and conduct joint studies in order to benefit from as much information on as many risks as possible.

THE UNDERWRITING PROCESS

Risk selection requires a number of steps. Agents begin the underwriting process when they fill out an application with the proposed insured. After being sent to the home office, an application may be reviewed again before it is assessed by a home office underwriter. Some applications may never even be seen by an underwriter, as they undergo jet screening or computer screening. The next section of this chapter discusses the first steps of the process of underwriting individual life and health insurance.

Field Underwriting

The prospecting and selling activities of agents represent the beginning of the risk selection process. This process is often referred to as *field underwriting* because it involves a great deal of screening and selection, much like home office underwriting. ***Field underwriting*** occurs when an agent gathers pertinent information about the proposed insured and records that information on the application for insurance. The application then becomes an important factor in the risk selection decision.

Agents are essential to the underwriting process, because they deal directly with the insurance purchaser. Company agents keep certain underwriting principles and guidelines in mind whenever they complete an application with a potential customer. Agents are trained, for example, to make sure that all questions on the application for insurance are answered and that descriptions of any health problems are complete and exact. When health problems are noted on an application, agents can make the underwriting process easier by seeking the following types of additional information:

- the precise name of any medical problems
- the date, duration, and frequency of any attacks or episodes
- aftereffects and complications of any problems, such as any loss of time from work
- the dates and types of any treatment or medication
- full names and addresses of physicians visited and dates of such visits
- dates of hospitalizations and names of hospitals

Agents are also expected to secure additional information from proposed insureds if the answers to any application questions are unusual. In addition, agents must report anything they know or suspect about a proposed insured that could influence the risk selection decision, but which the applicant or proposed insured may not have mentioned. The agent reports such information in the *agent's statement,* or *agent's report,* portion of the application or in a separate letter.

Application Processing and Preliminary Review

Each application that is received, either in the home office or a field office, is usually assigned an identification number. This number is used at first for control purposes and later as the policy number, if a policy is issued. The application and supporting materials are reviewed to make sure the file is complete. Certain other information is verified at this time: does the proposed insured's age meet the criteria for the type of plan requested? Is the agent licensed to sell the requested type of policy?

After such verification, the company's records are searched for additional information about the proposed insured. If the proposed insured is covered by one of the company's health insurance policies or another life policy, the underwriter can review information such as health insurance claims filed or prior life insurance applications. In most companies, a computer does the preliminary review and search for information about the proposed insured, and subsequently generates a worksheet. The **worksheet,** sometimes called a *data sheet,* is a printout of all available information about the proposed insured and, in some companies, pertinent information about the agent who submitted the application. A sample worksheet is shown in Figure 9-3.

In many companies, before an application and worksheet go to an underwriter, the application goes through either *jet screening* or *computer*

Figure 9-3
Sample underwriting worksheet.

UNDERWRITING WORKSHEET

NAME	SEX	AGE	POLICY NO.	SFX SCD

DATE OF BIRTH			REGIONAL OFFICE	CONTACT	DATE OF APP.
PLACE OF BIRTH		RESIDENCE		CURR.	IMPAIRMENT CODE PRIM. SEC. ASS. RSN
PLAN				S	NS

REWRITE ☐ ☐ F P OTHER D M Y

REWRITE ☐ ☐ F P OTHER D M Y

REWRITE ☐ ☐ F P OTHER D M Y

UNDERWRITER

	BASIC POLICY	REINS. REQ'D	INDEX
LIFE			
LIFERIDER			
WP			
ADB			
OTHER			

UNDERWRITING INFO	REC'D	REQ'D
APPLICATION		
NON MEDICAL		
MEDICAL		
SECOND MEDICAL		
URINALYSIS		
ECG		
CHEST FILM		
APS		
APS		
APS		
SMA-12		
IR		
B.B.R.		
FINANCIAL INFO		
QUESTIONNAIRE		

PURPOSE: ☐ PERSONAL ☐ BUSINESS TYPE:

PARTNERS/RELATIVES

PARA ☐ BUILD ____________

MD ☐ B.P. ____________

E=AP ☐ URINE ____________

DATE: OTHER ____________

OCCUPATION | HABITS, AVIATION AND/OR AVOCATIONS

IN FORCE: PERSONAL BUSINESS | INSUR. HIST. | FAMILY HIST.

NET WORTH INCOME

DATE		RATE

FORM 207 (1/84)

screening. These methods of analyzing proposed insureds' applications improve the efficiency of a company's underwriting operations.

Jet screening

Many insurance companies have underwriting personnel that specialize in *jet screening*—that is, processing simple cases as quickly as possible. If an application for insurance meets certain strictly defined criteria, then the jet screening staff, or *jet unit*, can approve the application and call for immediate policy issue. If the application does not meet the criteria for immediate issue, then the file is passed on to an underwriter for evaluation. Jet screening personnel are typically not authorized to decline or rate an application. In some companies, though, jet units can rate a policy for aviation hazard, avocation, or occupation. The following criteria are representative of those used by companies to choose applications for jet screening:

- The proposed insured must be within a certain age range—generally between 15 and 50 years old.
- The amount of the insurance applied for cannot exceed a specified amount—anywhere from $50,000 to $100,000, depending on the applicant's age and the company.
- All questions on both Parts I and II of the application must be answered.
- The proposed insured must have no significant health problems.
- The company's records and the Medical Information Bureau report must contain no adverse underwriting information on the proposed insured. The role of the Medical Information Bureau is discussed later in this chapter.
- The proposed insured's height and weight must be within acceptable standards.
- The proposed insured's occupation must be acceptable.

Jet screening reduces underwriting costs, because an experienced underwriter is not needed to review all applications. Companies that use jet screening can approve applications and issue policies quickly, which helps improve customer service. Some companies now use jet screening to process as much as 30 percent of their applications.

Computer screening

Computer screening uses automated systems to perform simple underwriting. Instead of using underwriters, underwriter trainees, or even a jet unit, insurance companies program computers with the necessary criteria to screen applications. In some companies, agents transmit application information directly from a field computer to a computer at the home office. In other companies, the information is entered when the application is received at the home office.

As applications are received and key information from the applications is processed, a computer evaluates the applications according to the required criteria. (Computer screening is one application of an *expert system*, which is discussed further in Chapter 16.) Applications that are approved can be prepared immediately for printing as policies, or the computer can send the applications to an underwriter for review.

ADDITIONAL INFORMATION SOURCES FOR RISK SELECTION

As mentioned earlier, the primary source of underwriting information is the application for insurance, which includes a great deal of medical and nonmedical information. However, when the insurer wants more information than is provided on the application or in a medical or paramedical examination, several other sources for information and verification are available. These sources include the Attending Physician's Statement (APS), inspection reports, motor vehicle reports, financial statements, interviews with the applicant, and the records of the Medical Information Bureau (MIB). In the following pages, we will discuss some of these additional sources of underwriting information.

Attending Physician's Statement (APS)

An underwriter who wants more specific information about the proposed insured's health history than is provided by a medical examination or by the application can request an Attending Physician's Statement (APS). An ***Attending Physician's Statement (APS)*** is a report from a physician consulted by the proposed insured either for routine physical examinations or for a specific health problem. Although an APS can be a valuable source of information, underwriters and agents agree that the APS is the single greatest hindrance to the swift processing of an application. Because doctors have other priorities and tend to respond slowly to requests for such information, underwriters request an APS only when necessary.

Medical Information Bureau (MIB)

Another source of information for the underwriter is the *Medical Information Bureau (MIB)*. The MIB serves as a clearinghouse of medical information for the life and health insurance industry. This bureau carries out two basic functions:

- maintaining information on proposed insureds regarding medical impairments and other risks admitted or discovered during underwriting; this information has been previously reported by member companies
- reporting such information upon request to member companies

Insurance companies request information from the MIB to find out whether a proposed insured has significant impairments or other risks that were previously admitted to or discovered by another insurer but were not acknowledged when the proposed insured made the current application for insurance. No member company can request information unless the individual being investigated has given written consent on a form that identifies the MIB as an authorized source of information.

As an example of how insurers use the MIB, suppose Jane McCormick applies to the Early Life Insurance Company for life insurance coverage on herself. A physical examination reveals that Ms. McCormick has a significant heart condition. Early Life rejects her application and reports the heart condition to the MIB. Ms. McCormick later applies to the Ultimate Life Insurance Company and does not mention the heart condition. Upon requesting information from the MIB, Ultimate Life would learn about the condition and would be alerted to conduct its own investigation.

Under MIB rules, an underwriter cannot base an underwriting decision solely on information provided by the MIB. The information from the MIB should serve only to alert the underwriter to the possible need for further investigation of a proposed insured's insurability. Companies reporting information to the MIB do not indicate what action they took on each insured's case, whether they issued the policy on a standard or rated basis or whether they declined it. The MIB does not restrict itself to only unfavorable information about a proposed insured, but also stores and reports favorable information submitted by member companies.

The MIB uses codes for the different impairments and test results on proposed insureds. Access to MIB-coded information is restricted to authorized medical, underwriting, and claim personnel in member companies. If a company finds any discrepancies in the MIB's coded information, the company is required to update the MIB records. In addition, proposed insureds have the right to correct the MIB's information about themselves.

Any information an insurance company receives from the MIB must be kept strictly confidential.

Inspection Reports and Telephone Interviews

Sometimes an underwriter wants to know personal or financial information about the proposed insured before deciding whether to accept the risk. One source of such nonmedical information is an *inspection report,* also called an *investigative consumer report.* An ***inspection report*** is prepared by a consumer reporting agency and contains information about a proposed insured's occupation, personal habits, hobbies, driving record, health, and finances. To prepare an inspection report, the investigating agency interviews the proposed insured and his or her friends, neighbors, and business associates. Depending on the answers given by these sources, other types of information may also be part of an inspection report.

Insurers in the United States and Canada are required by law to tell a proposed insured that an inspection report may be prepared and that the report will include information about the proposed insured's character and background. The proposed insured has the right to see a copy of the completed report and must be told if information contained in the report is the reason that the insurer declined or rated the application for insurance.

Because of growing costs and time delays, inspection reports prepared by consumer reporting agencies are being used more selectively. In many insurance companies, underwriters or other home office personnel gather information by telephoning proposed insureds and interviewing them directly. Such telephone interviews are more cost-effective and more timely than inspection reports and are an effective way to obtain needed information. Companies that do their own telephone inspections still use consumer reporting agency reports when the amount of insurance applied for exceeds a specified limit.

RISK FACTORS FOR LIFE INSURANCE

Many factors affect the degree of mortality risk presented by a proposed insured. As described above, the underwriter's task is to determine whether these factors are present and the extent to which they affect the degree of risk. ***Underwriting impairments*** for life insurance are factors that tend to increase a proposed insured's risk of death above that which is normal for his or her age.

One of the major factors in risk selection for life insurance is age. All other things being equal, a 60-year-old man poses a greater mortality risk than a 30-year-old man. Although the standard premium structure itself allows for this age-based difference, the age of the proposed insured still affects the underwriter's risk selection because as a person ages, the likelihood of physical impairment increases.

In addition to age, many other factors affect mortality risk. These factors can be classified as medical and nonmedical risk factors. A sample of extra-risk policies issued in 1988 by insurance companies in the United States showed that 82 percent of rated policies were rated for medical reasons, and the remaining 18 percent were rated for nonmedical reasons, such as occupation.

Medical Risk Factors

Medical risk factors for underwriting life insurance include

- weight
- physical condition other than weight
- family history
- smoking

Weight

A person who is significantly overweight represents a greater mortality risk than does a person of average weight. A proposed insured who is underweight causes less concern about mortality risk, but if an application indicates that a proposed insured has recently lost a significant amount of weight—especially over a short period of time—underwriters usually investigate to determine whether the weight loss occurred because of illness.

Physical condition other than weight

A proposed insured's health history sometimes indicates a higher-than-average mortality risk. For example, a person who has already had a heart attack is more likely to have a shorter life, all other factors being equal, than a person who has not had a heart attack. Numerous other factors—such as high blood pressure, kidney disease, heart or lung disorders, or diabetes—can produce higher-than-average mortality.

In order to make risk selection as accurate as possible, insurance companies maintain statistics on the various causes of death and rate their policies accordingly. Underwriters also keep informed about recent mortality and public health trends; some diseases have a higher mortality risk, and the relative risk represented by these diseases changes over time. For example, cancer presents a much greater mortality risk today than tuberculosis or influenza. The AIDS epidemic poses new challenges to underwriters. INSIGHT 9-2 details some of the issues underwriters face in attempting to deal with AIDS in the risk selection process.

INSIGHT 9-2

The AIDS Epidemic and AIDS Testing

Without a doubt, the acquired immune deficiency syndrome (AIDS) epidemic poses a serious threat to the insurance industry from all fronts—economic, social, and political. The AIDS epidemic now presents life and health insurers with a variety of serious concerns arising from both claims being made under policies that were already on the books before the epidemic broke out, and claims from insurance yet to be sold. Because claims against policies in-force were not anticipated when the policies were priced, and because it is difficult to predict the number of new claims that will be made against new policies issued, the financial impact on life insurers will become increasingly severe as the epidemic evolves.

In an effort to control the escalating threat, insurance companies have resorted to implementing stricter tests of insurance eligibility—specifically, HIV and T-Cell testing. A nationwide debate now pits the industry's efforts to retain control and solvency against the privacy and civil rights of individuals. Sero-positive individuals, AIDS activists, and the government have all spoken out in an attempt to restrict antibody

testing for a variety of reasons. These include (1) claims that the tests are inaccurate; (2) assumptions that insurers will not keep the test results confidential, resulting in discrimination at the workplace and elsewhere; and (3) the belief that insurance coverage should be readily available for those in society who need it the most.

In general, the insurance industry believes that (1) the tests are the most accurate measure available; (2) a high level of confidentiality has been met and will be ensured by requiring informed consent from the applicant; and (3) insurers must prevent adverse selection in order to offer adequate life and health coverage to the most people.

By 1988, state legislators were attempting to ban AIDS testing in response to growing community awareness and compassion for AIDS individuals. Since then, in an unprecedented maneuver, the industry has largely reversed legislative testing restrictions through active lobbying and educating the public.

Today, life insurers are permitted to conduct AIDS testing in all 50 states. Clearly, the insurance industry's swift and effective utilization of its internal resources and political leverage indicated that it recognized the severity of the AIDS epidemic. In its desire to stay ahead of legislative change, the industry must continue to move rapidly to establish and shape its operating environment.

Source: Excerpted with permission from the article, "The Impact of AIDS on the Insurance Industry," by Kenneth A. Getz, M.B.A., and Judith D. Bentkover, Ph.D., which appeared in the March 1992 issue of the *Journal of the American Society of CLU and ChFC,* Vol. XLVI, No. 2. Copyright 1992 by the American Society of CLU & ChFC, 270 Bryn Mawr Avenue, Bryn Mawr, PA 19010.

Family health history

The health history of a proposed insured's family can be important in identifying current and potential impairments. Family history is usually considered an important factor if it reflects a characteristic that also appears in some form in the proposed insured. For example, if both parents of a proposed insured died of heart attacks before they were 60 years old, then the history would probably be significant only if the proposed insured has high blood pressure or some other condition that increases the chance of heart attack. If such a condition exists, the underwriter would probably rate the policy. Except for rare conditions, such a family history by itself would not usually result in a rated policy.

Smoking

Research indicates that cigarette smoking significantly increases mortality risk. Many companies now have separate actuarial tables and premium rates for smokers and nonsmokers, and some insurance products are issued to nonsmokers only.

Nonmedical Risk Factors

The nonmedical factors that most frequently affect the underwriting decision are

- occupation
- avocation or hobbies
- moral hazard
- insurable interest
- antiselection
- aviation
- substance abuse
- foreign residence or travel
- finances

Occupation

Although advances in safety standards and industrial medicine have reduced the effects of accident and health hazards, some occupations are still inherently more dangerous than others. For example, steeplejacks and miners experience a higher mortality rate as a group than do office workers. Workers exposed to hazardous substances, such as asbestos or silicon dust, have a greater incidence of disease than do unexposed workers.

Aviation

If the applicant is a pilot, the type of flying done is important to risk classification. Pilots on scheduled airlines are standard risks; crop dusters are not. Flying as a fare-paying passenger on regularly scheduled airline flights is not sufficiently hazardous to affect a person's mortality risk.

Avocation or hobbies

Leisure activities that present unusual hazards increase a proposed insured's mortality risk. For example, an amateur sports car racer, or a person who explores caves or skydives as a hobby, presents a higher-than-average risk.

Substance abuse

Another important facet of a proposed insured's risk is the use of drugs or alcohol. The excessive use of drugs or alcohol, called *substance abuse,* can damage a person's health, thereby increasing the risk of death. Substance abusers also have a much higher rate of violent death than do people who do not abuse drugs or alcohol. In addition, substance abuse presents an element of moral hazard.

Moral hazard

Certain past histories may cause an insurer to rate or deny a policy based on perceived moral hazard. Moral hazard has two elements. First, moral hazard refers to the danger that the proposed insured is making a deliberate attempt to conceal or misrepresent information that might result in an unfavorable underwriting decision. Moral hazard also refers to the possibility that a proposed insured may act in a morally or ethically unacceptable manner. Thus, proof of a prior criminal record, compulsive gambling, dealing in drugs, and prostitution are examples of moral hazard risk. For some companies, too, a proposed insured's personal financial history (such as a recent bankruptcy filing or a poor credit rating) is considered in determining moral hazard.

Foreign residence or travel

A person living in an area with an extreme climate or severe political unrest can be considered a higher-than-average risk. Frequent travel to such areas also presents higher mortality risk.

Insurable interest

Underwriters must evaluate each application for **insurable interest** in the potential loss, which means that the intended policyowner will suffer an emotional or financial loss if the event insured against occurs. Insurable interest is especially important when the intended owner of the policy and the proposed insured are not the same person. The presence of an insurable interest can usually be found by applying the following general rule: if the potential policyowner has more to gain if the proposed insured continues to live than if the proposed insured dies, an insurable interest is considered to exist.

Without the presence of an insurable interest, the contract is not formed for a lawful purpose and, thus, would be void from the start. If the underwriter cannot detect an insurable interest, then the application must be declined. The presence of insurable interest is important when the insurance contract is formed. After the policy has been issued, the insurable interest that originally existed between the insured and the applicant may change over time and does not have to continue in order for the contract to be valid.

Legally, people possess an unlimited insurable interest in their own lives and can name whatever beneficiaries they choose. However, an underwriter will inquire fully about the reasons for naming a beneficiary who appears to have little insurable interest in the life of the proposed insured, even if the proposed insured is also to be the owner of the policy.

Antiselection

Antiselection, also called *adverse selection* or *selection against the insurer*, is the tendency of people with a greater-than-average likelihood of loss to apply for or to continue insurance coverage. Antiselection not only occurs at the time of policy application, but also occurs once policies are issued.

Antiselection is possible because people know more about themselves than they may reveal to the agent or underwriter. On the basis of their own personal knowledge, applicants can withhold significant information and choose amounts and plans of insurance that are most favorable for themselves. Because of the possibility of antiselection, the underwriter must analyze the available information about each applicant to determine whether the company has an accurate picture of the applicant's insurability. The tendency of insureds whose health has deteriorated to continue their insurance at a higher rate of persistency than those whose health has not changed is a form of antiselection. This form of antiselection is beyond the control of the underwriter.

Finances

Aside from medical considerations, the aspect of a case that most concerns an underwriter is typically a financial one: in particular, are the applicant's insurance wants in line with his or her insurance needs? To the underwriter, an application for an amount of insurance that is excessive in relation to the applicant's income sometimes indicates antiselection or questionable insurable interest. Another aspect of underwriting an applicant's finances is whether or not the applicant can afford the insurance for which he or she is applying. An applicant who cannot afford the policy premiums may allow the policy to lapse.

RISK CLASSIFICATION FOR LIFE INSURANCE

After reviewing all the pertinent information about a proposed insured, the underwriter assigns the proposed insured to a risk class. A *risk class* is a group of insureds who present a substantially similar risk to an insurance company. Among the most common risk classes used by life insurance companies are *standard, preferred, nonsmoker, substandard,* and *uninsurable.* Companies may use some or all of these risk classes in classifying proposed insureds.

- *Standard*—People in the standard risk class present an average mortality risk and pay standard insurance premium rates. Most insureds are included in the standard risk class. In some companies that have a *nonsmoker* risk class, the standard class is used for smokers, and "standard" risks who do not smoke are assigned to the nonsmoker class.

- *Preferred*—People in the preferred risk class present a lower-than-average mortality risk. A variety of factors are used to identify people in this risk class. People in the preferred risk class typically are in excellent physical condition, have good personal and family medical histories, and are nonsmokers. Preferred risks pay lower-than-standard premium rates.
- *Nonsmoker*—People in the nonsmoker risk class are individuals who have not smoked cigarettes—or in some companies used tobacco in any form—for a specified period of time before applying for insurance, usually 12 months. People in the nonsmoker risk class may be preferred, standard, or substandard risks.
- *Substandard*—People in the substandard risk class have medical or nonmedical impairments that make their mortality risk higher than average. Insurance companies divide impaired risks into several substandard classes. Substandard risks pay higher-than-standard premium rates of varying amounts, depending on the degree of extra risk presented to the company.
- *Uninsurable*—People in the uninsurable risk class run a risk of early death so great that companies do not insure them. Underwriters decline the applications of people in this risk class.

Every insurance company has its own standards for classifying risks, and a person classified as a substandard risk by one company might be a standard risk for another insurer. A person classified as uninsurable by one company might be classified as substandard by another. Some companies are known for their conservative risk classifications, and others have liberal risk classifications.

The degree of risk a company is willing to accept is a basic operational decision for the company. If a company's risk classifications are too strict, then the company may realize reduced mortality expenses, but it may also lose profitable business to its competitors. On the other hand, if a company's risk classifications are too lenient, then the company may increase its mortality expenses and jeopardize its financial position.

In 1988, 93 percent of all applicants for ordinary insurance in the United States were offered standard or better-than-standard rates, 4 percent were offered substandard rates, and only 3 percent were declined.

Underwriting Manuals

The *underwriting manual* is a summary of the guidelines used by a particular company to evaluate and rate risks. It provides underwriters with background information on underwriting impairments and serves as a guide to suggested underwriting actions when various impairments are present. The major portion of the manual discusses common medical impairments. For each impairment listed, the manual provides descriptive information and suggested ratings.

Many manuals also include a glossary of symptoms and medical terms, as well as a list of medical and insurance abbreviations and definitions, to help the underwriter interpret medical information in an applicant's file. In addition, underwriting manuals may include an index that lists synonyms and derivative terms for impairments, as well as a laboratory section that lists basic laboratory test information and a normal range of values for the most commonly used tests. Many manuals have additional sections that provide suggested ratings for nonmedical impairments, such as dangerous hobbies or extensive foreign travel. Figure 9-4 shows sample pages from an underwriting manual.

Figure 9-4
Sample pages from an underwriting manual.

ATRIOVENTRICULAR (AV) BLOCK

- SOME SECOND DEGREE AND ALL COMPLETE AV BLOCKS ARE ASSOCIATED WITH ORGANIC HEART DISEASE, e.g. ISCHEMIC AND HYPERTENSIVE HEART DISEASE, FIBROSIS OF CONDUCTING TISSUE, AMYLOIDOSIS, MYOCARDITIS, HEART SURGERY AND CONGENITAL ANOMALIES

Requirements — Medical examination, ECG, chest X-ray, APS

Rating		ADB	WP
No known cardiovascular disease Partial AV block (1st degree)			
PR 0.22 to 0.26	+0	Std.	Std.
PR 0.27 to .32			
—pulse < 66/min.	+25 to +50	Std.	Std.
66–80	+50 to +75	2	2
81–90	+75 to +100	2	2
over 90	+100 up	Dec.	Dec.
PR over 0.32	add +50 to above rates for PR interval of 0.27 to 0.32		

Figure 9-4 *(continued)*

Rating		ADB	WP
Partial AV block (2nd degree)			
Mobitz Type I (Wenckebach)	+0	Std.	Std.
Mobitz Type II	usually decline		
Complete AV block (3rd degree)			
Acquired	usually decline		
Congenital, long standing, stable ECG, no Stokes-Adams attacks			
—up to age 50	+100	Dec.	Dec.
—over age 50	+50	Dec.	Dec.
History of Stokes-Adams attacks	Dec.		
—with pacemaker	rate as "CARDIAC PACEMAKER"		

BUNDLE BRANCH BLOCKS—RIGHT AND LEFT

- RIGHT BUNDLE BRANCH BLOCK (RBBB) MAY BE AN INNOCENT CONGENITAL PHENOMENON ASSOCIATED WITH CONGENITAL HEART DISEASE, MAY ALSO RESULT FROM CARDIAC SURGERY
- AT OLDER AGES MAY INDICATE HEART DISEASE DUE TO ISCHEMIA OR FIBROSIS
- LEFT BUNDLE BRANCH BLOCK (LBBB) IS ALMOST INVARIABLY DUE TO ORGANIC DISEASE

Requirements — Medical examination, ECG

Rating		ADB	WP
No rateable cerebrovascular, cardiovascular, peripheral vascular or blood pressure impairment			
Right Bundle Branch Block			
Complete Right Bundle Branch Block with well documented history			
5 years or more	+0	Std.	Std.
with poorly documented or no history			
5 years or less			
—to age 45	+75	2	Dec.
—over age 45	+50	2	2

Figure 9-4 *(continued)*

Rating		ADB	WP
Incomplete Right Bundle Branch Block	+0	Std.	Std.
Left Bundle Branch Block			
with well documented history			
—to age 45	+100	Dec.	Dec.
—over age 45	+50	Dec.	Dec.
if present over 5 years reduce ratings by ½			
with incomplete history			
—to age 45	+150	Dec.	Dec.
—over age 45	+100	Dec.	Dec.
if present over 5 years reduce ratings by ½			
with ischemic heart disease	refer Med. Dir. rate for cause and add +100 up	Dec.	Dec.

The Numerical Rating System

One risk classification method that has been used since the early 1900s is the *numerical rating system,* which is based on the following assumptions:

- Many medical and nonmedical factors affect the composition of a risk.
- The impact of each of these risk factors on mortality can be determined by a statistical study of people affected by these factors.
- A numerical value can be assigned to each risk factor according to its impact on mortality.

In the numerical rating system, most companies assign an average risk a numerical value of 100, or 100 percent of standard mortality. Favorable factors are assigned negative values, called *credits.* Unfavorable factors are assigned positive values, called *debits.* Credits are subtracted from the basic rating value; debits are added. The sum of the basic rating value (such as 100), the credits, and the debits equals the numerical value of the risk presented by a proposed insured. The following discussion assumes a base value of 100.

Assigning numerical values to risk factors

The values assigned to risk factors are estimated from mortality studies of people with those factors. For example, assume that the factor being studied is the impact of body weight on the mortality rate. A study determines that the mortality rate for people who are 25 percent overweight for their age, sex, and height is 130 percent of the mortality for people of standard weight. This degree of overweight, therefore, merits a debit of +30. Figure 9-5 illustrates the rating process used for a 50-year-old man.

Because standard risks are usually represented by ratings between 75 and 125 or 130 when using a base of 100 for standard mortality, the proposed insured in Figure 9-5 would probably be accepted as a standard risk. If a company also writes substandard insurance, it has to decide on a cutoff point—a numerical rating of 500, for example—above which it considers a risk to be uninsurable. Some companies underwrite policies with ratings in excess of another company's cutoff point.

Figure 9-5
Using the numerical rating system.

DATA

Sex	Age	Height	Weight	Abdominal Girth	Family History
male	50	6'0"	256 lb.	3" less than expanded chest	good health

Factor	Rating	
	Debit	Credit
Basic rating	100	
Build	50	
Girth		10
Family history		10
Subtotal	150	20

Total rating (debit − credit) = 130

Risk classes and the numerical rating system

After a proposed insured's numerical rating is established, he or she is assigned to one of the risk classes. If a substandard rating is indicated, the proposed insured is classified, according to rating tables, with other substandard risks who have the same expected mortality rates. Most companies have 14 or more rating tables, and each table represents a different level of risk. If the numerical rating of a proposed insured exceeds the maximum number in the highest rating table, that person is usually declined for insurance or told to reapply after the conditions that caused the rejection have changed or improved.

By classifying an individual as part of a rated risk group, the insurance company is not predicting the longevity of that person. However, the company is predicting that, on average, the risk group to which the applicant belongs will show a higher-than-average mortality rate.

Premiums for Substandard Risks

Once a proposed insured has been classified as a substandard risk, the insurer must determine the extra premium amount to charge for coverage. However, it would be impractical and costly for each company to develop a specific extra premium amount for every impairment. In addition, the effects of all impairments on mortality are not known well enough to compute such premiums accurately. Therefore, most companies proceed on the assumption that the hazards leading to a substandard risk classification fall into three broad groups:

- hazards that *remain about the same* as people grow older—for example, partial deafness or partial blindness
- hazards that *increase* with age—for example, untreated high blood pressure
- hazards that *decrease* with time—for example, conditions corrected by successful surgery

A number of methods have been devised for determining the premium rate to charge for those insureds classified as substandard risks, but only two are commonly used today: (1) *extra-percentage tables* and (2) *flat extra premiums*. Use of these methods varies from company to company.

Extra-percentage tables

The ***extra-percentage tables*** method is by far the most commonly used plan for computing premium rates for substandard risks. Under this method, substandard risks are divided into broad classes, according to their numerical ratings, and extra premiums are calculated for the average extra percentage mortality anticipated for each class. For example, all proposed insureds with a numerical rating of 145 to 155 might be put in one class. Substandard extra premiums would then be calculated for each issue age in that class by assuming 50 percent extra mortality for all ages and policy years. The total premium charged in such cases, except for some term policies, would be less than 150 percent of the gross standard premium, because expense loading on such policies is the same amount as loading charged on a standard policy. Also, the formula for applying the extra mortality percentage takes into account the fact that the net amount at risk on the policy decreases over time. The **net amount at risk** is calculated by subtracting from the policy's death benefit the amount of the policy's reserve at the end of the policy year.

The extra-percentage tables method is well suited for situations in which the extra risk increases as the insured grows older. Certain physical impairments, such as being overweight, show a pattern in which the risk of extra mortality increases slowly while the insured is fairly young but increases much more rapidly as the insured ages. The method is not as well suited to situations where the extra risk is constant or actually decreasing.

Flat extra premiums

The **flat extra premium** method of rating a substandard life insurance risk is used when the extra risk is considered to be constant or temporary. The underwriter assesses a specific extra premium for each $1,000 of insurance. This extra premium does not vary with the age of the proposed insured. For occupations and hobbies in which accidents are the chief cause of higher mortality rates, the flat extra premium is particularly appropriate. Usually, this method is not appropriate to cover the extra risks associated with most medical impairments, because such risks rarely remain constant. However, temporary flat extra premiums are used in connection with certain medical risks that are deemed to decrease over time. For example, a company might assess a flat extra premium of $5 per $1,000 for two years for someone who had tuberculosis one year previously but shows no signs of current infection.

The extra premium amount charged in both the extra-percentage tables method and the flat extra premium method covers only the increased mortality associated with the risk and, in most companies, does not affect the policy's cash value or dividends.

Reducing substandard premium rates

Policyowners who have been issued insurance on a substandard basis sometimes become eligible later to buy insurance at standard rates or at least at better rates than the original premium rates that were assessed. In some cases, the policyowners have been paying an extra premium because of some medical or physical impairment that has improved or disappeared since the policy was underwritten. However, if all the insureds whose conditions have improved were removed from the original risk group, the average mortality rate of those remaining in this group would rise. Nonetheless, a company must be ready to consider a premium reduction for any policyowner who demonstrates an improvement. Otherwise, the policyowner may let the original substandard policy lapse and apply for a new one at a lower rate, perhaps from a competing company. In either case, the substandard group's future mortality rate will increase when this policyowner leaves the group. The company protects itself against these increased mortality rates for groups by establishing a margin of safety in the premium rates for the various substandard groups.

When the risk is reduced because of an insured's change in residence or occupation, a few companies require a probationary period of six months to two years before considering the change permanent. At the end of this period, the company refunds the extra premium paid during the probationary period and changes the premium rate, making the change effective from the date when the change in occupation or residence was made.

UNDERWRITING INDIVIDUAL HEALTH INSURANCE

Essentially, the process and tools of underwriting are the same in both life and health insurance. In several areas, however, there are some significant differences, which are discussed in the following section of this chapter.

Assessing Risk Factors for Health Insurance

Because of the differences in assessing morbidity and mortality, some risk factors are considered differently in underwriting health insurance. For example, because the proposed insured is nearly always both the applicant and the proposed beneficiary of a health insurance policy, insurable interest

Figure 9-6
Basic steps involved in the underwriting process.

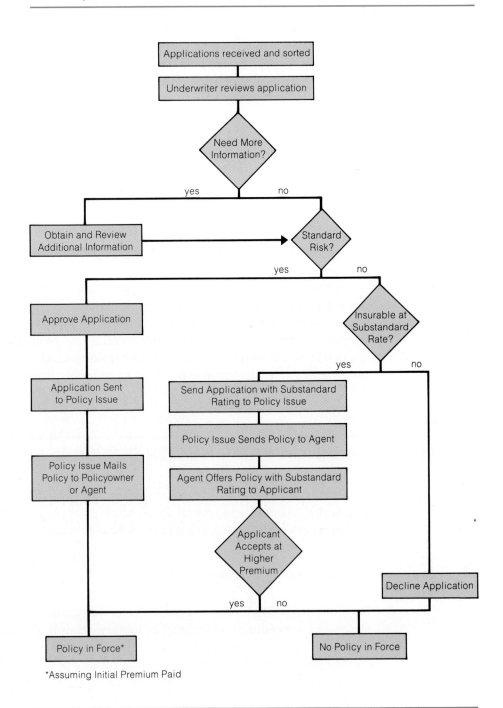

*Assuming Initial Premium Paid

is not as much of a concern as it is for life insurance. On the other hand, *occupation, antiselection, moral hazard,* and *finances* can be more important underwriting factors in health insurance than in life insurance. Furthermore, although the likelihood of a life insurance claim increases as the insured grows older, both the likelihood *and* severity of health insurance claims increase as the insured's age increases.

Occupation

Health insurance underwriters are concerned with any type of occupation that can increase the risk of accident or illness. ***Accident risks*** include exposure to fire, the use of dangerous machinery, the handling of heavy objects, and the risk of falling. ***Illness risks*** include exposure to dust, poisons, dampness, and extreme temperatures. The list below provides examples of risk classifications used for different occupational hazards.

- *Least Hazardous*—professional and office workers, such as lawyers, secretaries, and accountants
- *Hazardous*—manual laborers, such as house painters, plumbers, and carpenters; people who transport passengers in motor vehicles, such as cab drivers and bus drivers
- *Most Hazardous*—structural steelworkers and boilermakers
- *Uninsurable*—test pilots and war correspondents

Antiselection

Antiselection is another factor that is even more important for underwriting health insurance than it is for underwriting life insurance. Some people buy health insurance to provide benefits for a health problem that the insurance company is not aware of, but that the insured is. Insurers protect themselves from this type of antiselection by including pre-existing condition provisions in their policies. A ***pre-existing condition provision*** states that until coverage is in force for a specified period—usually one or two years—no benefit is payable if the condition that produces a claim (1) manifested itself before the issue date and (2) was not disclosed on the application.

Moral hazard

The danger that a proposed insured or an insured person might deliberately attempt to conceal or misrepresent pertinent information is a moral hazard that a health underwriter must consider as an important risk factor. For example, in order to receive financial benefits, an insured person could easily exaggerate the extent or duration of a disability. Therefore, the character of the proposed insured is one of the most important factors in health insurance underwriting, particularly disability income underwriting.

Finances

Health underwriters try to make certain that insureds are not purchasing more insurance than necessary. Disability income insurance, particularly, is intended to pay claimants a slightly lower after-tax income than they earned before they were disabled. The lower income provides insureds with an incentive to overcome their disabilities so they can begin working again and earning their previous income. An underwriter must determine a proposed insured's current income so that the insured is not sold a policy that will provide more income after disability than was earned before disability. In order to avoid an overinsurance situation, the underwriter must also determine if the proposed insured is already covered by a disability income policy.

Rating Substandard Risks in Health Insurance

Like life insurance underwriters, health insurance underwriters can accept, rate, or decline proposed insureds. In addition, health underwriters can modify the coverage originally requested and thereby offer proposed insureds some coverage, even if it is on a more limited basis. Health underwriters can modify insurance coverage by

- reducing the policy's benefit paying period
- reducing the benefit amount
- increasing the period of time that the insured must wait before benefits are payable
- attaching an **impairment rider,** also called an *impairment waiver,* to the contract in order to exclude or limit coverage for a specific health impairment

UNDERWRITING GROUP LIFE AND HEALTH INSURANCE

Most life and health insurance companies separate group underwriting from individual underwriting because of basic differences between them. With individual insurance, the underwriter is concerned solely with an individual applicant. In contrast, unless the group is small, group underwriting does not address the individual health, mortality or morbidity risk, or any other factor of each group member. In small groups—usually groups with fewer than 10 members—each member must provide evidence of insurability and be individually underwritten. For larger groups, however, the group underwriter evaluates the risk presented by the group as a whole.

Any large group of people includes individuals with medical impairments that would make them substandard or uninsurable risks if individual underwriting standards were used. The group underwriter is primarily concerned that the group proposed for insurance presents a *good distribution of risk,* meaning that the good health of a large number of individuals offsets the claim experience of the unhealthy group members. Because few groups are large enough to provide entirely predictable experience, insurers try to provide coverage to enough groups so that the accumulated number of insured people provides predictability. Underwriters usually reevaluate insured groups each year when the groups apply for renewal of their contracts.

New Business

The objective of the group underwriter is to make sure that the insured group or the aggregate of insured groups meets underwriting standards. The group underwriter relies on information supplied by the group representative and by the employer-applicant; such information is occasionally supplemented by inspection reports. Information collected by the insurer includes the group's prior claim experience, if any, and the distribution of men and women in the group. When evaluating an application, the group underwriter also considers the

- nature of the group
- age distribution of group members
- level of participation
- benefits applied for
- occupational hazards common to the group
- size of the group

Nature of the group

The purchase of insurance should be incidental to a group's primary purpose. If the purchase of insurance coverage were the main purpose for the group's existence, adverse selection would be more likely, because high-risk persons would naturally be attracted to membership. Standard risks would have less incentive to join or remain in the group. Purchasing insurance is obviously incidental to the purpose of an employer-employee group, which is the most common type of group covered by group insurance.

Age distribution of group members

Another important criterion of an eligible group is an expectation that a sufficient number of young members will be entering the group. Young new members are needed to replace those who leave the group and to keep the age distribution of the group stable. If a group did not add young new members for a number of years, then the increasing age of the group's original members would adversely affect the group's age distribution, and the group's claim rate would increase. However, if young new members are continually joining the group, the age distribution of the group and the expected claim rate should remain more stable.

Level of participation

To reduce the possibility of adverse selection, a group insurance policy must cover a large proportion of the people in the group. In a *noncontributory* plan—in which the policyholder, not the group members, pays the entire premium—broad coverage is not a problem; all eligible members of the group are covered. However, under a *contributory* plan—in which the group members must pay a portion of the premium—antiselection can occur because those in poorer health have a greater incentive to enroll than those in good health. A higher-than-average percentage of participants who are in poorer-than-average health will also eventually result in higher premiums for the group coverage, which will discourage those in good health from participating. Insurance companies reduce this antiselection risk by requiring that a certain minimum percentage of the total employees participate. The required percentage may vary by the size of the group; a smaller group requires a higher percentage of participation.

Benefits

Individual members of a group must not be allowed to choose the amount of their insurance protection. This rule guards against adverse selection, because people who would be classified as substandard risks are more likely to seek higher coverage than those who would be classified as standard risks.

Occupational hazards

The underwriter must evaluate any occupational hazards that could affect the group's claim rate. If the hazards are limited to a few group members and the group is small, the hazards may result in a slightly higher premium for only those members who represent an added risk. If such hazards are common throughout the group, they will be reflected in higher premiums for all group members.

Size of the group

If the group is comparatively small—25 or fewer members—special underwriting requirements are often imposed. For example, if the plan is contributory, the underwriter often requires a higher percentage of employee participation than under a large group plan. As mentioned earlier, if the group has fewer than 10 members to be insured, the underwriter may require some evidence of insurability from each individual member. These special requirements are necessary because such a small group cannot ensure a good distribution of risk.

Renewals

When a group life or health insurance policy is issued, the premium rate is guaranteed for a specific period, usually one year. At the end of the initial period, and usually each year thereafter, the underwriter must reevaluate the contract. At a minimum, this reevaluation focuses on two factors: the group's claim experience and, in contributory plans, the degree of participation.

If the claim experience for the previous year was favorable, the premium rates for the coming year may be reduced. If the experience was unfavorable, the underwriter can propose higher premium rates for the next year. This process of using a group's own experience to develop premium rates is known as *experience rating*, as discussed in Chapter 8.

The degree of importance an underwriter assigns to a group's claim experience varies with the size of the group. For a very large group, such as one with more than 1,000 members, the group's own claim experience is the primary factor in setting the group's premium rate. For a smaller group, the underwriter places less emphasis on the group's experience. For very small groups, such as those with fewer than 25 members, the underwriter pools the experience statistics from many small groups in order to develop accurate ratings. (This review of a group's experience can take place at the time of initial underwriting as well as at renewal. If an insurer is underwriting a group for the first time, the group's claim experience with its previous carrier is analyzed.)

In contributory plans, the degree of employee participation is verified to make sure that a sufficiently high level of participation exists and that chances of adverse selection are reduced. If the degree of participation has dropped below the acceptable level, the underwriter can require increased participation before the contract is renewed.

REINSURANCE

Just as individuals buy insurance to share risks, insurance companies also buy insurance to share their risks. This type of insurance is called *reinsurance.* One insurance company buys reinsurance from another insurance company to cover part or all of a risk that the original company will not or cannot undertake itself. The company seeking to reinsure a risk is the *ceding company,* or *direct-writing company.* The company accepting the risk is the *reinsurer,* or *assuming company.* Insured individuals whose policies have been reinsured are rarely aware that their protection involves reinsurance. The policyowners buy their policies from the ceding company, which remains legally responsible for the entire amount of any claim made under the policies.

Generally, insurance companies reinsure their policies for two reasons:

1. If an applicant wants a policy with a larger death benefit than the insurer can safely guarantee using its own resources, the company can seek a reinsurer to assume part of the risk.
2. If an insurer receives an application that would normally be classified as a substandard or uninsurable risk, the insurer may seek a reinsurer that specializes in such risks and which can offer better premium rates. By submitting substandard business for reinsurance, insurers can help their agents compete with other companies.

Some large insurance companies have personnel dedicated solely to reinsurance. In such companies, a *reinsurance officer* is responsible for arranging and administering reinsurance agreements. Other insurers use a committee of underwriters, actuaries, lawyers, and company executives to arrange reinsurance agreements; the agreements themselves are usually administered by underwriters or actuaries.

Retention Limits

Although a company may issue enough policies to be able to predict—with a good degree of accuracy—the number of claims it will receive each year, the dollar amount of the claims can fluctuate significantly, especially if the company issues policies for large amounts of coverage. A rapid succession of large claims can severely damage a company's financial position.

To protect itself against severe fluctuations in earnings caused either by large individual claims or by a high number of average-sized claims—perhaps from natural disasters or epidemics—the ceding company sets a *retention limit*. A **retention limit** is the maximum amount of insurance that a company carries at its own risk on any individual. Amounts above the retention limit are placed with a reinsurer. Reinsurers also have retention limits, and when the total amount of reinsurance in force and applied for on any one life exceeds the reinsurer's limits, the reinsurer cedes the excess amount of insurance to still another reinsurer. The process of one reinsurer's ceding its excess risk to another reinsurer is called **retrocession** (see Figure 9-7). The reinsurance company that accepts the excess risk of another reinsurer is called the **retrocessionaire.**

Figure 9-7
Reinsuring the risk.

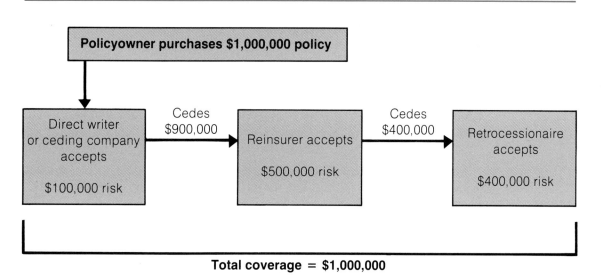

In setting retention limits, a company is influenced by several factors, which include the

- amount of surplus available in the company
- distribution of the company's insurance in force—by amounts, plans, age groups, geographical areas, and underwriting classifications
- probable distribution of new business, including the average death benefit per policy
- quality of the company's agency force
- quality of the home office underwriting staff
- cost of the reinsurance ceded
- type of product

There is no simple formula for setting a retention limit. Retention limits for life insurance typically range from as little as $10,000 in small, recently established companies to $10,000,000 or more in the largest companies. Many companies set a lower retention limit for substandard risks and older insureds. As ceding companies grow, they usually raise their retention limits. Therefore, agreements between ceding companies and reinsurers customarily include provisions allowing the ceding companies to *recapture* or take back from the reinsurers a portion of the reinsured business.

Some companies cede entire blocks of business to reinsurers. For example, assume that a company that has had no underwriting experience with substandard risks decides to improve the competitive position of its agents by accepting substandard risks. Through a reinsurance agreement, this company can pass its substandard business on to its reinsurer and use the reinsurer's underwriting facilities and experience to assess the substandard risks.

Most reinsurance companies employ experienced underwriters, and reinsurers can advise ceding companies about underwriting guidelines, rating classifications, and risk factors. Many insurance companies adopt and use the underwriting manuals developed by reinsurance companies rather than developing their own manuals.

Reinsurance Treaties

A reinsurance contract, also known as a **reinsurance treaty,** is the legal document between the ceding company and the reinsurer that specifies the risks that will be reinsured and the terms and conditions of reinsurance, including the reinsurance plan. A reinsurance treaty commonly provides for risk assumption under one of two primary methods: *automatic* and *facultative.* A ceding company can use one or both of these risk transfer methods with one or more reinsurers.

Automatic reinsurance treaty

Under an ***automatic reinsurance treaty,*** the reinsurer agrees to provide reinsurance automatically for all amounts in excess of the ceding company's retention limit up to some specified amount, called the ***automatic binding limit.*** For example, a reinsurer may give a ceding company an automatic binding limit for life insurance that is three times the ceding company's retention limit, with a maximum of $100,000. If a ceding company with a retention limit of $25,000 per individual decides to issue a $100,000 policy, then the ceding company would retain $25,000 of the coverage itself and cede the remaining $75,000 to its automatic reinsurer. If the amount of reinsurance needed exceeds the automatic binding limit, then the coverage is submitted to the reinsurer for consideration on a facultative basis (discussed below).

In an automatic reinsurance treaty, the ceding company agrees to cede to the reinsurer all accepted, eligible policies that are larger than the ceding company's retention limit. Because the reinsurer does not have to review and approve each application, the ceding company can issue policies for large amounts without delay. In fact, an automatic reinsurance agreement usually provides reinsurance coverage even if the insured dies before the ceding company has notified the reinsurer that the risk has been ceded.

In an automatic reinsurance treaty, the reinsurer relies on the accuracy of the ceding company's risk selection. However, the reinsurer is protected from too great a risk by the requirement that the ceding company must carry at its own risk the full retention limit on each policy issued. The reinsurer is also protected by reviewing ceding companies' underwriting standards and practices. In a sense, before obligating itself to accept their business, the reinsurance company "underwrites" the direct companies by auditing their underwriters and verifying the quality of their work.

Facultative reinsurance treaty

Under a ***facultative reinsurance treaty,*** the reinsurer makes an independent underwriting decision on each risk sent to it by the ceding company. The ceding company submits to the reinsurer copies of each application and any other information influencing the risk. The ceding company must then await the reinsurer's underwriting decision. The drawbacks created by the possible delays accompanying the reinsurer's underwriting process are offset to some extent by the fact that the ceding company is receiving a second underwriting opinion before issuing the policy. In some cases, the reinsurer has more information about a proposed insured than does the ceding company. For example, a reinsurer could receive concurrent applications for the same proposed insured from several ceding companies, none of which knows about the other applications.

In some cases, a ceding company submits a questionable risk to its automatic reinsurer on a facultative basis rather than bind the reinsurer automatically. As mentioned earlier, a ceding company also submits—on a facultative basis—amounts that exceed the ceding company's automatic binding limit.

Facultative-obligatory (fac-ob) reinsurance treaty. A variation of a facultative reinsurance treaty, called a *facultative-obligatory (fac-ob) reinsurance treaty*, combines the features of automatic and facultative treaties. With a *fac-ob treaty,* the ceding company does all the underwriting on the risks to be reinsured, sending no underwriting papers to the reinsurer. The facultative aspect of the fac-ob treaty is that the ceding company is sending only selected risks to the reinsurer, rather than all the risks, as with an automatic treaty. The automatic, or obligatory, aspect of the fac-ob treaty is that the reinsurer is obligated to accept submitted risks unless it does not have the retention capacity to cover the risk submitted.

Fac-ob treaties are uncommon and tend to be used by insurance companies that have high retention limits. Because of their high retention limits, such companies seldom need reinsurance. However, when they do need reinsurance for certain risks, they want an arrangement that requires little effort on their part. Fac-ob treaties provide such an arrangement.

Reinsurance Plans

Reinsurance plans differ in the risks assumed, the benefits paid, and premium payments. In this respect they are similar to the plans of insurance offered to the general public. Reinsurance plans can be grouped into two major categories: proportional and nonproportional. Under **proportional reinsurance plans,** which tend to be used with individual insurance, the different proportions of the risk that will be carried by the ceding company and by the reinsurer are specified when the reinsurance treaty is made. Under **nonproportional reinsurance plans,** which tend to be used with group insurance, the proportions of the risk to be carried by each company are not specified in the reinsurance treaty.

The most common types of proportional reinsurance are *yearly renewable term, coinsurance,* and *modified coinsurance.* Two common types of nonproportional reinsurance are *stop-loss reinsurance* and *catastrophic reinsurance.*

Yearly renewable term (YRT)

Under a *yearly renewable term (YRT) plan,* also called a *risk premium reinsurance (RPR) plan,* the ceding company purchases yearly renewable term insurance from the reinsurer. The amount of reinsurance coverage is equal to the net amount at risk on that portion of the original policy being reinsured. Typically, a reinsurance schedule is developed showing the YRT premiums and the portion of the net amount at risk to be reinsured each year.

The premium rate charged to the ceding company is often the result of negotiations between the ceding company and the reinsurer. Under a YRT reinsurance plan, the reinsurer is liable for its share of the net amount at risk when the insured dies, but the reinsurer does not contribute to any cash value payable when a reinsured policy is surrendered. Yearly renewable term premium rates sometimes provide for an experience refund, like those used in group insurance. For example, if the experience on a company's ceded business is good, the reinsurer refunds a portion of the premiums.

The YRT reinsurance plan has two distinct benefits: (1) it is easy to administer and (2) the ceding company retains the investment portion of the premium and, therefore, increases its assets. On the other hand, with a YRT plan the ceding company must establish reserves for the entire amount of the insurance, not just for the amount of insurance that it does not cede.

Coinsurance

Under a *coinsurance plan,* the ceding company pays the reinsurer part of the premium paid by the insured, minus an allowance for the ceding company's expenses. In return, the reinsurer agrees to pay the ceding company a proportionate part of the death benefit when a claim is filed and to contribute to all other policy benefits, including dividends, on a scale determined by the ceding company. In addition, the reinsurer agrees to accumulate the required reserves for the reinsured portion of the policy. For example, assume that a company with a life insurance retention limit of $100,000 issues a $250,000 policy and cedes $150,000 of the policy to a reinsurer under a coinsurance plan. The reinsurer is entitled to 60 percent (150,000 ÷ 250,000) of the gross premium, minus the expense allowance, and is liable for 60 percent of the claims, nonforfeiture values, reserves, and dividends relating to the policy. Thus, if the policy is terminated voluntarily, the reinsurer is liable for 60 percent of the policy's cash value.

An important benefit of coinsurance is that the reinsurer shares the strain on surplus that new business places on the ceding company. A major drawback of coinsurance is its effect on the assets of the ceding company. Asset growth is reduced because a portion of the premium must be transferred to the reinsurer and, therefore, is not available for investment by the ceding company. In addition, coinsurance plans can be more difficult to administer than YRT reinsurance plans, especially for companies that sell participating policies.

Modified coinsurance (modco)

Modified coinsurance (modco) plans are an attempt to overcome the adverse effect of coinsurance on asset growth. In a ***modco plan,*** the reinsurer receives its share of the gross premium minus an allowance for the ceding company's expense. However, the reserves for the entire policy are held by the ceding company. At the end of each year, the reinsurer transfers back to the ceding company an amount equal to the increase in the reserve for the reinsured portion, less the interest earned by the ceding company on the reinsured portion of the reserve fund. Except for the fact that the reserves are held by the ceding company, modco plans are similar to coinsurance plans.

Stop-loss and catastrophic reinsurance plans

Under a ***stop-loss reinsurance plan,*** also called an *excess-loss plan*, the reinsurer agrees to pay a percentage of all claims paid by the ceding company during a specified period that, in total, exceed a specified amount. For example, Argyle Reinsurance agrees to pay 90 percent of the amount by which Basilica Life's 1993 claims exceed $10 million. If Basilica paid $11 million in claims in 1993, Argyle would be obligated to pay Basilica $900,000 (90 percent of [$11 million − $10 million]).

Under a ***catastrophic reinsurance plan,*** when a specified minimum number of claims result from a single accidental occurrence—such as more than two claims resulting from an airplane crash, hurricane, or earthquake—the reinsurer pays losses in excess of the plan deductible. The reinsurer's liability is limited to a maximum amount per catastrophe.

RELATIONSHIPS WITH OTHER COMPANY PERSONNEL

Underwriters are in close contact with many other insurance company personnel. Their most frequent contacts are generally with the company's agents, marketing department, actuaries, policy issue personnel, customer service staff, and claim examiners. Figure 9-8 illustrates some of the essential contacts between underwriters and other company personnel.

Figure 9-8
Relationship of the underwriting department with other departments.

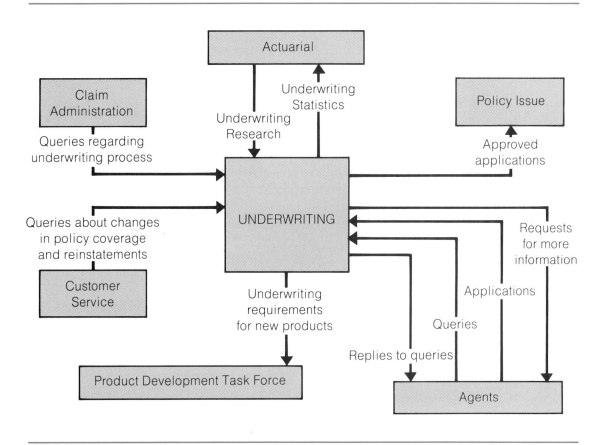

Sales and Marketing

Underwriters probably interact with insurance agents more often than they do with other company personnel. A steady stream of communications passes between the agent force and underwriters. Branch managers and managing general agents usually communicate with underwriters to

- ask about the status of certain applications
- determine why certain applications are being rated instead of being issued at standard rates
- ask the underwriters about the significance of an unusual answer on an application

- alert the underwriters that an agent is sending an unusual application to the home office

Similarly, underwriters frequently contact agents to ask for more information about an application or to explain why particular applications were rated or declined. Underwriters may not, however, discuss any medical information they have received from the MIB or the proposed insured's personal physician. When agents and underwriters have different opinions about underwriting decisions, compromises between these two parties may allow the agent to make a sale without jeopardizing the risk position of the company.

More experienced underwriters may also be asked to conduct training sessions and explain underwriting principles and guidelines to agents and marketing staff. In addition, underwriters usually inform the marketing staff about the underwriting skills and deficiencies of the company's agents and suggest ways to improve agents' field underwriting.

Actuaries

As seen in the previous two chapters, underwriters rely on actuaries for the statistics that are used to develop underwriting guidelines and risk classifications. Underwriters usually inform actuaries about the effectiveness of the guidelines and suggest changes that are appropriate from an underwriting standpoint. Medical directors' staffs are especially important in working with actuaries to develop appropriate underwriting guidelines.

Policy Issue

The policy issue unit is usually a part of the underwriting department. Wherever policy issue is handled, when an application is approved, the underwriters must transfer documents and any electronically stored information to the policy issue unit. That unit then makes sure that a policy is prepared and delivered to the correct person.

Customer Service

Sometimes underwriters must review requests for policy changes that are directed first to customer service personnel. For example, if a policyowner requests an increased amount of coverage, an underwriter may have to evaluate the additional risk. In those cases, the underwriter decides whether additional evidence of insurability is needed before the increase can be approved.

Another aspect of cooperation with the customer service area concerns former policyowners' requests to have their policies reinstated. Simple reinstatements are often done by customer service staff. However, if the request for reinstatement presents any complications—such as a significant change in the proposed insured's health or occupation—or if the reinstatement request is made after a specified time has passed, the case is referred to an underwriter for review. Under certain circumstances, the underwriter requires current evidence of insurability before authorizing the reinstatement.

Claim Administration

Underwriters and claim specialists usually work together when claims are made during a policy's contestable period. If claim investigators find any misrepresentation on the original application, they ask the underwriters to reevaluate the application to see if they would have approved the application with the same rating or if they would have issued a policy on any basis had the truth about the applicant been known.

KEY TERMS

underwriting	credit
rating an application	debit
field underwriting	extra-percentage tables
worksheet	net amount at risk
jet screening	flat extra premium
computer screening	accident risk
Attending Physician's Statement (APS)	illness risk
Medical Information Bureau (MIB)	pre-existing condition provision
inspection report	impairment rider
underwriting impairment	good distribution of risk
substance abuse	reinsurance
insurable interest	ceding company
antiselection	reinsurer
risk class	retention limit
underwriting manual	retrocession
numerical rating system	retrocessionaire

reinsurance treaty
automatic reinsurance treaty
automatic binding limit
facultative reinsurance treaty
facultative-obligatory (fac-ob)
    reinsurance treaty
proportional reinsurance

nonproportional reinsurance
yearly renewable term (YRT) plan
coinsurance
modified coinsurance (modco) plan
stop-loss reinsurance plan
catastrophic reinsurance plan

NOTE

1. The following section is adapted from Richard Bailey, *Underwriting in Life and Health Insurance Companies* (Atlanta: LOMA, 1985), Chapter 1.

Chapter 10

The Customer Service Function

After reading this chapter, you should be able to

- List several types of customers that insurance companies serve
- Describe some skills needed by employees who provide effective customer service
- Discuss different ways to organize the customer service function in a company
- Describe customer service functions that must be performed for individual and group insurance

Life and health insurance companies spend considerable time, effort, and money to market insurance protection and other types of financial products to prospective policyowners. This investment in a customer's business is wasted, however, if that customer becomes dissatisfied with the quality of service the company provides and stops doing business with the company. *Customer service* refers to the broad range of activities that a company and its employees undertake in order to keep customers satisfied so they will continue doing business with the company and speak positively about the company to other potential customers. Providing customer service involves learning what customers want and taking whatever reasonable steps are required to make sure they get it.

The service relationship between an insurance company and an insurance customer begins before a sale is made and continues throughout the life of the insurance policy or other financial product. In recent years especially, competition among insurers and other financial services providers has made good service vital to the successful operation of a life and health insurance company.

In this chapter, we will begin our discussion by presenting some basic concepts of customer service: who the customer is and who provides customer service. Then, we will discuss the manner in which customer service departments are organized and the assistance that people in these areas provide for their customers.

WHO IS THE CUSTOMER?

The perception of who exactly the customer is has widened considerably to embrace virtually all people who come into contact with a life and health insurance company—that is, all of the company's clients and constituents. An insurance company's customers can be divided into two general categories: external customers and internal customers.

An *external customer* is any person or business who is not on the insurance company's employee payroll and who is in a position either to (1) buy or use the insurance company's products or (2) advise others to buy or use its products. The best known among these customers are, of course, the people who actually use insurance products. For example, individual policyowners, annuity contract owners, insureds, beneficiaries, and group policyholders (such as corporations and unions that buy insurance coverage for their group members) are classified as external customers. Other external customers include insurance brokers, employee-benefits advisers, and insurance consultants who help group insurance purchasers choose the products they need.

Insurance company employees who keep the business of policyowners in force may be customers, too. These employees who receive service from other employees of the company are referred to as *internal customers.* For example, accounting, information systems, and human resources employees provide essential services to internal customers such as underwriters and customer service representatives.

In addition to those groups of customers who can be classified strictly as either internal or external, there is a group of customers who can be both internal and external customers. These are the people who actually sell insurance products and who are compensated by an insurance company for making sales. This category includes career agents, agent-brokers, licensed brokers, home service agents, personal producing general agents (PPGAs), and salaried sales representatives. These people are among an insurance company's most important customers because they are responsible for the sales that produce the company's income.

We will now look more closely at four major categories of life and health insurance company customers—policyowners/insureds, agents, beneficiaries, and account holders—to examine the nature of the customer service

Figure 10-1
Some relationships of the customer service department.

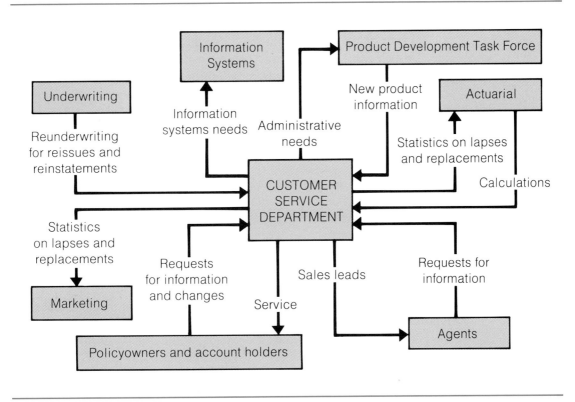

relationship and look at the types of transactions with which these customers might need assistance (see Figure 10-1).

Policyowners

Policyowners typically contact the customer service area to notify the company of address changes, to change beneficiary designations, and to change the coverages that their policies provide. Policyowners can, for example, ask questions about the cash value of their whole life policies or the benefits provided by their health insurance. They can ask about the investment results being realized on their equity-based insurance policies, their annuities, their pension plans, or their 401(k) plans. When insurance is marketed through direct response methods, without field agents or brokers, policyowners receive almost all of their information and assistance from the company's customer service department.

In most companies that use the agency distribution system, part of the agent's role is to provide continuing service to the individuals and businesses who bought insurance policies from that agent. Sometimes, however, policyowners and agents lose contact with one another. For example, the policyowner or the agent might move, or the agent might retire or change jobs. In such cases, the insurance company often assigns a new agent to the policyowner. Occasionally, it becomes the responsibility of the customer service department to provide such orphaned policyowners with complete insurance service.

Agents

Customer service personnel provide agents with a number of valuable services. Policyowners often contact their agents for either policy information or changes. Agents may then forward the policyowner's request to the customer service area. Also, complex questions—regarding, for example, the contractual terms, the design of the contract, the intent of contract language, and the administration of each aspect of a contract—are sent to a customer service employee who specializes in such questions.

Providing agents with prompt, accurate information is one of the most important functions of the customer service department, because the agent's relationship with the policyowner depends on the quality of this service. If responses from the customer service department are slow or incomplete, the policyowner may blame the agent. In order to reduce possible delays, many companies now provide agents in branch offices and agency offices with electronic access to policy information. Computer terminals tied into the home office's records and files give agents direct access to information on policyowners and contracts. An essential function of the customer service staff in this situation is to keep the company's files up-to-date.

In addition, customer service representatives provide agents with a variety of sales leads and can help agents conserve policies that have already been sold. For example, if a policyowner asks the customer service department to add a newborn child to a life insurance policy that covers the entire family, such a request could indicate that the policyowner needs to increase coverage. By passing this information on to agents, the customer service area can enhance the service that the agents provide and potentially bring new business to the company.

Beneficiaries

When an insured dies, the beneficiary may contact the customer service department to ask for clarification about the policy's benefits. Beneficiaries may want to know when they will receive their benefits, exactly how much the benefits will be, and what steps, if any, must be taken to receive the benefits. Many of these questions can be answered by claim administrators, but customer service personnel must be prepared either to answer such questions or to help the beneficiaries find the answers. Beneficiaries may also have questions about optional modes of settlement. Customer service specialists can describe each mode and identify the procedures for selecting one. Members of the customer service staff must remember that before the death of the insured, the beneficiary is entitled to only basic information about the policy, unless the beneficiary is an irrevocable beneficiary.

Account Holders

Insurance companies that administer 401(k) plans, mutual funds, individual annuities, and pension plans must provide their customers with service, although the type of service differs from that provided to insurance policyowners. Generally, financial account holders need periodic investment reports, and they often have questions about their financial holdings. For example, account holders may ask if they can transfer funds among the available investment funds without being charged handling fees, or they may want to know the current value of their single-premium deferred annuities. Customer service specialists must be familiar with the different financial products that their company offers and be prepared to answer questions about them.

WHO PROVIDES CUSTOMER SERVICE?

Anyone in an insurance company may be called upon at any time to provide customer service. However, a customer service representative is usually the first person that comes to mind when we think of customer service. To provide complete, prompt, accurate, courteous, and confidential service to policyowners, insurance companies establish customer service departments, or customer service areas within different operating units. Frequently, these departments or areas have both an administrative and a customer service function.

The customer service staff is responsible for administering contract values, maintaining policy records, informing policyowners of developments affecting their contracts, and processing any policyowner-requested changes. In some companies, customer service personnel are also responsible for underwriting, policy issue, premium billing and collection, agent compensation, and claim administration. Other names for a customer service department include the *policyowner service department, client service department, service and claim department,* and *policy administration department.* These other names, once again, reflect how broadly the customer service function is perceived.

Because administrative services are part of what customers purchase when they buy insurance policies, performing such tasks will always be an important part of what customer service representatives do. However, a growing number of insurance companies are asking their customer service representatives to do more. They want their representatives to think not only of the specific request that a customer brings them, but to go beyond that request and consider the entire array of customer needs that the company can fill. Customer service representatives are being trained to understand the full range of a company's products and activities and to recognize marketing opportunities. Customer service representatives are expected to have or to develop skills and knowledge in the following areas:

- *Communication skills.* Not only must customer service personnel be able to write effective letters, but they must also be able to communicate effectively on the telephone and in person.
- *Broad interpersonal skills.* Interpersonal skills are closely related to communication skills and help customer service staff listen more effectively, negotiate mutually satisfactory solutions, and gauge the effect their service has on their customers. Highly developed interpersonal skills also allow customer service employees to work with a variety of personality types and a variety of situations, such as dealing with upset customers.
- *Understanding of customers' motivations.* To serve their customers better, customer service representatives should understand their customers' wants and needs. People who work in the customer service area should use their experience to ask questions that may elicit more information from their customers. They should also understand what sort of service customers expect to receive and how customers perceive the service they are given. Many companies today either conduct their own surveys or contract with outside firms to determine their customers' expectations and service perceptions.
- *Computer skills.* Customer service personnel must typically be able to use computers to perform, or retrieve the results of, policy value calculations. Also, computers can help customer service personnel develop and present alternatives to help solve customers' problems.
- *Knowledge of company products.* Customer service personnel must be

able to grasp not only the basic features of traditional and nontraditional life products but also the complexities of many health insurance coverages. The nontraditional life products are especially service-intensive. Because these policies are less standardized, customers have more questions, and because the values of these policies change more frequently than those of traditional products, customers require more frequent information about them. Also, customer service representatives can be more helpful when they have knowledge of the interrelationships among a company's products and how to meet the potential needs of a customer with a variety of company products.

- *Knowledge of the company's position relative to the industry.* Knowing about the products offered by competitors and how these products compare with those of their own company is important for customer service personnel, because customers want this type of information. Many customers also want to know about the company's financial stability and performance as compared to other companies.

Customer service representatives are being given more authority to make customer service decisions and are being encouraged to come up with creative solutions to customers' problems. In short, customer service representatives are being trained to provide sophisticated customer service, rather than being limited to administrative assistance.

ORGANIZATION OF CUSTOMER SERVICE DEPARTMENTS

Customer service departments may be structured in a variety of ways. The most common organizational structures are functional organization, product organization, customer organization, geographical organization, and team organization.

Functional Organization

When customer service departments were first established, most were organized along functional lines. Although many companies continue with some form of functional structure, strict functional structures are becoming less common. In a functional structure, each customer service specialist performs one task—such as changing a policy's beneficiary or providing information on cash values—or a few tasks that are similar in nature. If the customer's request involves more than one area of inquiry, then the customer

Figure 10-2
Organization chart of a customer service department organized by function.

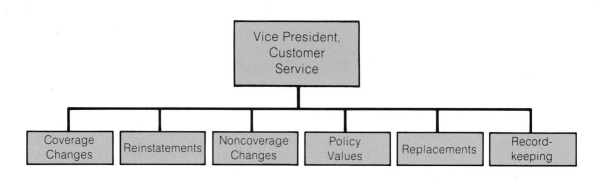

is transferred or referred to another specialist. This structure allows customer service specialists to become very proficient at their work, but in many companies customer service personnel are also rotated from one task to another on a regular basis. This cross-training allows customer service personnel to develop a broad base of job-related skills. Figure 10-2 illustrates a functional organizational structure.

Product Organization

As insurance products changed and insurers began offering more types of products, many companies began to organize customer service departments by product line, such as individual insurance, group insurance, health insurance, annuities, and pensions. In this type of organization, customer service personnel are trained in certain product lines and work only with those products. A product-based organization for the customer service function can be an effective structure for policyowners who concentrate their policy portfolios in a particular product.

A product-based customer service structure can be particularly useful in a company that markets investment-based products. Such products have a number of changeable aspects that policyowners and company personnel monitor closely. For example, variable universal life insurance has a savings element that is largely separated, or *unbundled*, from the insurance element. Savings elements fluctuate in value with the investment earnings of the insurance company, and policyowners watch their values closely. Customer service personnel are expected to understand how these unbundled policies work and to provide policyowners with information about the savings elements. For example, customer service specialists must

- be able to tell policyowners the value of the savings elements in their policies and the minimum premium or cost of insurance they need to pay to keep the policies in force
- make sure that the cash value does not exceed the guidelines established for a life policy to qualify as insurance
- send periodic reports to policyowners, showing the current value of each policy and the amount of interest being earned on the savings element

In addition, many insurance products allow for variable premium payments, as long as the payments meet the minimum policy requirements. Customer service personnel must be able to advise a policyowner about the minimum payments needed to keep a policy in force and the effects on the policy if larger payments are made.

Finally, because of the service-intensive nature of investment-based products, customer service professionals are more involved than ever before in the development and revision of new products. As mentioned in previous chapters, customer service personnel frequently serve on product design task forces. They advise actuaries about the administrative requirements for a new or revised product. They collaborate with information systems specialists and accounting staff in developing an effective computer system to help the customer service department administer the product.

One drawback to a product-based customer service structure is that a customer who has more than one policy with a company must deal with more than one customer service representative.

Customer Organization

Some companies have found that organizing by customer is an effective method of structuring the customer service function. In this form of organization, each agent and policyowner is assigned to a specific unit, or, more often, to a specific staff member in the customer service department. This staff member is responsible for processing all but the most unusual transactions for that agent and policyowner. Organizing by customer is popular with policyowners and agents alike, for they know exactly who to contact in the company. This type of organization requires customer service staff to be highly skilled and become experts in certain insurance products and in all aspects of customer service. From the customers' viewpoint, they do not have to know about a company's organization in order to find out who can answer their questions.

Some drawbacks to the customer-based organization are that it is expensive to maintain and that balancing the workload among customer service employees can be difficult.

Information systems that allow a single customer service representative to complete most customer transactions on-line have helped increase the practicality of customer organization.

Geographical Organization

Customer service departments can also be organized with geographical or decentralized structures (see Figure 10-3). Some companies that market their products over large areas and across several time zones have established regional service centers staffed with customer service personnel and other insurance professionals. More often, however, customer service departments are maintained only in the home office and may be divided into sections that serve only specific regions. By establishing computer networks for agents and toll-free (800) numbers for policyowners, many decentralized companies have found that regional service centers are not needed. The

Figure 10-3
Organization chart of a customer service department organized by region and function.

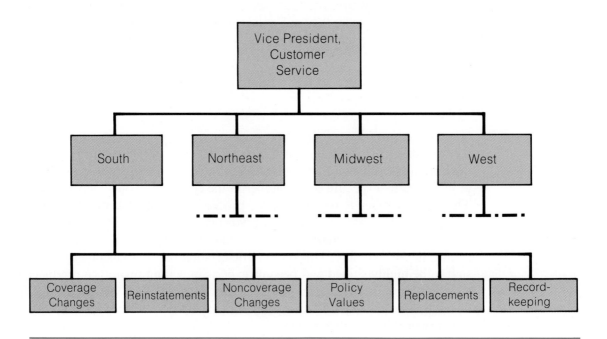

starting time for employees can be scheduled to accommodate the hours needed to provide service to a specific geographic region. For example, people serving the East Coast start work earlier than those servicing the West. Also, products sold and service demands may differ among geographic areas.

Each of the preceding organizational structures can be used in combination with the others to make customer service operations more effective. For example, a customer service department might be organized by region, but each region might then be organized by customer or function. Alternatively, a department that is organized by product line might then be organized by function, region, or customer (see Figures 10-4 and 10-5).

Team Organization

A number of insurance companies use the team structure for the customer service area. In a team structure, the customer service department is divided

Figure 10-4
Organization chart of a customer service department organized by product and function.

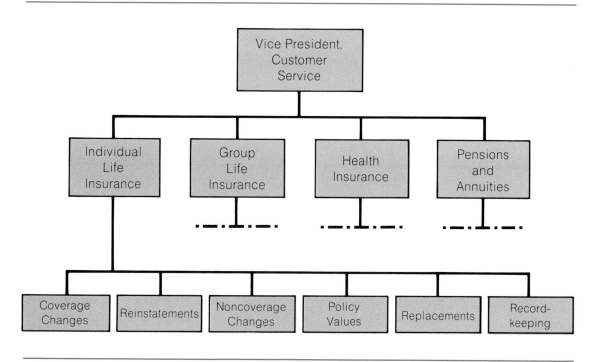

Figure 10-5
Organization chart of a customer service department organized by customer and product.

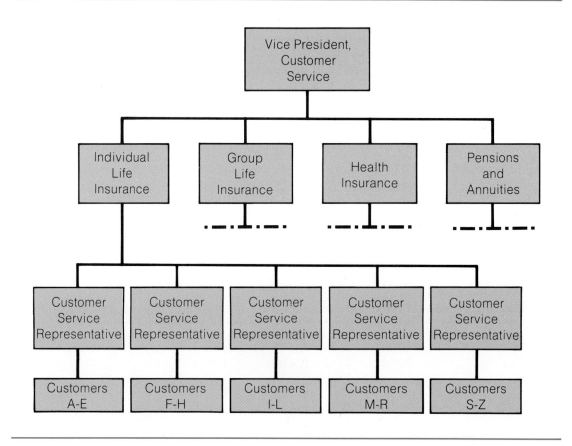

into several teams, with each team usually serving a particular region or group of customers. Within the team (which often consists of four to eight members), each member is trained to handle any typical customer service function. What sets the team organizational structure apart, however, is that the team members also plan their own work and vacation schedules, recommend improvements in operating procedures, and even address disciplinary matters within the team. In many ways, team members are expected to manage themselves. Their managers' functions are to ensure that proper support is available and to approve or disapprove team decisions. This structure gives team members more autonomy and leaves managers with more time for planning and dealing with unusual occurrences. A team organization generally requires a large customer base and a large staff.

CUSTOMER SERVICE FOR INDIVIDUAL LIFE INSURANCE

Customer service personnel working in individual life insurance perform a variety of administrative functions. Some of the most common are

- changing policy coverage, such as adding supplementary benefit riders to policies
- reinstating lapsed policies
- quoting cash surrender values and policy loan values and processing relevant transactions
- administering policy replacements
- making administrative changes (name, address, beneficiary, and ownership changes, for example)
- keeping necessary records

In the next few pages, we will discuss these functions and how they are carried out. Look at INSIGHT 10-1 for an example of how one company *initiates* customer service rather than waiting for a customer to call.

INSIGHT 10-1

Multipurpose Welcome Letter

In recent years, Great-West Life observed that, with today's complex insurance products, its customer service department was receiving many telephone calls and letters from clients who did not fully understand the insurance product they purchased. Whether they did not comprehend the policy's variable interest rates or did not get a complete explanation of policy features from the agent, the potential result was a disgruntled client.

To help solve the problem, Great-West Life's customer service department began sending a modified form of welcome letter. The letter goes out 45 days after the policy has been recorded in force at the company's home office. Each letter is product-specific to a large extent and gives the highlights of the particular product purchased.

Great-West provides its clients with their customer service 800 number in the letter. The customer service department also uses the letter to enclose one of their service brochures, which highlights the services that are available through the home office.

Source: Adapted with permission from an Activity Report submitted to LOMA by Ted Gacek of Great-West Life, June 1991.

Changing Policy Coverage

The customer service staff usually administers policyowners' requests to change the coverage provided in their policies. Three common ways to change coverage on individual life insurance policies are through policy conversions, benefit riders, and reissues.

Policy conversions

Many insurance policies contain a conversion privilege, which may take a number of forms. In a group insurance policy, a **conversion privilege** gives an insured group member the right to convert his or her group coverage to coverage under an individual insurance policy. The conversion can be made when a person leaves the group or when the group master policy is terminated. The conversion privilege in an individual insurance policy gives the policyowner the right in certain prescribed situations to change coverage from one type of policy to another—for example, from a term insurance policy to a whole life insurance policy on a prespecified date or event.

When a policyowner or insured group member invokes the conversion privilege, the customer service department can often process the request. If the conversion does not require an increase in the net amount at risk or if the increase in the net amount at risk is minimal, the conversion generally does not require any evidence of insurability. However, before a conversion can be processed, customer service representatives must typically do the following:

- verify that the conversion has taken place during the conversion period, if the company has limited that period
- verify that the new policy is from the approved list of plans if the company limits the plan type
- if the policyowner paid a full year's premium on the old policy, credit the policyowner with any premium amount that was not used during the final year of the old policy
- calculate a new premium rate for the converted policy
- calculate any special conversion credit offered by the company

Most calculations are generated from actuarial records, and customer service personnel can access this information electronically.

Once the conversion is approved, a new policy is issued to replace the old one. Some companies require payment of the first premium at the time a conversion is requested. Most companies, however, allow the agent to collect the first premium payment when the new policy is delivered to the policyowner.

Supplementary benefit riders

Policyowners sometimes want to revise the conditions of their coverage. Such changes can be made by purchasing additional policies that incorporate the added benefits. At other times, however, riders are added to an existing policy. A *rider* is an addition to an insurance policy which expands or limits the benefits payable and which becomes a part of the insurance contract. In particular, *supplementary benefit riders* are added to insurance policies in order to provide additional benefits. Some typical supplementary benefit riders are accidental death coverage, a waiver of premium benefit, and term insurance. Some companies also offer an increasing coverage benefit to assist in countering the effects of inflation. In evaluating a request for a supplementary benefit rider, customer service representatives usually consider the following information:

- type and amount of current coverage
- type of supplementary benefit rider and amount of coverage requested
- risk classification of the insured, based on factors such as age, health, and occupation
- length of time the present policy has been in force
- amount of time since the last evidence of insurability was submitted

Frequently, customer service representatives evaluate supplementary benefit rider requests by using guidelines that show acceptable ranges in these areas. If all the risk factors are favorable and if the rider amount is not unusually large, the request is often approved immediately. However, if the risk factors are less favorable or if the requested amount is large, additional steps are taken.

At the simplest level, the additional steps involve no more than an evaluation by a customer service supervisor, manager, or senior staff member. If the risk is large, the policyowner may be told that additional evidence of insurability is required. Sometimes this requirement involves a medical examination of the insured. Such cases are usually referred to the company's underwriters. In other cases, approval of the request is delayed pending an investigation. For example, a request for a large accidental death benefit rider might be held until the company verifies the insured's occupational status. Once the company approves the issue of the supplementary benefit rider, the customer service department mails the rider, an endorsement, or an entirely new policy to the policyowner.

Just as a policyowner can add a supplementary rider to a policy, a policyowner can also cancel a supplementary rider. Canceling a rider is easier than adding one, because appraisal factors do not need to be considered. When a policyowner cancels a rider, some adjustments to the premium amount may have to be calculated and, in some cases, a refund paid.

Reissues

At times, a policyowner may want to change a policy's coverage without having to undergo all the steps involved in reapplying for insurance. In such cases, the insurance company may agree to reissue the current policy with certain changes that fit the needs of the policyowner. For example, a policyowner may want a reissued policy if the original policy contained an error, such as the misspelling of a name or the recording of an incorrect beneficiary designation. Two other reasons for reissue are to reduce the death benefit of the policy and to change the insured on a key-person insurance plan.

Reducing the death benefit.   When policyowners decide that they are overinsured or that they cannot afford the cost of their current policies, they can request a reduction in the death benefit of their current policies. This change can usually be handled by customer service personnel, who perform the following activities:

- reissuing the policy
- paying the policyowner any required refund of premiums paid on the old coverage
- paying any difference in cash values between old and new policies

No underwriting is required to reduce a policy's death benefit. In some companies, reductions in death benefits are treated as replacements. Replacements will be discussed later in this chapter.

Changing insureds.   Many businesses buy key-person insurance to insure the lives of employees who are considered essential to the successful operation of the business. However, if a key person leaves a company and someone else is hired or promoted who is also considered essential, the company must insure the new key person. Rather than surrender the policy on the former key person and buy a policy for the new key person, the company may want to transfer coverage from the former insured to the current insured. If the insurance company agrees to reissue the policy for the new insured, the customer service department must ensure that the appropriate name changes are made and that policy values and premium charges are recalculated according to the new insured's mortality risk.

Reinstatements

Nearly all insurance companies handle reinstatements of lapsed policies in the same way, although specific criteria for approval vary. Each company reviews the reinstatement request, giving consideration to several factors.

First, the policyowner must send a signed request form within a specified time after the policy has lapsed. This period may vary from two to five years, depending on the type of life insurance policy involved. Next, the policyowner pays all unpaid premiums in arrears. Insurance companies can require the policyowner to pay interest on the unpaid premiums, but not all companies do so. Some states limit the interest rate that companies can charge on unpaid premiums. If a loan against the lapsed policy is unpaid, that loan must either be repaid or restored. If the loan is restored, the policy is reinstated with the unpaid policy loan still outstanding.

More complex is the requirement for the applicant to show evidence of insurability. The type of evidence required depends on several factors:

- length of time the policy has been lapsed
- type and amount of coverage
- risk classification of the insured at the time the policy was issued

When considering these factors, the company goes through a process similar to the consideration of requests for supplementary benefit riders. The customer service area uses guidelines to help make reinstatement decisions. In most cases, if the lapse period is short—say, 10 to 90 days—and the amount of coverage is not unusually large, the customer service unit is authorized to approve the reinstatement immediately. However, as the lapse period lengthens, the company will more likely require evidence of insurability.

Sometimes, the policyowner is advised that applying for a new policy may be better than reinstating the old one. Reinstatement frequently requires the payment of all unpaid back premiums. Therefore, when the duration of the lapse is long, applying for a new policy may sometimes be cheaper. On the other hand, the old policy may contain provisions that are not currently available to the policyowner or insured. Loan interest rates, for example, may be lower in the old policy, or the old policy may offer options and benefits no longer available under new policies. Also, premiums for a reinstated policy would be based on the original age and would therefore be lower than a new policy, especially if the original policy had been in force for a long period of time.

A reinstated policy's original suicide and contestable periods may have expired. Reinstated policies, however, have a new suicide period as well as a new contestable period for statements made in the reinstatement application. In at least one state in the United States, a reinstated policy must measure the suicide and contestable period from the *original* policy date.

Policy Values

Probably the most common inquiry a customer service department receives is a question about a policy's financial value. These inquiries might be about the current loan value or cash surrender value of a policy, the rate of interest credited to accounts, or the company's current policy dividend schedule. Other examples of policy value inquiries include currently available retirement incomes, future death benefit values based on a certain level of premiums paid, and the surrender value of paid-up additions to a policy. In most companies, customer service personnel can retrieve policy value information electronically and, if the caller gives proper identification, can give the information over the telephone. Customer service representatives must also be familiar with the degree to which policy values are subject to taxation in order to answer inquiries on that matter.

Just as it is important to notify agents of potential sales leads resulting from customer service requests, as mentioned earlier, it may also be important to notify agents of client inquiries regarding policy values. These types of inquiries may be signals that a customer's financial position has changed. An experienced agent who is notified of such inquiries knows when and how to follow up with the customer to help the customer solve any problems and to conserve the customer's business if possible.

Policy loans

When a policyowner requests a policy loan, customer service personnel examine the policy record to be sure that the proper person has made the request. If ownership of the policy has been assigned to another individual or organization or if the owner has designated an *irrevocable beneficiary*, additional signatures must be obtained. An **irrevocable beneficiary** is one whose rights to the proceeds of a life insurance policy cannot be canceled by the policyowner unless the beneficiary consents. In effect, the loan reduces the irrevocable beneficiary's interest in the policy. Once the loan request is verified as legitimate, the cash value of the policy is computed, to be sure the amount of the loan does not exceed the amount available for borrowing.

Depending on company requirements, policy loan requests can be made by mail or telephone. Sometimes the policyowner requests a loan for the maximum amount available. At other times, the policyowner requests a specific amount. If the policyowner requests a loan for more than the loan value of the policy, most companies process a loan for the highest possible amount and notify the policyowner of the reason for not granting the full amount of the request.

Premium loans

In some cases, policyowners establish a program to use policy loans to pay each premium. Policies on which premiums are systematically paid in this manner are referred to as ***minimum deposit business,*** or *leveraged business.* In minimum deposit business, a policyowner instructs the insurance company to pay premiums out of the policy's cash value and to send a premium notice only if the cash value is insufficient to pay the premium. Customer service staff must know how to handle the administration of minimum deposit business.

Some life insurance policies have an automatic premium loan provision. If a premium is not paid on time, a loan to pay the premium is automatically made against the cash value of the policy, thus preventing the policy from lapsing. The automatic premium loan is also beneficial to the company because it keeps policies in force and prevents the additional administrative cost of restoring lapsed policies. When an automatic premium loan is applied, the customer service representative needs to be prepared to explain to the customer the contractual provisions of such a loan and its impact on the policy's cash value and death benefit.

Policy dividends

The owners of participating life insurance policies may elect any of several basic dividend options. Depending on the options offered by their companies, policyowners can

- receive the dividends in cash
- leave the dividends with the company to accumulate with interest
- use the dividends to reduce the amount of the policy premiums
- use the dividends to buy paid-up additional insurance of the same kind as provided by the policy
- use the dividends to buy one-year term life insurance up to the amount of the cash value

Policyowners choose one of these options when they apply for insurance. Many policies also have a default option if one of these options is not chosen. Policyowners can change the option, usually at any time during the life of a policy. However, most companies require evidence of insurability if, after a policy is in force, the policyowner asks to use the dividends to buy one-year term life insurance.

Customer service representatives must be prepared to tell policyowners the amount of any dividend payment that the company has declared for the coming year. Customer service personnel must also answer questions about past dividend payments and resolve any problems that policyowners have in receiving their dividends. Customer service personnel can also inform policyowners about the current value of their accumulated dividends. Another part of the customer service function involves sending policyowners and taxation authorities the necessary tax information forms for reporting any interest that the dividends have earned in the current year. The customer service department also administers changes from one dividend option to another and processes policyowners' requests to withdraw dividends.

Surrenders

When customer service personnel receive a request for the cash surrender of a policy, they must make certain that the person making the request has the legal right to do so. Ordinarily, the policyowner has such a right, but the right has sometimes been transferred by assignment of ownership. Before processing a surrender, customer service representatives usually contact the policyowner and the policyowner's agent in an attempt to conserve the policy or to determine whether the policyowner has new insurance needs that require a new policy.

Once the surrender request is processed, customer service personnel calculate the net cash value of the policy, and they mail a check to the policyowner. The company may ask the policyowner to return the policy in order to receive the payment, but this requirement may be waived.

Some companies have established conservation units that are staffed with personnel specially trained to conserve policies and to monitor lapse and replacement activity. Statistics on lapses and replacements are sent to the company's marketing and actuarial specialists to help them find the best ways to make the company's products more attractive and cost-effective.

Replacements

For many reasons, a policyowner may decide to cancel a current life policy and purchase a new one. *Replacement* is the act of surrendering an insurance policy or changing the coverage of that policy in order to buy another policy. Customer service personnel have a number of duties associated with replacements of life insurance policies: determining the current policy's cash value, adding accumulated dividends, deducting any loan balances, and determining the policy's final value for the policyowner. Customer service representatives must also be familiar with any tax implications that replacement may have for the policyowner.

When a policyowner is considering replacing a policy with another company's policy, the customer service department has additional duties. When informed of the pending replacement, the customer service staff usually contacts the policyowner and the policyowner's agent in an attempt to conserve the policy or offer a competitive replacement product. If the policyowner still decides to replace the current policy with another company's policy, customer service representatives must make the same calculations as mentioned earlier and arrange to send the policyowner a check for the policy's value.

Insurance companies have various strategies for dealing with replacements. One strategy that U.S. companies promote is the *1035 exchange,* which insulates the policyowner from any tax effect in exchanging one policy for another. Companies may also promote *policy updates,* which provide an opportunity for policyowners to improve their current policies so that replacement is a less attractive alternative.

1035 exchanges

Based on Section 1035(a) of the Internal Revenue Code, 1035 exchanges can help a policyowner avoid some of the tax disadvantages that may occur with replacement of a life insurance policy. For example, when a policyowner surrenders a policy and receives the cash value in a lump sum, a portion of the sum is taxable as ordinary income if the sum exceeds the cost basis of the insurance policy. Assume, for instance, that a policyowner surrenders a 12-year-old permanent life insurance policy after paying $13,000 in premiums and receiving $2,000 in dividends. If the cash surrender value paid to the policyowner is $15,000, then the policyowner would have a taxable gain of $4,000 ([$15,000 − $13,000] + $2,000 = $4,000). However, under the provisions of Section 1035(a), if the policyowner actually exchanges the policy for a like policy as defined in the IRS code, there would be no gain and, thus, no taxable income.

When a 1035 exchange is requested, customer service representatives determine the values of the two insurance policies and handle the administrative details of exchanging one policy for the other. Because most 1035 exchanges occur with an exchange of policies between two companies, the value of the terminating policy must be calculated and transferred to the new company. Administrative procedures for 1035 exchanges vary from company to company, and customer service staff must keep abreast of changes in the tax laws that may affect such exchanges.

Policy updates

To make their policies more attractive and thereby protect themselves against policy replacements and surrenders, insurance companies have the option of updating their in-force policies. Updating a policy usually allows a policyowner to increase the policy's death benefit and earn interest and dividends at a current yield without increasing the premium. Customer service representatives inform policyowners of the opportunity to update their policies and administer the policy updates for those who request them. These updates are particularly useful to insurance companies in times of rising interest rates.

Noncoverage Changes

When the customer service staff receives a request to make a noncoverage change, such as a name or address change, a customer service representative must make sure that the person requesting the change has the right to do so. This process usually involves checking the policy number, verifying the requester's identity, and making sure that the policy has not been assigned to another owner. Some companies require policyowners to make all change requests in writing. Other companies accept certain changes by telephone. Usually, the caller must give certain policy information and personal identification.

Name and address changes

Notifications of changes in name or address are the most routine transactions that customer service personnel process. Some companies accept such notification over the telephone. Other companies require completion of a prepared form. Companies may request a certified copy of a marriage license, divorce decree, or court order to verify a name change. When adequate evidence is received, the name change is usually processed electronically, thereby changing all appropriate company records. If a signed form and written evidence are required, these materials are kept as part of the policyowner's permanent records. Finally, either a corrected copy of the face page of the policy or an *endorsement* with the correct information is prepared and sent to the policyowner for attachment to the policy. An *endorsement* is a document that is attached to a policy and that subsequently becomes a part of the contract.

Address changes do not ordinarily call for any substantiating evidence. However, an address change can signal the customer service staff that other changes may be necessary. For example, a policyowner who has moved may have been paying premiums under a preauthorized check (PAC) plan. In such a case, a customer service representative must determine whether the policyowner has also changed banks, and whether the new bank can continue to supply PAC service.

A change in address can also mean that another field office, agent, or regional service center may now provide service to the policyowner. If the customer service responsibility needs to be transferred from one field office to another, both field offices must be informed. If a broker is involved, the broker's consent for such a transfer may be necessary. When no agent or broker is available to provide service for the policyowner, the policyowner may be assigned directly to a customer service representative until an agent is available.

Beneficiary changes

When the company receives a request to change a policy's beneficiary designation, a customer service representative must check the request to be sure that all necessary conditions are met. First, the policyowner must sign the request. In addition, if the original beneficiary was an irrevocable beneficiary, then the original beneficiary must also sign the change request. If an irrevocable beneficiary's permission is not obtained, under most circumstances the company cannot make the change. Although policies that allow designation of irrevocable beneficiaries are available, policyowners rarely exercise the option to designate an irrevocable beneficiary.

In Canada, policyowners who own policies issued before June 30, 1962, may designate preferred beneficiaries. The class of *preferred beneficiaries* consists of the spouse, children, parents, and grandchildren of the insured. A policyowner can make a beneficiary change from a preferred beneficiary to another preferred beneficiary without the consent of the designated preferred beneficiary. However, the policyowner must obtain the consent of the designated preferred beneficiary in order to make a beneficiary change from a preferred beneficiary to a nonpreferred beneficiary. Customer service representatives must be prepared to administer beneficiary changes on such policies that are still in force.

In order to change a beneficiary designation, most insurance companies merely require the policyowner to notify them of the change in writing. This method of changing the beneficiary is called the ***recording method,*** or *filing method*. Some insurers may also require that a change of beneficiary request be signed by a disinterested witness or that the documents requesting the change be notarized. A few insurance companies require a beneficiary change procedure called the *endorsement method*. Two possible procedures can be followed for the ***endorsement method:***

- The policyowner returns the policy to the insurance company, and the endorsement with the name of the new beneficiary is attached to the policy.
- The policyowner requests the change by letter, and the company sends the policyowner an endorsement that can be attached to the policy. The beneficiary change form—that is, the endorsement—must be signed by the policyowner.

Among companies that use the endorsement method, the second procedure is more common.

Ownership changes

The ownership of a policy can change in several ways, and the customer service staff is responsible for administering such changes correctly. For example, to transfer all rights of ownership of a policy, a policyowner can make an ***absolute assignment,*** authorizing another person or organization to own the policy. In order for the insurance company to be bound to act in accordance with an absolute assignment, the policyowner must provide the insurer with written notification of the assignment. Some insurers include a clause in the policy specifying that the insurer will change the policy's ownership upon written request from the policyowner. Other companies require the policyowner to request an absolute assignment form that the policyowner must complete and return to the insurance company.

Policyowners may also make a collateral assignment of an insurance policy. A ***collateral assignment*** transfers some ownership rights in a contract from one party to another. The assignment is made on condition that upon payment of the debt for which the contract serves as collateral, all transferred rights shall revert to the policyowner. Customer service personnel handle the administration of such an assignment.

In states with community property laws, an insurance policy can be considered community property. For example, assume a married person living in a community property state buys an insurance policy. If the couple later divorces, the spouse can claim equal ownership in the insurance policy if the policy was paid for from community funds, such as a joint checking account. A court usually decides on ownership, but the insurer's customer service staff administers a change in ownership.

Customer service personnel also administer split-dollar insurance plans. Employers use these plans to help certain employees obtain large amounts of permanent insurance that they could not otherwise afford. Under a split-dollar plan, the employee is the insured and can name the beneficiaries, usually the insured's family. The employer and the employee each pay part of the premium. If the employee dies, the employer receives an amount of the proceeds equal to the cash value of the policy, and the beneficiaries receive the remaining benefits. However, if the plan is terminated before the employee dies, the employee usually has the right to buy the policy from the employer for an amount equal to the policy's cash value. The customer service staff calculates the policy's cash value and administers the transfer of ownership.

Recordkeeping

Customer service specialists are responsible for extensive recordkeeping. They maintain up-to-date records electronically and may be responsible for storing original policy documents. These records are needed both for day-to-day departmental business and for periodic audits that may be conducted by the company's auditors, state or provincial regulators, or independent auditing firms. State and provincial regulators also require insurance companies to record all consumer complaints, to identify the complaints by type, and to indicate when a complaint was received and when and how it was resolved. More and more insurers are using these complaints to find out what customers want, what they perceive, and what they expect from the companies.

Insurance program updates

As mentioned in this chapter, requests for policy changes and record changes may indicate a need for additional insurance. A beneficiary change or name change can mean that the insured was recently married, thus indicating an insurance review. A simple address change may mean a bigger house, greater mortgage, a larger family, or a promotion—all of which may translate to a need for increased insurance coverage. An effective customer service representative thinks beyond the simple recordkeeping transaction in order to provide complete service to a policyowner, insured, or agent, as described in INSIGHT 10-2.

INSIGHT 10-2

Customer Service in Action

Amelia Jones, a customer service representative in the home office of an insurance company, recently received a letter of appreciation from Joel Kennedy, an account representative in the Boston sales office. Amelia had worked through her lunch hour to gather facts that helped Joel prepare for an upcoming meeting with a policyowner. In his letter, Joel said he was thrilled about being able to handle all the policyowner's questions as easily as he did, and that his success was largely due to the information Amelia gave him.

Amelia says she treats customers the way she would like to be treated. "Whatever a person asks for, I'll try to do," she says. "A field person is as much a customer as a policyowner. No matter which one you help, the effort goes toward our company's success."

* * * * *

Brand-new group health insurance coverage and a brand-new baby in need of eye surgery meant a lot of questions for the Young family. Mr. Young called his insurer's regional claim office and spoke with Pat Copeland, a claim representative. Pat worked closely with the Youngs to explain their group policy's benefit provisions and limitations and to address their concerns.

In a letter to Pat's supervisor, the Youngs expressed their gratitude, "Pat has helped our family understand many of the important aspects of the insurance business. She always takes the time to answer our questions and to return a phone call promptly. It's nice to know there is someone you can count on!"

Pat Copeland believes that an ounce of prevention is worth a pound of cure. Said Pat, "If you provide customer service on the front end, you'll have fewer customer relations problems to contend with in the long run."

Source: Adapted with permission from *Shining Moments,* provided by Provident Life and Accident.

CUSTOMER SERVICE FOR GROUP INSURANCE

Many of the concerns that affect customer service for individual life insurance also affect group life and health insurance. Service should be prompt, courteous, accurate, and confidential. However, because of the differences between individual and group insurance contracts, as well as between life and health coverages, most insurance companies train separate customer service staffs for group insurance. The customer service unit for group insurance business is usually separate and distinct from the individual insurance customer service staff. The remainder of this chapter covers a number of factors that specifically affect customer service for group insurance.

Opening a New Group Insurance Account

When administering new group insurance accounts, customer service personnel (1) establish policyholder service records, (2) process enrollment forms, and (3) issue contracts and certificates. In some companies, the customer service area might also be in charge of administering the payment of commissions and bonuses to brokers or group representatives.

Establishing policyholder service records

When an application for group insurance is approved by the company's underwriters, the customer service department opens a new policy file to maintain records for that policy. Such a file contains all pertinent information about the contract and the group involved. The policy file indicates the

- number of group members
- benefits stated in the contract
- date coverage begins for each member
- premium rate for the policy

Processing enrollments

To become insured under a group insurance plan, each group member must complete an enrollment card that identifies the beneficiary of the insurance policy and provides the insurance company with demographic information about the new member. If the insurance plan is administered by the insurance company, the enrollment cards are maintained by the customer service department. If the plan is self-administered, the cards are maintained by the group policyholder.

Maintaining Policy Records

The customer service department also changes and updates group insurance records as needed. As group members and their dependents are added to or deleted from coverage, customer service representatives change the policy records. Customer service personnel must also maintain records on the amount of premiums received and the dates they were received, and the claims, commissions, and other payments made that affect the policy. The staff also prepares and sends premium billing statements to the policyholder, processes premium payments, and notifies the policyholder and the group representative when premium payments are overdue. Finally, the customer service department handles complaints and answers inquiries and requests from the policyholder and individual group members. Group members may ask questions about the exact coverage available for certain medical procedures or the procedure for filing claims. As with individual insurance, the ability of customer service representatives to deal quickly and politely with direct complaints, requests, and inquiries is becoming more and more essential to the successful operation of the insurance company.

Terminating Group Coverage

When a group policyholder does not renew its group contract, the customer service staff closes the files for that contract and informs the group members of their right, if any, to convert their group insurance into individual insurance. Most employees with group health insurance now have the right to continue medical and dental coverage for themselves and their dependents for up to 18 months, and dependents may in some cases continue coverage for up to 36 months.

As mentioned earlier, when an employee insured under a group plan stops working for the company that owns the group plan, the employee frequently has the right to convert coverage to an individual policy within 30 days of terminating employment. Such a right is exercised by signing a form requesting the coverage. The form is forwarded by the employer to the insurance company, which issues an individual policy. The new policy is issued at current rates and for an amount or extent of coverage that is no greater than the coverage the individual was insured for under the group plan. The customer service department handles the individual's inquiries about rates, premium payment arrangements, and beneficiary designations.

KEY TERMS

customer service
external customer
internal customer
conversion privilege
rider
supplementary benefit rider
irrevocable beneficiary
minimum deposit business

replacement
endorsement
preferred beneficiary
recording method
endorsement method
absolute assignment
collateral assignment

Chapter 11

Claim Administration

After reading this chapter, you should be able to

- Describe several different ways in which the claim area can be organized
- Outline the basic steps involved in the claim decision process
- Discuss the types of information available to claim examiners during the investigation of an insured's death
- Give some reasons why insurance companies might deny individual life insurance claims
- List and describe six features of medical expense claims that are not normally found in life insurance claims
- Distinguish between the factors involved in processing medical expense claims and those in processing disability income claims
- Explain the concepts of coordination of benefits and deductible amounts

The claim area of an insurance company is responsible for carrying out the financial promises that the company makes in its insurance policies. To fulfill the company's responsibilities to its policyowners, beneficiaries, and insureds, the claim area must ensure that benefits are paid promptly and to the correct party. However, in order to protect the insurance industry, the general public, and the company from abuses of the insurance contract, the claim area must also guard against paying fraudulent or improper claims.[1]

Claim examiners consider all the information pertinent to a claim for insurance benefits and make decisions about the company's payment of the claim. Also called *claim analysts, claim approvers, claim specialists,* and *claim consultants,* these professionals are trained to consider all practical reasons for approving or denying a claim for policy benefits.

The person who submits a claim is referred to as the ***claimant.*** This person may be the policyowner, the beneficiary, or a person acting on behalf of the policyowner or beneficiary. Because claim personnel interact directly with claimants and other customers of the company, they must have excellent human relations skills. Interactions with claimants often require special sensitivity on the part of claim personnel because such interactions occur at a time when the claimant has experienced a loss—emotional, financial, or both. Thus, both the conduct of claim personnel and the efficiency of the claim operation are important factors in an insurance company's image. In order to assure a high level of service and professionalism in claim administration, many companies have established a claim philosophy to guide employees as they perform their work. Companies frequently use or adapt the "Statement of Principles" of the International Claim Association.

In this chapter, we will discuss the structure of the life and health insurance claim function. We will describe the basic claim decision process and look at claim investigation. We will then apply these claim processes to three types of insurance: life insurance, medical insurance, and disability insurance.

STRUCTURE OF THE CLAIM FUNCTION

Although life and health insurance companies can organize their claim functions in a number of ways, most companies that sell a variety of products establish units that correspond to the different types of products that the companies provide. For example, a large company that sells individual life, group life, individual health, and group health insurance might have a separate claim unit for each type of product.

Some companies have regional claim offices that can provide quick, personal service to customers in particular geographical locations. Figures 11-1 and 11-2 show claim administration organizational structure by product and by region. Regional claim offices are usually given authority to process and pay certain types of claims up to a specified dollar amount. For example, regional claim offices might be permitted to process—without approval from the home office—routine individual life insurance claims of $100,000 or less and group life insurance claims of $250,000 or less. Similarly, regional claim offices might be authorized to approve health and disability claims up to specified dollar limits. Claims for amounts above those limits are submitted to a central claim department in the company's home office.

The authority and responsibility of a claim examiner is directly related to the size and types of claims the examiner can approve. The levels of authority in a claim area often begin with an examiner trainee and progress to examiner, senior examiner, specialist, consultant, and so on. At each

Figure 11-1
Organization chart of a claim administration department organized by product.

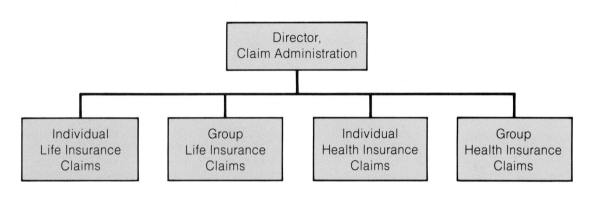

Figure 11-2
Organization chart of a claim administration department organized by region.

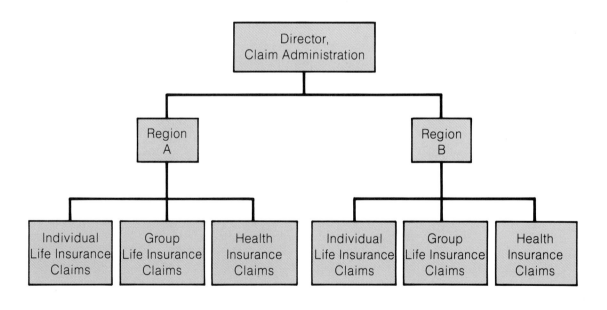

Figure 11-3
Example of levels of authority in a claim administration department.

Type of Claim	Approval Authority
Routine claims that do not involve the contestability provision	Examiner Trainee . . . . $ 50,000 Examiner . . . . $100,000 Sr. Claims Examiner . . . . . $200,000 Asst. Manager . . . . no restrictions Manager . . . . no restrictions
Claims that involve the contestability provision or the accidental death benefit provision	Examiner Trainee . . . . no authority Examiner . . . . $ 50,000 Sr. Claims Examiner . . . . . $100,000 Asst. Manager . . . . no restrictions Manager . . . . no restrictions
Claims that involve suspicion of fraud or unusual legal complications	Examiner Trainee . . . . no authority Examiner . . . . no authority Sr. Claims Examiner . . . . . no authority Asst. Manager. . . . . $100,000 Manager $1,000,000

authority level, claim area staff members are authorized to approve claims up to a certain dollar value. Figure 11-3 indicates the claim approval authority held by personnel at various authority levels in a typical claim area.

Many life and health insurance companies require their claim area staff to complete courses on life and health insurance products, the administration of claims, the management of claim operations, and the medical, dental, and legal matters affecting the administration of claims. Such courses are included in educational programs offered by ICA, LOMA, and the Health Insurance Association of America (HIAA). Most companies also have extensive in-house training programs and procedures manuals to help claim staff understand the company's unique products and claim procedures so that they can process claims correctly and consistently.

THE CLAIM DECISION PROCESS

Given the wide variety of insurance products available and the even wider variety of situations that could result in claims for the benefits of those policies, a complete discussion of every possible claim process is beyond the scope of this text. However, claim examiners generally follow a basic claim decision process in their work. This process is applied to most life and health insurance claims, regardless of the specific insurance product type, claim amount, or situation. The claim decision process basically requires the company to obtain satisfactory answers to these questions prior to approving a claim:

1. Was the policy in force when the loss was incurred?
2. Was the insured actually covered by the policy?
3. Is the policy contestable?
4. What was the nature of the loss?
5. Is the loss covered by the policy?
6. What benefits are payable?
7. Who is entitled to receive the benefits?

Verifying Policy Status

As the first step in the claim decision process, the examiner verifies that the policy under which the claim is filed was actually in force at the time the loss occurred. This verification is usually routine because most companies maintain this information electronically.

Verifying Coverage of the Insured

Once the in-force status of the policy has been established, the next step is to verify that the person suffering the loss was actually covered under the policy. This step is necessary to protect the insurance company from fraudulent and mistaken claims. A *fraudulent claim* occurs when a claimant intentionally uses false information in an attempt to collect policy benefits. However, the majority of problems encountered by examiners during this stage of the claim decision process stem from mistakes made by the claimant. Claims for benefits under family policies or group policies, for example, can present situations in which persons making claims mistakenly believe that they are included under a policy that does not actually cover them.

Examining for Misrepresentation

An insurer ordinarily relies on statements made in policy applications. If such statements are false, they may result in the company's issuing a policy it would not otherwise have issued. Upon learning the truth, the insurer may have the right to cancel the policy on the grounds that no valid contract ever existed. The legal remedy of canceling an insurance contract because of material misrepresentation in the application is called ***rescission.*** Companies in both the United States and Canada must meet strict legal requirements in order to rescind a policy. One of these requirements is a limit on the time during which an insurer may contest or challenge the validity of a policy because of misrepresentation in the application. This time limit, usually two or three years, is called a ***contestable period.***

As a standard practice, many companies scrutinize any claims arising during the contestable period. Such claims, of course, may be perfectly legitimate; as such, they would be honored. However, the claim examiner must consider whether the possibility exists that the insured or policyowner withheld or falsified information at the time of application. Most often, falsified information involves the medical history or condition of the insured; however, the insured's occupation, hobbies, or any other factor that influences insurability could have been falsified.

Verifying the Loss

The claim examiner seeks proof that the loss did occur, along with sufficient detail to describe the exact nature of the loss. Much of the necessary information is supplied by the claimant on the claim form. The ***claim form*** is an application for payment of benefits under an insurance policy. A typical claim form requires the claimant to provide general information about the insured person and the loss. Claim forms and the information requested on them differ according to the type of claim being submitted. The claimant also must attach supporting documentation. Such proof of loss also takes different forms, depending on the nature of the loss and the kind of coverage.

Determining the Amount of Benefits

Insurance companies adhere closely to the provisions of the insurance contract in order to protect the interests of all parties concerned and to provide benefits exactly as intended. Usually, the amount of liability for any particular claim can be easily determined. The claim examiner has to take into account numerous factors including premiums paid in advance, deductibles, coinsurance, and interest payments, which affect the final benefit amount.

Determining the Recipients of Benefits

The company is responsible for getting benefit payments to the proper party. Life insurance policy proceeds are payable, in the manner designated, to the beneficiary or beneficiaries named in the policy. In many cases, the company can distribute the policy proceeds in exactly the way specified by the policyowner, but such distribution may not always be possible. For example, a beneficiary may be a minor or may be disqualified from receiving the policy proceeds because of statutory law. Companies can also create different plans under which a beneficiary can receive policy proceeds, as shown in INSIGHT 11-1. Medical expense and disability benefits are ordinarily payable under policy terms to the insured person but may be assigned to a provider of services, such as a doctor or hospital.

INSIGHT 11-1

Claim Payment Options at Life of Georgia

In 1988, Life of Georgia began using a new method of paying beneficiaries of individual life policies proceeds amounts in excess of $10,000. Instead of sending these beneficiaries a claim check, Life of Georgia sets up a fully guaranteed money-market-type checking account, called a Future Account, for each of these beneficiaries. The insurer deposits the total claim amount into the account.

Life of Georgia establishes Future Accounts only for beneficiaries, not assignees. Also, such accounts are not established if the proceeds are payable under an alternate mode of settlement, such as a Special Interest Option or Installment Pay-Out.

The Future Account provides no-cost checking for the beneficiary. The beneficiary receives a checkbook and may write one check for the entire amount or any number of checks up to the amount of the funds in the account. Any funds left on deposit earn interest. A primary benefit of this claim payment system is that the beneficiary earns interest on the claim proceeds from the date of claim approval. Under the previous system, the beneficiary did not have the opportunity to begin earning interest on the proceeds until the claim check cleared through banking channels.

At the time the account is opened, Life of Georgia sends the beneficiary a letter explaining that the claim has been approved and the account has been opened. The letter tells the beneficiary to expect to receive a kit and checks from the bank within 48 hours, and gives a toll-free number for the beneficiary to use if he or she has any questions regarding the Future Account.

The field district office and [servicing] agent receive a copy of the beneficiary's letter and use this as an indicator to schedule a follow-up visit with the beneficiary to verify that the kit has been received and to assist the beneficiary with any questions or insurance services needed. This follow-up visit can be made at the convenience of the beneficiary and the agent, without the pressure of delaying the claim payment. The kit includes a card the beneficiary can use to indicate the person to receive the remaining proceeds if the beneficiary dies before the Future Account is closed. In that case, the new payee sends Life of Georgia a copy of the beneficiary's death certificate, and

the insurer instructs the bank to issue a Treasurer's Check to the new payee to close out the account.

Each month, the beneficiary receives a statement of the account, showing interest credited, all checks processed, and the current account balance. There is a space on the statement for the insurer to put in either a sales or a general message. At the end of the year, the bank prepares and mails the 1099 interest forms for each beneficiary.

Source: Adapted with permission from an Activity Report prepared by Lynn Kent, ALHC, FLMI, and submitted to LOMA by Ben Ransbotham of Life of Georgia, July 1988.

INVESTIGATING CLAIMS

Although not part of the formal decision process, investigation is a critical step in processing certain claims. In the majority of cases, the claim examiner evaluates a claim from the claimant's statement and from the submitted proof of loss. Using that information, the examiner determines whether the claim is legitimate and whether it meets the requirements of the policy. If the examiner has reason to doubt any aspect of the claim, further information may be required before a decision is made. The process of obtaining necessary claim information is known as a *claim investigation.* The purpose of a claim investigation is not to directly decide the merit of the claim, but rather to supply the information necessary to reach that decision. The process of investigation, then, is one of fact finding, not one of decision making.

The majority of claims do not require investigation. Of those that do, most require only short, simple searches that may involve no more than checking one medical record or interviewing one person. Investigations of this sort are typically performed by claim examiners themselves, working through written correspondence or by telephone.

Some claims require extensive investigation in order to verify all the relevant information. For example, a case in which an insured's death might have been accidental or suicidal would require extra investigation. Sometimes a claim examiner is able to conduct a complete investigation from the company office. Often, however, a company representative must pay a visit to the place where the insured lived or where the loss occurred. Some insurance companies have their own staffs of claim investigators for such field work; other companies use outside professional investigation agencies.

The extent of the investigation to be conducted in connection with a claim depends on the exact type of claim involved, the kind of information needed to make a proper decision about the claim, and the difficulty encountered in obtaining that information. More specifically, the extent of an investigation is influenced by the

- amount of the insurer's liability
- cause of the loss
- circumstance of the loss
- amount and type of information already available
- age of the insured
- place where the loss occurred
- length of time the policy has been in force
- policy provisions

The extent of the investigation, the information sought, and the techniques used to gather that information necessarily depend on the situation. Sources of information include hospitals and attending physicians, employers and unions, banks and neighboring businesses, landlords and tenants, and neighbors, relatives, and friends of the insured. Government agencies at all levels may also have important information about either the insured or the event of loss.

In recent years, concern has grown over an individual's right to privacy within society. One result of this concern has been the need for insurers to secure valid authorizations to obtain claim investigation data from various sources. Also, a number of statutes and court rulings affect the techniques that may be employed in an investigation. For example, conducting an investigation under a false pretext is now prohibited in many jurisdictions. Many of the privacy regulations only formalize practices that insurers had already adopted on their own initiative, but those regulations have the weight of law. Violations may leave the insurer liable for the payment of damages.

Each step of a claim investigation is carefully documented and retained in the claim file for that case. The documentation of an investigation should include

- the policy number and claim number, if any
- the source contacted: hospital, physician, employer, or other source
- the date of contact
- the authorization to obtain necessary information, if such authorization is necessary

- a copy of the request for information, if the request was made through correspondence
- a report of the interview with the source, if one was conducted
- other material information that has been obtained, such as police reports, vital statistics records, or newspaper clippings

The documentation of an investigation should contain only information that is relevant to the claim. *Hearsay evidence,* or evidence based on what someone has been told but has not actually witnessed, that is uncovered during an investigation may properly be documented as a lead to more substantive evidence. Investigation reports, however, should not contain the personal opinions of the investigator or examiner. In the event of litigation over the claim decision, the contents of the claim file would likely be open to the claimant's counsel, and the inclusion of personal opinions in the file is both unprofessional and potentially prejudicial to the position of the company.

LIFE INSURANCE CLAIM PROCEDURES

The life insurance claim form is an application for payment of the policy proceeds. A typical claim form requires the claimant to provide general information about the insured person, the attending physician, if any, and the basis on which the claimant is submitting the information. An example of such a claim form is shown in Figure 11-4.

Along with the completed claim form, the claimant must send proof that the insured is deceased. A death certificate is the generally accepted proof of death. In the United States, the death certificate indicates the cause of death and is signed by a physician or is issued by a government official, such as the Registrar of Vital Statistics or the local coroner. In Canada, the death certificate is issued by the Registrar of Vital Statistics and does *not* generally indicate the cause of death. In both the United States and Canada, the death certificate can be either an original or a certified copy. Some companies, especially in Canada, also accept as proof of death certificates provided by funeral directors. If the claimant cannot immediately secure a valid death certificate, many companies also accept an Attending Physician's Statement, a coroner's statement, or a hospital's death certificate.

In addition to the claim form and the death certificate, the insurance company may request an Attending Physician's Statement from the doctor who treated the deceased before death. If the situation requires, the

Figure 11-4
Sample claim form.

CLAIMANT'S STATEMENT	INDIVIDUAL LIFE CLAIMS **Remarkable Life Assurance Company of America**

NOTE: The Company and its Agents are prepared to assist in the completion of Proofs of Claims, and settlement can readily be obtained by direct communication with the Company or its nearest local representatives.

This form is to be completed by the person or persons to whom the policy is legally payable as beneficiary. If the beneficiary is the insured's estate, the statement should be completed by the executor or administrator and a certified copy of the appointment issued by the proper court and bearing the clerk's signature must be furnished. If the beneficiary is not of legal age, a guardian should complete the form and submit a certified copy of the appointment issued by the proper court and bearing the clerk's signature.

A certified copy of the Official Certificate of Death, certified by the issuing agency, must be furnished the Company.

If the beneficiary is entitled to receive and desires settlement under an optional mode of settlement a form 1400 should be completed. If the proceeds are to be paid as a life income, proof of age of the beneficiary must be furnished.

For policies with a CHILDREN'S RIDER or FAMILY and PARENT AND CHILDREN policies, see instructions on Supplemental Statement 123.

If death occurred within the two year period following the date of issue of the policy, form 34(a), Death Claim Medical History form, executed by the Insured's next of kin, must be furnished.

1. POLICY NOS.			
2. NAME OF DECEASED	3. RELATIONSHIP TO INSURED (IF OTHER THAN INSURED)	4. RESIDENCE AT TIME OF DEATH	
5. CAUSE OF DEATH	6. PLACE OF DEATH	7. DATE OF DEATH	
8. DATE OF BIRTH	9. PLACE OF BIRTH	10. EMPLOYER	

FRAUD STATEMENT REQUIRED BY SOME STATES

Any person who knowingly and with intent to defraud any insurance company or other person files a statement of claim containing any materially false information, or conceals for the purpose of misleading, information concerning any fact material thereto, commits a fraudulent insurance act, which is a crime.

BENEFICIARY'S TAX IDENTIFICATION NUMBER*
(see explanation on reverse side)

Under penalties of perjury, I certify:
That the number shown on this form is my correct taxpayer identification number; and

☐ Check box if you are NOT subject to backup withholding under the provisions of
section 3406 (a) (1) (C) of the Internal Revenue Code.

FAILURE TO CHECK BOX WILL RESULT IN COMPANY WITHHOLDING 20% OF INTEREST PAYMENT ON LUMP SUM PROCEEDS.

AUTHORIZATION TO OBTAIN INFORMATION

Name of Deceased _____
(Please print)

To all doctors; medical professionals; hospitals; clinics; other health care providers; insurers; insurance support organizations; and other persons who have information about the patient.

I authorize you to give the Remarkable Life Assurance Company of America and/or the Remarkable Life Assurance Company its reinsurers or its agents: (a) all information you have as to illness, injury, medical history, diagnosis, treatment and prognosis with respect to any physical or mental condition of the patient; and (b) any non-medical information about the patient which the Company believes it needs to perform the business functions described below.

The information obtained will be used to determine if the patient is eligible: (a) for insurance; or (b) for benefits under a Company policy. It will also be used for any other purpose which relates to the insurance or benefits.

This form will be valid for the duration of the claim. I know that I may request a copy of it. I agree that a copy is as valid as the original.

DATE SIGNED	SIGNATURE OF BENEFICIARY
	RELATIONSHIP TO DECEASED
BENEFICIARY'S TAX ACCOUNT NO. (SOCIAL SECURITY NO.)	ADDRESS (NO. & STREET, CITY & STATE)

insurance company may also request an autopsy report. Such documents are usually necessary under the following circumstances:

- the insured died during the contestable period
- the policy includes accidental death benefits
- claim personnel have reason to question the mode or cause of death

If additional information is needed, the claim examiner has several sources of information: the deceased's physician, the coroner, police reports, hospital records, accident reports, and newspaper accounts. Claim examiners may gather this information themselves or contact a consumer reporting agency to solicit information. Fewer than 5 percent of all life claims require the use of consumer reporting agencies. Figure 11-5 shows the steps that a

Figure 11-5
Illustration of a typical procedure for approving a life insurance claim.

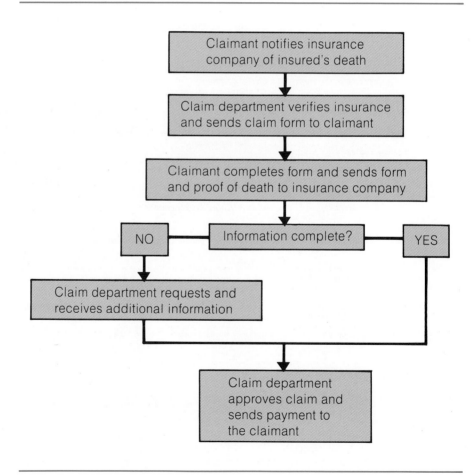

company usually follows when a claim is processed. After the required information is gathered and reviewed, the claim is either approved or denied.

Paying a Life Claim

If the claim is approved, a check for the correct amount of money—including any applicable interest—is sent directly to the claimant or to an agent who then delivers the check to the claimant. In cases where the proceeds are payable to the insured's estate or to a minor child, additional documentation may be required to support the right of the claimant to receive the proceeds.

Denying a Life Claim

Fewer than 1 percent of all life insurance claims are denied. When insurance companies deny individual life insurance claims, they usually do so for one of the following reasons:

- The policy was not in force at the time the insured died.
- Death occurred within the contestable period, and information that was material to underwriting the policy was not disclosed when the policy was applied for.
- The insured committed suicide during the exclusion period, and the insurer is liable only for a refund of the premiums paid.
- In a claim for accidental death benefits, death was not deemed to be accidental according to the terms of the accidental death benefit provision of the policy.

If a claim is denied, the claim examiner sends a letter to the claimant, explaining why the claim was denied (see Figure 11-6). Before the letter is mailed, a draft of the letter may be forwarded to the insurance company's legal department for review and approval. A claimant who does not find the company's reasons for denial acceptable may institute legal proceedings against the company, and these proceedings may ultimately lead to litigation. Few life insurance claim disputes, however, reach the stage of litigation. Before litigation occurs, the insurance company and the claimant or the claimant's attorney generally attempt to negotiate an acceptable resolution to the dispute. Occasionally, the company and the claimant reach some form of compromise settlement.

When there are conflicting claimants to a policy's benefits, the insurance company may file a *bill of interpleader* with a court. ***Interpleader*** is a legal

Figure 11-6
Illustration of a typical procedure for denying a claim.

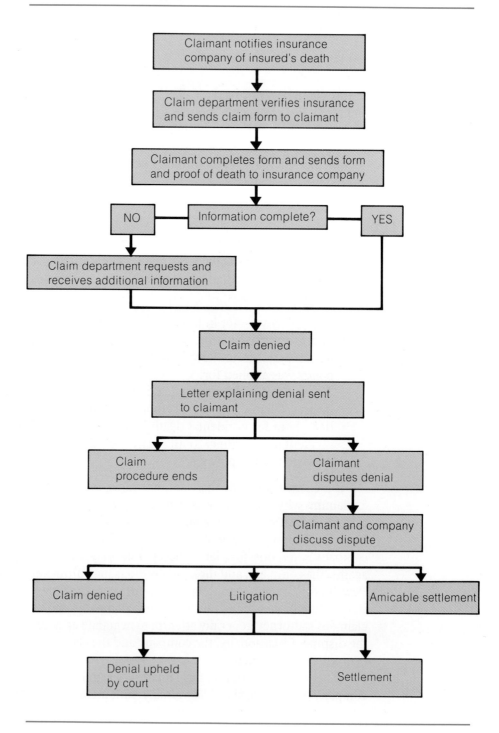

remedy that allows an insurance company to pay the policy proceeds to the court. The court then decides the proper recipient of the claim settlement. Generally, however, the courts address a bill of interpleader only if the conflict cannot be resolved by the parties themselves. In Canada, where the term *interpleader* is not commonly used, all the provinces except Quebec provide for deposit of proceeds into a Court. In Quebec, the deposit may be made with the provincial Finance Minister.

If a life insurance claim results in litigation, the claim area works with the company's attorneys to provide any information needed to defend or prosecute the case. The claim examiner or a senior manager of the claim area may be required to appear in court to provide testimony. Company underwriters and medical directors might also appear in court to provide evidence.

HEALTH INSURANCE CLAIM PROCEDURES

The risk that an insurance company incurs for health insurance coverage differs from the risk incurred for life insurance coverage. When a person covered by life insurance dies, a specific life insurance benefit is paid to the insured's beneficiary. However, when a person insured under a health insurance policy is sick or injured, the benefits payable to that person can vary widely, depending on the following factors:

- the type of sickness or injury
- the seriousness of the sickness or injury
- the cause of the sickness or injury
- the length of time that the sickness or injury continues
- specific conditions of the health insurance coverage

As mentioned in Chapter 8, health insurance can be divided into two broad categories: medical expense insurance and disability income insurance. For the remainder of this chapter, we will discuss claims submitted under coverage provided by each of these categories of health insurance. In health insurance claims, the claimant is usually the person who is insured or a dependent of the insured person.

Medical Expense Insurance Claims

A claim examiner processing a claim for medical expense benefits is concerned about many of the same factors an examiner considers for life claims, such as the in-force status of the policy and whether the policy covers the loss. However, a claim examiner checking a medical expense claim must consider six specific features of medical expense insurance that are not characteristic of life insurance coverage: *exclusions, waiting periods, pre-existing conditions, deductibles, coinsurance,* and *coordination of benefits.*

Exclusions

When a medical expense insurance contract is created, the insurance company identifies in the contract certain *exclusions,* which are expenses that the policy does not cover. Expenses caused by the following conditions are usually excluded from payment in most medical expense insurance contracts:

- cosmetic surgery, unless corrective surgery is required following an accidental injury
- treatment for any injury or sickness that occurs while the insured is in military service or that is the result of an act of war
- treatment for injuries that are self-inflicted or that are caused by attempted suicide
- pre-existing conditions disclosed by the applicant that, by rider or endorsement, the company has declined to cover
- any hospital-surgical procedures for which expenses are paid by other organizations or which are provided free of charge in government facilities, if the insured receives treatment in government facilities

Each type of medical expense contract has different exclusions, and claim examiners must check the contract involved before a claim can be processed to make sure that excluded expenses are not paid.

Waiting periods

Waiting periods are used in both medical expense and disability income insurance. Before approving a claim, the claim examiner must make sure that the waiting period has ended.

In medical expense insurance policies, the **waiting period** is a prescribed amount of time following policy issue, during which the insured's medical expenses are not covered by the policy. The purpose of the waiting period for medical expense insurance is to protect the insurance company from charges that occur because of a sickness that the insured may have known about before the insurance contract was signed. The waiting period for medical expense insurance usually lasts from 14 to 30 days following policy issue and normally applies only to medical expenses arising from sickness, not accidents. Longer waiting periods, which may last three to six months, are established for specific medical conditions such as appendicitis and tonsillitis.

Pre-existing conditions

A *pre-existing condition* is usually defined as an injury that occurred or a medical condition that first appeared before an insurance policy was issued. Most medical expense insurance policies contain a *pre-existing conditions provision,* which states that until the insured has been covered under the policy for a specified period, no benefit is payable for pre-existing conditions. Generally, this provision does not apply to conditions disclosed on the application. The pre-existing conditions provision is designed to prevent people from buying insurance to provide benefits for health problems known to them but not disclosed to the insurance company. In many states, if the insurer is aware of the condition when the policy is issued, an insurer can use an impairment rider to exclude benefits for a pre-existing condition. Otherwise, exclusion of benefits is limited to the period defined in the pre-existing conditions provision.

The pre-existing conditions provision on long-term disability coverage under a group insurance policy is meant to give the insurer protection from antiselection based on existing medical problems or conditions. This provision helps insurers avoid the expense of securing a health statement from each eligible employee and then having to underwrite each individual covered by the policy.

Deductibles

Many medical expense insurance policies specify that, before any benefits become payable, the insured must pay a portion of the medical expenses that result from an accident or sickness. The portion that the insured must pay before the insurance company makes any benefit payment is called the *deductible,* or *deductible amount.*

Deductibles may be either per cause deductibles or calendar year deductibles. A *per cause deductible* applies to all eligible expenses resulting from a single sickness or injury. A *calendar year deductible* applies to any eligible medical expenses incurred by the insured during any one calendar year. For example, assume that an insured person is covered by a medical expense insurance policy that includes a $100 per cause deductible. If the insured has a tonsillectomy and an appendectomy in the same year, the insured pays the first $100 of expenses for each operation before the insurance company pays any benefits. If, on the other hand, the insured is covered by a policy with a $100 calendar year deductible and has those same two operations in one year, the insured pays only the first $100 of total medical expenses for that year before the insurance company pays any benefits. The claim examiner must make sure that the appropriate deductible has been paid before any portion of a claim is paid to a claimant.

Coinsurance

Coinsurance, which is also called *percentage participation,* requires both the insurer and the insured to pay a percentage of all eligible medical expenses that result from a sickness or injury. Under a typical policy, the insurer pays 75 or 80 percent of medical expenses in excess of the deductible amount, and the insured pays 20 or 25 percent of the expenses—known as the *copayment*—as well as the deductible amount. For example, if an insured files a major medical insurance claim of $1,100, and the insurance policy calls for a $100 per cause deductible and for the insured to pay 20 percent coinsurance, the insurer pays $800 of the claim (80 percent of [$1,100 claim − $100 deductible]). The insured is thus responsible for $300: the $100 deductible plus the $200 copayment (20 percent of $1,000).

Another common feature in medical expense policies is the *stop-loss provision.* Under this provision, after an insured has paid a specified maximum amount of medical expenses, the insurer pays 100 percent of the balance of medical expenses for the year, up to the contract limit. For example, a policy may have a provision stating that an insured must pay only $2,000 in out-of-pocket expenses during any one year. After that $2,000 level is reached, the insurer is liable for all medical expenses up to a certain specified limit.

Coordination of benefits

Sometimes claimants are insured under more than one medical expense insurance policy. In such cases, claimants are said to be *overinsured,* because they might collect more money in benefits than they actually paid in medical expenses. Because it is not in the public interest for insureds to profit from sickness or injury, most group medical expense policies, and some individual policies, contain a coordination of benefits clause. A *coordination of benefits (COB) clause* is a method of integrating benefits payable under more than one group medical expense insurance policy so that the insured's benefits from all sources do not exceed 100 percent of eligible medical expenses. A COB clause defines the plan of insurance that is the primary provider of benefits when an insured group member has duplicate coverage under another group medical expense policy. Once the plan designated as the primary provider has paid the benefit amounts promised, then the insured can submit to the secondary plan a claim and a description of the benefit amounts already paid by the primary plan.

Processing Medical Expense Claims

Many companies now have highly automated systems for processing routine health insurance claims. An input clerk can enter claim processing information electronically on as many as 150-200 routine claims each day, and the computer system does most of the calculations as well as a great deal of routine claim analysis.

Claim examiners administer most health insurance claims, but some companies also employ one or more doctors, physician's assistants, and dental assistants to examine certain nonroutine health insurance claims. Other insurance companies retain the services of consulting physicians or dentists who visit the company periodically—usually once a week—to provide the company with expert analyses of complicated or unusual claims.

Most companies require claimants to submit with the claim form originals of receipts for medical expenses. Original documents are required because claim examiners can more easily spot changes that might indicate tampering. Fraud, however, is not the most frequent reason for denying a medical expense insurance claim. More often, claims are denied because they are made for treatments that are not eligible for coverage under the terms of the insurance policy. INSIGHT 11-2 describes a system for automating the claim filing process and a procedure for ensuring the accuracy of claim processing.

INSIGHT 11-2

Paperless Health Insurance Claims

A new health insurance card system may mean that patients and doctors will never have to file a paper claim.

Health Information Technologies, Inc.

(HIT), a Princeton, New Jersey-based designer of magnetic card systems for the health insurance industry, has contracted with The Travelers (Connecticut) to custom-

,, fc

ize and install HIT's Health Link System in The Travelers' managed-care networks.

The pilot program, scheduled to begin in December, will electronically transmit health claims to The Travelers from doctors' offices in Sacramento, California, and Austin, Texas.

Each doctor's office will have a Health Link system consisting of two components: a magnetic-card terminal and a printer. Before treatment, a patient's health card is run through a terminal—a procedure similar to credit card authorization for retail purchases. The card then connects with The Travelers' membership data base, which is updated daily. Within seconds, a terminal message indicates whether an appropriate referral has been made. After treatment, the system electronically files a claim with The Travelers.

Based on the success of the Sacramento and Austin pilots, Health Link may be incorporated in The Travelers managed-care networks across the country. In the future, the system is designed to become an all-payors system, interfacing with the computer networks of multiple insurers.

Claim Quality Review

Metropolitan established its Accuracy Assurance Review (AAR) program in the mid-1980s in response to the growing need for a formal system-generated quality assurance claim review program. Both medical and dental claims offices participate in the AAR process. Because the selection and review processes have been automated, AAR units can focus on the job of preventing errors, rather than just recording and reporting them.

Every week, an electronic Audit/Quality computer trail selects a sample of each claim approver's daily claim production. The system maintains an on-line file of the claims selected in this main sample. Each claim selected is accessed, on line, for review. Any errors detected are coded into the system right on the review screen. The system then generates an array of statistics and reports at several levels: the individual approver, team, office, and national operations.

The weekly main sample review assures that claims are being processed both correctly and without unwarranted delay. Specific errors uncovered by the review are corrected by the approver. If the review discloses patterns of an approver's errors, immediate retraining is initiated for that approver. Local claim office management is immediately advised of any problem and can take remedial action.

Source: First article adapted with permission from "Current Practices," *LIMRA's MarketFacts,* November/December 1990, p. 54. Second article adapted with permission from an Activity Report submitted to LOMA by Jack B. Helitzer of Metropolitan Life, October 1990.

Generally, when a medical expense claim is denied, the claim examiner sends a standardized letter that gives the company's reasons for denying the claim. If the claimant disputes the denial, then a claim supervisor can send a second letter, restating the insurance company's position. If the company receives notice that the claimant intends to challenge the denial in court, all correspondence thereafter is checked by the legal staff. Because of the relatively small dollar amounts of many medical expense insurance claims, many resisted claims are disputed in small claims court. In small claims court, a claim supervisor, rather than a company lawyer, usually represents the company.

Disability Income Insurance Claims

Disability income claims are usually more difficult to process than medical expense claims, primarily because a claim examiner must determine whether disability actually exists within the company's definition of that term. Payment of medical expense insurance claims is more straightforward, because such insurance covers expenses for medical services, and copies of bills for such services must accompany any such insurance claim. With these bills as evidence, a claim examiner can usually decide whether or not the company should pay the claim and, if so, the amount of money the claimant should receive.

Disability income insurance claims, however, can be extremely complicated. As described in Chapter 8, *disability income insurance* provides for benefits to be paid in regular installments to an insured person in order to replace some of the insured's income when the insured is disabled by sickness or accident. The disability income benefit is specified in the policy. Usually the amount of disability income insurance that a company allows an individual to purchase is a percentage, such as 67 or 75 percent, of the individual's earned income. If the disability benefit equaled the claimant's previous income, the claimant would have little incentive to return to work.

The waiting period for disability income insurance differs from the waiting period for medical expense insurance. The waiting period for disability income insurance is called the *elimination period* or *probationary period,* and is a specified amount of time, beginning with the *onset of each disability,* during which benefits are not payable. The elimination period for disability income insurance can last from seven days to six months, or more. The purpose of the elimination period for this type of insurance is to eliminate small or unnecessary claims that would be disproportionately expensive to administer, thus causing insurers to increase their premium rates. Longer elimination periods are also often used to coordinate benefit payments with salary continuation plans or other short-term disability plans already in force.

One difficulty in processing disability income claims arises from various interpretations of the definition of *total disability.* Most disability income policies relate the definition of total disability to an insured's ability to work. For example, most older disability income policies define total disability as the insured's inability to work in any occupation. However, this definition is now considered too restrictive, and modern definitions are more liberal. The definition of **total disability** included in most policies issued today provides that insureds are considered totally disabled if, at the start of disability, their disability prevents them from performing the essential duties of their regular occupation. However, at the end of a specified period after the disability begins, usually two years, insureds are considered totally disabled only if their disabilities prevent them from working at *any* occupation for which they are *reasonably fitted* by education, training, or experience.

Many contracts now also provide benefits for partial disability. **Partial disability** can be defined as a condition that prevents an insured from working full-time or completing one or a number of important job duties. Residual benefits are made available to persons with a partial disability. A **residual benefit for partial disability** is a disability income benefit payment that is made to a partially disabled insured. This payment varies according to the percentage of the insured's income that is lost during the period of partial disability.

A major problem for disability insurance claim examiners is that any two medical specialists can disagree on whether a person is unable to work because of a disability. Claimants, lawyers, doctors, and claim examiners can all interpret total disability in various ways. Depending on a claimant's age, occupation, and emotional, mental, and physical characteristics, a condition that is disabling to one person may not be disabling to another.

Processing and investigating disability claims

In order for claim examiners to begin processing a disability claim, the insurance company must receive a statement from the claimant that describes the reasons for the claim. The statement must be accompanied by a report from the claimant's attending physician, describing the diagnosis and treatment for the disability and including an estimate of the duration of the disability.

After the insurance company receives the claim and the proof of disability, the claim examiner verifies the validity of the claim. In some situations, the claim examiner must contact the claimant or the attending physician.

Contact with the claimant may be made in person, on the telephone, or by letter. The claim examiner usually asks the claimant to describe in detail his or her (1) medical condition and how long it has existed, (2) current sources of income, (3) occupation before the disability and the types of duties performed, and (4) plans to return to work. The claim examiner also explains the claimant's coverage and answers any questions that the claimant might have.

The claim examiner contacts the attending physician in order to verify information about the claimant's condition, diagnosis, suggested treatment, and proposed medications. The claim examiner also asks the attending physician if the claimant is totally disabled. Information as to total disability is difficult to obtain, because many physicians are cautious about making such a judgment. However, if the claim examiner obtains enough information from the physician, the insurance company can decide whether the claimant is totally disabled according to the policy's definition of total disability.

Some companies do not ask the physician if a person is disabled and unable to work. The reasoning behind not querying the physician is that the answer to the question is as much a function of the work the claimant performs as it is a medical decision. Instead, the physician is asked only for the specifics of the medical problem and the extent of physical or mental limitations imposed by the medical problem. Then, the claim examiner—in conjunction with the company's own medical or rehabilitation staff—decides whether the person has satisfied the test of being unable to perform a job for which the person is qualified by education or training.

When group insurance is involved, a claim examiner can contact a claimant's employer to verify that the claimant is not working and to determine (1) the claimant's job title and duties before the disability, (2) if the disability occurred because of a work-related activity, thereby determining whether Workers' Compensation applies, (3) if the claimant is receiving any income from the employer during the disability, and (4) if the claimant's employment will be reactivated when the disability ends.

After the claim examiner has verified disability information with the claimant, the attending physician, and—if necessary—the claimant's employer, the examiner may still have questions about the disability. In such cases, the claim examiner may ask for an independent medical examination of the claimant by a medical specialist other than the attending physician, or the claim examiner may request an investigation of the claimant's activities. In addition to verifying the claimant's condition, such evaluations may also be used to help determine a plan for the claimant's vocational rehabilitation. Such independent evaluations may be expensive, and because the cost of these services is absorbed by the insurance company, a claim examiner must be selective in requesting them.

In the small number of claims in which fraud is suspected, the claim examiner may request surveillance of the claimant. Surveillance is more common in Canada than in the United States, primarily because of the number of privacy laws in the United States that restrict when and how surveillance may be used. Also, high costs are involved with surveillance. Surveillance is normally conducted by a consumer reporting agency.

Making a disability claim decision

When claim examiners have gathered adequate information, they can make one of the following decisions:

1. *Approve the claim.* This decision is the most common for a disability claim.
2. *Settle the claim.* The claim examiner may believe that complete payment of the claim is not required and that the insurance company should pay only a portion of the claim. A settlement usually calls for a lump sum to be paid to the claimant rather than for periodic payments to be made for the duration of the disability. This settlement option is rare for group disability claims in Canada.
3. *Deny the claim.* The claim examiner must be absolutely sure that the claimant is not totally disabled. Only a small percentage of all disability claims in the United States and Canada are denied.

Vocational rehabilitation programs

Many insurance companies have become actively involved in helping their claimants become rehabilitated. Because complete rehabilitation is difficult to achieve, insurance companies usually seek vocational rehabilitation for their claimants. ***Vocational rehabilitation*** is intended to help the disabled person return to an occupation that provides some income.

Generally, vocational rehabilitation can take a number of forms:

- retraining disabled people to do the work that they did before they became disabled
- encouraging the employers of disabled people to modify working conditions so that the disabled persons can return to their former duties
- training disabled people to do work that may be entirely different from the work that they did before they became disabled
- training disabled people to be self-employed in another line of work or endeavor

Some companies with disabled employees have established rehabilitation units that work closely with insurance company claim areas. The purpose of a rehabilitation unit is to evaluate claimants who have long-term disabilities and to determine whether they can be rehabilitated. The staff members of the rehabilitation unit, often called *counselors*, do not provide rehabilitative therapy themselves. Instead, the job of rehabilitation counselors is to see that each claimant has opportunities to receive the therapy necessary to return to complete good health or at least to a productive occupation.

Some insurance companies operate their own rehabilitation facilities. Because operating such facilities is costly, most insurance companies prefer to identify a rehabilitation center that is located near each claimant and to pay the rehabilitation center for providing therapy.

KEY TERMS

claim examiner	pre-existing conditions provision
claimant	deductible
fraudulent claim	per cause deductible
rescission	calendar year deductible
contestable period	coinsurance
claim form	stop-loss provision
claim investigation	coordination of benefits (COB) clause
hearsay evidence	total disability
interpleader	partial disability
waiting period	residual benefit for partial disability
pre-existing condition	vocational rehabilitation

NOTE

1. Portions of this chapter have been adapted with permission from Jo Ann S. Appleton, FLMI, ALHC, *Claim Administration: Principles and Practices* (Atlanta: International Claim Association, 1986).

Chapter 12

The Investment Function

After reading this chapter, you should be able to

- Explain why an insurance company's investments are important both to that company's operations and to society
- Describe different ways insurers can organize their investment function
- Explain the purpose of asset-liability matching and some methods of accomplishing this matching
- Describe the procedure for setting and implementing investment policy
- Explain the factors that insurance company investment analysts consider in choosing investments
- Distinguish between stocks and bonds, and between different types of stocks and bonds
- Describe investments other than stocks and bonds that are part of an insurer's investment portfolio

Life and health insurance companies are among the most important institutional investors in the United States and Canada. In 1990, life and health insurance companies in these two countries acquired approximately $116 billion worth of new investments, which helped fuel the U.S. and Canadian national economies. The total invested assets of life and health insurance companies in the United States and Canada in 1990 were worth over $1.5 trillion.

Through their investments, insurance companies help provide the impetus for economic growth. A large number of business ventures are funded, directly or indirectly, by insurance companies. Insurance companies provide funds for building office complexes, manufacturing plants, shopping centers, new homes, and apartments. They invest in oil exploration and in the development of new sources of energy. How insurance companies manage their investments impacts not only policyowners and stockholders, but also vast numbers of other people throughout the societies in which insurance companies operate.

Insurance companies also bolster their own operations with investments. In the early 1990s, life and health insurance companies received about 30 percent of their gross income from investment earnings, with most of the remainder coming from premium payments. Figure 12-1 illustrates the growth over the years of insurers' investment income as a proportion of their total income.

As noted in Chapter 8, the price of an insurance product is affected by the amount of income that actuaries expect the insurance company to earn on its investments. As insurers earn more money on their investments, they can lower the cost of their products or provide higher rates of return. Insurance

Figure 12-1
Investment income as a percentage of life insurers' total income, 1980-1990.

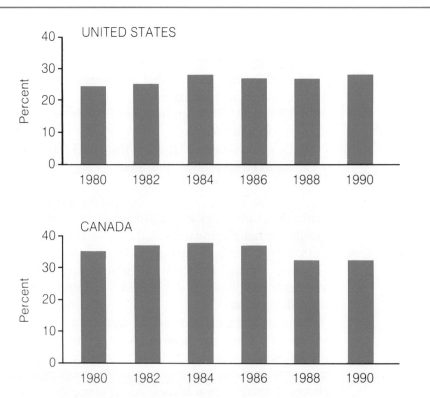

Source: American Council of Life Insurance, Canadian Life and Health Insurance Association.

companies must balance the pressure to earn high levels of investment income with the need to guarantee that their investments are relatively safe from the risk of financial loss.

In Chapter 1, we noted that in some areas insurance companies compete directly with other types of financial institutions, such as banks and investment companies, for consumers' business. Besides marketing traditional insurance products, insurers also manage pension funds and offer consumers pure investment opportunities through investment management services and money market funds. In addition, insurance companies offer investment-based insurance products such as variable life insurance, and companies must maintain a certain level of investment earnings for these products to be successful.

In this chapter, we will discuss the investment function: typical structures and operations of the investment function, factors that affect life and health insurers' investment policies, and the types of investments that insurers make.

ORGANIZATIONAL STRUCTURE OF THE INVESTMENT FUNCTION

As we have noted for other functional areas, the structure of an investment function depends on the size of the insurance company. For example, a large company can have employees that specialize in administering each specific type of investment, but small companies may assign several investment activities to each employee. Some insurance companies may even hire independent investment consultants to perform investment functions that in other companies would be performed by salaried personnel. As we address the organizational structures presented in this chapter, keep in mind that many structures are possible, but the actual functions performed are generally the same for most insurance companies.

Departmental Structure

Many insurance companies organize their investment function as depicted in Figure 12-2. In this structure, an investment department is directed by a vice president of investments, who reports to the president of the company and who follows the general investment policies established by the investment committee of the board of directors. Under the vice president are the *portfolio*

Figure 12-2
Traditional investment department structure.

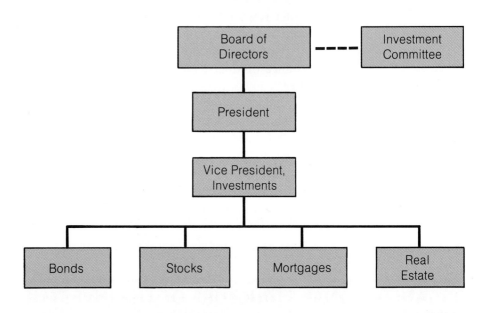

managers, each of whom is responsible for administering a group of investments, called a ***portfolio,*** in one of four areas—bonds, stocks, mortgages, and real estate. In each of these investment areas, employees evaluate investment opportunities and make appropriate investments for the company, according to the company's general policies and specific guidelines set by the vice president of investments.

Many investment departments have separate units for conducting research and handling the administrative details of the investment department, such as recording bonds and mortgages held and stock owned. Some large insurance companies employ a full-time economist or staff of economists to research and forecast economic trends. The company economist may work in the investment area or may report directly to the executive office. Because of the reliance on automation in today's investment environment, some information systems specialists may also be assigned to an investment department.

Insurance companies that manage pension funds frequently add a unit to their investment departments that is concerned solely with pension fund investments. In this situation, the investment department frequently uses one of the two structures illustrated in Figures 12-3 and 12-4. These figures show that the investment department can be divided into two parallel units,

Figure 12-3
Investment department with parallel pension fund.

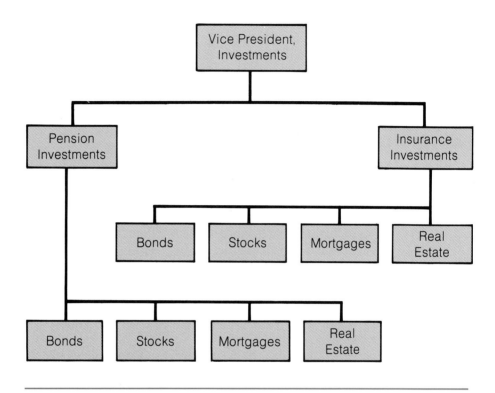

Figure 12-4
Investment department with integrated pension fund.

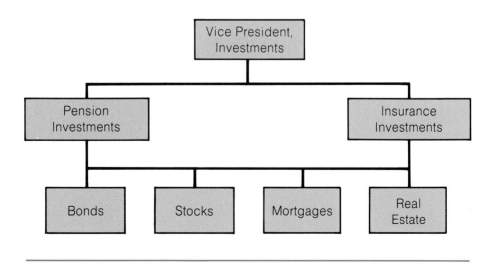

one for making pension fund investments and one for making insurance-related investments. This structure provides clear lines of accountability, responsibility, and control, but such an organization can also lead to a large staff and some duplication of tasks. To avoid the drawbacks of the parallel structure, some companies establish pension fund units with portfolio managers who determine the type of pension fund investments that should be made, but who depend on the investment department support personnel to make and administer the actual investments.

Asset Management Structure

Some insurance companies want a more direct correlation between investments and products so that company managers can determine and control the amount of investment income needed for each line of business. Traditional investment operations, though relatively simple to administer, may not permit close accounting between products and investments. In addition, some analysts contend that in a traditional structure, one line of business can actually operate at a loss while being subsidized by the premium and investment income of profitable lines of business. Therefore, many insurance companies organize their investment function in a manner similar to that shown in Figure 12-5.

As Figure 12-5 indicates, the asset management structure inserts another tier of management between the vice president of investments and the portfolio managers of the investment area. People at this additional tier of management are called *asset managers*. An asset manager's job is to monitor not just investments but all of the assets and liabilities of each specific line of business. (As noted in Chapter 8, actuaries provide much of the information about liabilities.) An asset manager is thus aware of all the money coming into and going out of each line of business. In consultation with the portfolio managers, the asset manager determines the best way to match assets and liabilities—that is, the best way to invest and adjust the company's asset holdings so that cash is available as it is needed. This process is known as *asset-liability matching.*

The main purpose of an asset management structure and asset-liability matching is to carry through the company's goals for earning a certain amount of money on its investments within a certain level of risk. From a regulator's viewpoint, the most important purpose of asset-liability matching is to help control the risk that the company will suffer disintermediation (discussed in Chapter 2).

An asset management structure can be established through separate

Figure 12-5
Investment department with asset managers.

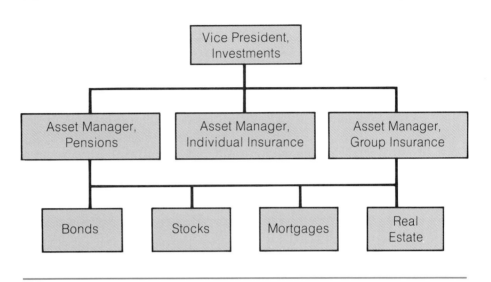

accounts, which are discussed in Chapter 13, or through a process known as segmentation of accounts. Under a policy of ***segmentation of accounts,*** asset portfolios are organized so that they support specific lines of business and specific products. Asset managers must make sure that cash is available to meet the marketing and servicing expenses of each line of business or product. These expenses include policy surrenders, claims, and dividends, if any.

Segmentation of accounts can be a challenging task because of the difficulty of (1) projecting the number of surrenders or lapses in a certain product or product line and (2) forecasting interest rates and returns on a company's investment portfolio. Both of these factors affect the amount of money coming in for a product. Asset management can also be more difficult for one product than another. For example, an asset manager who is working on a traditional whole life product for an established company has the benefit of a great deal of experience with surrenders and interest rates relative to that type of policy. On the other hand, an asset manager who is trying to match assets and projected liabilities for a newly introduced and untested product has a more difficult task because not as much information is available on which to base projections. Another drawback of asset-liability matching is its high cost. The expense of performing asset-liability matching also increases substantially when assets are managed along major product lines.

Independent Investment Companies

Some large insurance companies have created independent investment companies that may be properly classified as *spin-offs*. As noted in Chapter 2, **spin-offs** are former units or departments of a company that operate as independent companies whose primary customer is their parent company. Spin-offs can, however, offer their investment services to other individuals and organizations. They provide the parent company with all the necessary investment services, but they have their own accounting operations, information systems, and human resources areas. Some insurance companies have spun off their investment departments entirely, and others have separated only certain portions. A number of insurance company pension fund and real estate units now operate as independent investment management firms.

SETTING INVESTMENT POLICY

By law, a life and health insurance company's board of directors is responsible for establishing the broad guidelines for investing company funds. The board of directors usually appoints board members to a committee, often called the *investment committee* or *finance committee*, to develop and implement the company's general investment policies. Although the investment committee must oversee the investment policies of the insurance company, this overseer role may be an active or a passive one.

The actual makeup of a company's investment committee often influences the role that the committee plays in policymaking. Generally, an investment committee includes a few key company executives—such as the president, the chief financial officer, the chief actuary, and the vice president of investments—as well as individual board members from outside the company. These *outside directors* may be influential stockholders (in the case of a stock company) and may have backgrounds as lawyers, bankers, or any of a number of other professional occupations. Usually, the number of outside directors exceeds the number of company executives on the investment committee, so the role that the investment committee takes in the investment policies of a company often depends on the personalities and professional backgrounds of the outside directors.

Policies Set by the Investment Committee

In setting the broad guidelines for investing the company's assets, the investment committee first researches certain aspects of the company's financial position and investment status. Among the subjects studied at this time are the company's latest financial reports, the economic environment, the market position of the company, and the company's position relative to goals that the board of directors has set. Guidelines set by the investment committee typically incorporate the

- objectives that the company should achieve through its investments
- goals for specific, long-range planning periods (for example, the next year or the next five years)
- minimum standards for safety and investment earnings
- general types of investments needed to achieve the company's objectives
- types of risks that investment personnel can or cannot take in making investments
- dollar amount of an investment that each level of investment personnel can approve before having to seek approval from the next higher level of authority

In some companies, the investment committee also monitors the federal, state, and provincial regulations that constrain investment activities. Such monitoring may also be conducted by company lawyers and investment personnel. Periodically, the investment committee evaluates the performance of the company's investment program. Generally, however, the investment committee sets policy and establishes long-range plans, leaving day-to-day investment decisions in the hands of the vice president of investments and his or her professional staff.

Operational Planning

Whether an investment committee develops strategic investment policies for the company, or simply approves or disapproves the strategic policies suggested by the investment department, investment personnel must carry out those policies. The investment staff follows through on the operational plans that carry out the company's investment objectives.

The development of operational plans is the responsibility of (1) the vice president of investments, (2) asset managers (if such an organizational structure is used), and (3) portfolio managers from each of the functional areas. These investment professionals have extensive training in finance, mathematics, and economics. Many are Chartered Financial Analysts (CFAs), and many have earned master's degrees in business administration (MBAs).

Generally, the vice president and the asset managers continuously monitor the company's liabilities and generate information about the specific asset requirements needed to match the liabilities. Portfolio managers are told (1) the amount of money available for them to invest during the coming fiscal period and (2) the guidelines and goals set by the investment committee. The portfolio managers then discuss with other members of the investment staff the various investments and investment strategies needed to achieve their goals.

When choosing investments, a portfolio manager generally considers the following factors:

- expected **rate of return,** or *yield*, on the investment, which is the expected return of an investment expressed as a percentage of the cost or purchase price
- safety of the investment, which indicates the relative amount of risk involved in making an investment
- **diversification,** which is an investment strategy through which companies purchase many different types of investments to lessen the chance that the poor performance of any single investment will have a significant negative effect on the company's portfolio
- general economic conditions, including the expected inflation rate
- **liquidity** of the investment, which is the ease with which the investment can be converted into cash quickly and at a reasonable price
- tax laws that may affect the investment, especially the after-tax rate of return on the investment
- liabilities of the insurer and how the insurer's assets should match those liabilities
- regulations that limit the insurer's investments

TYPES OF INVESTMENTS

Life and health insurance companies place funds in a variety of investments. Because the management of each type of investment requires special expertise, investment operations in most companies are divided into functional investment areas: *stocks, bonds, mortgages,* and *real estate.* Throughout the next section of this chapter, we will describe these types of investments and some methods of investing in these assets. INSIGHT 12-1 offers a closer look at the investment environment for insurers as a specific point in time.

INSIGHT 12-1

A Move to Quality Investments

The economic environment for insurers during 1991 dictates a move to high-quality, conservative investments, according to respondents to a recent *Resource* magazine survey.

Jeff Seel, vice president and chief investment officer, Security Life of Denver, maintains that a life insurance company's policy concerning investments must support what the market demands. Therefore, "all investments need to be of high quality. Currently, Treasury or U.S. Government Guaranteed Investments are very appropriate."

Catherine B. Husman, FSA, vice president and corporate actuary for American United Life (AUL), believes that if companies did not make a choice to invest conservatively, the rating agencies would force them to do so. "The influence of the rating agencies is such that companies will be looking for as much quality in their portfolios as they can afford," she states. "Investments will be along traditional lines rather than into subsidiaries in non-insurance businesses as was popular in the 1980s. Marketable bonds may be preferred to private placements in order to provide companies with sources of liquidity."

Jim Robinson, vice president and controller, USAA Life and Health Insurance Division, says the companies that will attract business in the coming years are the ones with a conservative investment posture. "The public is demanding rock-solid financial institutions and they want investments to be stodgy, conservative and safe. A small percentage in well-chosen, below-investment-grade bonds makes sense. Also, well-chosen real estate properties or commercial mortgages make sense, especially those that are diversified geographically and by business type," he notes.

Bob Buckingham, FSA, vice president and valuation actuary at Century Life of America, and Robert Schneider, executive vice president and chief financial officer, The New England, both think independent rating agencies are the way to convince the public that the insurance industry is financially sound. Says Buckingham, "The life insurance industry must convince unbiased third parties such as major rating agencies within the country that the industry's investments are sound. Reliance on these third parties to corroborate the soundness of these investments will provide much more credence to the strength of the industry than simply declaring ourselves healthy." Schneider adds that, according to the latest Standard & Poor's compilations, "the insurance industry is by far the soundest—out of itself, banks, and S&Ls—in terms of asset quality."

Source: Adapted with permission of the publisher from Tim Kelley, "Profitability a Key Concern of Industry," *Resource,* July 1991, pp. 7-9.

Figure 12-6 shows the percentage of the different types of investments held by U.S. and Canadian life and health insurance companies in 1990.

Figure 12-6
Percentage of different types of investments held by life and health insurance companies in 1990.

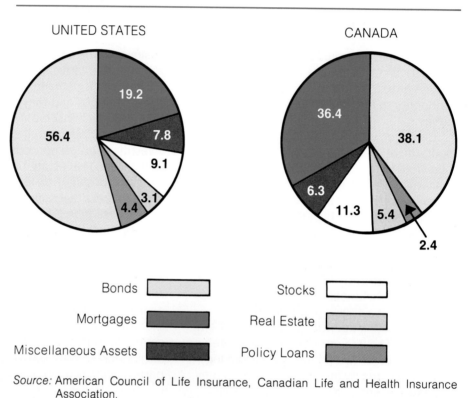

Source: American Council of Life Insurance, Canadian Life and Health Insurance Association.

Note that Figure 12-6 includes the percentage of policy loans held by insurance companies. Policy loans constitute a significant proportion of insurers' investments, but they are not generally administered by the investment staff. Policy loans are governed by provisions in the insurance contract and are made available to policyowners at interest rates stated in the contract. They are normally administered by customer service personnel.

Stocks

Stocks, more commonly called *shares* in Canada, are investments that represent ownership in a corporation. When a corporation is organized, the money needed for its operation can be raised by selling shares of its stock to people or organizations that want to invest in the corporation. These investors, called *stockholders* or *shareholders*, have **equity** in the corporation, which means that they are part owners of the business. Therefore, stocks are referred to as *equity investments*. (The term *equity-based insurance products* refers to insurance products that feature investments in a portfolio of stocks.)

Through ownership in a business, stockholders assume the risks of the business venture. If the business prospers, then the value of the stockholders' equity should increase accordingly, and the value of the stock should rise. If the business fails, then the stockholders could lose the entire amount of their investment.

Life and health insurance companies invest in two different types of stocks—*common stocks* and *preferred stocks* (see Figure 12-7). In the next few pages, we will discuss these two types of stocks and the main way that they are bought and sold.

Common stock

The most prevalent kind of stock issued today is **common stock.** Owners of a company's common stock have the following rights:

- voting in the election of the company's board of directors and on certain major questions affecting the firm
- sharing in the profits of the firm through dividends declared by the board of directors
- sharing in the distribution of assets when the company is dissolved

For years, various state and provincial regulations placed strict limitations on the total percentage of common stocks that a life and health insurance company could include in its assets. One reason for this limitation was the fact that common stocks are subject to wide fluctuations in value, depending on the profitability of the corporation and the general state of the economy. Because policyowners depend on life and health insurance companies to provide security from economic risk, regulators felt that too much reliance on the market performance of common stocks could threaten the ability of insurers to meet their obligations.

However, to allow insurance companies more freedom to compete as financial institutions, some states have eased their limitations on common stock purchases. For example, for a number of years the state of New York would not allow any insurer domiciled in the state to hold more than 10 percent of its assets in common stock. Now, New York simply requires that companies follow a **prudent investor rule,** which mandates that companies exercise sound and reasoned judgment in making their investment decisions. Nonetheless, restrictions still exist on trading certain types of stock-related products, such as stock futures and stock options. As of this

Figure 12-7
Stocks as a percentage of life and health insurers' assets, 1940-1990.

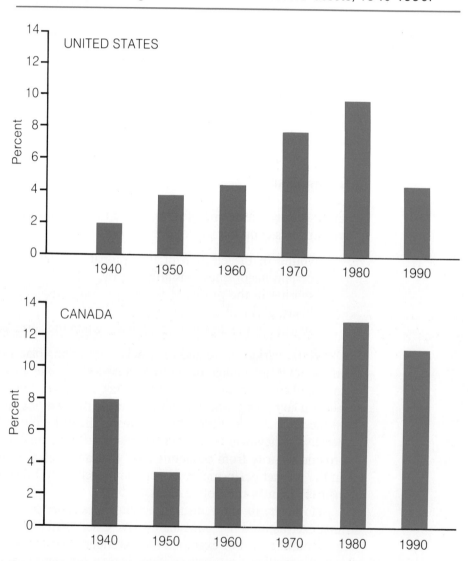

Source: American Council of Life Insurance, Canadian Life and Health Insurance Association.

writing, legislation was pending in the Canadian Parliament that would require financial institutions, including insurance companies, simply to follow prudent judgment when investing policyowners' money.

Preferred stock

Preferred stock is stock that usually carries a fixed, specified dividend payment. The dividend rate on preferred stock is specified as one of the terms of the preferred stock issue and is given as part of the identification of the stock, as in *General Motors 8 percent preferred;* this name indicates that this particular issue of preferred stock of the General Motors Corporation would pay a fixed annual amount of dividends equal to 8 percent of the preferred stock's par, or face, value. The declaration of a dividend on preferred stock, as on common stock, is always made at the discretion of the corporation's board of directors.

In general, preferred stockholders do not have voting rights as do common stockholders. However, preferred stockholders are given certain preferences over common stockholders in the distribution of the company's profits and assets. If the corporation goes out of business and must sell its assets in order to pay its debts, the preferred stockholders have a claim on the assets of the business. This claim ranks behind the claims of creditors but ahead of the claims of common stockholders. Preferred stockholders must be paid their dividends before any dividends can be paid on common stock.

Certain types of preferred stocks grant the stockholder additional rights. A *participating preferred stock* is one that grants stockholders the right to receive dividends above the stated rate if the company has good earnings and declares an extra dividend. A *cumulative preferred stock* is one on which the amount of any stated dividend that is not declared in one period is added to the dividend due in the following period. This obligation to pay cumulative preferred stockholders their dividends must be met before dividends can be paid to common stockholders. A company's preferred stock can have one, both, or neither of these features. Some preferred stocks, called *convertible preferreds,* can be converted into shares of common stock. *Floating rate preferreds* belong to a class of preferred stock that does not have a fixed dividend rate.

Preferred stocks do not have the certainty of income that is guaranteed to bondholders (discussed later) nor the liquidation preference of creditors. In addition, preferred stocks do not offer the capital gains potential of common stocks. As a result, despite some tax benefits that are available to holders of preferred stocks, these stocks are usually a small part—1 to 2 percent—of life and health insurers' investment portfolios.

Stock investment operations

The **stock market** is a network of intricate relationships through which stockholders, potential stock investors, and stockbrokers gather information about stocks, look for potential buyers and sellers, and make stock trades. Life and health insurance companies make most of their stock investments through the stock markets.

Many stocks are bought and sold through **stock exchanges.** The New York Stock Exchange and the American Stock Exchange are the best-known exchanges for stock transactions in the United States. In Canada, the best-known stock exchanges are the Toronto Stock Exchange and the Montreal Stock Exchange. Only the members of a stock exchange can buy and sell at the exchange. Members of stock exchanges are typically brokerage firms that take buy and sell orders from their clients—who may be individuals, investment clubs, financial institutions such as insurance companies, or governments—and carry out those orders through an auction process on the floor of the exchange.

Periodically, the portfolio manager in charge of stock investments for an insurance company is told the amount of money available to invest in stocks and the broad guidelines that should govern the choice of stock investments. Portfolio managers then make the day-to-day decisions about stock investing: when to buy or sell stocks, which stocks to trade, and how much to invest in particular stocks. Portfolio managers usually have a specific financial limit to their authority. For example, if a proposed stock purchase will cost the company more than $500,000, then the portfolio manager will ask the treasurer or vice president of investments to authorize the purchase.

If the proposed purchase is beyond the financial authority of the vice president of investments, then the purchase may require authorization by the president of the company, the company's investment committee, or its board of directors. Presentation to the board of directors takes time, and time is important in most investments. Many companies, therefore, give their investment staffs a high level of approval authority so that investment opportunities are not missed because of delays in obtaining approval.

When portfolio managers make their decisions, they do so based on information gathered for them by *investment analysts,* or *securities analysts.* Like other members of the investment staff, investment analysts have extensive knowledge of economics, finance, mathematics, and management. Many investment analysts have earned MBAs and have work experience in the industries they analyze, such as forest products, retail sales, and banking. Investment analysts are sometimes assigned directly to a functional area, such as the stock section of an investment unit, or they can be assigned to a central investment research section.

Investment analysts examine annual reports and frequently interview the management of companies issuing stocks. They read financial publications, such as the *Wall Street Journal,* the *Financial Post, Forbes,* and *Value Line Investment Survey,* to identify economic trends and investment opportunities. They study stock market averages and indexes, which measure the general behavior of stock prices. Using the most recent financial statements of individual companies, investment analysts evaluate the various financial accounts within a company, compare that information with general industry information that they have gathered, and try to determine a company's actual strength and the value of its stock as an investment. Investment analysts also use a number of computer software packages to gain easy access to investment tools, such as daily stock information, historical data on a variety of stocks, charts of stock activity, and formulas for calculating financial ratios and projecting economic trends.

After receiving sufficient information from investment analysts, the portfolio manager may discuss proposed investments with other portfolio managers, asset managers, and the vice president of investments. The portfolio manager then tells the department's trader which stocks to buy or sell, the price limitations for buying or selling, and the deadline for the transaction. The trader then contacts a *registered representative,* who carries out buy and sell orders on the stock exchange floor.

Usually at the end of each day, particularly in very large companies, the entire staff of the investment area's stock unit meets to discuss the transactions made during the day and to plan the next day's activities.

Bonds

Whereas stocks represent ownership, bonds represent debt. Governments and corporations, like individuals, often need more money than they have at any particular time. Organizations that need money can borrow it by issuing bonds to investors. A **bond** is a *debt investment* that represents a promise on the part of its issuer to repay the borrowed money to the bondholder at a stated time in the future and, in the meantime, to pay interest to the bondholder at either a specified rate or a floating rate. Bonds are usually issued in multiples of $1,000, and interest is usually payable semiannually.

The investor who purchases a bond is lending money to the issuer, and the investor is, therefore, a creditor of the issuer. The **bond certificate** is the evidence of the issuer's debt to the owner of the bond. The bond certificate states the amount of principal (also known as the bond's *face amount* or *par value*), the rate and timing of interest payments, and the **maturity date,** which is the date on which the principal will be repaid to the bondholder.

Some bonds are **callable,** which means that the issuer has the right to pay them off at a date earlier than the maturity date at a price specified on the bonds. Some bonds are **convertible,** which means that they can be converted into shares of the bond issuer's common stock at a stated conversion rate. Both equity investments (stocks) and debt investments (bonds) are called *securities.*

The risk of loss is normally less for a company's bondholders than for a company's stockholders. Because bondholders are creditors, they are said to have prior claim to the assets of the business. Having **prior claim** means that if a business fails and its assets are sold to raise money to pay its debts, certain investors' claims on the business assets will be met before the claims of other investors. Bondholders' claims on a business's assets are met before stockholders' claims. Stockholders, being part owners, receive only what is left of the assets after all business debts, including those to bondholders, are paid.

However, if a business is profitable, bondholders receive only the stated interest payments and the return of the principal amount of their bonds. Holders of common stock, on the other hand, stand to gain from the company's increased profitability. Their portions of the company's profits, which the company pays periodically to the stockholders in the form of *dividends,* can increase, as can the market value of their stock. In contrast, dividends on preferred stock do not generally increase.

Bonds constitute the largest category of investments held by most North American insurance companies. As shown in Figure 12-8, life and health insurers have historically invested a fairly large portion of their assets in bonds. In 1990, U.S. life and health insurance companies held 56.4 percent of their assets in bonds, and Canadian companies held 38.1 percent of their assets in bonds. The two primary issuers of bonds are governments and corporations.

All levels of government issue bonds: federal governments, states, provinces, territories, possessions, counties, cities, and towns. In the United States, government bonds other than those classified as federal bonds are usually called **municipal bonds,** even when cities are not the issuers. In Canada, only those bonds that are backed by city governments and sold in the municipal markets are called *municipal bonds.* In 1990, Canadian life and health insurance companies held 22 percent of their assets in government bonds, and U.S. companies held 15 percent of their assets in government bonds.

Most government bonds are called **general obligation bonds,** because they are backed only by the credit and taxing power of the government unit that issued them. However, not all government bonds are backed by credit or taxing authority. Some bonds issued in the United States, called **revenue**

Figure 12-8
Bonds as a percentage of life and health insurers' assets, 1940-1990.

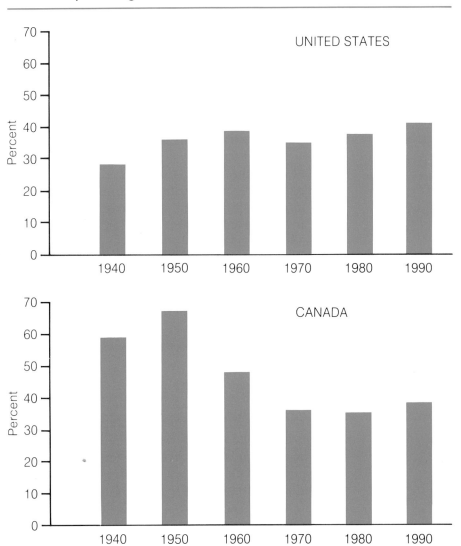

Source: American Council of Life Insurance, Canadian Life and Health Insurance Association.

bonds, are backed only by the income the issuer expects to receive from the project for which the bonds were issued. For example, if a city issues a revenue bond to raise money to build a convention center, then the bond is backed by the income that the city expects to receive from operating the convention center.

Bonds issued by the federal government are considered among the safest of any investments available to the public. That benefit is somewhat offset, however, by the fact that they usually pay relatively low rates of interest compared with riskier types of bonds. Generally, riskier investments pay higher rates of return, but because of the nature of the insurance business, safety is an important factor in an insurer's investment portfolio.

Corporate bonds are secured or unsecured bonds issued by corporations. When a corporation issues *secured bonds,* it pledges that some or all of its assets or properties will be used to meet the bondholders' claims if payment is not made when due. In case of such default, the bondholders have first claim on the specified assets and can have them sold to provide funds for meeting the bond obligations. Unsecured bonds, called *debentures,* are backed only by the corporation's promise to pay, that is, by the full faith and credit of the issuer. When a corporation issues debentures, no specific assets are pledged to support the bonds. Payment depends entirely on the corporation's earning power and net worth. All other factors being equal, a company's secured bonds are regarded as a safer investment than the same company's debentures. However, the debentures of a financially strong corporation may be regarded as safer than the secured bonds of a company in a weaker financial position.

Bond investment operations

Investors who buy bonds are not required to hold those bonds until the maturity date. A bond can be bought and sold by different investors over and over again as long as some investor is interested in buying the bond. When interest rates and the economy are fairly stable, insurance companies tend to buy bonds and hold them until they mature. However, when interest rates fluctuate widely and financial markets are volatile, insurance companies trade bonds almost as frequently as they trade stocks.

Bonds that are offered for sale to the general public are known as *public offerings,* and they must be registered with government agencies (such as the Securities and Exchange Commission [SEC] in the United States). However, some corporations issue investments that are not offered to the general public. These investments, called *private placements,* or *direct placements,* are offered by the issuer directly to specific financial institutions and do not need to be registered with government agencies. A private placement can occur with or without an investment banker's acting as an agent between the investor and the issuer. In addition to bonds, stocks and mortgages can also be issued as private placements.

Private placements provide a number of benefits for both the issuer and the investor. The issuer does not have to spend time and money paying registration fees and registering the issue with government securities agencies. When an investment banker's services are not needed, the issuer does not pay the investment banker's distribution fees. The issuer is saved the uncertainties of trying to sell the investment to the general public. If the terms of a private placement need to be renegotiated at some date, the issuer usually has to negotiate with only one investor or a small group of investors.

Because the issuer is saving the costs of a more expensive means of distribution and because, in many cases, the investor is giving up liquidity, the investor can usually obtain a higher rate of return on a private placement than is normally available on public offerings with otherwise similar terms. Finally, both the issuer and the investor can negotiate the terms of agreement to suit their specific needs. For example, the issuer of a privately placed bond issue can negotiate to obtain a favorable repayment schedule, and the investor can negotiate to include provisions that allow the investor to convert the bonds, within a stipulated period, into a specified number of shares of the issuer's common stock.

Information about bonds

Bond analysts obtain information about bonds from many sources. The following publications and reports provide most of the information needed to evaluate bonds for investment:

- the annual reports of companies issuing bonds
- brokerage reports
- for public offerings, 10-K and 10-Q reports that U.S. companies must file with the SEC
- articles in newspapers and business journals
- meetings with officials of companies that issue bonds

Bond analysts also evaluate bond yields and bond ratings for public offerings. **Bond yields** indicate the rate of return that a bond is expected to earn. By comparing the yield of a bond with the yields of other bonds of a similar type, quality, and maturity, analysts can obtain information to help them time their bond purchases and sales. *Barron's*, a financial news publication, quotes average yields for a variety of corporate and municipal bonds.

Bond ratings, which are letter grades that indicate the credit quality of bond issues, are assigned by rating agencies, such as Standard & Poor's, Moody's Investor Services, and Dominion Bond Rating Service. The National Association of Insurance Commissioners (NAIC) has also adopted a system for rating bonds. Bond ratings are based on a variety of factors, such as the earnings record of the issuing corporation, the size of the company, the amount of the company's bond indebtedness, and the property—if any—pledged to back up the bonds.

The meaning and interpretations of bond ratings vary only slightly from agency to agency. Standard & Poor's ratings, for example, are AAA, AA, A, BBB, BB, B, CCC, CC, C, DDD, DD, and D. Ranked in this way, AAA bonds have the highest rating and are the safest possible bond investment. Bonds grade BB and below are considered speculative, and bonds in the D grade are in *default,* which means that the bond issuer is unable to make either payments of interest or repayments of principal to bondholders. In general, the higher the rating, the lower the rate of return; the lower the rating, the higher the rate of return.

Mortgages

One of the most common reasons that individuals and organizations borrow money is to finance the purchase of real property or real estate—land, a home, an office building, a factory. The person or organization that lends the money seeks to minimize the investment risk, and the customary way of doing this is to have the loan secured by a pledge of the property. A *mortgage* is a legal instrument under which a lender can claim the real property pledged for a loan if the borrower does not make the loan payments when due. In 1990, mortgage loans were generally the second-largest category of investments held by insurers (see Figure 12-9).

Most mortgage loans are long-term, with the period to repay the loan lasting as long as 30 years. In the United States, the interest rate on the loan can be fixed for up to the full 30 years, but in Canada, the interest rate is typically fixed for a shorter period of time, such as 6 months to 5 years. In order to provide reasonable safety for the lender, the amount of the mortgage loan is usually less than the appraised value of the property. Also, most states in the United States limit the amount that an insurer can invest in a mortgage to 80 percent of the property's appraised value.

Mortgage loans are usually *amortized,* which means that the borrower gradually pays off the loan by making periodic payments of principal and interest throughout the life of the mortgage. Each mortgage payment consists partly of interest and partly of principal in predetermined amounts.

Figure 12-9
Mortgages as a percentage of life and health insurers' assets, 1940-1990.

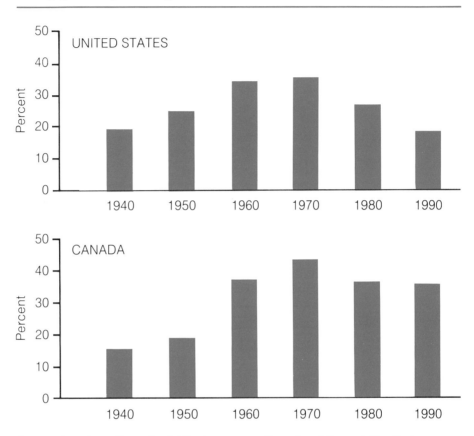

Source: American Council of Life Insurance, Canadian Life and Health Insurance
            Association.

Frequently, the lender collects money for property taxes and property insurance along with the monthly mortgage payments and holds this tax and insurance money in a special account, called an ***escrow account.*** The lender pays property taxes and insurance premiums as they come due with the money in the escrow account.

Life and health insurance companies have always been an important source of mortgage loans, although the distribution of insurers' mortgage loans has shifted over the years. Before the 1920s, most insurers' mortgage investments were farm properties. With changes in the economy, a decrease in the number of farms, and an increase in residential and commercial construction, the predominant area of mortgage loans shifted from farms to private residences, then to apartment houses, and now to nonresidential commercial buildings. At the end of 1990, the mortgage loans of U.S. insurance companies were distributed as follows:

Nonresidential property	81 percent
Multifamily property	11 percent
One- to four-family property	5 percent
Farm property	4 percent

In the past, mortgages provided profitable long-term investments for insurance companies. However, in the late 1970s interest rates began to rise quickly, and the long-term nature of mortgages became a burden for insurance companies. A large portion of many insurance companies' assets were invested in 20- and 30-year mortgages that were yielding fixed interest rates of 4, 6, or 8 percent per year while the prevailing interest rates were 10, 15, and even 20 percent. Insurers could not earn competitive interest rates on their old mortgages, and they could not sell the old mortgages without losing money. Today, insurance companies still hold a large portion of their assets in mortgages, but as their old, fixed-interest, 30-year mortgages mature, insurance companies are investing in shorter-term mortgages that mature in 5, 10, or 15 years. Another type of mortgage that insurers can invest in is an ***adjustable-rate mortgage (ARM),*** which allows the interest rates to rise or fall with prevailing interest rates in the national economy.

Mortgage operations

Insurance companies acquire mortgages either by dealing directly with borrowers or by dealing with mortgage brokers or mortgage bankers who represent borrowers.

Direct acquisition of mortgages. Under the direct acquisition method, the insurance company must generally establish its own regional mortgage offices, called *branch offices*. These branch offices are staffed with mortgage analysts and inspectors who look for mortgage investment opportunities. The branch office staff evaluates the possible risks and earnings of proposed mortgage investments, inspects the properties under consideration, and makes recommendations to the home office mortgage unit about specific mortgage investments. Unless the mortgage is especially large or of a type not usually accepted by the insurance company, the recommendation of the regional mortgage analyst is normally accepted by the home office. Uncommonly large or complex mortgages, however, are generally reviewed by company attorneys to assure that the mortgage contract is legal and enforceable.

Once a mortgage loan is approved and the loan is made, the insurer must administer or service the mortgage loan. Servicing a loan includes (1) mailing mortgage payment notices, (2) collecting payments, (3) putting money into an escrow account, and (4) paying insurance premiums and taxes from the escrow account. The branch office, a local mortgage servicing company, or the home office can service the mortgage.

Acquisition through mortgage correspondents. Although a number of large insurance companies have established branch office systems to seek and acquire mortgage investments, many companies, both large and small, obtain their investments indirectly through *mortgage correspondents.* Mortgage bankers and brokers are both called *mortgage correspondents* because they act as correspondents between borrowers, such as building contractors, and lenders, such as insurance companies. The mortgage correspondent receives a fee consisting of a small percentage of the outstanding balance of the loan. In return, the correspondent performs all the various functions involved in mortgage investment operations, including locating the loan prospect, appraising the mortgage property, and servicing the loan. By paying someone else to find and obtain mortgage investments for them, many insurance companies, especially small companies, feel that they can reduce their expenses and make their operations more efficient.

Mortgage-backed securities. Since the late 1970s, mortgage-backed securities have become a major portion of the mortgage investment market. One type of mortgage-backed security is a *pass-through certificate,* which represents fractional ownership, such as 10 percent, in a pool of mortgages. Another type of mortgage-backed security is a collateralized mortgage obligation (CMO). A *CMO* is a type of bond backed by investments in mortgages. Holders of CMOs are grouped according to the length of investment desired. Short-term investors are entitled to the first distributions of principal, then intermediate-term investors, and then long-term investors. Instruments such as pass-through certificates and CMOs are bought and sold as if they were bonds.

Real Estate

Real estate investments differ significantly from the mortgage loan investments discussed earlier. When making a real estate investment, an insurance company actually buys real property in the form of land or buildings. The company is not lending money to some other party to buy or build real property. Because ownership is involved, real estate investments are classified, like stocks, as equity investments.

Real estate investments account for only a small percentage of the assets of life and health insurance companies. In fact, in some jurisdictions, investment in real estate for other than the insurance company's own use has been limited by statute. In 1990, real estate investments accounted for 5.4 percent of Canadian companies' assets and 3.1 percent of U.S. companies' assets (see Figure 12-10). About 20 percent of this real estate investment consisted of property used by the insurance companies themselves—their home and field offices. Despite the small proportion of insurers' portfolios that real estate investments represent, real estate provides insurers with additional risk diversification and an opportunity for high after-tax returns.

Restrictions on real estate other than that for the company's own use were originally established in the early 1900s. Regulatory authorities believed that real estate was not a safe investment for insurance companies, especially after several companies suffered large losses on their real estate holdings. More recently, however, regulators have decided that prudently managed real estate investments can be appropriate investments for insurers. Therefore, regulators have eased investment limitations on many kinds of real estate properties, but strongly discourage speculative investments. Today, insurance companies are buying warehouses, shopping centers, apartment complexes, and office buildings. Pension funds especially are investing in real estate. Because of their large cash flow and the long-term nature of their liabilities, pension funds are well suited to real estate investments, which usually require large initial cash outlays and provide high rates of return if held as long-term investments.

The following factors are especially important in an insurer's decision to invest in real estate:

- *Current income.* Real estate offers investors current income at rates that are generally higher than the rates paid on most other equity investments, especially common stocks.
- *Stability of value.* Real estate values do not fluctuate as much as the values of common stocks, or even fixed-income bonds. Although inflation tends to reduce the value of many securities, the value of real estate has remained stable and has even increased during periods of inflation. One reason for the stability of real estate prices is that the market for real estate is not very liquid.
- *Tax aspects.* Insurers can benefit from owning improved real estate by using depreciation to shelter income from federal and state income taxes.

Figure 12-10
Real estate as a percentage of life and health insurers' assets, 1940-1990.

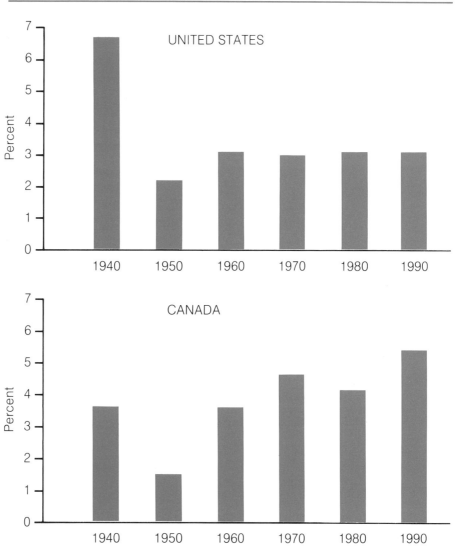

Source: American Council of Life Insurance, Canadian Life and Health Insurance Association.

- *Liquidity.* As mentioned earlier, real estate is generally not a very liquid investment. As a result, prices are not measured on a daily basis as they are with some other types of investments. Technology makes it possible to sell common stocks in a matter of seconds, but real estate sales may take many months to complete. Only those funds that can be committed for a number of years should be invested in real estate.

All of an insurer's real estate must, by law, be purchased either for the insurer's own use or as income-producing property. Thus, an insurer cannot buy undeveloped land for speculative purposes. However, an insurer can buy undeveloped land if it plans to develop the property.

Methods of acquiring real estate

The simplest method of acquiring real estate is outright purchase. Sometimes such a purchase is made directly by the insurer; in other cases, the insurer forms a subsidiary company that specializes in real estate investments. If the amount of an investment is too large for an individual insurer to provide by itself, the insurer may join with other companies, insurers or noninsurers, to pay for the investment together. This arrangement, in which an individual or organization becomes a partner and part owner in a business enterprise, is a form of joint venture. Joint ventures, which were discussed in Chapter 2 and which will be mentioned again in Chapter 17, are particularly common when property is being developed for a noninsurance partner.

Life and health insurers also invest in real estate by participating in a *sale-and-leaseback transaction,* under which the owner of a building sells the building to an investor but immediately leases back the building from the investor. For example, property may be built by a developer, who then sells the property to an insurance company and immediately leases the property back from the insurance company. Maintenance and operation of the property become the responsibility of the *lessee,* which is the individual or organization that is leasing the building from the owner. The insurance company, as *lessor,* is freed from administration of the property—such as collecting rent and maintaining the property—while still collecting income from the lessee's rental payment. Frequently, the lessee is also required to pay the taxes and insurance on the property. Such an arrangement means that the lease is a *net lease.*

A sale-and-leaseback transaction has benefits for both the developer and the insurance company. By selling the building to the insurance company, the developer recovers the cost of construction. The developer then can use the recovered costs either to operate the building as a lessee or else to finance the development of another property. The insurance company benefits because it thus obtains a sizable investment in a single income-producing real estate asset. Also, as discussed earlier, the insurance company obtains tax benefits from depreciation of the property.

RELATIONSHIPS WITH OTHER DEPARTMENTS

Actuarial, marketing, and accounting personnel frequently work with the investment staff, especially when investment-sensitive products are being developed. In addition, because investment operations are so important to the financial stability of the company, the executive office and the board of directors also have a close relationship with the investment staff.

Generally, accountants are responsible for reporting the company's financial results, and actuaries project the company's expected assets and liabilities, the frequency with which liabilities must be paid, and the frequency with which assets will be replenished. Both the accountants and the actuaries depend on investment specialists to report to them the rate of return that company investments are currently earning and the rate they are expected to earn in the future. Combining all this information allows company managers to match the company's assets with its liabilities and to help assure that the company remains financially sound.

Communications between the investment department and other company departments are especially important when the product design task force is planning a new product or revising a current one. With advice from many different areas of the company, the product design task force outlines a product and describes it to the investment staff. This description includes the (1) rate of investment earnings needed to make the product successful, (2) types of liabilities associated with the product, (3) frequency with which claims will probably be made on the product, and (4) projected cash flow generated by the product. After studying its current investments, the conditions of investment markets, and the general state of the economy, the investment staff advises the product design task force about the types of investments necessary for the success of the product and the expected rate of return on those investments.

Figure 12-11 illustrates some of the most important relationships between the investment function and other areas inside and outside the company.

Figure 12-11
Relationship of the investment department with other departments in the company and with organizations outside the company.

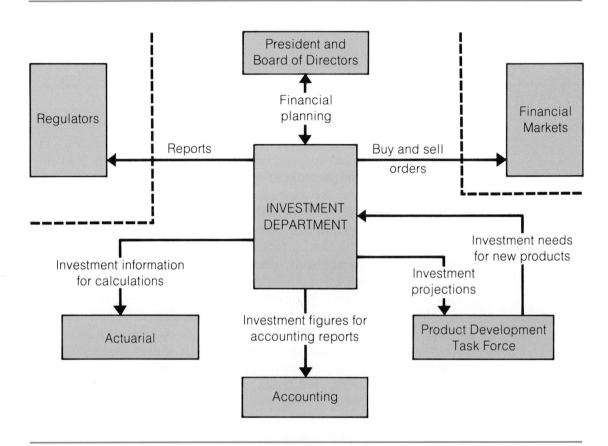

KEY TERMS

portfolio
asset-liability matching
segmentation of accounts
spin-off
rate of return
diversification
liquidity
stocks
equity

common stock
prudent investor rule
preferred stock
participating preferred stock
cumulative preferred stock
convertible preferred stock
floating rate preferred stock
stock market
stock exchange

bond
bond certificate
maturity date
callable bond
convertible bond
prior claim
municipal bond
general obligation bond
revenue bond
corporate bond
secured bond
debenture
public offering
private placement

bond yield
bond rating
default
mortgage
amortized loan
escrow account
adjustable-rate mortgage (ARM)
mortgage correspondent
pass-through certificate
collateralized mortgage obligation
  (CMO)
sale-and-leaseback transaction
lessee
net lease

Chapter 13

The Accounting Function

After reading this chapter, you should be able to

- Identify the parties that use or are interested in accounting information
- Define the term *solvency* and explain why this concept is particularly important to insurance companies
- Describe the responsibilities of the company's controller and the rest of the accounting staff
- Identify the elements of the basic accounting equation and explain their relationship and interaction during an accounting transaction
- Distinguish between statutory accounting practices (SAP) and generally accepted accounting principles (GAAP)
- Identify three accounting reports that most companies issue
- State the purpose of separate, or segregated, accounts
- Explain the purposes of financial analysis and auditing

The accounting function provides some of the most essential information used in business management. **Accounting** is a system for collecting, analyzing, and summarizing financial data. This system provides information needed to make business decisions and to satisfy financial reporting requirements. People studying a company's accounts and financial statements can learn about the organization's financial activities and can project in a more informed way what the company's financial prospects might be. Accurate financial reports help show whether or not a company is financially sound and whether or not it is making a profit. By analyzing these reports, a company's management can identify trends and problem areas in company activities and can develop appropriate strategies for improving performance.

In this chapter, we will discuss the accounting function, accounting fundamentals, and the most important accounting reports. In addition, we will describe accounting principles and practices that apply to insurance companies; the ways in which accounting helps with company analysis, planning, and control; and the use of audits in the accounting function.

WHO USES ACCOUNTING INFORMATION?

Many people and organizations are interested in accounting information. Within a company, *board members, officers,* and *managers* need accounting information to establish company goals and policies and to monitor company financial performance. *Employees* at many levels use accounting information to carry out their jobs, such as billing customers, paying for purchases, and preparing paychecks, claim payments, and commission payments.

Company owners examine financial statements derived from accounting information to determine if the company is operationally and financially secure, because the owners can lose part or all of their investment in the company if the business fails. The owners are also interested in the company's financial performance. If returns on their investment in the company are not adequate, the owners may consider selling their interest in the business and placing their money in an investment with better prospects of success.

Insurance consumers are concerned primarily with the premiums the company charges and with the company's ability to survive and meet its future obligations. *Creditors* are primarily concerned with the company's **solvency,** which is the ability to meet financial obligations as they come due. *Potential creditors* may want to analyze the company's financial strength before deciding whether and under what terms to extend the company credit.

Finally, various *government agencies* use the company's accounting information. Income taxes that a company must pay are based on accounting data that shows what the company has earned. In addition, government regulators analyze a company's accounting information in order to help determine whether the company is meeting legal requirements that apply to the operation of an insurance company.

ACCOUNTING PERSONNEL AND THEIR ACTIVITIES

Accounting personnel are responsible for planning, controlling, and analyzing many financial activities. *Controller* is the title typically given to the executive in charge of a company's accounting department. Depending on the company, the controller may report to the company's chief financial officer, the vice president in charge of finance, or the company president. The controller is generally a certified public accountant (CPA) in the United

States or a chartered accountant (CA) in Canada. Reporting to the controller may be an associate or assistant controller, an accounting manager, or a chief accountant, each of whom usually has a recognized professional designation in accounting as well. Senior accountants, accounting analysts, and assistant accountants also participate in the accounting function.

The accounting function in an insurance company generally includes the following major areas:

- policy accounting
- investment accounting
- tax accounting
- general accounting
- budget planning and control
- cost analysis
- management information reporting
- internal auditing

As shown in Figure 13-1, most of these areas are the responsibility of the controller. Frequently, however, the internal auditing unit reports directly to the auditing committee discussed in Chapter 3. This reporting relationship, which maintains the independence and objectivity of the internal auditing unit, is necessary because internal auditors examine the accounting function as well as all the other functions in the company.

Figure 13-1
Organization chart of an accounting department.

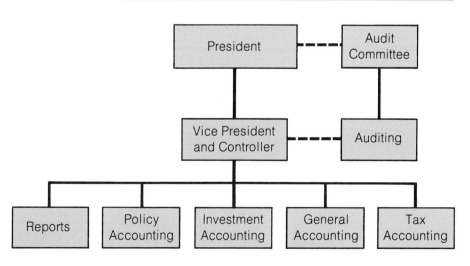

In a life and health insurance company, the accounting staff is responsible for activities such as

- establishing the system of accounts used to classify assets, liabilities, income, and expenses
- maintaining the company's accounting records
- recording receipts and disbursements
- preparing accounting and financial reports
- preparing tax returns
- planning and controlling budgets
- analyzing operating costs
- allocating costs and expenses to areas throughout the company
- conducting audits of records and procedures

Accountants may also assist with strategic planning by helping to develop long-term plans and goals for the entire organization. Later in this chapter, we will discuss in some depth the work performed by accountants specializing in policy accounting, investment accounting, general accounting, and tax accounting.

People throughout an insurance company interact with the accounting staff. Accountants help plan and control operating budgets for each of a company's divisions. The accounting staff may also administer the company's cash funds, reimburse employees for travel expenses, and prepare functional expense analyses for different divisions, products, or profit centers. In addition, the internal auditing unit periodically sends staff members throughout the company to evaluate records, operations, and reporting procedures.

ACCOUNTING FUNDAMENTALS

Although this chapter is concerned primarily with accounting operations, certain accounting fundamentals, terms, and principles must be described before we go on to more detailed discussions. In the next few pages, we will briefly introduce these accounting fundamentals.

The Basic Accounting Equation

The basic accounting equation contains three components: *assets, liabilities,* and *owner's equity.*

- **Assets** are all things of value owned by the company. Examples of assets include investments, cash, and data processing equipment.
- **Liabilities** are the company's debts and future obligations. A life and health insurance company's liabilities include the actual and expected claims of its policyowners and their beneficiaries and the amounts owed to creditors.
- **Owner's equity** is the difference between a company's assets and its liabilities and represents the owner's financial interest in the company. Owner's equity includes the company's *capital* and its *surplus*.

Assets are equal to liabilities plus owner's equity. This relationship is expressed in the basic accounting equation:

$$Assets = Liabilities + Owner's\ Equity$$

When recording monetary transactions on its books, a company always keeps both sides of this accounting equation in balance. This process is shown in the following example:

1. ***Jack Crane and James Good form a business by investing a total of $1,000 of their own money.***

   Assets = Liabilities + Owner's Equity
   $1,000 = 0 + $1,000

   The investment of $1,000 provides the company with that amount of assets in the form of cash. The sum is attributable solely to the owners, so the owner's equity in the company is $1,000. Liabilities are zero. If the company were to go out of business at this time, the entire amount of its capital would be returned to the owners, Jack Crane and James Good.

2. ***The company purchases merchandise on credit for $400.***

   Assets = Liabilities + Owner's Equity
   $1,400 = $400 + $1,000

   The assets of the company now include $400 worth of merchandise, plus $1,000 in cash. However, the company has incurred a debt of $400, which is recorded as a liability. Note that the owner's equity did not change. If the company were to go out of business at this time, $400 would be paid first to the creditor who financed the purchase of the merchandise. After the creditor is paid, the assets and liabilities would be reduced by $400, and the owners would receive only their original investment of $1,000 ($600 in cash and $400 in merchandise).

3. The company sells the merchandise for $700 cash.

Assets = Liabilities + Owner's Equity
$1,700 = $400 + $1,300

The sale of the merchandise has two effects on assets. First, the asset total is decreased by $400 because the company no longer owns the merchandise. Second, the company increases its asset total by the $700 in cash received from the sale. The effect is a net increase of $300 in assets. No creditor is involved in this transaction. Therefore, the liabilities do not change. Because the equation must always be kept in balance—that is, the left side must equal the right side—the owner's equity is increased to $1,300. If the company were to go out of business at this point, the creditor would be paid the debt of $400, leaving $1,300 in cash to be paid to the owners.

4. The company pays its creditor the $400 owed.

Assets = Liabilities + Owner's Equity
$1,300 = 0 + $1,300

Because the creditor has been paid, the assets are reduced by $400 and the company no longer has any liabilities. The owners are entitled to all of the company's assets. The amount of capital has risen from the original investment of $1,000. This increase is directly attributable to the $300 profit made on the sale of the merchandise.

Note that each transaction uses the technique of *double-entry bookkeeping*—that is, each transaction has two effects on the basic accounting equation. For example, the purchase of merchandise on credit increases both assets and liabilities, and the sale of merchandise increases assets and owner's equity.

Accounting Terminology

The basic accounting equation (Assets = Liabilities + Owner's Equity) provides the framework for classifying accounting data. However, these three categories do not sufficiently classify accounting data for most practical purposes. *Assets*, for example, is a broad category that includes cash, amounts receivable, equipment, supplies, inventories, investments, and other things of value to the company. Even some of these classifications are too broad to be useful and need to be further subdivided by establishing a series of accounts.

An *account* records the transactions involving a particular asset, liability, or owner's equity item. Traditionally, accounts have been

Figure 13-2
T-Account for cash assets.

Cash

Debit Side (Incoming Cash)		Credit Side (Outgoing Cash)	
July 1, 1992	5,000.00	July 31, 1992	2,651.19
July 31	3,500.00	August 31	1,102.53
August 31	8,246.75		

---

represented in the form of a T. A T-account for cash assets is shown in Figure 13-2. When an account is shown in this manner, the title of the account is centered above the T. Monetary transactions for the account are recorded as accounting entries. Accountants use the terms *debits* and *credits* for entries recorded in accounts.

- A **debit** is an entry made on the left side of an account.
- A **credit** is an entry made on the right side of an account.

Debits increase asset and expense accounts, but decrease liability, income, and owners' equity accounts. Credits increase liability, income, and owners' equity accounts, but decrease asset and expense accounts.

When financial transactions first occur, they are usually recorded in a **journal,** also called a *book of original entry*, which is a chronological listing of all of a firm's financial transactions. The record of each transaction is called a *journal entry*. After journal entries are made, they are *posted*, or recorded, in the appropriate accounts. The collection of all of a company's accounts is the **ledger,** also called the *general ledger* and the *book of final entry*.

In the past, journals and ledgers were maintained manually and kept in large bound books. Today, business accounting records are typically stored and updated electronically.

Accounting Principles

Life and health insurers have historically and by law used accounting principles that focus on the requirements of insurance regulators and the interests of policyowners. The accounting principles followed by insurance companies are based on *statutory accounting practices (SAP)*. Most businesses other than insurance companies use *generally accepted accounting principles (GAAP)* instead of SAP. The main difference between SAP and GAAP is that statutory accounting is primarily designed to show a company's financial solvency—that is, could the company pay its debts if it needed to sell its assets and go out of business today? GAAP statements measure the company's financial condition using the **going-concern concept,** which assumes that the company will remain in business in the future.

To provide uniform financial reporting in most of the business community in the United States, the Securities and Exchange Commission (SEC) requires virtually all stock insurance companies, as well as any type of insurance company that sells equity-based products, to file financial statements based on GAAP as well as statements based on SAP. By studying GAAP financial statements, investors can more easily compare the financial positions of insurance companies with the financial positions of other types of businesses.

Canadian insurers follow the statutory accounting practices prescribed by the federal Canadian and British Insurance Companies Act and its related regulations and forms. This Act's objective is the same as that of statutory accounting practices in the United States: to help ensure the solvency of insurance companies and thus protect policyowner interests. Canadian insurance companies began moving to GAAP-based reporting in 1992.

ACCOUNTING REPORTS AND STATEMENTS

As mentioned earlier, reports produced by the accounting staff provide an essential source of information for an insurance company's managers, owners, policyowners, customers, regulators, and competitors. In the next few pages, we will talk about some of the reports and statements that provide this information.

Accounting Reports

Accounting reports are prepared for both internal and external uses. Certain accounting reports are prepared solely for the company's management. Such reports include operating budgets, financial forecasts, analyses of the source and use of funds, expense analyses, and analyses of the profitability of product lines, individual products, or sales territories.

The primary accounting report that a company makes public is the statutory *Annual Statement.* Governmental authorities prescribe the exact form of this statement, which includes a balance sheet, income statement, and detailed schedules of investments and insurance activities. Many companies also publish an *annual report.*

Balance sheet

A ***balance sheet*** shows a company's financial condition as of a particular date. The date, always shown in the heading of the report, is usually the end of a fiscal period, such as a year or a quarter of a year. The balance sheet consists of a general listing of the firm's assets, liabilities, surplus, and capital. Figure 13-3 shows a simple balance sheet.

Balance sheets are based directly on the basic accounting equation:

Figure 13-3
Example of a balance sheet.

Assets:	
Cash	$ 8,000
Accounts Receivable	4,500
Equipment	20,000
Building	15,000
Total Assets	$47,500
Liabilities:	
Accounts Payable	$ 5,000
Mortgage Payable	10,000
Total Liabilities	$15,000
Capital:	
Capital Stock	$20,000
Surplus	12,500
Total Capital	$32,500
Total Liabilities and Capital	$47,500

Assets = Liabilities + Owner's Equity. The total of both sides of the balance sheet must equal each other, just as in the basic accounting equation.

Income statement

During its normal business activities, a company generates income and incurs expenses. The company's profit or loss depends on the relationship between income and expenses. An ***income statement*** reports on the profitability of a company for a given period by summarizing the company's income and expense accounts during that time. This report is sometimes called a *profit and loss statement,* an *income and expense statement,* or a *revenue statement.* Figure 13-4 shows a simple income statement.

Figure 13-4
Example of an income statement.

Widget Computer Corporation

Income Statement
For the Year Ended December 31, 1991

Income:
Computer sales income	$ 8,500,000
Consultant fee income	2,000,000
Total income	$10,500,000

Expenses:
Wages and salaries	$7,200,000	
Telephone	500,000	
Supplies	280,000	
Insurance	120,000	
Depreciation of computers	100,000	
Repairs	200,000	
Total expenses		$8,400,000
Net income		$2,100,000

Annual report

Any company that is publicly owned is required to prepare an annual report for its owners. The ***annual report*** contains a balance sheet, an income statement, and any other financial data that the company's management is required to or chooses to include. For example, some companies may present graphs that illustrate premium income or insurance in force. In addition, the annual report usually includes a narrative account of the year's activities, a description of current conditions and operations, and a general discussion of future prospects and plans.

The Annual Statement

As mentioned earlier, the accounting practices of life and health insurance companies have been influenced by regulatory requirements. These requirements are reflected in the Annual Statement, which companies prepare for regulatory authorities. The ***Annual Statement,*** portions of which are shown in Figures 13-5 and 13-6, contains detailed accounting and statistical data that authorities need to evaluate a company's solvency and compliance with insurance regulations.

In the United States, the Annual Statement's format and contents are specified by the state insurance commissioners. In Canada, the Office of the Superintendent of Financial Institutions and provincial governments determine the form and content of the Annual Statement. The Annual Statement differs from a company's annual report in that the Annual Statement is compiled according to SAP, and the annual report is typically prepared according to GAAP.

The Annual Statement in the United States

The Annual Statement form used in the United States includes the following reports and other information:

- a balance sheet in the form of an assets page and a liabilities, capital, and surplus page
- a summary of operations (statement of income and expenses)
- a surplus statement
- supporting exhibits, schedules, and supplemental reports

The Annual Statement's exhibits and schedules support the totals shown in the primary financial statements, such as the balance sheet. Examples of

Figure 13-5
Assets page of an Annual Statement.

ASSETS

		1 December 31, 1991	2 December 31, 1990
1.	Bonds (less .... liability for asset transfers with put options)	284,688,300	248,322,813
2.	Stocks:		
	2.1 Preferred stocks	58,887,384	40,571,423
	2.2 Common stocks	95,700,722	63,549,605
3.	Mortgage loans on real estate	2,698,951	2,975,210
4.	Real estate:		
	4.1 Properties occupied by the company (less .... encumbrances)		
	4.2 Properties acquired in satisfaction of debt (less .... encumbrances)		
	4.3 Investment real estate (less .... encumbrances)	6,381,301	6,768,775
5.	Policy loans	14,632,633	13,350,554
6.	Premium notes, including .... for first year premiums		
7.	Collateral loans		
8.1	Cash on hand and on deposit	10,355,836	8,614,388
8.2	Short-term investments	8,934,494	
9.	Other invested assets	4,073,107	4,467,303
10.	Aggregate write-ins for invested assets..		
10A.	Subtotals, cash and invested assets (Items 1 to 10)	486,352,728	388,620,071
11.	Reinsurance ceded:		
	11.1 Amounts recoverable from reinsurers	39,474	55,076
	11.2 Commissions and expense allowances due		
	11.3 Experience rating and other refunds due		
12.	Electronic data processing equipment		
13.	Federal income tax recoverable		
14.	Life insurance premiums and annuity considerations deferred and uncollected ...	6,629,643	6,612,981
15.	Accident and health premiums due and unpaid	35,255	63,721
16.	Investment income due and accrued	8,778,567	7,904,045
17.	Net adjustment in assets and liabilities due to foreign exchange rates		
18.	Receivable from parent, subsidiaries and affiliates	525,799	393,380
19.	Amounts receivable relating to uninsured accident and health plans		
21.	Aggregate write-ins for other than invested assets	440,494	375,351
22.	Total assets excluding Separate Accounts business (Items 10A to 21)	502,801,960	404,024,625
23.	From Separate Accounts Statement		
24.	Totals (Items 22 and 23)	502,801,960	404,024,625

DETAILS OF WRITE-INS AGGREGATED AT ITEM 10 FOR INVESTED ASSETS			
1001. MORTGAGE LOAN ESCROW $156,987 LESS TRUST FUND LIABILITY $156,987			
1002.			
1003.			
1004.			
1005.			
1098. Summary of remaining write-ins for Item 10 from overflow page			
1099. Totals (Items 1001 thru 1005 plus 1098) (Page 2, Item 10)			

DETAILS OF WRITE-INS AGGREGATED AT ITEM 21 FOR OTHER THAN INVESTED ASSETS			
2101. INVESTMENT RECEIVABLE		418,424	361,964
2102. GUARANTY ASSESSMENT		22,070	13,387
2103.			
2104.			
2105.			
2198. Summary of remaining write-ins for Item 21 from overflow page			
2199. Totals (Items 2101 thru 2105 plus 2198) (Page 2, Item 21)		440,494	375,351

NOTE: The items on this page to agree with Exhibit 13, Col. 4.
The Notes to Financial Statements are an integral part of this statement.

Figure 13-6
Liabilities, surplus, and other funds page of an Annual Statement.

LIABILITIES, SURPLUS AND OTHER FUNDS

	1 December 31, 1991	2 December 31, 1990
1. Aggregate reserve for life policies and contracts $251,633,988 (Exh. 8, Line H) less included in Item 7.3	251,633,988	215,702,695
2. Aggregate reserve for accident and health policies (Exhibit 9, Line C, Col. 1)	6,544,627	6,615,747
3. Supplementary contracts without life contingencies (Exhibit 10, Part A, Line 2.3, Col. 1)	1,422,166	1,224,304
4. Policy and contract claims:		
4.1 Life (Exhibit 11, Part 1, Line 4d, Column 1 less sum of Columns 9, 10 and 11)	2,732,171	2,110,529
4.2 Accident and health (Exhibit 11, Part 1, Line 4d, sum of Columns 9, 10 and 11)	6,279,116	5,437,158
5. Policyholders' dividend and coupon* accumulations (Exhibit 10, Part A, Line 3 plus Line 4, Col. 1)	3,945	3,714
6. Policyholders' dividends and coupons due and unpaid (Exhibit 7, Line 10)		
7. Provision for policyholders' dividends and coupons payable in following calendar year — estimated amounts:		
7.1 Dividends apportioned for payment to ... DECEMBER 31 ... , 1992	181	179
7.2 Dividends not yet apportioned		
7.3 Coupons and similar benefits		
8. Amount provisionally held for deferred dividend policies not included in Item 7		
9. Premiums and annuity considerations received in advance less discount; including $169,448 accident and health premiums (Exhibit 1, Part 1, Col. 1, sum of Lines 4 and 14)	628,552	599,339
10. Liability for premium and other deposit funds:		
10.1 Policyholder premiums, including deferred annuity liability (Exhibit 10, Part A, Line 1.1, Col. 1)	31,659	36,805
10.2 Guaranteed interest contracts, including deferred annuity liability (Exhibit 10, Part A, Line 1.2, Col. 1)		
10.3 Other contract deposit funds, including deferred annuity liability (Exhibit 10, Part A, Line 1.3, Col. 1)		
11. Policy and contract liabilities not included elsewhere:		
11.1 Surrender values on canceled policies		
11.2 Provision for experience rating refunds		
11.3 Other amounts payable on reinsurance assumed		
12. Commissions to agents due or accrued — life and annuity $319,998 accident and health $24,471	344,469	459,941
12A. Commissions and expense allowances payable on reinsurance assumed		
13. General expenses due or accrued (Exhibit 5, Line 12, Col. 5)	1,041,470	981,426
13A. Transfers to Separate Accounts due or accrued (net)		
14. Taxes, licenses and fees due or accrued, excluding federal income taxes (Exhibit 6, Line 9, Col. 5)	533,091	547,837
14A. Federal income taxes due or accrued, including $231,398 on capital gains (excluding deferred taxes)	10,228,207	5,926,561
15. "Cost of collection" on premiums and annuity considerations deferred and uncollected in excess of total loading thereon		
16. Unearned investment income (Exhibit 3, Line 10, Col. 2)	263,895	314,591
17. Amounts withheld or retained by company as agent or trustee	603,714	769,781
18. Amounts held for agents' account, including $41,099 agents' credit balances	41,099	33,934
19. Remittances and items not allocated	1,473,313	1,223,529
20. Net adjustment in assets and liabilities due to foreign exchange rates		
21. Liability for benefits for employees and agents if not included above		
22. Borrowed money and interest thereon		
23. Dividends to stockholders declared and unpaid		
24. Miscellaneous liabilities:		
24.1 Mandatory securities valuation reserve (Page 29A, final Item)	39,632,840	4,363,633
24.2 Reinsurance in unauthorized companies		
24.3 Funds held under reinsurance treaties with unauthorized reinsurers		
24.4 Payable to parent, subsidiaries and affiliates	868,164	654,283
24.5 Drafts outstanding		
24.6 Liability for amounts held under uninsured accident and health plans		
25. Aggregate write-ins for liabilities	425,830	856,644
26. Total Liabilities excluding Separate Accounts business (Items 1 to 25)	324,732,497	247,862,630
27. From Separate Accounts Statement		
28. Total Liabilities (Items 26 and 27)	324,732,497	247,862,630
29. Common capital stock	1,500,000	1,500,000
30. Preferred capital stock		
31. Aggregate write-ins for other than special surplus funds		
32. Gross paid in and contributed surplus (Page 3, Item 32, Col. 2 plus Page 4, Item 44a, Col. 1)	2,000,000	2,000,000
33. Aggregate write-ins for special surplus funds		
34. Unassigned funds (surplus)	174,569,463	152,661,995
35. Less treasury stock, at cost:		
(1) shares common (value included in Item 29)		
(2) shares preferred (value included in Item 30)		
36 Surplus (total Items 31 + 32 + 33 + 34 − 35)	176,569,463	154,661,995
37. Totals of Items 29, 30 and 36 (Page 4, Item 48)	178,069,463	156,161,995
38. Totals of Items 28 and 37 (Page 2, Item 24)	502,801,960	404,024,625
DETAILS OF WRITE-INS AGGREGATED AT ITEM 25 FOR LIABILITIES		
2501. SECURITY DEPOSITS	2,208	2,208
2502. INVESTMENT PAYABLE		498,513
2503. RETIRED LIVES RESERVE	7,720	7,148
2504. BONUS LIABILITY	415,902	348,775
2505.		
2598. Summary of remaining write-ins for Item 25 from overflow page		
2599. Totals (Items 2501 thru 2505 plus 2598) (Page 3, Item 25)	425,830	856,644
DETAILS OF WRITE-INS AGGREGATED AT ITEM 31 FOR OTHER THAN SPECIAL SURPLUS FUNDS		
3101.		
3102.		
3103.		
3104.		
3105.		
3198. Summary of remaining write-ins for Item 31 from overflow page		
3199. Totals (Items 3101 thru 3105 plus 3198) (Page 3, Item 31)		
DETAILS OF WRITE-INS AGGREGATED AT ITEM 33 FOR SPECIAL SURPLUS FUNDS		
3301.		
3302.		
3303.		
3304.		
3305.		
3398. Summary of remaining write-ins for Item 33 from overflow page		
3399. Totals (Items 3301 thru 3305 plus 3398) (Page 3, Item 33)		

*Includes coupons, guaranteed annual pure endowments and similar benefits.

information that can be found in a company's Annual Statement exhibits and schedules are

- analyses of operations by lines of business
- premiums and annuity considerations
- dividends applied, reinsurance ceded, and commissions incurred
- listing of investments and investment income
- dividends to policyowners
- analysis of nonadmitted assets
- expenses

A company must file its Annual Statement in each state, and in the District of Columbia if applicable, in which it is licensed to do business.

The Annual Statement in Canada

Canadian companies registered under the Canadian and British Insurance Companies Act are required to file an Annual Statement with the federal Department of Insurance. The Canadian Annual Statement has the same general form as that used in the United States; it consists of the basic financial statements supported by exhibits and schedules. Canadian companies file information about their total business. Non-Canadian companies report only their Canadian business on the specified form, but this form must be supplemented by the total business statement that is submitted to their home jurisdiction.

A company must also file an Annual Statement in each province where the company is licensed to do business. A provincial company that is not federally registered must complete a prescribed form, which is modeled closely after the federal form. Companies that are federally registered submit a shorter and simpler form of the federal Annual Statement to the provincial authorities.

UNIQUE ASPECTS OF LIFE AND HEALTH INSURANCE ACCOUNTING

Although many typical accounting procedures apply to life and health insurance companies, insurance accounting differs from general commercial accounting in several ways. In the next few pages, we will talk about some unique aspects of life and health insurance accounting.

Accrual-basis and Cash-basis Accounting

Most businesses record their financial transactions through the use of accrual-basis accounting. In an *accrual-basis accounting* system, income items are recorded when they are earned and expense items are recorded when they are incurred, even if cash has not actually changed hands.

For example, assume that CompuBuilder, a computer products distributor, orders and receives 3,000 microchips from MicroMaker, a manufacturer of computer parts. The price for these microchips is $30,000. Using accrual-basis accounting, CompuBuilder's accountants would record that the company has spent $30,000, even though the cash will not be paid until the company receives an invoice from MicroMaker. Similarly, Micro-Maker's accountants would record that the company has sold $30,000 of merchandise, although it may not receive the cash for another month. Because the company that buys the goods is legally liable for payment, the seller is generally assured of receiving payment. Therefore, accrual-basis accounting is a reasonable procedure and is recommended for most businesses.

In a *cash-basis accounting* system, entries are not made until cash actually changes hands. Cash-basis accounting is used in some insurance companies because of the nature of insurance products. Insurance policies are unilateral contracts, in which the policyowners make no promises and are not liable for premiums. If policyowners choose not to pay their premiums, they owe nothing to the insurance company. The contracts can be terminated whenever the policyowners choose. Therefore, when a premium comes due for payment, the insurance company cannot assume that the premium will be paid and, thus, does not record the premium as income until it receives the actual cash payment.

Some insurance companies use a mixture of accrual- and cash-basis accounting for their daily accounting records; others use the accrual method only. The nature of a company's accounts and the practicality of accruing income and expense items usually determine the accounting method that a company uses.

Suspense Accounts

The use of cash-basis accounting causes certain peculiarities in insurance accounting. For instance, although insurance companies process many cash payments and receipts every day, not every transaction can be fully processed when cash is paid or received. For example, when a premium payment is received in advance for a new policy that has not yet been issued, the cash payment cannot be considered as premium income until the application is approved and the policy is issued. Therefore, the premium payment is recorded temporarily in a liability account called a *suspense account*. **Suspense accounts** are used to record transactions that cannot be credited immediately to a permanent account.

Nonledger Accounts

Statutory accounting practices require that an insurance company's Annual Statement be presented on an accrual basis. In order to make such a presentation, companies that do use cash-basis accounting must convert their general ledgers from a cash basis to an accrual basis. They must also report certain nonledger accounts that have been maintained on an accrual basis. **Nonledger accounts** are generally used to record assets and liabilities that are not affected by cash transactions. The most important of these accounts is the policy reserve, which constitutes an insurance company's largest liability. Policy reserves cannot be maintained on a cash basis because they are estimated figures based on actuarial calculations, not the sums of actual cash payments and expenses.

Examples of nonledger assets and liabilities that appear on the Annual Statement include

- policy reserves
- deferred and uncollected premiums
- investment income due and accrued
- dividends due and accrued
- federal income taxes

Nonadmitted Assets

Statutory accounting practices restrict certain types of assets from being included in the balance sheet of a company's Annual Statement. The purpose of restricting the presentation of these assets is to assure that an insurance company's assets are valued on a conservative basis. Assets that, according to government regulations, are not acceptable for inclusion on the balance sheet of a life insurance company are called **nonadmitted assets.** Nonadmitted assets are classified in two general categories:

- *Assets for which no portion of the value is admitted.* These assets generally include furniture, equipment, automobiles, computer software, office supplies, and loans to employees of the company. Because the realizable value of such items is uncertain, they must be identified as nonadmitted assets on the Annual Statement.

- *Assets for which a portion of the value is admitted and the remainder is nonadmitted.* Most of the assets in this category are investments. Because investments fluctuate in value, insurance companies are allowed to admit only amounts prescribed by law. When an investment has a lower market value than its current value shown on the company's books, the difference is considered nonadmitted.

TYPES OF ACCOUNTING IN INSURANCE COMPANIES

The accounting activities in life and health insurance companies can be divided into four broad categories:

- policy accounting, including claim and reserve accounting
- investment accounting
- general accounting
- tax accounting

In the following pages, we will discuss these different types of accounting and the challenges they pose to life and health insurance accountants.

Policy Accounting

Policy accounting, also called *premium accounting,* is responsible for the largest number of accounting transactions within a company—frequently millions of transactions each year. Policy accounting includes premium billing and collection, commission accounting, policy loan accounting, and policy dividend accounting. Claims that are filed on policies also result in accounting transactions.

Premium billing and collection

Although premium accounting systems differ among companies, every insurer must have a premium accounting system that performs the following functions:

- billing premiums properly as they become due
- controlling premium collections and properly accounting for cash
- recording premium collections on policyowner records

- recording premium income by appropriate categories so that the data can be used for computing taxes and preparing accounting reports and statements for management and regulatory agencies

Diversity among premium accounting systems results from differences in company organization and management preferences. For example, some insurance companies centralize premium collections at the home office. Other companies have several collection centers throughout their marketing territories. Insurers also differ in the way they prepare lapse notices and statistical reports. Furthermore, premium accounting systems vary significantly among each of the three major lines of insurance business: ordinary, group, and industrial.

Ordinary premiums.   The premium accounting system for traditional life and health insurance policies generally involves the billing and collection of one premium at a time by mail. Premium notices are prepared before the premium due date but after policyowner records have been updated for dividends and premium deposits.

The premium billing system, which is sometimes managed by the customer service staff, generally includes procedures designed to help conserve policies that are about to lapse. If the company does not receive a premium by a certain date, a reminder is mailed to the policyowner. The agent may also receive a notice about the impending lapse. This notice gives the agent time during the grace period to initiate conservation efforts with the policyowner.

When the overdue payment is not received by the end of the grace period, the policy record is examined to determine whether the policy provides for an automatic premium loan. If so, the company adjusts the accounting records to advance the premiums on the policy and indicates such a loan on the master file. If there is no automatic premium loan provision or no cash value, the policy lapses. The procedure is different with universal life insurance products. No automatic premium loan is applied, but coverage under the policy continues if the policy has a sufficient cash value.

Many life and health insurance companies have methods of collecting premiums other than sending a notice and waiting for payment. Two common methods are preauthorized payments and lock-box banking.

- Under a ***preauthorized payment*** system, the policyowner signs a two-part authorization form. The first part authorizes the insurance company to withdraw future premiums from the policyowner's savings or checking account as they become due. The second part of the form authorizes the bank to honor such withdrawals. The authorization copy is provided to the bank only once. Future withdrawals do not require the policyowner's signature.

Frequently, preauthorized payments are implemented through the use of *electronic funds transfer (EFT)* systems in which funds are transferred from the customer's bank to the insurer's bank via computers. No paper documents are required. A preauthorized payment system that is implemented through the use of checks is called the *preauthorized check (PAC)* system.

- Under a **lock-box banking** system, the insurer's bank opens premium payment envelopes and immediately deposits the payments to the company's account. Payments, which are received at a specified post office box to which the bank has access, are credited to the company's account sooner with this system than they otherwise would be because processing and recordkeeping are handled by the company after the deposit is made.

Group premiums. The accounting procedures for group premiums depend on whether the billing plan is self-administered or insurer-administered. In a **self-administered billing plan,** the policyholder performs most of the administrative work. The policyholder maintains detailed records of group membership; processes routine requests, such as requests for beneficiary changes and name and address changes; and in some cases, prepares certificates for new group members. Each month the group policyholder prepares a premium statement that shows the computation of the premium due, which is sent along with the premium payment to the insurance company. The home office periodically audits these computations.

If the group plan is an **insurer-administered billing plan,** the insurance company performs the administrative work, which includes computing the amount of the premium due and mailing a statement to the group policyholder, usually on a monthly basis. The total amount of a group's premium may change each month because of people joining and leaving the group. If the group is comparatively small, the billing statement can list each insured group member and the premium for that member. In a large group, the statement often shows only the number of persons in each of several classifications, along with the total premium for each classification.

Industrial insurance premiums. Industrial insurance premiums are usually collected through the home service method, in which agents personally collect premiums from policyowners. The premium accounting system most commonly used for industrial insurance is the cash premium accounting system. The advance and arrears system has also been associated with industrial insurance premium collection, but fewer companies are using this system.

- *Cash premium accounting system*—The agent informs the home office of the amount collected on each policy. After the agent remits to the insurer the premiums collected, the home office updates the policy records to reflect this income and prepares new route collection records.
- *Advance and arrears accounting system*—The home office charges an agent with the amount of all premiums due on the policies the agent services. When the agent remits the collected money, the agent is credited with the amount of premiums collected. Ideally, the amount collected by the agent matches the amount of the premiums due. Usually, however, there are differences: some policyowners cannot be reached, some do not wish to continue their insurance, and others make payments in advance. As a result, the agent's balance is likely to be either in *advance* or in *arrears*. From time to time, the agent reports to the home office on all policies for which premiums are either in advance or in arrears. The home office records are then reconciled with the agent's records.

Commissions

Because of the direct relationship between premium collections and agents' commissions, premium accounting and commission accounting are closely linked. The basic policy records used for premium billing usually indicate the agent's commissions for the policy. In many accounting systems, the collection of a premium immediately updates both the policy record and the commission record. In other systems, the commission records are separately updated, usually once or twice each month. For tax reporting purposes, the system also maintains a year-to-date record of total commissions paid.

Policy loans

Policy loan accounting involves keeping records of the principal and interest on each loan. The principal amount of a policy loan—that is, the amount borrowed—plus the interest due or accrued cannot be greater than the policy's cash value. The interest is usually payable on the policy anniversary date, and the amount due is shown on the premium notices. Some companies charge the interest in advance; others charge it at the end of the policy year. If interest is charged in advance and the policyowner repays all or part of the principal during the year, then the policyowner is entitled to a partial refund of the interest already paid. If interest on a policy loan is not received by the insurance company when due, then the unpaid interest is added to the amount of the loan, provided the policy's cash value is sufficient to cover the principal plus interest.

Policy dividends

Policy dividends are usually declared, on participating policies only, by the company's board of directors once each year according to a dividend schedule recommended by the company's chief actuary. Dividends for ordinary policies are generally payable on the policy anniversary. The accounting transaction for policy dividends depends on the dividend option that the policyowner has chosen:

- If the dividend is paid in cash, a check for the dividend amount is prepared and mailed to the policyowner.
- If the dividend is applied to pay premiums due, the next premium notice shows the amount of the premium minus the amount of the dividend. If the dividend is greater than the premium, the excess is paid in cash to the policyowner or applied under one of the other dividend options.
- If the dividend is left with the company to accumulate at interest, the policyowner is mailed a notice of the amount of the dividend and the total accumulation.
- If the dividend is applied to purchase paid-up additions, the policyowner is informed of the amount of additional insurance accumulated under the option.
- If the dividend is applied to purchase one-year term insurance, the amount needed is used automatically to buy one-year term insurance—usually subject to a maximum amount of insurance not to exceed the policy's cash value—at the insured's current age. Any excess dividend may be paid in cash or applied under one of the other dividend options available.

Claim accounting

Because the amounts of claims and other contract payments—such as payments on annuities and supplementary contracts—are often quite large, requests for these payments must be examined carefully and approved by a qualified person before money is paid. The responsibility for authorizing payments and accounting entries in connection with claim settlements is assigned to a claim examiner. When a company makes claim and contract settlements, cooperation between the claim examiners and accounting personnel helps control the company's settlement process.

Accountants must also establish and maintain a claim reserve account for claims in the course of settlement—that is, claims about which the company has been notified but that have not yet been paid or denied. This reserve account is required by statutory accounting. Journal entries are also made when a claim is approved. If a check is issued, the entry is made in connection with issuance of the check. If the proceeds are left with the company under a settlement option, the entry is made as soon as the amounts and conditions of the settlement contract are established.

Investment Accounting

After premium income, investment income provides the largest amount of income for an insurance company. In cooperation with investment specialists, a company's accountants must record the following amounts:

- investment income
- purchases and sales of investments
- gains and losses from investments
- investment values that will be used in the company's Annual Statement

Investment accounting procedures change to keep pace with changes in the investment environment itself. For example, accountants had to develop new procedures to keep track of investment-sensitive, variable, and equity-based products, for which the relationships among premiums, cash values, and investment returns are subject to change. As a result, accounting for such products can be more complex than accounting for more traditional products.

Separate accounts and general accounts

Until the 1960s, life and health insurance companies were generally required, because of statutory accounting practices, to pool or group together their accounts. No single asset or group of assets could be designated to support a specific liability or group of liabilities.

Then insurance companies began to market variable annuities and pension funds. Investors, not the insurance company, assumed the investment risk for these financial products. To improve their competitive position in the variable annuity market and the pension fund market during the 1960s, insurers needed to use more aggressive investment strategies than those designed for traditional insurance products. Insurance companies thus obtained permission to establish separate accounts. A **separate account,** usually called a *segregated account* in Canada, is an account maintained separately from a company's general account. Separate accounts are established to manage the funds used to support nonguaranteed insurance products.

By maintaining separate accounts, insurance companies are able to pursue more aggressive investment strategies without affecting the funds in the general accounts. Assets in separate accounts can be invested without regard to the usual restrictions that are placed on the investments of life company assets. All income, gains, and losses of a separate account are directly attributed to the contracts backed by the separate accounts.

In 1990, Canadian insurance companies held more than $17 billion, or 13.8 percent of their assets, in segregated accounts. During the same year, U.S. insurance companies held almost $160 billion, or 11 percent of their assets, in separate accounts.

Segmentation of general accounts. Another accounting procedure used by some insurance companies to match specific invested assets with specific liabilities is called segmentation. **Segmentation,** used in association with asset/liability matching (see Chapter 7), is a process by which insurance companies divide their general accounts into distinct parts, or *segments*, that correspond with each of the insurer's major lines of business. For example, one segment can be used to account for group life insurance investments, and another can be used to account for individual life insurance investments. In a company that uses segmentation, all accounts except separate accounts are still pooled, but the company has a clearer idea of where its assets and liabilities originate.

Segmentation allows insurance companies to monitor the cash flow of each product line. In this way, accountants, investment analysts, and actuaries can determine both the types of investments that are needed to maintain each product line's profitability and which lines of business are generating positive cash flows and profits.

Segmentation can also be used to determine the degree of investment liquidity needed to meet the claims of each product line. For example, claims on health insurance products are usually made more frequently and less predictably than claims on life insurance products. An insurance company can match its health insurance assets to its liabilities by trying to make sure that cash is coming in to match the cash that is going out. Investment personnel would thus invest at least some of the company's health insurance money in assets that can be turned into cash at short notice.

General Accounting

Life and health insurance companies perform the same basic accounting functions that all businesses do. Two examples, accounting for payroll and accounting for disbursements, are briefly presented here to give an idea of the scope of general accounting functions.

Payroll accounting

Payroll accounting involves calculating employees' pay, preparing paychecks, maintaining payroll records, and producing reports for management and government agencies. A payroll record for each employee includes such information as wage or salary rate, number of dependents claimed, deductions, and year-to-date totals of income and deductions. The record also indicates whether the employee is entitled to receive overtime pay.

Accounting personnel must record federal, state, provincial, and local tax deductions for each employee so that this information can be included in quarterly reports to the government and in annual withholding statements to employees. These records must also show deductions, such as those for health insurance and savings or pension plans.

Paychecks are produced before the actual payroll date so that they have time to reach the various work locations. Some companies use EFT systems to deposit paychecks directly in employees' bank accounts. Companies may also use banks and other independent firms to process the payroll records and to prepare paychecks.

Disbursements

The objectives of accounting for disbursements are to (1) provide a permanent record of all disbursements, (2) confirm that all disbursements are properly authorized, and (3) ensure that all disbursements are charged to the proper account. Disbursements fall into a number of categories:

Policy-related disbursements	policy loans
	benefits
	surrenders
	withdrawals
	policy dividends
Compensation-related disbursements	employee payroll
	agents' commissions
Investment-related disbursements	purchases of stocks, bonds, and real estate
	purchases or granting of mortgage loans

> **General operating disbursements**   supplies and equipment
> office rentals
> utilities
> taxes
> travel advances
> physicians' fees for medical
> examinations ordered by the
> company

Small disbursements may be handled through cash funds that are controlled by managers throughout the company. Larger expenditures must usually be supported by a *voucher* or check request signed by someone with the authority to disburse the amount involved. Large, continuous disbursements—such as payroll, commissions, and policy dividends—are generally made electronically. Built-in controls ensure the correctness of payees, amounts, and accounts to be charged.

Tax Accounting

Life and health insurance companies pay the same kinds of taxes—income taxes, property taxes, and unemployment taxes, for example—that other companies pay. Accountants must keep records for all the company's taxes and prepare the necessary returns.

In addition to the usual kinds of taxes paid by corporations, insurance companies must also pay premium taxes. State and provincial governments impose premium taxes on life and health insurance companies in the form of a percentage of the premiums that each company collects. At first, states and provinces imposed premium taxes only on insurance companies located outside of their jurisdictions, with the intention of giving domestic companies a competitive advantage. Later, premium taxes began to be considered a source of funds to pay for the cost of supervising the industry and as a source of additional tax revenue; as a result, premium taxes were imposed on all insurance companies doing business in the state or province. Recent U.S. court decisions have tended to equalize the rates at which domestic and out-of-state insurers are taxed.

In the United States, the definition of *taxable premiums* varies from state to state. Some states impose the tax on gross premiums; other states allow companies to deduct the amount of policy dividends from the gross premium amount before the premium tax is computed. Some states require that the insurer pay the larger of the premium tax or the state income tax. In general, considerations—that is, payments received—for annuities are taxed at a lower rate than insurance premiums. Some states do not tax annuity considerations at all.

All Canadian provinces levy a tax on life insurance premiums but not on considerations for annuities.

PLANNING AND CONTROLLING FINANCIAL OPERATIONS

Accounting personnel are essential in helping company managers gain a complete understanding of their business and in providing them with the information needed to plan and implement business strategies. In the next few pages, we will discuss some of the ways in which the financial analyses, budgets, and audits produced by accountants help insurance companies plan and control their operations.

Financial Analysis

Financial analysis is the process of evaluating financial records to determine a company's profitability and stability. Financial analyses are used by a company's officers and managers to help them make decisions about the company's activities. Industry analysts also use financial analyses to help them compare one company to another.

Brokerage houses analyze the financial performance of stock insurance companies to determine the best investments for the broker's clients. Such analysis considers a company's earnings, the ratios of share price to earnings, and the amount of dividends paid per share of stock. In addition, state regulators use certain financial ratios suggested by the National Association of Insurance Commissioners (NAIC) to determine the stability of insurance companies. State and provincial regulators and the NAIC use the Annual Statement, stockholder reports, audited financial statements, and other financial reports to analyze a company's financial position.

Financial analysis conducted for the company's own management uses even more detailed financial information. Three common analytical procedures that management uses are the comparisons of

- the financial results of two or more financial periods—for example, comparing the first three months of the current year with the first three months of the previous year

- the financial results of one period to that same period's budgets
- the company's financial results to the results of other companies

By making these comparisons, management can determine if the company is performing as expected and can help identify the company's strengths and weaknesses.

Other important analyses are *ratio analyses*, which show the proportionate relationship between two different amounts. A ratio is computed by dividing one amount by another. The following comparisons or ratios are often used by insurance companies to measure financial performance:

- sales production to sales targets
- benefit disbursements to premium income
- actual investment yield to anticipated investment yield
- cash surrender values paid to premium income
- actual expenses to budgeted expenses
- claim costs to anticipated claim costs
- investment expenses to investment income

All of these ratios help show the company's managers how the company is performing and how it compares to other companies.

Budget Planning

A *budget* is a detailed plan showing how resources should be allocated during a specified period. In order to achieve a well-planned budget and budgeting process, company managers and other employees must cooperate in the following areas:

- formulating goals and strategies
- coordinating activities to achieve common goals
- planning a workable pattern of activities for various levels of management
- evaluating managerial effectiveness in achieving goals

When preparing budgets, financial planners work with other departments to estimate, for a specific period, (1) the amount of income the company expects to earn, (2) the amount of work that must be done, and (3) the cost of doing that work. For example, financial planners consult with marketing and actuarial personnel to estimate the amount of premiums the company should receive and the impact of those premiums on policy reserves. Financial planners also consult with investment specialists to estimate the amount of investment income expected during the upcoming period. The marketing staff helps financial planners determine the expected costs of selling policies; underwriters estimate the cost of evaluating applications; and claim personnel determine the anticipated volume of claims and claim expenses. All of these estimates are used to allocate appropriate funding to each department, product line, or profit center.

Types of budgets

Most companies develop several types of budgets. For example, companies may prepare a *cash receipts and disbursements budget* to help monitor cash flow, as well as a *capital expenditures budget* to allocate funds for significant purchases and acquisitions. In addition, many companies develop departmental budgets, which can be subdivided into *revenue budgets* and *expense budgets*. Such departmental budgets may apply to a department, a product, or a profit center. In the following section, the term *departmental budget* will be used to refer to the general grouping of revenue and expense budgets, regardless of the company's form of organization.

The revenue budget. Generally, the first step in preparing departmental budgets is to prepare the entire company's **revenue budget,** which projects the amount of income that the company expects to receive in the upcoming year. Because the revenue budget determines the restraint that must be placed on all other budgets, it must be prepared before expense budgets can be completed. The revenue budget consists primarily of premium and investment income estimates. Methods of projecting revenue can range from relatively simple estimates based on prior experience to more complex estimates based on computer simulations.

Expense budgets. Three primary types of insurance company expense budgets are benefits budgets, sales expense budgets, and general and administrative expense budgets.

- The **benefits budget** indicates the amount of money a company expects to pay for claims, cash surrenders, policy dividends, and policy loans in the upcoming year. Actuaries are generally responsible for developing the benefits budget.
- The **sales expense budget** is based primarily on the costs incurred in selling insurance. In addition to commission costs, these expenses include the costs of advertising, promotion, travel, branch office operations, and salaries for marketing personnel.
- The **general and administrative expense budget** includes the other

expenses of operating the company. Usually, this budget is the aggregate of all departmental expense budgets.

Budgets as Evaluation and Control Devices

Budgets are used as evaluation and control devices to provide managers with financial guidelines for operating their areas of responsibility. Budgets are also used to indicate whether managers are meeting the goals set for the company. To assess this information, many companies' accounting departments include control and expense analysis units. These units review each area's operating expenses and compare these expenses to assigned budgets. Such reviews are generally conducted monthly and are based on computer-generated expense reports sent from each area to the accounting staff. If an area's expenses vary significantly from its budgeted totals, the area's manager will meet with accountants in the control and expense analysis unit to discuss the variance.

Sometimes budget and cost variances are beyond a manager's control. For example, assume that an insurance company spends $8 to process each claim. If the claim area estimated in its budget that it would process 7,000 claims in April but actually processed 10,000, then the claim area's actual claim processing costs would exceed the budgeted amount by $24,000:

7,000 budgeted claims x $8 per claim = $56,000 budgeted costs
10,000 actual claims x $8 per claim = $80,000 actual costs
$80,000 - $56,000 = $24,000 over budget

In such a situation, the claim expense budget would be adjusted for the variance, and new budget estimates might be made for the remainder of the year.

On the other hand, assume that the same area processed 7,000 claims but spent $70,000 processing those claims. This expenditure would indicate that the cost of processing each claim was $10, not $8 as originally budgeted. In such a case, a claim manager and the accounting control and expense analysis manager would determine the reason for the cost overrun. It could be that the claim area was overstaffed, that the claim process itself was inefficiently organized, or that an unexpected occurrence—such as the introduction of a new product—had temporarily affected staff efficiency. Whatever the reason, the claim manager would be expected to make the necessary corrections to control future variations from budgeted costs.

Expense analysis also evaluates costs according to factors such as product type and function, thereby providing essential information for product pricing.

Auditing

All company managers are responsible for establishing controls in order to monitor the activities in their departments, product lines, or profit centers. Managers must make sure that corporate policies and procedures are being followed, that records are being kept correctly, and that the firm's assets are being properly protected. The auditor's role is to verify that these controls are in effect throughout the organization. *Auditing* is the process of examining and evaluating company records and procedures to ensure the reliability of the accounting reports. All companies undergo periodic accounting audits—both *internal audits,* which are conducted by company employees, and *external audits,* which are conducted by public accounting firms hired by the company and regulatory bodies.

In general, an auditor has the following major responsibilities:

- verifying that the company's assets are accounted for and that they are safeguarded from loss
- assessing the soundness and the application of financial and operating controls within the company
- ensuring that the company's established policies and procedures are being followed
- verifying the reliability of data, records, and reports
- evaluating the efficiency of operating procedures

Internal auditing unit

Internal auditors examine a company's financial affairs and general operations, even those operations that do not directly involve the expenditure of funds. In many companies, the internal auditing unit makes a detailed examination of each area in the company. An auditor spends several weeks or even months within a single company area, examining not only its financial records, but all of its operating and reporting procedures. Afterward, the auditor submits a detailed report to the manager, the manager's superiors, and the controller, describing every function of that area and how that function is carried out. The report indicates which functions are carried out efficiently, which are not, and how improvements can be made. For example, an auditor may suggest new procedures for handling beneficiary changes in the customer service function or more efficient ways for underwriters to process insurance applications. Most recommendations in the report are discussed with the manager before the report is submitted to the manager's superior.

Because of the internal auditing unit's responsibilities, the unit must have the independence to be objective in its judgments. Therefore, the auditing unit is usually not directly attached to the other accounting functions. If the unit is part of an accounting department, the auditors typically report to the controller. In many companies, however, the internal auditors report directly to the audit committee of the board of directors.

External auditors

Besides employing their own internal auditing personnel, companies retain the services of external auditors, usually CPA firms in the United States or CA firms in Canada. The use of external auditors helps assure that the company's financial performance is evaluated impartially. External auditors conduct independent annual audits of the firm's financial statements and accounting records to determine whether the statements present a fair and reliable picture of the company's financial position and the results of the company's operations. In addition, some insurance companies employ accounting firms to prepare tax returns and suggest improvements in operating procedures. For some companies, external auditors are also hired to augment the work of the internal audit staff.

In the United States, an NAIC Model Bill mandates that all companies undergo an external audit. In addition, all U.S. companies reporting to the SEC must have their GAAP-based financial statements audited by a CPA firm. In Canada, all federally licensed companies are required to file independent auditors' reports. In addition, in some provinces, all foreign life insurers with a branch in Canada must file an independent auditor's report.

Auditing methods

Examining every operation and verifying every financial transaction within a company would be impractical and costly. Instead, auditors rely on a system of statistical sampling in which they examine only a portion of the accounts, transactions, or operations in a company. The samples are chosen according to sound statistical methods, giving the auditor a reasonable level of confidence that all the accounts, transactions, or operations are as valid as those in the sample. The art of auditing has been refined to such a point that, in many cases, the auditor reviews transactions at only two or three key points in the processing system. This review should indicate if other transactions within the system have been processed accurately.

KEY TERMS

accounting
solvency
assets
liabilities
owner's equity
account
debit
credit
journal
ledger
going-concern concept
balance sheet
income statement
annual report
Annual Statement
accrual-basis accounting
cash-basis accounting
suspense account
nonledger account
nonadmitted asset

policy accounting
preauthorized payment
lock-box banking
self-administered billing plan
insurer-administered billing plan
cash premium accounting
advance and arrears accounting
separate (segregated) account
segmentation
financial analysis
ratio analysis
budget
revenue budget
benefits budget
sales expense budget
general and administrative expense
    budget
auditing
internal audit
external audit

Chapter 14

Legal Operations

After reading this chapter, you should be able to

- Describe the different ways to organize a legal department in a life and health insurance company
- Discuss the different responsibilities assigned to life and health insurance company lawyers and legal staff
- Differentiate among and describe the areas of law with which an insurance company's legal department is concerned
- Describe several ways in which the legal department interacts with other insurance company functional areas

Life and health insurance companies are guided by laws that affect their relationships with policyowners, beneficiaries, stockholders, prospective customers, employees, agents, other corporations, and governmental authorities. Therefore, most insurance companies have a legal department that reviews company actions to ensure that the company fulfills its legal responsibilities to all parties. The legal department also helps the company protect its legal rights. This department might also be called a *law department* or *legal services department*.

In this chapter, we will discuss the operations of legal departments in life and health insurance companies. We will describe the various ways in which a legal department may be organized, the functions that the legal department performs, and the relationships of the legal department with other areas of the company.

ORGANIZATIONAL STRUCTURES OF LEGAL DEPARTMENTS

The structure that an insurance company establishes for its legal department depends on a number of factors, including the size of the company, the

389

extent of its operations, and the geographical areas in which it does business. For example, a small home service company operating in only a few states might have a one-person legal department, or might rely completely on the services of outside law firms rather than having a legal department of its own. Large companies, too, may retain outside attorneys. In many cases, not even the largest companies can keep enough lawyers on staff to cover every specific problem that may arise. Even so, a national or multinational company that sells many lines of insurance and holds extensive investments across a broad geographical area would almost certainly have a legal department staffed by numerous lawyers with responsibilities in different areas of law.

Insurance company legal departments typically follow one of three structures: the *traditional structure,* the *regional structure,* or the *functional structure.*

Traditional Structure

In the traditional structure, still used today by many companies, legal work is handled by the home office legal department (see Figure 14-1). The department is usually headed by a lawyer called the *vice president and general*

Figure 14-1
Traditional organizational structure of a legal department.

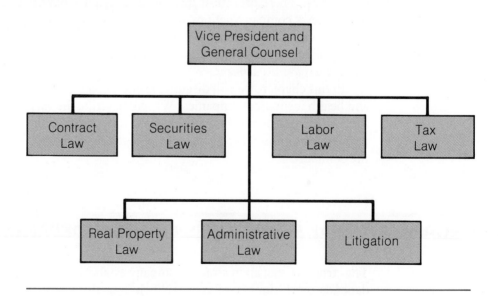

counsel, also known as the *chief counsel.* The vice president and general counsel oversees the department, delegates work to appropriate staff members, and usually serves as an adviser to the company's board of directors. The staff of the legal department can consist of one or more lawyers, plus paralegals and other support staff, such as clerks, librarians, and administrative assistants. Some large insurers may have more than 100 lawyers in their legal departments.

Paralegals are people specially trained in techniques of legal research and the formalities associated with various legal transactions. Paralegals are not, however, permitted to give legal advice and usually have not attended law school or passed a *bar examination,* which is a licensing test that a person must pass before practicing law. Some larger companies may also employ a special law librarian for the legal department library, because maintaining a law library usually requires specialized knowledge.

The lawyers in the legal department have graduated from law school and have passed a state or provincial bar examination. As mentioned earlier, depending on the size of the company, legal matters may be handled by one lawyer, or they may be apportioned among members of a staff of lawyers, with each lawyer specializing in one or more functions or areas of law, such as real estate law, securities law, litigation, or tax law.

Regional Structure

As the operations of life and health insurance companies have expanded, some companies have established regional or branch offices to carry out some of the functions traditionally associated with the home office. This trend has been especially strong among larger companies in the United States. Companies that first began to decentralize usually organized only claim offices on a regional basis. Eventually, however, companies moved more and more functions to regional offices, so that now nearly every function traditionally performed in the home office, including the legal function, can be found in a regional office (see Figure 14-2).

Certain functions in particular are delegated to lawyers in the company's regional offices. Regional office lawyers perform the following functions:

- maintaining governmental relations at the state or provincial level
- providing routine assistance to the regional claim department
- arranging for outside counsel to handle litigation originating in that region

They also advise policyowners on the local laws regarding taxation of their insurance and financial services products.

Maintaining governmental relations

In the United States, insurance companies monitor and try to have an impact on legislation and regulations in their own jurisdictions. Similarly, in Canada, insurers submit comments to the government on proposed legislation and regulations. In a company that operates in numerous

Figure 14-2
Regional organizational structure of a legal department.

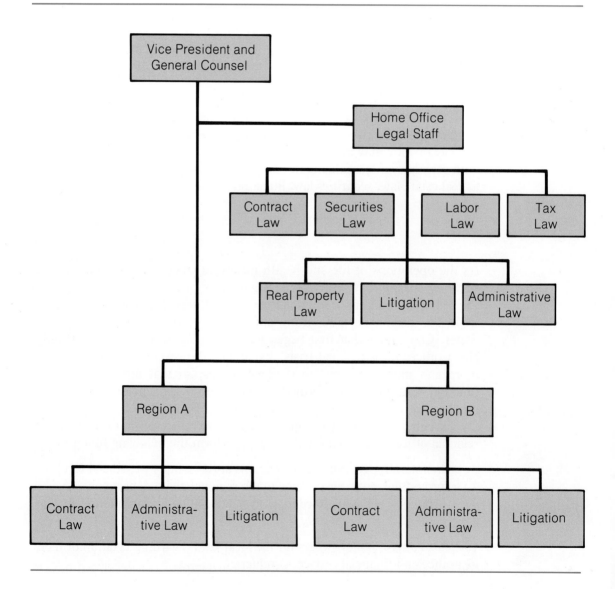

jurisdictions, lawyers in regional offices can more readily keep up with changes in local laws that affect the industry, such as laws relating to the wording of policy contracts. By keeping up with legal developments in each jurisdiction, the company can update its policies and products on a timely basis and remain in compliance with applicable laws. Lawyers in a regional office are also available, in addition to home office lawyers, to present the viewpoint of the insurance industry to state legislators and regulatory agencies when statutes or regulations are proposed that would affect the insurance business.

Assisting the claim department

When a company's claim processing function is handled through regional offices, lawyers in these offices can help resolve disputed claim situations. Lawyers in a regional office are probably more familiar with applicable local laws affecting claims than lawyers in the home office. The company also keeps travel expenses lower by using lawyers from a regional office.

Arranging for outside counsel

When a company believes that a lawsuit the company is involved in is not likely to be settled easily, regional office lawyers are well placed to arrange for local outside counsel to handle the lawsuit. *Outside counsel* are lawyers who are members of a private law firm that has been hired to represent or provide advice to the insurer. Lawyers in the regional office may find it easier than home office lawyers to establish good working relationships with local outside counsel.

Functional Structure

As the life and health insurance business becomes more complex, insurers deal with more legal questions than ever before. Many questions range far beyond the traditional bounds of insurance contract law. In response to the increasing number and diversity of legal questions, many insurers have begun to assign lawyers to various functional or product areas throughout the company, rather than concentrating all the lawyers in a single legal department (see Figure 14-3). In larger companies, one or two lawyers might be assigned to each unit or division that has a substantial need for legal advice. For instance, a product development unit might need its own lawyer to keep up with taxation changes so that the company can develop products

Figure 14-3
Functional organizational structure of a legal department.

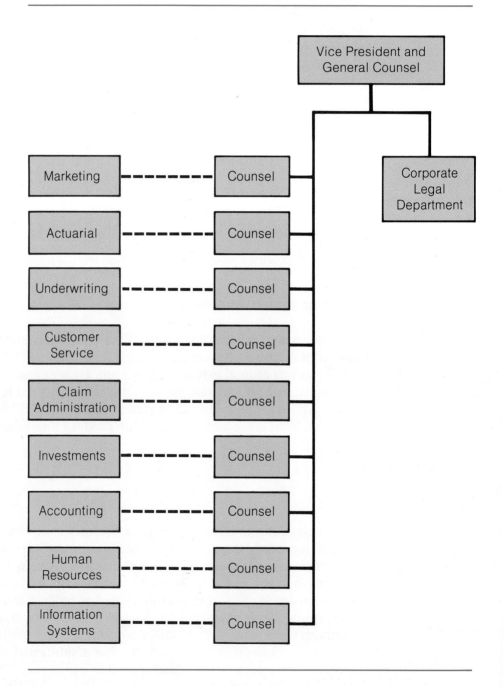

that take advantage of tax-saving opportunities. A company with large real estate operations might assign lawyers to work in the real estate investments division to develop and review leases, property management agreements, sales contracts, and so on.

A functional structure does not necessarily result in the dismantling of a central legal department. In most cases, the central legal department must still handle litigation, coordinate the work of any lawyers in regional offices, and deal with matters of general corporate law. However, by focusing the efforts of the home office attorneys, the functional structure streamlines the organization of the central legal department.

LEGAL DEPARTMENT FUNCTIONS

In addition to laws specifically governing insurance, the aspects of law that insurance company lawyers most frequently deal with are contract law, claims law, agency law, securities law, employment law, tax law, real property law, corporate law, administrative law, and litigation. Some of the more routine situations requiring the guidance of the legal department are described in INSIGHT 14-1. In the next few pages, we will describe the various aspects of law and how they affect the functions of a life and health insurance company.

INSIGHT 14-1

Procedures on Common Legal Problem Cases

Astral Life recently reviewed its procedures on some of the more common legal problem cases. In order to strike a balance between legal risk and operating efficiency, the company established the following guidelines for these situations.

Divorce

If Astral Life is notified that there may be a divorce involving a policyowner, a determination must be made as to whether the divorce action is in a "critical period" with respect to any action or service the policyowner requests. Astral Life defines the "critical period" for exercising care in a divorce situation as the period beginning when the divorce is filed until six months after it is final. During this time, ownership of the husband and wife's property is subject to change at the discretion of the court, and therefore, the policyowner can not unilaterally deal with his or her policy.

Legal or customer service staff should ask when the papers were filed or when the divorce was final and, if within this critical period, document the file with the information. A "Special Handling" caution is placed in the policy file and recorded on the master computer file. All activity pertaining to the policy must be approved by a first-line supervisor. An attempt is made to obtain a photocopy of the divorce decree and property settlement, if any. If the policyowner refuses to provide this documentation but insists on making a change, the only other option is to obtain written authorization for the change over the notarized signature of the spouse.

Bankruptcy

Astral Life treats the situation with a bankruptcy similar to divorce by defining a "critical period" as beginning when bankruptcy is filed until it is declared. During this time, all property owned by the person filing bankruptcy is under the custody of the bankruptcy court and is subject to a determination by the court as to whether it will be distributed in payment of debts. Exemptions vary from state to state, and if the company is on notice, any request for a distribution or change during the "critical period" requires the approval of the bankruptcy trustee.

If bankruptcy is mentioned in connection with a service request, an attempt is made to determine if the bankruptcy is in the "critical period." If so, legal staff should document the contact in the policy folder and refer the case to a first-line supervisor. At that point, a legal caution is placed on the case and further actions are planned. No action is taken, however, until it is determined if the court will include the policy among the bankruptcy assets.

Conservatorship/Guardianship

If Astral Life receives a service request from someone asking to act for a policyowner on the basis of his or her position as a conservator or guardian, legal or customer service personnel should ask for a photocopy of the legal papers appointing that person as conservator or guardian. When the papers are received, the case is referred to a first-line supervisor for approval of handling and any cautions.

Astral Life does not accept a conservator's or guardian's authority to change the beneficiary of the policy unless the papers specifically give the person that right or the company receives official court approval for that specific change. If a question arises as to authority for any disbursement or change, lawyers should consider asking for court approval before proceeding, but keep in mind the expense that this would put on the conservator or guardian.

Power of Attorney

A power of attorney is a written legal document giving one person the power to act on another's behalf. If someone claims to have a power of attorney to act for an Astral Life policyowner, that person should be asked to send the company a photocopy of the legal document granting that power. When it is received, the case is referred to a first-line supervisor for approval of any change.

While in-house counsel is available for consultation for these and other cases, these guidelines give some discretion and control to Astral Life's supervisory staff in some of the more common situations.

Source: Adapted with permission from an Activity Report submitted to LOMA, March 1989.

Insurance Law

In the United States, insurance is primarily regulated by the state governments. In Canada, both the federal and the provincial governments have authority to regulate insurance. Each of these governmental units has enacted laws and regulations pertaining to (1) the financial stability of insurance companies, (2) the products an insurance company offers, and (3) the manner in which insurance companies conduct their business. These laws and regulations, as well as the court decisions that have been based on them, make up the body of law known as *insurance law.*

Insurance laws and regulations affect almost every aspect of an insurance company's operations. These laws and regulations, for example, require the insurer and its agents to be licensed by each state or province in which they do business. Insurers must also comply with insurance laws and regulations that govern their dealings with agents and employees, proposed insureds, policyowners, and beneficiaries. Many of these insurance laws overlap with a variety of other aspects of the law. For example, although insurance contracts are governed in many respects by general contract law, insurance laws modify many aspects of contract law as it applies to insurance contracts. Insurance contracts must also be drafted in compliance with a variety of insurance laws. These laws affect how an insurer performs its contractual obligations by paying claims as they come due. Most of the areas of law that we will discuss in the remainder of this section are affected in some respects by insurance laws.

Contract Law

The basis of the business in which insurance companies are engaged is the insurance policy, which is the written evidence of a contract. A ***contract*** can be defined as a legally binding agreement between two or more parties. As written contracts, insurance policies are subject to the principles of contract law, although these may be modified by insurance laws. ***Contract law*** is the body of legislative enactments and previous court decisions that governs the interpretation of the rights and duties of the parties to a contract. Life and health insurance policies are contracts in which the insurer agrees to pay a stated benefit when a certain event—for example, the death of the insured—occurs. The policy also includes other contractual provisions relating to premium payments, contestability, and so on.

Other familiar types of contracts, such as those for the sale or purchase of a home or automobile, differ from life and health insurance contracts in that once agreement is reached in a sale or purchase contract, both parties have made promises to do something. If either party fails to do what it has promised, the other party can sue for damages. This type of contract is called a **bilateral contract,** because both parties have exchanged promises. An insurance policy, however, is a **unilateral contract,** because only one party, the insurer, promises to do something. The insurer cannot maintain a suit for damages if the policyowner fails to pay the premiums and the policy lapses. The insurer, however, is liable if it refuses to pay the policy proceeds, provided that the policy is in force.

Two areas where contract law is especially important to insurance legal departments are *policy drafting* and *claims*.

Policy drafting

Initial drafts of policies are usually developed by the insurer's marketing specialists and actuaries. Company lawyers review these drafts in order to ensure that they comply with the laws of the jurisdiction where the company is located and all other jurisdictions where the company intends to make this type of policy available. In the United States, after lawyers review these policy drafts, they are submitted for approval by the appropriate state insurance departments.

If the drafts do not exactly comply with all applicable laws and regulations, state regulators may ask for changes. Usually, the company defends each policy and explains why it believes that the policy meets the requirements of the particular jurisdiction. If the regulators are not persuaded, the company may (1) add a rider to the policy to modify its terms in accordance with that jurisdiction's requirements, (2) draft an entirely new policy for use in that jurisdiction, or (3) decide not to issue that policy in the objecting jurisdictions. The same policy, however, may be submitted to other jurisdictions for approval.

In Canada, insurers need not submit a policy for formal approval in every province where the product will be sold, except for variable insurance products, which must always be submitted for approval.

The legal department may also be involved in simplifying policy language. Easy-to-read policies have been mandated by law in a number of states—though not in Canada—and insurance company lawyers have worked to draft policies that are easy to understand while remaining in compliance with the law. Figure 14-4 shows a passage from a policy written in traditional legal terms and the same passage written in the "easy-to-read" style now required by the laws of many states.

Figure 14-4
Examples of policy language before and after changes made for readability.

Before readability legislation	After readability legislation
Death of Beneficiary. If the last surviving beneficiary for any death benefit proceeds payable under this policy predeceases the insured, the beneficial interest in such proceeds shall vest in the Owner. If any beneficiary dies simultaneously with the Insured or within fifteen days after the Insured but before due proof of the insured's death has been received by the Company, the proceeds of the policy will be paid to the same payee or payees and in the same manner as though such beneficiary predeceased the insured.	**Death of Beneficiary.** If no beneficiary for the life insurance proceeds, or for a stated share, survives the Insured, the right to these proceeds or this share will pass to you. If you are the Insured, this right will pass to your estate. If any beneficiary dies at the same time as the Insured, or within 15 days after the Insured but before we receive proof of the Insured's death, we will pay the proceeds as though that beneficiary died first.
Protection against Creditors. To the extent allowed by law and subject to the terms and conditions of this policy, all benefits and money available or paid to any person and relating in any manner to this policy will be exempt and free from such person's debts, contracts and engagements, and from judicial process to levy upon or attach the same.	**Protection against Creditors.** Except as stated in the Assignment provision, payments we make under this policy are, to the extent the law permits, exempt from the claims, attachments, or levies of any creditors.

Claims

Typically, when a policyowner or beneficiary presents a claim under an insurance policy, the insurer verifies that a covered loss has indeed occurred and then pays the benefits. The insurer, however, may deny the payment of certain claims if, for example, it believes that the party presenting the claim is not entitled to the proceeds or that a covered loss did not actually occur. In such cases, company lawyers must aid the claim department in interpreting the language of the policy and analyzing the facts of the situation to determine the insurer's liability. As discussed in Chapter 11, once the claim examiner decides to deny a claim, the legal department advises the claim area about the legal aspects of the denial.

Agency Law

Insurance companies are corporations that can act only by delegating authority to individuals, such as the company's officers, directors, and employees. In addition, insurance companies must retain agents to act on their behalf in contractual dealings with applicants for insurance. In legal terminology, an *agent* is a person who is authorized by another party, known as the *principal*, to act on the principal's behalf in contractual dealings with third parties. **Agency law** is that body of law that governs the rights, duties, and liabilities that arise among the parties when an agent represents a principal in contractual dealings with third parties. Certain insurance laws and regulations also govern how agents conduct their businesses and affect insurers' relationships with their agents.

Many duties of insurance company lawyers are concerned with agency law. When an agent is hired to represent an insurer, for example, the parties typically enter into an agency agreement that spells out the agent's duties and responsibilities, as well as how the company compensates the agent for performing those duties. The legal department is usually responsible for drafting the agency agreements that an insurer and each agent enter into when the agent is hired. Insurance company lawyers are also involved in many other situations involving agents. For example, when an agent acts improperly, the legal department is called on to advise the insurance company on how to deal with the agent to ensure that the company complies with the applicable laws and the agent's agreement.

Securities Law

A growing area for insurance company legal departments, especially in the United States, is the area of securities law. **Securities law** involves the interpretation and application of legislative and regulatory requirements regarding the sale and purchase of investment vehicles, especially stocks and bonds. As more investment-oriented products are developed, insurers come under increased scrutiny in the United States from the Securities and Exchange Commission (SEC). The legal department is responsible for advising the product development staff on SEC regulations and indicating the products that may be sold legally by various types of agents. For example, laws prohibit agents without SEC licenses from selling certain variable annuities.

In Canada, legal departments of insurers have similar functions in the investments area. Canadian companies that sell investment products in the United States must comply with SEC regulations in the same way as U.S. insurers. Variable products sold in Canada must be approved by each province's Department of Insurance. In order to sell mutual funds in Canada, agents must be accredited by the applicable provincial securities commissions.

Company lawyers also assist in the legal formalities associated with private placements and the purchase and sale of stocks and bonds. For example, if a corporation is interested in the private placement of a $500,000 bond issue and an insurer's investment analysts recommend that the insurer invest in the bond issue, the insurer's lawyers may be called on to help negotiate the terms of the agreement. The agreement specifies matters affecting the repayment schedule, such as any privileges to convert the bonds to common stock. When the insurer and the issuing corporation reach agreement on the terms, the lawyers draft a contract setting forth the details of the transaction and the rights and duties of the parties involved. They also make certain that the contract is properly signed.

Another investments-related responsibility for a stock company's lawyers is to keep the company informed about and in compliance with regulations regarding issuance of the company's own stock. Particularly important in the United States is IRS Rule 16-B, which regulates the purchase and sale of company stock by the company's officers and directors, and certain stockholders of the company.

Employment Law

Employment law is that area of the law that governs the relationship between an employer and an employee. As employers, insurance companies must comply with applicable employment laws. Most of the legal department's work in the area of employment law concerns the company's own employment practices. Company lawyers advise the human resources area in establishing and implementing sound guidelines and policies.

Employment law can be divided into three major categories: human rights legislation, employment standards legislation, and pension benefits legislation. Each type will be described briefly below.

Human rights laws are concerned with protecting the personal rights of the individual worker. Such laws prohibit unfair discrimination in employment on the grounds of a number of stated factors, such as race, religion, sex, age, marital status, physical or mental disability, and national origin. Human rights legislation also mandates that workers doing the same or similar work must receive the same pay, and it protects employees of both sexes against sexual harassment. The privacy and security of employees are afforded protection by human rights laws.

Employment standards laws mandate certain employment standards for covered employees. These statutory employment standards concern a variety of issues, such as minimum wage rates, overtime pay, and, in Canada, required amounts of paid vacation, and required amounts of parental leave.

Pension benefits laws govern the terms and operation of private pension plans used by employers for their employees.

For those insurance companies that have employees who are members of a labor union, company lawyers must be prepared to represent the company in the collective bargaining process. In *collective bargaining,* a company negotiates with a labor union to reach an agreement about the pay, work hours, benefits, and working conditions for company employees who are represented by the union.

Equal employment opportunity in the United States

Title VII of the Civil Rights Act of 1964 prohibits U.S. employers from discriminating in employment practices. As amended by the Pregnancy Discrimination Act of 1972, Title VII prohibits discrimination on the basis of race, color, religion, sex, or national origin. The human resources staff is responsible for assuring that company employment practices are conducted according to these and other equal employment opportunity laws. However, charges of discrimination are still sometimes brought against companies and supervisors.

Employees or potential employees in U.S. companies who feel that they have been discriminated against can bring their complaints to the local or federal *Equal Employment Opportunity Commission (EEOC).* The EEOC investigates job discrimination complaints. If the EEOC finds that a complaint is justified, an attempt is made to eliminate the discrimination and bring all interested parties into agreement. If such conciliation efforts fail, the local EEOC may hold a public hearing on the complaint. The EEOC is also empowered to file a suit in a court of law on behalf of the aggrieved individual. However, only the courts have the power to order an employer to discontinue a discriminatory practice.

Generally, three categories of discrimination exist: disparate treatment, disparate impact, and perpetuation of past discrimination.

- **_Disparate treatment_** is intentional discrimination. Disparate treatment involves the creation and application of different rules concerning hiring, promotion, and compensation of people based on factors such as sex, race, age, and national origin. A company's refusal to hire a qualified applicant for a clerical position because that applicant is a man would constitute disparate treatment. However, a church can require its priest or minister to be a member of that religious denomination.

- **_Disparate impact_** occurs when an employer has an employment policy or practice—not justified by business necessity—that appears to be neutral but results in a disproportionately negative impact on a group of people who are protected by law from employment discrimination. It does not matter whether the employer intends for the policy or practice to be discriminatory. An example of disparate impact concerns the requirement of a college degree for an internal job posting when a college degree is not justified by business necessity. Such a requirement might eliminate a large proportion of minority candidates who, because of their economic status, were not able to attend college.

- **_Perpetuation of past discrimination_** involves the intentional or unintentional continuation of a discriminatory practice. For example, assume that a company's sales force previously had an advancement system, created before Title VII, that kept women from rising through the hierarchy. If the company continued using this advancement system into the 1990s, perpetuation of past discrimination would exist.

If the EEOC takes a discrimination case to court and wins the case, the court can choose a number of remedies for the discrimination. The two most common remedies are orders to the discriminating company to provide back pay and to discontinue discriminatory practices.

Back pay consists of all the payments—including wages and fringe benefits—that the victims of discrimination would have received had they not been discriminated against. Requiring the company to discontinue its discriminatory practices may include such remedies as removing supervisory personnel, posting antidiscrimination posters, and rehiring former employees against whom the company discriminated.

Two more recent acts that are enforced by the EEOC are the Age Discrimination in Employment Act of 1967 (ADEA; amended in 1978 and 1986) and the Americans with Disabilities Act of 1990 (ADA). ADEA specifically prohibits discrimination in employment practices against people who are 40 years of age or older. ADA bans discrimination in employment practices against persons who are mentally or physically disabled.

Equal employment opportunity in Canada

The federal and provincial governments in Canada have passed human rights acts that prohibit employment discrimination on the basis of an individual's race, national origin, color, religion or creed, sex, marital status, or age. Discrimination is specifically prohibited in such employment-related areas as hiring, promoting, training, transferring, advertising for employees, and using employment agencies.

The enforcement of human rights legislation in Canada is the responsibility of provincial human rights commissions, which investigate complaints about discrimination. If a commission determines that an individual has a valid complaint, then the commission attempts to settle the complaint through conciliation. If conciliation fails, a board of inquiry is usually appointed. This board may either (1) issue orders for compliance or compensation or (2) prescribe other legal remedies.

Tax Law

Insurance company lawyers must be well versed in the various tax laws applicable to the company and to its policyowners. Tax law is a broad field that may be subdivided into the following categories:

- personal income tax law
- employee benefits tax law
- estate tax law
- corporate income tax law

The insurer's legal department has important responsibilities in each of these areas.

Personal income tax law

To determine which products are likely to be attractive to consumers, company lawyers must have an understanding of personal income tax law. *Personal income tax law* deals with those sections of the tax code that specify the types of income that are taxable to individuals, as well as the expenditures that can be deducted from taxable income. Any insurance or financial services product that can make money for an individual while maintaining or reducing the amount of income on which taxes must be paid is likely to attract customers. Lawyers in the United States helped develop individual retirement accounts (IRAs), for example, which allow many individuals to invest money that will not be taxable until the individuals retire.

The legal department also helps to arrange compensation packages to attract top executives. Legal expertise is needed both in understanding how to make the maximum use of tax-saving strategies and in drafting the agreement that explains the details of the compensation package. These packages are quite complex. In addition to the usual salary and benefits, packages for executives may include various forms of incentive compensation in money or in stock options. If such compensation is based on company earnings, for example, lawyers must work with the company and the executive to negotiate and settle on a contract that will define such terms as *company earnings*. Also, the lawyers may work with the executive to try to defer certain aspects of compensation in such a way that they would meet tax code regulations.

Employee benefits tax law

Insurance companies devote a good deal of time to employee benefits—both as employers and, for many companies, as providers of such benefits. Pensions, retirement plans, and group life, health, and disability programs are products with major markets for many insurers, who must design these products and services to fit applicable tax laws and regulations. Thus, attorneys must contribute to the marketing and administration of products and services dealing with employee benefits. Compliance with the constant flow of tax laws and regulations requires an ongoing effort by trained legal professionals.

Income tax law affects the way insurers provide benefits for their employees. The legal department works with human resources staff members to determine which employee benefits are not taxable as current income. Some types of employee benefits that the government determines are in the public interest may be currently deductible from the employer's taxable income but not currently taxable to the employees who receive the benefits.

Estate tax law

Estate tax law deals with taxes levied on a person's assets at the time of death. The legal department helps develop products that reduce the taxes owed by an individual's estate at his or her death. For example, a life insurance policy may be designed so that, when used to fund a trust, it provides an income to the insured while he or she is alive and then a lump sum to a beneficiary at the insured's death. The policy proceeds would not be subject to estate tax when the lump sum is paid to the beneficiary. Company lawyers must be familiar with ways to use life insurance as an estate-planning vehicle so that they can help train agents to present the tax benefits of insurance products to prospective customers.

Corporate income tax law

Like any other taxpayer, an insurance company must pay taxes on its income. However, determining what is and is not taxable income is a much more difficult task for an insurance company than for an individual. **Corporate income tax law** is the body of laws and regulations that defines income for a corporation and how that income is taxed. Corporate tax lawyers help company accountants interpret the tax laws that apply to insurance companies. These interpretations allow the accountants to calculate the company's tax liability and maximize the company's tax-saving opportunities.

An insurance company receives income from various sources, such as premium payments, stock and bond investments, mortgage investments, real estate operations, and the sale of various assets. Not all of this income is treated in the same way for tax purposes. Company lawyers must be thoroughly familiar with the complicated tax provisions that apply to each of these types of income.

Real Property Law

Because most insurance companies invest in real estate, insurance company lawyers must be well versed in the principles of real property law. **Real property law** deals with the ownership and transfer of rights in real estate. In the real estate area, the legal department handles contracts and deeds for the purchase and sale of property. Also, insurers often buy and sell mortgages, and attorneys are involved in the negotiations of these contracts. Company lawyers also perform the following functions related to mortgage operations:

- drafting the mortgage documents
- negotiating the purchase and sale of blocks of mortgages
- handling foreclosure proceedings

At times, the legal department advises the company's investment specialists about the best way to handle a particular real estate asset. For example, the legal department might advise the company to enter a sale-and-leaseback arrangement for one of the office buildings it occupies. A sale-and-leaseback arrangement could be beneficial to a company that needs cash and owns a building that has appreciated in value. By selling the building, the company realizes the building's appreciated value at once and obtains the cash it needs. Meanwhile, the company can rent its same office space from the new owner.

In another situation, the company might be better off to manage and operate a foreclosed property rather than sell it. For example, if the insurer has foreclosed on a poorly managed office building located in an area where rents are high, the insurer's property management group may be able to manage the building effectively and achieve a high rate of return on the company's investment. The legal department might also advise such a course of action in circumstances in which property values are depressed and selling the property would not enable the insurer to recoup its investment.

The legal department provides assistance to the real estate unit when the company undertakes a real estate development. Lawyers may be involved in negotiations to acquire the land the company needs. Legal staff may also be involved in drafting and reviewing the sales and rental agreements for the development.

Corporate Law

The legal department becomes involved in mergers and takeovers in which the insurance company absorbs or is absorbed by another corporation. Lawyers may be consulted early in the merger process to help determine whether the merger would violate antitrust legislation that protects against the existence of monopolies in certain products or markets. During the negotiation process, lawyers help explain to the insurer's top management the ramifications of various offers and counteroffers. Once a merger or takeover is agreed to in principle, the lawyers draft the contracts, spelling out the terms of agreement, such as

- the consideration that will be exchanged by the parties
- the timetable for the merger
- details of stock issue, purchase, and redemption
- the status of certain top executives

Lawyers also can advise an insurer on how to make itself an unattractive target for a takeover attempt.

If an insurance company is investigating mutualizing or demutualizing, the legal department researches the issue and tries to answer any legal questions that management might have. The legal department advises management about the differences in regulation of stock companies and mutual companies, especially regarding matters such as taxation, capital and surplus limits, and dividends. If the company decides to change its operating structure, the legal department provides specific advice on how to accomplish the change. For example, top management of a mutual company in the demutualization process would need the legal department's advice on how to value the equity in the company held by policyowners and how to represent fairly that ownership interest in a stock issue. Company lawyers would assist top management in classifying stock to be issued and determining the voting and dividend rights of each classification.

Administrative Law

The legal department may be asked to render advice or appear before regulatory commissions or agencies. *Administrative law* involves interpreting and applying regulations established by state, provincial, and federal agencies. Company lawyers may be invited to comment on proposed regulations that affect company operations. Most of the time, however, administrative law duties are limited to seeking regulators' approval of different items, such as policy forms, rates, and advertising materials. If the regulators refuse to approve any of these items and if the company considers the regulators' reasons for not approving them to be insufficient, the company's lawyers can request a hearing from the appropriate agency so that the company can present its point of view.

Litigation

Litigation is the act or process of resolving a dispute by means of a lawsuit. Litigation is a legal specialty in itself and may involve disputes in any of the areas of law that we have discussed. Lawyers handling litigation for an insurance company are responsible for the following duties:

- instituting or responding to the lawsuit
- researching the facts of the case
- taking statements from involved parties
- researching relevant court cases
- filing for appeal if the insurer does not prevail at the trial level, or possibly defending an appeal if it does prevail

Some companies employ staff lawyers who specialize in litigation. Other companies hire outside counsel when litigators are needed.

Often, cases are settled before a trial actually begins. Still, an insurance company that resists a claim must prepare itself for litigation. As mentioned in Chapter 11, insurance companies are cautious about choosing to resist a claim. Litigation can have negative effects on a company's public image and can be extremely costly and time-consuming. Also, if a court determines that the company resisted a claim without sufficient reason, the company may be accused of bad faith and be forced to pay punitive damages. ***Punitive damages*** are fines awarded over and above the actual contract amount and are designed to punish a litigant insurer for its behavior. Another type of ruling that may be made against an insurer is an order to pay ***compensatory damages,*** which include the contract amount as well as damages for a wrong that an insurer is found to have committed.

Another common situation in which insurance companies become involved in litigation is a suit of interpleader, in which an insurance company pays the proceeds of a policy to the court and asks the court to determine the proper recipient.

ADDITIONAL RESPONSIBILITIES

The legal department provides legal assistance and advice to many different functional areas in an insurance company (see Figure 14-5). We have already discussed product development, claims, investments, and human resources. In addition to these areas, company lawyers also work with the marketing and underwriting functions.

The legal department works with the marketing staff in three primary areas: agent contracts and compensation, sales training, and advertising.

- ***Agent contracts and compensation***—The legal department drafts agent contracts after the marketing staff has stated its goals for the contracts. Company lawyers also review commission schedules to make sure that they conform to all applicable regulations.
- ***Sales training***—Lawyers sometimes assist company staff and agents in understanding how certain products work, particularly those that affect tax liabilities or have complex legal ramifications. Company lawyers may also help train agents in legal aspects of estate planning and wealth accumulation planning. In some companies, lawyers may even be asked to accompany agents on sales calls that might result in especially large contracts for the company.
- ***Advertising***—Because of the many laws and regulations regarding the content and presentation of advertisements and promotional materials,

Figure 14-5

Some relationships of the legal department with other company departments and interested parties outside the insurance company.

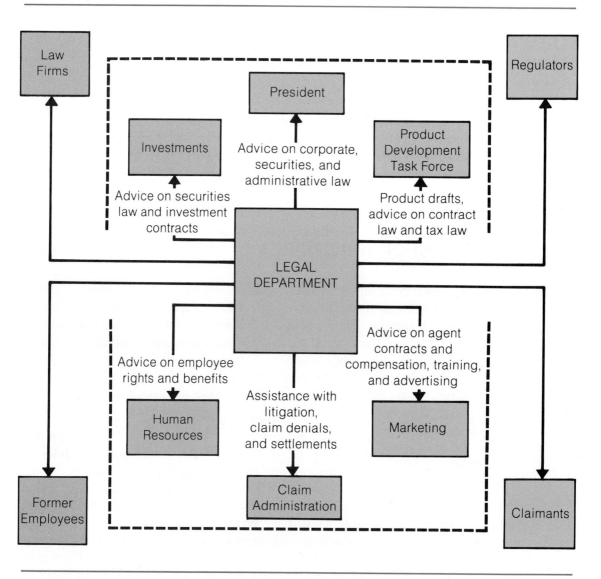

many insurers now have their lawyers review all such materials to make sure that they neither misrepresent the company's products nor seem susceptible to misinterpretation.

The legal department assists the underwriting area in a number of different ways. For example, the legal staff monitors state, provincial, and federal laws regarding discrimination and privacy, which are two issues that affect an underwriting operation. Also, attorneys may be called in to advise the underwriting department on a policy rescission matter, or a question regarding a claim and whether or not a policy was ever in force.

In addition to their insurance-related responsibilities, insurance company lawyers also perform functions that would be found in the legal departments of most large non-insurance-related corporations. These functions include helping review or obtain property and liability insurance on the company's own facilities and operations, and assisting with the lease or purchase of computer equipment. Because of the importance of internal resolutions and meeting minutes as legal documents, the corporate secretary of an insurance company is often an attorney. If the secretary is not a lawyer, the legal department helps the corporate secretary by advising about rules for annual meetings, drafting bylaws, preparing board resolutions, and researching the law on board actions, compensation, elections, and liability.

KEY TERMS

paralegal
bar examination
outside counsel
contract
contract law
bilateral contract
unilateral contract
agency law
securities law
human rights law
employment standards law
pension benefits law
collective bargaining
Equal Employment Opportunity
  Commission (EEOC)

disparate treatment
disparate impact
perpetuation of past discrimination
back pay
personal income tax law
estate tax law
corporate income tax law
real property law
administrative law
litigation
punitive damages
compensatory damages

Chapter 15

The Human Resources Function

After reading this chapter, you should be able to

- Describe the functions of the human resources area
- Explain the steps involved in human resource planning
- Compare the benefits and drawbacks of internal and external recruiting
- Describe the steps involved in the employee selection process and different types of selection tests
- Compare training, orientation, and professional development
- Describe some performance appraisal techniques and the benefits and drawbacks of each one
- Identify the factors considered in determining employee compensation

To operate in the best manner possible, an insurance company needs many resources—money, technology, information, a physical plant, products, a distribution system, and *people*. Throughout this textbook, we have discussed different types of resources and how they are managed to the best advantage. Wherever possible, we have discussed the people who make the business work, for without them there would be no business. The creativity, diligence, intelligence, and resourcefulness of a company's employees, managers, and officers provide the life and health insurance industry with the essential ingredients for success.

Recruiting, selecting, and maintaining a staff of qualified people are among the responsibilities of the human resources area. Most companies have a central human resources (HR) department, sometimes called a *personnel department*, that performs these functions for all of a company's divisions. Some companies dedicate human resources staff to each of a company's divisions, products, or functions, but, for ease of reading, this chapter assumes that an insurer has a central human resources department.

Regardless of its organization or place in the company, the human resources staff performs similar functions throughout an insurance company. Human resources staff members

- compile projections and forecast staffing needs for the company
- recruit potential employees
- help department managers select employees for open positions
- assist in orienting and training staff members and helping them develop professional and managerial skills
- administer a system for evaluating the performance of staff members
- plan and maintain a compensation system
- develop and administer benefit plans
- provide personal and professional guidance and counseling

In addition, the human resources function is responsible for implementing sound human resources policies and procedures that reflect current laws and regulations. For example, the human resources area, in consultation with company lawyers, establishes guidelines for employee selection, hiring, promotion, and termination to ensure that the company is not engaging in unlawful discrimination. Also, the human resources department produces reports for management about employee turnover, sick days, and usage of benefits. Finally, as described in INSIGHT 15-1, human resources departments might organize efforts or make charitable contributions on behalf of the company's employees.

INSIGHT 15-1

Insurers Support Desert Storm Troops

One way that human resources departments accommodate employees is to follow through on societal issues that affect the company's employees. For example, insurance companies throughout North America responded to the Persian Gulf conflict of 1990-91 with many innovative methods to support the troops and thus boost morale among their employees. Here are a few examples:

- Lincoln National Corporation (LNC) of Fort Wayne, Indiana, became a telephone lifeline for a few days in January 1991 for soldiers participating in Op-

eration Desert Storm. The company became a link for calls troops made from Saudi Arabia to dependents and family members living in Germany. Over a three-day period, more than 1,000 telephone calls were handled by LNC volunteers staffing the "Lincoln National Troop Line." This unique telephone hookup service was provided for U.S. military personnel transferred from Europe to the Middle East.

"Lincoln National was pleased to participate in this effort in support of the service men and women in the Middle East. During these dangerous times, we felt it was important to provide some peace of mind for military personnel and their families through this communications hookup," said David D. Allen, LNC executive vice president. More than 300 LNC volunteers staffed phone banks at LNC's home office facilities for four-hour shifts. They used local and long distance telephone network equipment normally used for the corporation's day-to-day business operations.

• Metropolitan Life's efforts to support the troops included a special two-day blood drive. Response was so great that not all donors could be accommodated during this two-day period. MetLife also printed stories in their home and head office magazines about salespersons and administrative employees involved in the Middle East operations. The company provided salary supplements and waived contributions for medical, dental, and group life insurance coverages for their employees participating in Desert Storm.

• In October 1990, Modern Woodmen of America launched a letter-writing campaign involving all Modern Woodmen camps, youth and teen clubs, agency field force, and home office staff. Modern Woodmen sent approximately 50,000 personal messages to those on active duty with Operation Desert Shield. Modern Woodmen provided special letterhead for all camps, clubs, agents, and home office staff to show their patriotism through morale-boosting letters to the troops. Once completed, all letters were returned to their home office for bulk shipment to the Persian Gulf. Home office employees volunteered their time to stuff letters in preparation for the mass mailing.

Source: Adapted with permission of the publisher from "Industry News," "LN Unites Troops and Families," *Resource,* April 1991, p. 40; and Activity Reports submitted to LOMA by Robert Luna of Metropolitan Life, March 1991, and by Gerald P. Odean and Gary A. Kruger of Modern Woodmen, April 1991.

The organizational structure of human resources departments may vary from company to company. However, the structure that is shown in Figure 15-1 illustrates most of the functional units in insurance companies' human resources departments. As you look at this organization chart, note that the marketing area usually provides human resources support for the company's agents and agency personnel. The human resources activities described in this chapter apply particularly to home office personnel management, although many of the activities are also appropriate for an agency environment.

In this chapter, we will discuss the human resources function and its activities. We will also look at how human resources are managed, not just by the human resources staff but by all managers in a life and health insurance company. Managing human resources is a responsibility that runs throughout every area of every organization.

Figure 15-1
Organization chart of a human resources department.

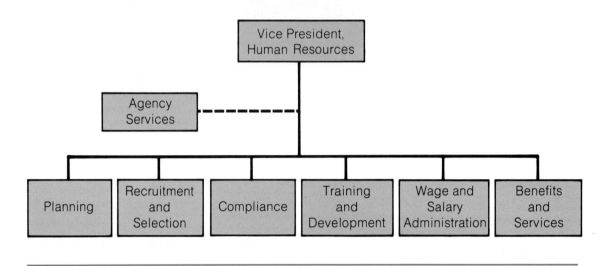

HUMAN RESOURCE PLANNING

When executives develop long- and short-term plans for their companies, they usually consider general economic conditions, the changing aspects of the marketplace, new products being produced by competitors, and the industry's experiences in the recent past. Market researchers conduct statistical studies of current and potential markets, and financial managers calculate financial ratios and project expected future income and disbursements. More and more companies now also forecast the availability of human resources and plan for recruiting the people that the company needs. *Human resource planning,* which is usually conducted by the human resources staff, is the process of determining the number of qualified people who are now available or should be available in the future to fill positions needed in a company. Human resource planning consists primarily of two broad functions: (1) forecasting the company's need for qualified employees and (2) determining the number of qualified people who are now or may soon be available for employment. Given ongoing demographic changes and the increasing diversity of the work force, human resource planning is becoming more challenging.

Forecasting Staffing Needs

Although human resources departments in some large insurance companies conduct studies to forecast staffing needs, most companies rely on estimates of staffing needs from each functional unit. Basically, staffing needs depend on and fluctuate with the demand for a company's products. The company must estimate the level of sales expected in the future and the number of employees—both agency personnel and home office employees—who will be needed to support those sales. In addition, the company must consider a number of other factors:

- the turnover rate caused by resignations, retirements, and other voluntary and involuntary terminations
- the performance of the employees currently working for the company
- new products marketed by the company that may require the support of specially trained employees or large numbers of new employees
- technological developments that might change the nature and size of the company's work force
- trends in labor force demographics
- economic factors, such as the unemployment rate
- the company's current and projected financial condition

This forecasting process should be integrated with the company's long-range planning so that the human resources staff can prepare for significant changes in the company, such as the elimination of a line of business, a change in the distribution system, or a merger with another company.

Forecasting techniques

Sometimes the forecasts of staffing needs are based solely on the educated guesses and estimates of managers. When a more measurable or *quantifiable* approach is needed, human resources professionals use forecasting techniques that employ statistical research and computer models. Two typical quantitative forecasting techniques for staffing needs are trend analysis and ratio analysis. These techniques are used more often in large companies than in small companies.

Trend analysis. To conduct a *trend analysis,* the manager analyzes data from past periods in order to predict future trends. For example, a manager might know that for the past three years the company's agency services staff has increased by five employees each year. Using trend analysis only, the manager would assume that the agency services staff will increase by five employees in the current year as well. Unfortunately, trend analysis assumes that employment levels are affected only by the passage of time. In reality, however, sales, productivity, technology, demographics, and many other internal and external factors greatly affect employment levels.

Ratio analysis. As discussed in Chapter 13, ***ratio analysis*** indicates the proportionate relationship between two different amounts. The ratio is calculated by dividing one amount by another. For example, a manager knows that each customer service representative can handle an average of 40 inquiries in a day. If the company receives 120 customer calls in an average day, then the manager divides the total number of customer calls received per day by the number of inquiries that one customer service representative can handle in one day. This calculation determines the number of service representatives needed.

$$\frac{\text{Total calls per day}}{\text{Calls per representative per day}} = \frac{120}{40} = 3$$

The company needs three customer service representatives in the office each day to handle inquiries. As with trend analysis, however, ratio analysis does not take productivity levels into account. Referring back to our example, if each representative were given additional tools, training, incentives, and motivation to become more productive, then the company may need fewer customer service representatives. Other factors can also affect the ratio, such as a change in the mix of the company's products.

Estimating the Labor Supply

After the various divisions determine the number and types of employees needed from one period to the next, the human resources staff estimates the number of people who might be available to fill certain types of positions. These estimates consider the supply of labor both inside and outside the company.

Internal labor supply

Human resources departments usually maintain detailed records on the labor supply in their own companies, although the means of monitoring the internal labor supply vary widely from company to company. In small companies, where the human resources manager knows every employee personally, the manager might maintain informal records regarding the abilities of each person in the organization. In larger companies, the human resources manager often maintains a skills inventory on the company's staff. A *skills inventory* is a manual or computerized data base of the education, training, and experience of each person working for an organization. This listing provides managers with information to help them identify employees and their qualifications for various positions in the company. Most skills inventories contain the following information about each employee:

- *education,* including high schools, colleges, and universities attended; degrees; scholarships; special awards and activities; and any work-related courses completed
- *work experience,* including present position, salary, responsibilities, positions formerly held with current and previous employers, and general salary history
- *special qualifications,* including professional organizations to which the employee belongs, authorship of work-related publications, participation on major task forces or special work teams, fluency in foreign languages, and knowledge in specialized areas, such as computer technology
- *potential,* including job performance evaluations, aptitude test results, health information, and number of years until retirement

Information that a company keeps about an employee cannot be used in a discriminatory fashion.

In addition to a skills inventory, many large companies also keep **succession charts,** which illustrate graphically the likely candidates for promotion to various key positions in a company. Figure 15-2 is an example of a succession chart. Notice that several candidates are listed in order of preference under each position. The order is determined by many of the items indicated on the skills inventory, such as experience, proven ability, potential, and education. By maintaining skills inventories and succession charts, human resources managers can identify the number of potential job candidates in their companies as well as their comparative qualifications. Skills inventories and succession charts are also used to plan career development of current employees. By giving employees opportunities to perform more challenging and rewarding jobs, a company helps keep employees motivated.

External labor supply

Estimating the number of people outside the company who have appropriate qualifications for specific jobs is difficult. However, estimates can be made by monitoring the following factors:

Figure 15-2
Example of a succession chart.

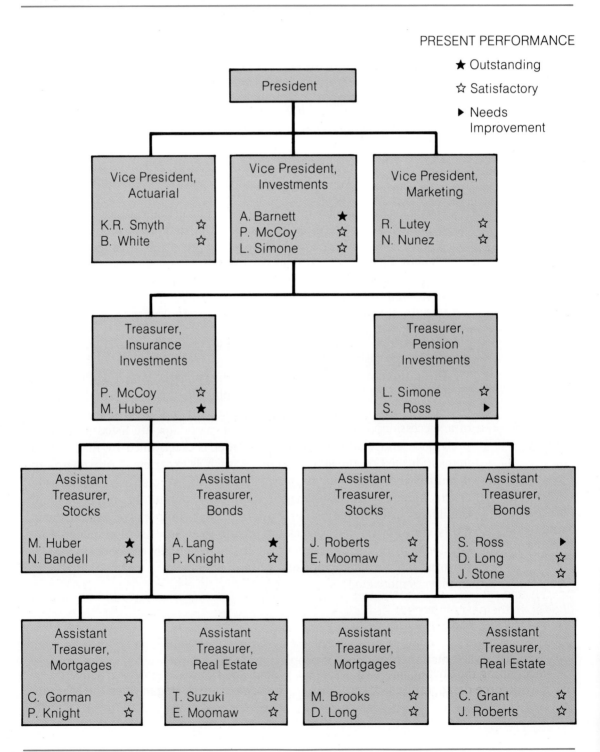

- national economic conditions and the expected unemployment rate
- local economic developments, such as the opening or closing of large businesses in the company's area of operations
- the supply of potential employees with certain job skills, such as the number of college graduates with accounting degrees or high school graduates with clerical skills

Such information can be obtained from local newspapers, national business and professional publications, government reports, demographic studies of the area's labor pool, and research studies conducted by educational organizations.

RECRUITING QUALIFIED PERSONNEL

Companies recruit job candidates by looking both inside and outside the company for the best-qualified people. In this section, we will describe the processes involved in recruiting candidates from inside the company and from sources outside the company, and the procedures companies use to select employees. INSIGHT 15-2 provides a closer look at how some companies are responding to changes in the work force from which employees are chosen.

INSIGHT 15-2

Capitalizing on Work Force Diversity

Capitalizing on diversity is the latest corporate response to changing work force demographics. To a growing number of insurance companies, capitalizing on (or valuing) diversity means developing the policies and procedures needed to attract and retain the best employees by becoming attuned to their differences. Diversity takes in not only differences in race and gender, but also in lifestyle and cultural background.

Recognizing the shifting nature of today's work force demographics, many insurance companies are taking action. Here is just a sampling of what companies are doing to capitalize on work force diversity to ensure that they have the employees they need to meet their changing business needs now and in the future.

Minnesota Mutual

Minnesota Mutual's efforts to actively manage diversity began when the Minority

Recommendations Task Force was formed to identify the obstacles to minority employees' career success at Minnesota Mutual. Shortly thereafter, Minnesota Mutual began developing a number of programs such as their Managing and Valuing Diversity Training Curriculum.

The overall objective of the "diversity" training program, according to Margaret O'Donnell, manager, corporate training and development, is to help participants develop an appreciation of the "people" differences within the organization, so that all of the company's human resources are utilized to their full potential.

Another instrumental force in Minnesota Mutual's diversity program is Minorities for Corporate Awareness (MCA), a network formed in mid-1987 to provide support to minority employees. George Robinson, MCA Network Committee cochair, said, "Although membership is limited to racial minorities, our group frequently sponsors special events open to all Minnesota Mutual employees. Our objective is to help provide a work environment where everyone can work together to meet corporate and personal goals."

Aetna Life and Casualty

Comprehensive staffing is the name for Aetna's multifaceted approach to meeting the effects of the demographic changes that are already being felt in many field locations as well as at the company's Hartford, Connecticut, headquarters. Comprehensive staffing means "finding ways—innovative ways as well as traditional ways—to staff your organization and to meet your business needs," said Ethan Loney, senior administrator, equal opportunity compliance.

Aetna's comprehensive staffing brings together a multitude of existing programs

to recruit and retain employees. Recruiting efforts range from Saturday Academy, a training program for inner-city youths, to college recruiting. Methods of retaining employees include alternate staffing options, such as job sharing, part-time work, home work, and temporary work; a plethora of education programs; and benefits such as child-care referral and a family leave policy.

As Loney explained, most of these programs have existed for a long time. What's new is that they're being grouped under one heading—comprehensive staffing. In addition, he said, some of the programs are now taking on a new emphasis because the company is putting extra effort into recognizing that it will be harder to recruit and retain people in the future.

Allstate

An employee survey is one of the latest steps in Allstate's efforts to explore companywide cultural diversity issues. The survey is part of a project that examines Allstate's Affirmative Action (AA) program and its impact on the company. Allstate wants to know how employees feel about diversity issues. It also wants to know what other companies are doing and wants to get input from community leaders.

Allstate is continuing to meet the changing needs of its employees. Susan Martin, assistant vice president of human resources, recently initiated the Work and Family Connections program, which includes three new policies—the Family Leave Policy, the Part-time Professional, and the Family Illness Allowance.

The new program recognizes the importance the family plays in an employee's overall performance and strives to help employees maintain a healthy balance between work and family life. Allstate believes that the new program gives the company a competitive advantage in the recruiting and retaining of employees.

Source: Adapted with permission of the publisher from Barbara Jones Newey, "Insurance Companies Capitalizing on Work Force Diversity," *Resource,* July/August 1989, pp. 7-12.

Internal Recruitment

Most companies have well-established internal recruitment procedures, and many companies prefer to fill job openings from within the company. Internal recruitment is accomplished in several ways, including promotion, upgrading, lateral transfer, and demotion.[1]

Promotion occurs when an employee is awarded a job at a level of the organizational hierarchy higher than his or her present job.

Upgrading involves educating, developing, and training a current employee to perform work duties more effectively or to take on new duties. When companies automate certain functions, they may upgrade the positions that previously performed the manual tasks to reflect the new skills necessary in the automated function. The company would then train incumbents so that they can fill the upgraded positions.

Lateral transfer is the act of moving an employee from a position at one level in an organization to another position at the same level of the hierarchy. In a lateral transfer, the employee is neither promoted nor demoted.

Demotion occurs when an employee is assigned to a job at a level of the organizational hierarchy lower than his or her present job. Although demotion is not a common method of internal recruitment, it is sometimes used as an alternative to separation when an employee with a good work record is found to have inadequate skills to perform his or her current job but qualifies for a lower-level job. Demotion is also sometimes used to preserve employees or positions during a downsizing or merger.

Internal recruitment has a number of benefits:

- Internal recruitment is usually less risky for the company than external recruitment. The company is already likely to have an accurate assessment of a current employee's skills and performance. A person hired from outside the company is an unknown quantity.
- Internal recruitment is less expensive than external recruitment. Help-wanted ads and job placement agencies are not needed with internal recruitment.
- Internal recruitment boosts morale. If a company has a policy of

staffing from within whenever possible, employees feel that they have a good chance for promotion and career development. Internal recruitment also boosts morale by giving everyone within an organization an equal opportunity to be considered for new positions.

- A current employee knows the company and its mission and does not need a corporate orientation program. Every company has its own procedures and traditions, and a current employee knows both the official and unofficial procedures for getting a job done. A current employee has personal contacts in the company and understands the values that the company's executives appreciate and encourage. For these reasons, internal recruitment tends to minimize the need for orientation and training.
- Internal recruitment increases current employees' experience and value by allowing them to move from one department to another.

Some companies conduct internal recruitment on an informal basis, contacting individual employees who are being considered for a vacant position in the company. Such informal recruitment practices, however, can overlook qualified employees and lead to employee dissatisfaction or charges of discrimination. Therefore, most companies have established regular job posting and bidding procedures to assure that all qualified employees have an opportunity to apply for any job openings in the company. Companies can also use their skills inventories to aid in internal recruitment.

In most *job-posting* programs, the human resources department announces a new job opening by placing a position description on the company's bulletin boards. The *position description* lists the job title, the duties and responsibilities of the position, and the qualifications that a candidate must have to be considered for the position. Generally, the job is posted for a specified period, usually three to five days, during which time employees can obtain additional information and apply for the job. After the time limit has passed, the posting is removed and applicants are screened and interviewed. In some cases, if no satisfactory internal candidate applies at first, the job posting may continue concurrently with external recruitment efforts.

External Recruitment

Sometimes a company has no qualified employees to fill an open position. In such a situation, a qualified candidate must be recruited from outside the company. Furthermore, some of the benefits of internal recruiting can become drawbacks that the company must counterbalance by recruiting externally. For example, hiring someone who understands the company's values, traditions, and procedures has its benefits, but such hiring can lead to managerial inbreeding and cause a situation in which everyone thinks in a similar way and no new ideas are developed. Hiring someone from outside the company can bring fresh energy and ideas to the company and stimulate creativity. In addition, even companies that are committed to internal recruitment must still recruit externally for entry-level positions.

Sources of external candidates

Human resources staff members use a number of means to recruit possible employees from outside the company. Among the most common methods for external recruiting are help-wanted advertising, contracting with private employment agencies, conducting job fairs and searches at educational institutions, and following up on staff referrals.

Help-wanted advertising. Probably the most prevalent way to recruit externally, especially when unemployment is high and a job's responsibilities are not overly demanding, is through *help-wanted advertising* (see Figure 15-3). In this form of recruitment, advertisements are placed in newspapers, magazines, and professional and trade journals. In some rare cases, recruitment efforts are made on radio and television. Help-wanted advertisements describe the available position, the necessary qualifications, and sometimes the position's proposed salary or wage.

Private employment agencies. For a fee that varies from 10 to 30 percent of a job candidate's first-year salary, *private employment agencies* help employers find qualified people to fill jobs and help individuals find the types of jobs they want. The fee is almost always paid by the employer, but the employer can usually reclaim all or part of the fee if the new employee proves to be unsuited for the job within a certain period, such as three months.

Other types of private employment agencies are temporary help agencies and executive search firms. Whereas private employment agencies usually concentrate on placing full-time job applicants, *temporary help agencies* provide companies with part-time and temporary workers—usually for clerical, office services, systems, or accounting positions—to fill immediate or seasonal demands for workers. *Executive search firms,* also known as *headhunters,* locate and place executives, upper-level managers, and specialized technical staff, such as underwriters and actuaries.

Educational institutions. Most large insurance companies look to colleges and universities as sources for potential managers, agents, and entry-level professional and technical employees. Large companies often send recruiters to college campuses to describe and promote the company and to interview potential job candidates. Human resources departments also mail job descriptions for posting in college placement offices. Some

Figure 15-3
Sample want ads.

INSURANCE CUSTOMER
SERVICE MANAGER

Rapidly expanding mass marketing insurance administrator with over 25,000 insureds (Hospital, Life, Medicare Supplement). Needs experienced Customer Service Manager to establish policyowner marketing system, direct the activities of administration and claims, including conservation and all other phases of administration. Will become the third person on a team in charge of converting our manual insurance processing and claims to an on-line computer system. Salary open—send resume and salary requirements to:

CHIEF UNDERWRITER

Central Fla. aggressive Life Co. seeks Chief Underwriter, FLMI or CLU preferred. Salary commensurate with experience. Send resume with salary requirements to:

VP PRODUCT DEVELOPMENT

Life insurance subsidiary of a major national corporation seeks a VP Product Development who will revamp existing product lines and make recommendations for new interest-sensitive annuity products. Individual must possess a broad financial services background with strong insurance fundamentals. Minimum experience seven years. College degree required. Excellent location. Salary commensurate with experience. Submit resume and salary requirements to:

PERSONNEL
ASST. PERSONNEL MANAGER
Immediate opening for highly motivated person. Requires excellent communication skills and minimum 2 years experience in human resources department to include group benefit administration, confidential record keeping, structured interviewing techniques, personnel policies, functional job descriptions, performance appraisal systems, and newsletter preparation.

SECRETARY
Fortune 500 insurer is seeking mature, intelligent person for legal dept. No legal exp. necessary. High School Grad w/good organizational skills & accurate typing. Exp. w/ word processing and dictating machine desirable.

RECEPTIONIST
Front-office position available for individual with exceptional communications skills. Responsibilities include operation of PBX switchboard, greeting visitors, and general clerical duties. Light typing required. No previous experience required. Will train right individual. Opening due to inside promotion.

companies maintain a special relationship with selected high schools and grade schools by participating in career days and similar activities, although such relationships are intended more to enhance public and community relations than to promote a recruiting effort.

Staff referrals. Another important source of new employees is a *staff referral,* in which a current employee suggests a job candidate to the human resources department. Staff referrals usually provide the company with high-quality employees, and many companies encourage staff referrals by paying bonuses to staff members who refer job candidates who are hired. Staff referrals are used extensively to recruit agents. However, caution must be exercised in using a staff referral. To avoid charges of discrimination, a company must apply appropriate screening and testing procedures when considering an applicant who is being considered as a result of a staff referral.

Selecting Employees

Companies usually establish a standard procedure for selecting employees to fill open positions in the organization. The procedure usually includes the following steps:

(1) The applicant completes an application form.
(2) Potential candidates are asked to return for a screening interview.
(3) The applicant is asked by the company to undergo employment testing.
(4) An employment interview is conducted.
(5) The company performs a reference check and may ask the applicant to undergo a physical examination.

Each of these steps is described below.

The application form

All companies require applicants to complete a job application form. The *application form,* which is designed or adapted for each company by its human resources staff, requests the specific information that the company needs to identify appropriate job applicants. Unlike a resume, which the job applicant designs to appear as favorable as possible and which can vary considerably in content and form from one applicant to another, the application form provides the company with the same type of information on every applicant.

As shown in Figure 15-4, a typical application form requests the following information:

Figure 15-4
Sample application form.

Employment Application

Federal and state law prohibits discrimination in employment because of *race, color, creed, age, sex, national origin or disability.*

PERSONAL

Name _____
    LAST   FIRST   MIDDLE INITIAL

Address _____
    NUMBER AND STREET

_____
CITY   STATE   ZIP CODE

Telephone _____ Social Security
Number _____ Number _____

GENERAL INFORMATION

Position _____ Salary _____ by the
Applied for   Expected   Week ☐
                              Month ☐
                              or Year ☐

Type of employment desired: If employed, when can you start work?
Full-time ☐ Temporary ☐ Part-time ☐ Date ____ / ____ / ____

If under 18, do you have a work permit? Yes ☐ No ☐

If you are not a citizen of the United States, do you have the legal right to remain permanently in the United States? Yes ☐ No ☐ Not applicable ☐

Have you ever been employed by this company? Yes ☐ No ☐ If so, when? ____ / ____ / ____

and in what capacity? _____

Have you ever been convicted of a felony? Yes ☐ No ☐

If yes, explain when and where, and describe the outcome of the case. _____

How were you referred for this position? _____

Do you have any serious physical or mental handicaps preventing you from performing any specific kinds of work that may be required by this job? Yes ☐ No ☐

If yes, you may describe handicaps and explain work limitations below.*

_____

EDUCATIONAL BACKGROUND

TYPE OF SCHOOL-NAME-LOCATION	DIPLOMA OR DEGREE	MAJOR FIELD OR COURSE OF STUDY	OVERALL GRADE AVERAGE
HIGH SCHOOL Name _____ Location _____			
COLLEGE Name _____ Location _____			
COLLEGE Name _____ Location _____			
GRADUATE SCHOOL Name _____ Location _____			
OTHER Name _____ Location _____			

Scholarships received* _____

Scholastic or other honors* _____

Extra-curricular activities* _____

Do you plan to continue your education? Yes ☐ No ☐

If so, when and in what field? _____

U.S. MILITARY

U.S. Military Service Experience: Yes ☐ No ☐

If your duties were job related, please describe _____

*Except those which would disclose race, religion, color, sex, national origin or ancestry.

*Furnishing the information is voluntary. It is being sought to provide opportunities for the handicapped, the information will be kept confidential; and refusing to provide the information will not result in unfavorable treatment.

Date

Name

Figure 15-4 *(continued)*

EMPLOYMENT HISTORY

Please list all part-time and full-time positions, giving present or last position first.
(Use an additional sheet of paper if necessary.)

1 DATES WORKED

FROM _____ TO _____

SALARY

STARTING _____ FINAL _____

Employer's Name _____

Supervisor's Name and Title _____

Employer's Address _____

Your Job Title and Duties _____

Reason for Leaving _____

Employer's Telephone No. _____
May the above employer be contacted at this time for a reference? Yes ☐ No ☐

2 DATES WORKED

FROM _____ TO _____

SALARY

STARTING _____ FINAL _____

Employer's Name _____

Supervisor's Name and Title _____

Employer's Address _____

Your Job Title and Duties _____

Reason for Leaving _____

Employer's Telephone No. _____
May the above employer be contacted at this time for a reference? Yes ☐ No ☐

3 DATES WORKED

FROM _____ TO _____

SALARY

STARTING _____ FINAL _____

Employer's Name _____

Supervisor's Name and Title _____

Employer's Address _____

Your Job Title and Duties _____

Reason for Leaving _____

Employer's Telephone No. _____
May the above employer be contacted at this time for a reference? Yes ☐ No ☐

Account for all periods of unemployment in excess of three (3) months:

_____

_____

WORK EXPERIENCE

What office machines do you operate? _____

Typing Speed _____

MANUAL _____ ELECTRIC _____ STENO SPEED _____

What special skills, knowledge, talents, business licenses, or other job-related experience, not covered elsewhere, do you have?

_____

_____

OTHER

Additional comments which you feel would be important in our consideration of your application:

_____

_____

_____

_____

If employed by _____, I will abide by its rules and regulations. I also agree to physical examinations at any time at the option of the company at no personal expense, and agree that the examining physician may disclose to the company or its representatives the results of such an examination. Further, I understand that my employment is not for a stated period of time. All of the foregoing information I have supplied in this application is a full and complete statement of facts and it is understood that if any falsification be discovered, it may constitute grounds for dismissal upon discovery thereof.

Signature of Applicant _____ Date _____

Printed by Life Office Management Association

- personal data, such as the applicant's name, address, and telephone number
- the job or type of work for which the applicant is applying
- the date the applicant will be available for work
- the salary that the applicant is seeking
- the educational and training background of the applicant
- the work history of the applicant, including companies worked for, dates employed, past salaries, and former supervisors

In designing or adapting an application form, human resources professionals must be sure not to ask any questions that might lead to a charge of discrimination by an applicant who was not awarded the job. Many job applications used to ask about information such as marital status, age, national origin, and religious affiliation. Such questions may no longer be asked.

The screening interview

After the human resources staff has examined the application forms completed for a particular job, some applicants are identified as potential job candidates. These candidates are asked to come to the company's offices for a screening interview. The *screening interview,* which is almost always conducted by a human resources employment specialist, is intended to eliminate those applicants who are obviously not qualified for the job. Human resources specialists are well trained in interviewing techniques, and their work in screening interviews can reduce the number of candidates that department managers must consider later in the screening process.

Employment testing

Another significant selection and screening approach is employment testing. For a test to be of any value to an employer in selecting new employees, the test should be valid and reliable. *Validity* refers to the degree to which a test is correlated with a job-related criteria. Thus, a selection test that possesses validity shows that applicants who do well on the test will also do well on the job. *Reliability* refers to the extent to which a test gives the same results on repeated administrations of the same or an identical test. That is, an applicant who scores a 90 on a test on Monday should score at about the same level on an identical or equivalent test on Tuesday.

Employment tests used for selection purposes can be categorized generally as aptitude tests, performance tests, and personality tests. All tests should comply, as necessary, with relevant U.S. federal regulations or the Canadian Provincial Human Rights Code.

Aptitude tests predict a person's ability to learn a specific job if sufficient training is provided. Such tests can measure clerical aptitude, manual dexterity, numerical aptitude, mechanical aptitude, and aptitude in other areas. Clerical aptitude tests are among the most common aptitude tests that insurance companies use. Aptitude tests often rely on the collection of biographical data, or biodata, which has proven to be a valid test predictor of job success of potential applicants. **Biodata** includes information about education, previous employment, and other past experiences that relate to the desired position.

One standard aptitude test used extensively by insurance companies is the *Job Effectiveness Prediction System (JEPS)*, developed by LOMA. JEPS is generally used to measure the aptitude of entry-level clerical and technical-professional applicants who are seeking nonsales positions.

Performance tests measure the work that a person can do and relate it directly to the job for which the person is applying. Although most other tests are standardized and are used by many different organizations without modification, performance tests are generally developed by each organization to suit its own needs. Small companies, without the time or resources to conduct extensive testing, tend to prefer performance tests. In one type of performance test, the **work sample test,** applicants perform a task, such as typing a letter, that is a necessary part of the job they want.

Another type of performance test that insurance companies use, particularly for management and customer service positions, is the situation management test. In the **situation management test,** the job applicant is asked to respond to a particular work-related situation. The situation can be presented on paper, verbally, or on videotape, and the applicant is evaluated on the basis of his or her response to the situation.

Personality tests identify a person's motivational, emotional, and interpersonal characteristics. Although personality tests are criticized for being too personal and for testing an area too subjective to be measured, some large companies have found these tests useful in identifying the type of person they want to employ. One type of personality test is the **interest test,** which is designed to identify a person's general interests. A side benefit of the interest test is that it can be used as a career planning tool after the applicant has been hired. Some companies also perform psychological assessments or administer honesty tests, also called *integrity tests,* on applicants for certain high-level or otherwise sensitive positions.

The employment interview

Whereas the human resources staff usually conducts the screening inter-view, the manager or supervisor of the unit in which the position is available usually conducts the employment interview. The purpose of the *employment interview,* which is often a series of interviews, is to provide the manager and the candidate with the chance to decide whether the candidate is qualified for the job and whether the job is suited for the candidate. Many managers and supervisors now receive training to help them keep their interviews job-related, effective, and within legal restrictions placed on the topics that can be covered in an interview.

Reference checks and physical examinations

For some companies, the final steps in the screening process include checking the applicant's references and having the applicant undergo a physical examination.

Reference checks. An applicant's references come from people or organizations that can verify the applicant's work history, job performance, and educational background. References may be characterized as business references, personal references, and academic references. Business refer-ences include the applicant's former employers. These references are usually considered the most important because they can provide prospective employers with detailed information about applicants' work habits, promo-tion records, and former responsibilities and salaries. Provincial legislation in Canada gives job applicants the right to see letters of reference that describe them. Similarly, the U.S. Privacy Act of 1974 requires federal employers to show letters of reference to employees upon request.

Knowing that former employees can see letters of reference and knowing that some organizations have been sued by former employees because of information contained in an unfavorable reference, many companies are now reluctant to provide business references. Companies usually must have the consent of a former employee before releasing information about him or her. Some companies that do provide references offer only limited information, verifying the former employee's dates of employment, positions held, and salary. Reference checks are usually conducted by human resources staff.

Physical examinations. Most companies do not require physical examinations for all of their applicants, because the expense of such examinations would be prohibitive. However, some companies require applicants for executive and upper-management positions to undergo physical examinations. Such physicals are usually conducted at the company's expense. Because of the passage of the American with Disabilities Act (ADA), U.S. companies must be careful not to administer physical examinations in a selective or discriminatory manner. Physical examinations, if they are given at all, must be required of all applicants for that position.

One specific type of physical examination that some companies perform is *drug testing*. Companies that have a policy of not hiring applicants who use illegal drugs may test the urine or blood of applicants to determine whether any evidence of drug abuse exists.

ORIENTATION, TRAINING, AND DEVELOPMENT

In an increasingly competitive and ever-changing business environment, an insurance company must establish and maintain effective programs for orienting, training, and developing employees. **Orientation** is the process of introducing new employees to an organization's procedures, policies, and other employees. **Training** is generally defined as activity directed toward learning, maintaining, and improving the skills necessary for current job performance. **Development,** by contrast, is generally defined as activity directed toward learning and improving the skills needed for future job performance.

Many companies centralize the training function within the human resources area and have at least one person on the HR staff who specializes in determining training and development needs. The training staff may develop and deliver all programs itself, or it may use experts from inside and outside the company to conduct all or part of its training offerings.

In some companies, the training function may be completely decentralized. Large functional areas, such as information systems and claim administration, may have their own training staffs, and in other areas the manager may take responsibility for training employees.

One other common configuration is a combination approach—the HR area offers general training and development programs on such topics as management development and human relations skills, and the line areas offer their own specialized technical training. In this section, we will look at various methods companies use to orient new employees, train them to do their jobs, and develop them for future responsibilities.

Orientation

Many organizations have found that the first few days—even the first few hours—a new employee spends at a job can have a powerful impact on that employee's viewpoint and attitudes (see INSIGHT 15-3). Early impressions and experiences can affect the employee's future performance within the organization. The orientation process is usually a joint effort of the human resources area and the new employee's department. The portion of the orientation conducted by the human resources staff is usually an introduction to the organization in general, including explanations of the company's

INSIGHT 15-3

MetLife's Orientation Program

From the employee's first day on the job, a companywide orientation program at MetLife emphasizes quality and accountability.

A video, "Working Toward Excellence," takes a new MetLife employee on a tour of the Big Apple Circus. The viewer meets the circus performers and the "behind-the-scenes" crew while they describe their work environment and discuss ways to exceed their customers' expectations. Using the circus as a metaphor, the video underscores the point that each employee, no matter what the work setting, is responsible for providing service excellence.

"Working Toward Excellence" is part of MetLife's *Quality From the Start* employee orientation program. Developed with the input of more than 2,000 MetLife personnel, *Quality From the Start* introduces the newcomer to the company's businesses, customers, expectations, and corporate values. The program consists of eight video presentations and a variety of printed materials that give the new employee an overview of MetLife's family of companies and its scope of business.

Quality From the Start officially begins with a welcome letter to the new employee after the individual accepts a job offer, and is completed on the employee's one-year anniversary.

Quality From the Start pairs the new employee with a mentor and builds in opportunities for the employee to talk with managers and associates. The program places responsibility on the new employee to take an active role in learning about the company and his or her job responsibilities.

Quality From the Start is designed to help employees

- develop a sense of pride in working at MetLife
- become aware of the scope of the company's businesses and its impact as a major financial institution
- reduce the anxieties associated with starting a new job
- become a productive, contributing member of the MetLife team quickly and efficiently
- understand that quality customer service is a primary source of competitive advantage
- understand the standards of quality by which performance will be measured
- share responsibility for individual growth and development

MetLife studied how other excellent companies, both in and out of the insurance industry, oriented the new employee at every level. "A unique and successful aspect of our program is that it's not directed at only clerical-level employees or professional-level employees," comments Susan Berger, assistant vice president responsible for MetLife's Human Resources Development and Training Department. "We built it to serve the entire employee population."

The emphasis on a manager's participation in *Quality From the Start* is evident by the 86-page management guide that details all facets of the program. In the guide's introductory letter to the managers, MetLife president and CEO John Creedon writes: "Your role in creating a good first impression of the company and in getting new

employees off to a good start is critical in helping newcomers play a part in making MetLife The Quality Company."

A new employee also receives an orientation checklist. Divided into categories titled "The Work Environment," "The Job," "The Company and Its Mission," "Our Business and Customers," and "Being the Best," the checklist is a roadmap the employee uses to chart orientation activities and the specific resources (e.g., organization charts, videotapes, etc.) available to accomplish the activities.

"At MetLife," Berger summarizes, "we want employees to be active in their orientation and career development. To deliver quality service to all customers, they must feel accountable for what they do. This feeling must start right at the beginning, and this is what *Quality From the Start* is all about."

Source: Adapted with permission of the publisher from Chris Breston, "MetLife Gives Employees 'The Best Possible Start,'" *Resource*, November/December 1988, pp. 22-27.

- history, organizational structure, current activities, and goals
- rules and operating procedures, such as dress code, safety regulations, working hours, and lunch and other work breaks
- compensation policy and practices
- benefits, such as group life and health insurance, pension and savings plans, vacations, and holidays

During this introduction, the employee may receive a company handbook that contains specific details about the information provided in the orientation session.

After being introduced to the company itself, the new employee is usually given an orientation to his or her work area. This orientation may be conducted by a human resources specialist, but more likely it will be conducted by a co-worker or supervisor from the employee's own area. This orientation usually includes an introduction to managers, supervisors, fellow employees, and the new employee's work station or office.

For employees who have never worked in life and health insurance, many companies provide a general introduction to the industry itself. This orientation, which can include classroom sessions, films or videotapes, and self-study materials, may be developed by the company's human resources staff, by the staff of the division where the new employee will work, or by outside educational organizations.

Training and Development

The first step in providing training or development for an employee or a group of employees is to assess whether training and development are actually needed and, if so, the skills or knowledge that must be acquired. In assessing training and development needs, the human resources training specialist seeks to find areas in which a difference exists between

- the knowledge and skills that employees currently have and the knowledge and skills they should have
- employees' daily performance and their optimal performance
- the organization's current performance and its optimal performance

Five approaches to assessing training and development needs are outlined below:

1. *Analysis of specific job requirements.* The job description established for a job is used to determine the training or development necessary for an employee to fulfill the stated requirements.
2. *Analysis of work performance.* A manager checks work completed by an employee in order to determine the areas in which the employee would benefit from training or development.
3. *Analysis of performance standards.* The performance standards set for a job are used to establish the type and depth of training or development that an employee needs in order to reach the standards.
4. *Administration of an organization opinion survey.* Some or all of the members of an organization, both managers and other employees, are surveyed to determine the types of work-related problems they are encountering.
5. *Organizational analysis.* Analyzing and comparing the organization's actual performance (as shown in production reports) to the organization's desired performance (as expressed in its goals and forecasts) can reveal areas in which training or development is desirable.

After training and development needs have been assessed, the organization next designs a training or development program. The responsibility for program design involves building the program's content and choosing appropriate training methods.

In deciding the content of a training or development program, a trainer first establishes specific learning objectives on which to base the content. *Learning objectives* are specific statements of the desired outcomes or results of training and development activities. For example, specific learning objectives for training courses for claim examiners might be to

- use a reference manual on state insurance regulations in order to determine whether or not to make payments for specific medical conditions in certain states
- calculate the benefit amount of a cost-of-living adjustment for a disability income policy

Learning objectives serve to motivate employees. Thus, it is important for training specialists to set these objectives at an appropriate difficulty level. Learning objectives also establish a level by which actual performance can be measured. The objectives should be expressed in terms that are observable or able to be calculated.

Using the learning objectives as a guide, the training specialist then develops the content of the training program or locates appropriate training materials. Training and development materials often include a *job aid,* which is a checklist, procedure guide, manual, or other item that employees can use for reference at work. A job aid is useful for presenting information needed for a task that is performed infrequently, that involves many steps, or that requires an employee to make numerous decisions.

Training and development methods

As we mentioned earlier, the primary purpose of training is to prepare employees to perform specific tasks. Development, on the other hand, tends to focus more on helping employees strengthen their general business and management abilities. Development usually provides employees with both technical knowledge and insights into the workings of human relationships in the business setting. Both training and development take a wide variety of forms, and many programs offered to employees contain elements of both training and development. Training and development are provided both on the job and off the job. Several training and development methods will be described below.

On-the-job training. ***On-the job training (OJT)*** is training provided while participants remain in the workplace and involves performing the actual work to be done on the job. In traditional on-the-job training, a new employee's co-worker or supervisor explains and demonstrates procedures and observes while the new employee performs the procedures. OJT is efficient because it can be done while the new employee is actually producing work for the company. Its one-on-one nature forces the new employee to take an active role in learning and enables the trainer to observe the level of the employee's learning and take action immediately to correct problems.

Another form of on-the-job training is job rotation. Also known as *cross-training*, **job rotation** involves moving an employee from one position to another at regular intervals in order to enable the employee to develop expertise in a variety of jobs. Although job rotation increases the variety of tasks that an employee can perform, it does not increase the complexity of the employee's job at any one time. Job rotation allows an employee to enjoy more job variety and to gain a more complete sense of the organization's functions, as described in INSIGHT 15-4. It also enables an organization to assign employees effectively during vacation or overload periods.

INSIGHT 15-4

Job Rotation Program

In order to provide senior technical and supervisory staff with exposure to different products and to maintain a challenging and interesting work environment, Canada Life's Group Pension area introduced a formal job rotation program. The program, which was introduced in January 1987, provides a method for the orderly transfer of senior technical and supervisory staff from one position to another at a similar job level. The program is intended to operate as a chain so that, as one person moves to a new position, the person replaced is free to move along to another position. In order to minimize disruption in work and productivity, the program permits an overlap period during which the incumbent trains the new person. The training time, if required, can be for a period of between eight to twelve weeks.

While some of the transfers are initiated by the department managers, most of the transfers between departments are initiated by the employees. Once a year, a letter is sent to each employee to explain the program and to provide the employee with an opportunity to express interest and preferences. Attached to the letter is a return form that asks employees to indicate if they are interested in being involved in the program during the next year and, if so, if there is a particular position to which they would like to move.

Matching people and positions, and getting the timing right, has not always been easy, but solutions have been found. Sometimes the linkage has been broken, but a means of perpetuating the rotation has always been developed. Flexibility is the essential ingredient.

During the '90s, Canada Life will be

increasingly faced with the challenge of dealing with "plateaued" employees. A job rotation program instituted along the lines described may prove to be an effective strategy for dealing with the plateauing phenomenon.

Source: Adapted with permission from an Activity Report submitted to LOMA by Howard H. Newman of Canada Life, March 1990.

On-the-job development techniques. As the name suggests, *on-the-job development techniques* take place at the work site during normal working hours. These techniques are similar to on-the-job training except they usually involve a wider range of activities. Several on-the-job development techniques are commonly used to develop professional and managerial skills:

- ***Coaching.*** In this technique, a junior manager or potential manager is assigned to work with an experienced manager. The junior employee is given some of the work and responsibility of the manager, and the manager provides the junior employee with instruction and encouragement.
- ***Understudy.*** This technique takes coaching one step further, because the junior employee, or *understudy*, is being trained to take over the job of the manager, or *mentor*.
- ***Job rotation.*** One purpose of job rotation is to give employees a broad understanding of a company by having them work in a variety of functional areas. Frequently, job rotation is used for management trainees who are recent college graduates. The trainee usually spends several months in each department, sometimes as an observer but usually as an active participant in department operations. Another purpose of job rotation is to offset plateauing. Employees reach a ***plateau*** when they have risen to a certain career level and have no position for upward movement within the organization. Job rotation provides variety for such employees and allows them to increase their value to the organization by becoming familiar with different work processes.

Training and development conducted "off-the-job". Many types of training and development are best conducted away from the work area. Often training is conducted in a group setting. Some typical methods of training commonly used in group situations are described below.

A ***lecture*** presents information to employees who attend class sessions. Lectures are often supplemented by discussion, readings, and audiovisual aids such as slides, films, and videotapes.

In the **conference method,** trainees interact in small groups with a trainer present to provide feedback and guidance. The conference method is used to generate solutions to problems or to gain understanding of specific new techniques or information.

When trainers use **case studies,** they give trainees descriptions of conditions or problems and ask them to evaluate the situation and offer solutions. This training method teaches employees to use logical, systematic approaches to resolving problems and enhances decision-making skills.

Role playing engages learners in a simulation technique so that they can act out specified roles. Learners are able to "try out" newly learned interpersonal skills and communication techniques in a hypothetical situation and receive immediate feedback.

Some of the group training methods discussed above, such as case studies, are appropriate for individualized training. Another commonly used training method appropriate for individualized training is programmed instruction. **Programmed instruction** uses educational devices—such as textbooks, workbooks, and computers—to provide trainees with (1) information about a subject, (2) opportunities to apply their knowledge of the subject, and (3) feedback about their progress in gaining knowledge. Programmed instruction presented in a computerized format is usually referred to as **computer-based training,** also called *computer-assisted instruction.* Some programmed and computer-based instruction may be developed by a company for its own use, but many companies buy such instructional tools from organizations that specialize in developing such training media.

A number of organizations provide off-the-job development programs. Among the more popular types of programs are university programs, company and professional organization programs, programs offered by independent management organizations, and company-sponsored management institute programs. Many of these programs provide college credit and continuing education units.

University programs, which can last from a few days to several weeks, are developed by universities and taught by college professors or other experts in their fields. These programs provide business people with a more sophisticated understanding of a wide variety of business subjects. Many companies now subsidize or pay for their employees' tuition to attend university programs and reward those who complete the programs successfully.

Company and professional association programs are developed to prepare people who are employed in specific businesses. The life and health insurance industry has numerous programs available to its employees. These programs include short conferences and seminars on topical subjects, as well as self-study and classroom programs that require participants to pass a series of examinations to prove that they have completed the courses successfully. Some of the best-known company associations and professional associations that provide development programs will be discussed in Chapter 18.

Independent management organizations usually provide short conferences and seminars on a wide variety of subjects.

Company-sponsored management institute programs are learning institutions that companies have developed for their employees. Frequently, these institutes are facilities with a college-campus atmosphere and classroom teaching. Companies use these institutes to provide most of the professional development that they think their employees will need to be successful in their work.

EVALUATING STAFF PERFORMANCE

Formal performance appraisal procedures are considered to be the best way to evaluate staff performance. Years ago, supervisors and managers evaluated their staff members' work on what they remembered from the past year. Few formal procedures were available, and little paperwork was required to document evaluations, the reasons for such evaluations, or reasons for promotion or termination. Now, however, many workers at all levels of an organization receive formalized and well-documented performance appraisals. Documentation is an increasingly important aspect of the appraisal process, particularly if any promotion, termination, or disciplinary action is being planned.

Performance Appraisal Methods

The method of performance appraisal that a company uses is usually chosen or developed by the human resources staff. Sometimes they are assisted by an advisory committee of company employees or by an outside consultant that specializes in human resource issues. The human resources staff trains the company's managers and supervisors to use the chosen appraisal system. The managers and supervisors of each functional unit are the people who actually conduct performance appraisals. In some companies, employees are also trained in performance appraisal administration so that they understand the system and how they are being evaluated. Some common performance appraisal methods will be discussed in the next few pages.

Essay appraisal

One of the simplest forms of performance appraisal is the essay. In the *essay appraisal technique,* managers and supervisors write a report about each of their subordinates, indicating the subordinate's job performance, strengths, weaknesses, accomplishments, and potential for promotion. An essay appraisal gives managers and supervisors great freedom in evaluating their subordinates. However, because the essays are unstructured, they are difficult to compare with one another. Another drawback is that using essay appraisals can lead to purely subjective assessments of the employee's performance, when more objective assessment methods may be appropriate. In addition, the effectiveness of an essay appraisal often depends on the appraiser's ability to write clearly. With the essay technique, an employee's evaluation can depend as much on the appraiser's writing ability as on the employee's performance. To offset its limitations, the essay appraisal is often used along with a more structured appraisal technique.

Critical incident technique

In the *critical incident technique,* a supervisor keeps a record of an employee's especially good or bad work behavior. Examples of such records include "Developed more efficient procedure for administering group life insurance claims" or "Misjudged upturn in the stock market and sold stocks at a loss." The supervisor then uses these examples, or *critical incidents,* to judge the employee's performance at the end of the evaluation period. A critical incidents record is useful in the evaluation interview because the evaluator can use specific examples of the employee's work performance. However, because this technique places so much emphasis on isolated incidents rather than day-to-day activities, the critical incident method of performance appraisal should never be used alone in judging performance. This appraisal method is often used for training and development purposes or to supplement other evaluation methods.

Ranking methods

One popular category of appraisal methods requires the appraiser to compare employees with one another and rank them, from best to worst, based on specific characteristics of their work or behavior. In the *alternation ranking method,* the appraiser first takes a list of employees and a list of characteristics, such as "completes work quickly" or "produces high-quality work." The appraiser identifies the employee who best typifies a certain characteristic. Then the appraiser identifies the employee who least typifies the same characteristic. After that, the appraiser picks the second-best and the second-worst employee for that characteristic, then the third-best and third-worst, until all the employees have been rated and the appraiser has a complete ranked listing.

A similar ranking method is the *paired comparison method,* in which each listed employee is compared to all other listed employees one at a time to determine which employee is the better of the two with respect to the particular job characteristic being rated. When all employees have been compared on each job characteristic, the employee who compared favorably most often is ranked first and so on until the last employee is ranked.

Ranking methods of performance appraisal tend to be subjective and are difficult to use if the group of employees being evaluated consists of twenty or more people.

Graphic rating scales

The most widely used of all appraisal techniques is the graphic rating scale. *Graphic rating scales* provide the appraiser with a list of basic characteristics that relate to job performance, such as "completes work on time," "cooperates with fellow workers," "maintains high standards," and "finds better ways to do work." The appraiser then determines the degree to which the employee exhibits the characteristic being rated. For example, the appraiser might choose to rate an employee as exceptional, commendable, satisfactory, or unsatisfactory in cooperating with fellow workers.

The advantage of the graphic rating scale technique is its standardized format. Because all employees are judged on the same criteria, one employee's performance should be comparable to another employee's performance. On the other hand, certain characteristics are more important for some jobs than for others. Many rating scales do not allow the appraiser enough flexibility to indicate or weight various aspects of performance.

Behaviorally anchored rating scales (BARS)

Behaviorally anchored rating scales (BARS) are similar in structure and format to graphic rating scales. BARS, however, contain job-related characteristics that are more specific to the job and more fully described. In addition, the scales for rating the employee on each characteristic are related to specific behavioral descriptions. Figures 15-5 and 15-6 show an excerpt from a BARS and an excerpt from a graphic rating scale, respectively. Although the BARS has the advantage of greater detail, the graphic rating scale is simpler to complete.

Figure 15-5
Excerpt from a behaviorally anchored rating scale.

	5—Outstanding top 5%	4—Superior 10%	3—At Expected Level 70%	2—Below Expected Level 10%	1—Marginal bottom 5%
Amount of Work	5	4	3	2	1
Consider number of assignments completed and volume of output in relation to nature and conditions of work performed. Disregard quality of work.	Extraordinary volume of work completed.	Consistently turns out a good volume of work.	Amount of work completed is satisfactory.	Output barely acceptable.	Amount of work entirely inadequate.
Quality of Work	5	4	3	2	1
Consider thoroughness, accuracy, and orderliness of completed job. Disregard amount of work handled.	Unusually high-grade work is consistently performed. Quality is exceptional in all respects.	Quality is of high grade, but not exceptional.	Work is reasonably complete, accurate and presentable.	Quality occasionally is unsatisfactory.	Work usually lacking in thoroughness, accuracy or neatness.
Dependability	5	4	3	2	1
Consider the manner in which worker applies self to work, if job is done timely, and the amount of supervision required to get the desired results.	Justifies utmost confidence. A minimum of supervision required.	Applies himself well but occasionally needs direction and supervision.	Fairly reliable and conscientious. Normal supervision required.	Cannot always be relied upon to get desired results without supervision.	Undependable. Needs constant supervision.
Judgment	5	4	3	2	1
Consider the wisdom of his/her decisions in the absence of detailed instructions and judgment in unusual situations.	Thinks quickly and logically in all situations. Judgment can always be depended upon.	Judgment usually of a high degree.	Judgment adequate in normal situations.	Makes frequent errors in judgment. Works best with detailed supervision.	Judgment entirely undependable.
Comprehension	5	4	3	2	1
Consider mental ability in mastering new routine, grasping explanations, and ability to retain this knowledge.	Brilliant and keen mind coupled with eagerness to learn.	Quick to grasp new ideas and methods.	Learns satisfactorily.	Learns by excessive repetition. Needs guidance.	Slow in learning even simple procedures. Needs constant guidance.
Attitude	5	4	3	2	1
Consider attitude toward job and company.	Enthusiastic about type of work; booster of company.	Happy on job; favorable attitude toward company.	Seems to be interested in company.	Shows little interest in either job or company.	Disgruntled on job; critical of company.
Cooperation	5	4	3	2	1
Consider extent to which employee works harmoniously and effectively with fellow employees, supervisor and others.	Exceptionally successful in working with and assisting others.	Quick to volunteer to work and assist others.	Generally works well with and assists others.	Cooperation must be solicited. Seldom volunteers to work with or assist others.	Fails to cooperate. Unwilling to work with or assist others.
Capacity and Ambition For Future Growth	5	4	3	2	1
Review all the factors previously considered and judge employee's capacity and ambition for future advancement both in present department or branch and in the organization.	Outstanding candidate for future development. Given opportunity, could be expected to go far in the organization.	Capable of developing beyond present level of work.	Has probably reached most suitable job or level of work.	Barely capable of handling present level of work.	Entirely out of place in present job. Should be moved to simpler work or dismissed.
Overall Job Accomplishment	5	4	3	2	1

Source: David J. Cherrington. *Personnel Management: The Management of Human Resources* © 1983. Allyn and Bacon. Boston, Mass. All rights reserved. Reprinted by permission.

Figure 15-6
Excerpt from a graphic rating scale.

1. Amount of work	5	4	3	2	1
2. Quality of work	5	4	3	2	1
3. Dependability	5	4	3	2	1
4. Judgment	5	4	3	2	1
5. Comprehension	5	4	3	2	1
6. Attitude	5	4	3	2	1
7. Cooperation	5	4	3	2	1
8. Capacity and ambition for future growth	5	4	3	2	1
9. Overall job accomplishment	5	4	3	2	1

5	4	3	2	1
Outstanding	Superior	At Expected Level	Below Expected Level	Marginal
Top 5%	10%	70%	10%	Bottom 5%

SEPARATION OF EMPLOYEES

Changes in employment are necessary in the life of an organization. *Separation* occurs when an employee leaves an organization. Separation can result from resignation, layoff, retirement, or discharge. A *resignation* occurs when an employee leaves an organization in order to pursue work with another organization or to take up an alternative occupation, such as parenting or education. A *layoff* results when an organization has no work for an employee to perform but expects to recall the employee when work becomes available. *Retirement* occurs when an employee withdraws from a position or an occupation, usually concluding his or her career or profession.

Discharge is the dismissal of an employee who does not otherwise wish to leave an organization. Discharge can occur as a result of a certain cause such as poor job performance, drug or alcohol abuse, or other undesirable, work-related behavior. Discharging unproductive or unprincipled employees is necessary in order to maintain consistent production within an organization and to prevent the development of resentful feelings on the part of other employees. In today's environment of corporate mergers, technological advances, revised job requirements, and increased competition, employee discharges also occur as an organization trims or retrains its work force at any level from entry-level employees to top-level managers.

The human resources area is notified of all separations and handles paperwork associated with ending the employment relationship. In addition, the HR department in many companies conducts an exit interview. An *exit interview* is a meeting between a manager (or a human resource director) and an employee who has resigned or who has been laid off, retired, or discharged. In an exit interview, the employee is questioned about working conditions and about ways of improving any problem areas. Information gained from an exit interview can be circulated to all managers and supervisors so that they can resolve difficulties that are reported, especially those that are mentioned on a consistent basis. An exit interview enables employees to vent frustration and anger, and provides an organization with information about employee grievances and current or potential problems in the workplace.

In some cases, especially when the company is forced to lay off employees, the human resources area may provide outplacement counseling services. *Outplacement counseling* usually involves providing career counseling, vocational testing and skills evaluation, and information about job searches. A program of outplacement counseling offered by a company does not, however, imply that the present employer is assuming responsibility for finding new employment for the terminated person.

The human resources area may analyze the kinds and numbers of employee separations to determine the causes of the separations and to decide whether changes are needed in an organization. A large number of resignations, for instance, may indicate that the organization currently has a noncompetitive wage scale or an unchallenging work environment. A large number of layoffs may indicate that management is failing to balance the number of employees hired with the amount of work available for those employees to perform. Excessive numbers of discharges typically indicate that the organization's staff selection and training procedures need review in order that the organization may make closer matches between the skills of employees and the work activities assigned to them.

ESTABLISHING COMPENSATION SYSTEMS

Many factors are considered in determining what each employee is paid. In order to establish a fair and equitable compensation system, the human resources department must evaluate the various jobs in the company, determine appropriate wage and salary scales, and establish and administer various benefits and services. The next section of this chapter will describe these activities.

Job Evaluation

Before the human resources department can develop an equitable pay scale, all the jobs in the company must be evaluated. This job evaluation is usually conducted by a committee of company executives, managers, and human resources specialists. Occasionally, an outside consulting firm will be hired to assist in the evaluation. In the job evaluation process, each job in the company is analyzed and rated according to the following factors:

- education required for the job
- training required for the job
- complexity of the job
- accountability of the job position
- authority of the job position
- duties and responsibilities of the job position

The most widely used job evaluation method is the *point factor comparison system,* in which points are assigned to each job based on the specific requirements and characteristics of the job. The number of points assigned to the job is then correlated with a pay scale that indicates the amount of money that people in jobs of different point ranges are paid.

Wage and Salary Administration

Once an equitable job evaluation system is established, wage and salary scales can be developed for a company. In addition to reflecting the job's relative importance in the company as recognized by the job evaluation, wages and salaries also take into consideration (1) the company's financial resources, (2) comparative pay in other companies, and (3) government requirements. Results of collective bargaining agreements, as may occur in a unionized workplace, can also be a factor in determining wages to be paid. In addition, some companies participate in salary surveys that determine the compensation levels for a certain industry or a specific job function.

The amount of money a company can pay its employees is limited by the amount of money the company earns. However, a company must also make its pay scale competitive with other companies. A competitive pay scale helps assure that the company pays enough money to attract and keep talented employees but not so much that it is paying more than necessary for the services provided by its employees. Industry wage and salary surveys provide a company with comparative pay information.

Government requirements also directly affect a company's wage and salary policies. For example, minimum wage standards set a limit on the minimum amount an employer can pay for a job, and antidiscrimination legislation in both the United States and Canada is intended to assure that all people of similar ability, seniority, qualifications, and performance levels receive equal pay for the same work.

Pay incentives

In addition to the normal salaries and wages paid to employees, many companies have developed pay incentive plans through which employees are rewarded for exceptional work. Some incentive plans reward individual employees for their personal efforts; some plans may reward all employees if the entire company met or exceeded a certain performance standard during the previous year. In insurance companies, individual pay incentives usually take the form of *production bonuses,* which reward an employee for achieving certain prescribed goals. The bonus is usually a percentage of the employee's hourly wage or annual salary. For example, some group insurance sales representatives receive bonuses whenever they sell a group insurance contract.

Production bonuses can also be awarded to groups. If a company's performance exceeds expectations, the directors can choose to award a bonus to all employees. This bonus is usually a percentage of annual salary. Another form of group pay incentive is the *profit-sharing plan,* in which each employee receives a stated share of the company's profit. Profit-sharing plans can be categorized as *current* or *deferred.* A *current profit-sharing plan* pays employees a share of the profits as the profits are earned. A *deferred profit-sharing plan* puts each employee's share of the profits in a trust fund where the money earns interest or dividends. An employee who retires, leaves the company, becomes permanently disabled, or meets some other requirement stated in the profit-sharing agreement, is paid the deferred profits, plus the interest or dividends earned on those profits.

Some companies also establish an *employee stock ownership plan (ESOP),* in which the company contributes money to a trust fund that is used to buy shares of the company's own stock for the employees. Each year, the company makes a contribution to the trust fund based on a percentage of each employee's annual salary.

Benefits and Services

Most companies also provide employees with a number of benefits and services that are not included in normal wages or salaries. In 1989, these benefits and services equaled about 38 percent of the amount paid in salaries and wages in the United States and Canada. Some of the most common of these benefits are listed below:

- *payment for time not worked,* including vacations, holidays, personal days, and sick leave
- *life insurance,* including accidental death and dismemberment insurance
- *health insurance,* including disability income insurance, medical expense insurance, and dental insurance
- *retirement income,* including private pension plans or profit-sharing plans, as described earlier
- *employee services,* including subsidized day-care and elder-care facilities; subsidies to help pay for employees' education; company-sponsored cafeterias; counseling, legal, and limited medical services; fitness programs; transportation subsidies, such as paid or free parking or subsidizing the cost of public transportation
- *government-required benefits,* including unemployment compensation, workers' compensation, and social security or other retirement programs

It is usually the responsibility of the human resources department to develop and administer these benefits and services. To fulfill this responsibility, human resources staff members must be knowledgeable about or have access to experts in a number of areas, including employment law, financial planning, and benefits counseling and administration.

KEY TERMS

human resource planning	demotion
trend analysis	job posting
ratio analysis	position description
skills inventory	help-wanted advertising
succession chart	private employment agency
promotion	temporary help agency
upgrading	executive search firm
lateral transfer	staff referral

application form

screening interview

validity

reliability

aptitude test

biodata

performance test

work sample test

situation management test

personality test

interest test

employment interview

orientation

training

development

learning objectives

job aid

on-the-job training

job rotation

plateau

lecture

conference method

case study

role playing

programmed instruction

computer-based training

essay appraisal technique

critical incident technique

alternation ranking method

paired comparison method

graphic rating scale

behaviorally anchored rating scale
  (BARS)

separation

resignation

layoff

retirement

discharge

exit interview

outplacement counseling

point factor comparison system

production bonus

profit-sharing plan

current profit-sharing plan

deferred profit-sharing plan

employee stock ownership plan (ESOP)

NOTE

1. Portions of the remaining sections of this chapter have been adapted with permission from Jane S. Lightcap, FLMI, ALHC, *Managing Claim Department Operations* (Atlanta: International Claim Association, 1991).

Chapter 16

The Information Systems Function

After reading this chapter, you should be able to

- Describe the components of an information system and an insurance company's sources of data for such a system
- Explain the data base concept and its importance to insurance company operations
- Discuss some recent developments in office systems technology
- Identify the different responsibilities of people who work in the information systems area
- Describe the purpose of a decision support system
- Describe the operations of typical insurance company information systems, including the information systems used by a company's different functional areas

Information is one of an insurance company's most important resources. Company managers need accurate and complete information to help assure the success of company operations. For example, managers in various areas have a need to know such information as the total monthly sales, the amount and distribution of company assets, and the company's projected and actual claim experience for the current quarter. In order to make this and other necessary information available on a timely basis to the people who need it, the company develops systems to manage information.

The systems used to process data and provide information are called *information systems*. These systems are now almost universally computerized systems. The technology that goes into a computerized information system can be viewed as a competitive strength or weakness for an insurance company. With an effective and efficient information system, a company can

- keep down costs for marketing and servicing its products
- have a more effective customer service operation
- more accurately track the performance of its operating areas and product lines

An insurance company with a poorly designed or poorly implemented information system is severely limited compared to companies with efficient information systems. Because of a fiercely competitive environment, a company with a technological edge may be in a position to secure and keep in force much more business than a company that lags behind in automation. For a description of what one company did to keep pace with technology, read INSIGHT 16-1. Also, a company with advanced computer capabilities is in a better position to develop new products than a company without such capabilities. Products such as universal life—for which the values change so often—would not be offered were it not for the advanced information systems now available to support the products. Nonetheless, a company must evaluate the cost of implementing new systems and weigh the expense against the benefits such technology would bring to the company. Even though the cost of new systems and new technologies is dropping, many smaller companies still find that the expense of new systems is too high to make investment in them worthwhile.

INSIGHT 16-1

Application Tracking System

After several months of investigation, programming, testing, and a pilot program, Western-Southern installed a fieldwide Application Tracking System (ATS) in October 1989. This system is designed to provide both field and home office users with information on the status of an application as it proceeds through underwriting and issue processing. ATS follows an application from the day it is submitted from the field office through home office processing, back to the field, and through delivery of the policy to the insured. Tracking is accomplished via a video monitor, light pens, and bar codes.

Before an application is mailed from a district office, a tracking system label, containing a unique bar-coded control number, is affixed to the application. A matching label is also attached to a control card containing the control number, plan amount, etc. By passing a light pen over the label, the application is registered on ATS as "application entry."

Upon receipt in the home office, the tracking record for each application is updated to reflect "received in underwriting." From that point in time, every action taken on the file, along with the date of that action, is added to ATS. For example, if the underwriter orders an attending physician's statement, the physician's name and address are included on the record. The date each ordered item is received is also added to the record. When the application is approved, declined, or withdrawn, such data is also entered on ATS. The complete or on going history of a file is visually summarized via the terminal.

The progress of the application through the issue department is tracked in the same manner. Via ATS, the field is advised of situations that may delay policy issue or mailing. The final entry from the home office is the date the policy is issued and the policy number.

The next record to ATS is entered by the field and reflects "policy received in district office." The final record indicates the date "policy delivered" or "policy returned as not-taken."

At any point in processing, the district manager can review the ATS record of every application pending in his or her office, every application from a particular account, or one particular application. Having this on-line capability greatly reduces inquiries to the underwriting and issue areas. Records are automatically purged 40 days after the final action date.

As with any systems-based processing, significant and reliable time service statistics are readily available. For the underwriting and issue departments, this has proven to be a valuable adjunct to other auditing checks. Prior to ATS, time service was calculated by manually reviewing less than 10 percent of the work.

For the field and Agency areas, reports are produced which summarize applications entered for the week, applications pending, policies issued but not received in the district office, and policies received but not yet placed. As a result of ATS statistics, a handwritten weekly report that required several hours to prepare has been completely automated.

Source: Adapted with permission from an Activity Report submitted to LOMA by M.L. Bradley of Western-Southern Life, April 1990.

The primary responsibility for electronic information systems rests with the information systems (IS) department, also known as the *information services department*. In the past, this department was often called the *data processing department*. However, because of the increased use of computer technology, the duties of this department have expanded, and the term *information systems department* is now more common.

In this chapter, we will first describe the components of an information system. Then we will discuss the data base concept and its importance for insurers. Later in the chapter, we will discuss the information systems department itself and the different types of information systems that are used throughout a life and health insurance company.

INFORMATION SYSTEMS

In order to manage information, companies develop systems. An ***information system*** processes data and makes the resulting information available to the people who need it. An information system consists of four components: input, processing, output, and control. **Input** is the data that is entered into the system. **Processing** is the act of performing specified operations on the input to produce meaningful results. **Output** is the data or information generated when the system processes the input. The **control** mechanism ensures that the system performs according to specifications and that the system operates under necessary levels of security.

For example, if a company wants to know its premium income for a given month, the amount of each premium payment received during that month can be entered as an *input* into the system. The system then *processes* this data by totaling the payments. The system *output* is the total amount of premiums received—the desired information. The *control* mechanism monitors the operation to ensure that all data is processed as specified and made available only to those people who are allowed access to it.

The data an insurance company uses comes from the company's various operating units as well as from sources outside the company. The most common sources of *internal data,* which is data derived from sources within the company, are

- *policy transactions*—applications, issued policies, policy loans, premiums received, dividends applied, claims
- *investment transactions*—investment income, mortgage records, and acquisitions and sales of securities
- *personnel records*—names and addresses of agents and home office employees, payroll and commission records, performance appraisal data, skills and experience records
- *accounting records*—cash receipts and payments, operating expenses, policy reserves, taxes

External data sources—that is, sources of data outside the company—include census reports, government economic forecasts, industry studies, and other published records.

Internal and External Information Needs

All areas of an insurance company, as well as organizations and individuals outside the company, need information. The two types of information needed internally by insurance companies are operational information and management information. **Operational information** comes from internal data included in the company's source documents. This data is used routinely by a life insurance company as it carries out its tasks. For an insurer, examples of operational information include lists of premium billings, account balances, and the amounts of agents' commissions. Managerial and nonmanagerial employees in the various functional areas of an insurance company both need operational information to perform their work.

Management information, on the other hand, is information that managers need to formulate objectives, to determine whether those objectives are being met, and to support the decision-making process. This type of information can come from external sources as well as analyses of operational information. For an insurer, examples of management information include percentage of claims processed accurately and in a timely manner, amount of insurance in force this year versus last year, and profitability of its competitors' products compared to the company's products.

External organizations that need information from an insurance company include regulatory agencies, consumer groups, and financial institutions. For example, regulatory agencies need a great deal of financial information from an insurance company to monitor its solvency. Individuals other than employees who may need information include policyowners, prospects, stockholders, and brokers.

DATA BASE AND DATA COMMUNICATIONS

As we noted earlier, the purpose of an information system is to assure that data and information are available, accessible, and understandable to system users. The ability to process, store, and retrieve data and information is an essential aspect of an information system. To perform these functions effectively, an information system usually includes a data base and a data communications network.

Data Bases

The data base is the cornerstone of a computer system. The corporate data bases are some of a company's most valuable resources and should be easily accessible to those who need them. A *data base* can be defined simply as a collection of data organized for easy access, updating, and retrieval. The data selected should be essential to the continuing operation of one or more particular functions of the firm. Storage of nonessential data hampers the efficiency of an information system.

A well-designed data base enables the information system to provide operational and management information on a timely basis. At one time, each department processed only the data required for its own files, which were physically and electronically separate from the files of other departments. By having a data base that includes data from all of a company's areas, a number of people and functional areas can use the same data simultaneously.

Establishing a data base, however, does not necessarily mean that one huge file is created. Instead, data can be organized either into separate files or into related files that are connected through a master file. The master file contains certain basic information and guides the user to other files that contain further information. For example, a policyowner data base would include a master file for each policyowner, containing the policyowner's name, policy number, address, birthdate, agent's name, etc. In addition, the policyowner master files contain references to other related files, such as the file that contains more information about the policyowner's agent. Organizing data files in this manner makes the data *nonredundant,* which means that the data appears a minimum number of times in the data base and yet is easily accessible to those who need to know more than the particular master file contains.

In a properly constructed data base, files that are used by more than one department are automatically updated for all departments when any one department changes the data. For example, if a policyowner's address is corrected in one file, the updated information is then available for all departments that use that information.

Decision support applications

Another benefit of data bases is that information generated by several departments can be easily used by the company's management in the decision-making process. For example, the company's chief financial officer can access the data base for (1) marketing information that compares projected sales to actual sales, (2) accounting information that describes cash expenditures and receipts, and (3) investment reports that identify pending acquisitions and the performance of the company's current holdings. With this information, the chief financial officer can compare the company's expected and actual cash flows and decide whether any of the firm's activities need to be modified because of changes in the company's income. When a firm's files are maintained separately, such diverse information is much more difficult to obtain.

In summary, the corporate data base is an integral part of the information system. In order to give people in different locations across the company access to this data base, however, a company must have a data communications network.

Data Communications Networks

Data communications, also known as *telecommunications*, is the transmission of data from one point to another through a transmission link. Data communication is needed whenever input/output units, such as terminals and printers, are located at some distance from the computer's processing units or data storage. This distance may be as close as on the premises or as far away as across town or even across the country. In most cases, telephone lines are used as the transmission link between the input/output units and the processing units. When telephone lines are used to transmit data, both the sending unit and the receiving unit must be attached to a device called a *modem*.

In some cases, satellite transmission can be used to send information, not by a direct link between electronic equipment, but over radio waves. Using a satellite network, an insurance company can transmit information to offices around the world. Figure 16-1 illustrates both kinds of network arrangements.

Figure 16-1
Examples of data communications networks.

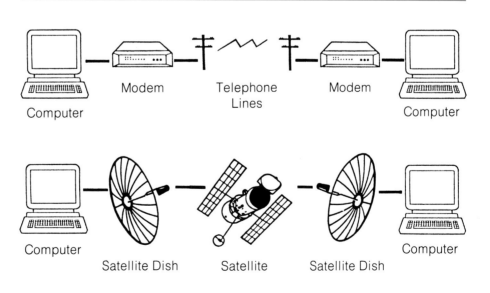

| Computer | Modem | Telephone Lines | Modem | Computer |

| Computer | Satellite Dish | Satellite | Satellite Dish | Computer |

In a data communications network, the sending and receiving units can be any type of computer or terminal. The terminals used can be either *dumb terminals,* which cannot process data without being connected to a computer, or *intelligent terminals,* which can process information without being connected to a mainframe computer.

Data communications applications

Data communications networks in most insurance companies connect home and field offices. The most common insurance company applications of data communications are queries to the corporate data base and requests for sales proposals. For example, a field office employee may, at the request of a policyowner, access the data base to find out the premium amount that the policyowner owes. The on-line query capability made possible by data communications has greatly improved insurance companies' customer service function.

On a broader scale, data communications networks link insurance companies to sources of useful information. For example, the National Electronic Information Clearinghouse (NEIC) serves as an on-line clearinghouse of health claim data for insurance companies. Examples of other data communications applications include

- gathering information on insurance applicants from the Medical Information Bureau
- finding out the market value of stock from financial information networks
- sending electronic mail messages between regional offices and the home office
- transferring funds electronically

AUTOMATED OFFICE SYSTEMS

Automated office systems use computers and other electronic equipment to improve productivity by increasing the speed, accuracy, and efficiency of information transfer among the various offices of a company. In the 1970s and 1980s, specific office automation technologies—such as word processing, electronic mail, facsimile (FAX) transmission, and teleconferencing—were first introduced into most insurance company offices. In the 1990s, a number of other office systems are finding their place in insurance companies. Two systems that we will discuss here are image processing and electronic publishing. Because of constantly improving technology and increased competition, new applications and systems will emerge as time goes on.

Image Processing

Beginning in the middle of the twentieth century, many futurists and forecasters predicted the coming of the *paperless society,* in which every business transaction and storage of all information would be handled electronically. Needless to say, the paperless society has not yet come about and probably never will. For example, more checks are now written for payment of goods and services than ever before. However, the increasing use of image processing technology is reducing the amount of paper files that insurance companies must maintain.

Image processing, or *imaging,* is the ability to capture, store, retrieve, display, process, and manage visual and printed images electronically. More and more insurance companies are converting paper files to electronic images via image processing. Using image processing and eliminating paper files has a number of benefits for life and health insurers.

- *Images can be retrieved immediately on a computer terminal,* and a number of employees can call up the same image at the same time. Virtually no search time is involved, and there is no need to make copies for paper files.
- *Image processing saves a great deal of space,* because many thousands of documents can be stored on various media, such as optical and digital disks. Paper files often require immense file rooms, or even off-site storage warehouses for which rent must be paid, climate must be controlled, lights must be lit, and so on. An image processing system becomes a part of space already devoted to information systems. Image processing systems can also be decentralized so that terminals for retrieving images are located at employees' workstations.
- *An image processing system improves security of a company's files.* Access to certain files or by certain users can be controlled electronically. Also, because documents need not be copied manually, fewer copies of confidential or sensitive documents exist.
- *Image processing enhances the kinds of information that insurance companies can maintain.* For example, in the health claim area, a

description of injuries suffered by a claimant can be supplemented with a photograph or an X-ray of the injuries.

Image processing can be used in any insurance company functional area that requires storing, retrieving, and accessing large numbers of documents. The underwriting, customer service, legal, investments, and claim processing areas are some examples. As with most new technologies, companies must evaluate the high cost of installing and maintaining an imaging system against the benefits its use would bring to the company.

Electronic Publishing

A second office automation technology that is being used more and more in insurance companies is electronic publishing. ***Electronic publishing*** uses computer programs and equipment to produce professional-quality visual and printed material without expensive typesetting and graphics equipment and in significantly less time than is required by traditional printing technologies. An electronic publishing system can (1) combine data, text, graphics, and other images (*input*), (2) format (or *process*) them into a design of the user's choice, and (3) *output* the result onto disk, paper, film, or other media of the user's choice.

Insurance companies are finding a number of uses for electronic publishing. Agents and brokers use electronic publishing to produce attractive proposals for potential customers. Once the policies themselves are ready to be issued, they can be produced electronically in the agent's or broker's office. If any changes need to be made at the time the policy is presented, the customer does not have to wait for a revised policy to come from the home office. Proposals made to potential policyowners or group policyholders can be customized by altering a basic text and printing the result on a high quality output device at the agent's or broker's office.

Electronic publishing is also helpful in issuing large numbers of checks. Using blank paper, an office with the proper printing capabilities can—in a single process—combine a company logo with check serial numbers and other data needed to prepare a large number of checks. Electronic publishing can also create policy forms. Any necessary changes can be made quickly and without having to return the forms to a printer outside the company. Electronic publishing can be used to produce only as many forms as the insurer needs at the present time, thus saving money on storage costs. If the form quickly becomes obsolete, the company has not wasted money and other resources by producing more forms than were required.

ORGANIZATION OF THE INFORMATION SYSTEMS DEPARTMENT

The IS department is responsible for developing, operating, maintaining, and modifying the computer systems used throughout the company. In addition, this department is responsible for helping other company employees who use computers—the **end users**—make the most effective use of their systems. IS personnel also share ideas on how other types of technology can help employees. Although each insurance company may organize the IS department differently, the following description reflects the organization and functions of many such departments. The organization chart in Figure 16-2 illustrates this structure.

The Information Systems Staff

In addition to the manager of the IS department, the IS staff is usually made up of personnel whose jobs fall within one of four broad categories: *operations*, *systems analysis*, *programming*, and *data administration*. The specific job titles usually found within each of these categories, and the responsibilities of each job, are described in the following sections.

Operations

Like most other machines or devices, a computer must have someone to operate it. A small computer requires only a single operator; a large

Figure 16-2
Organization chart of an information systems department.

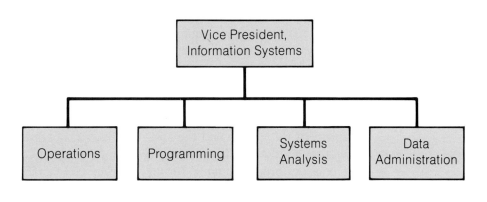

computer may require a number of operators. A computer operator typically performs all tasks needed to run a program on the computer. These tasks include communicating instructions to the computer; mounting, dismounting, and maintaining the data storage media (such as tapes or disks); and putting the correct paper or other output media in the printer.

Other members of the operations area include input clerks, input and control clerks, and output clerks. Input clerks operate terminals and other data input devices. Input and control clerks maintain controls over computer input and output, schedule jobs on the computer, and maintain records concerning tapes and disks. Output clerks deliver output, run machines that trim and separate paper forms, and check that all expected output is being produced.

Systems analysis

The primary responsibility of a systems analyst is to design the solution to a problem. More specifically, a *systems analyst* usually designs computer systems to meet the operational needs of the different functional areas or product lines in a company. For example, a systems analyst might be asked to develop a new accounting system for the accounting staff, or an administrative system for the human resources department or for a new product line.

When designing a computer system for any particular area, the systems analyst becomes familiar with that area's duties and responsibilities and designs a system that meets its needs. Typically, the analyst and the people in the functional area requesting help work together to develop a computerized solution to the problem. Once the solution is defined, it is communicated both orally and in writing to the *programmer,* who is responsible for translating the solution into a functioning program. The roles of systems analyst and programmer are becoming less distinct, and the systems analyst and programmer may now be the same person. An analyst who is also a programmer is called a *programmer/analyst.*

In some cases, a company's systems analysts are asked to evaluate and help choose systems and programs developed by outside vendors for implementation in the company's own information system. The benefits of purchasing commercially available systems and programs are that the time to implement the system and the cost of making it operational are often less than they would be if the systems were developed in-house. A drawback to systems and programs bought from a commercial vendor is that they may not be as well-suited to a company's particular needs as a system developed in-house.

Programming

As mentioned earlier, the people who write computer programs are called *programmers*. Depending on the size and scope of its needs, an insurance company may have one or many programmers. In some cases, each programmer specializes in writing certain types of programs, such as marketing programs, accounting programs, or programs to support the company's group life insurance business.

Programmers write programs in a variety of special computer languages. Because natural languages, such as English and French, contain ambiguous terms and words, special languages have been developed to enable programmers to communicate with computers. The choice of a computer language is determined primarily by the type of program being written and the type of problem being addressed. For any given type of problem, there are usually a number of computer languages from which to choose, and most insurance companies use more than one language. New programming languages are constantly being developed to meet changing needs, to try to simplify the analysis and programming process, and to improve system development and effectiveness. Among the most common computer languages that insurance companies use are

- COBOL (Common Business Oriented Language)
- COBOL II
- APL (A Programming Language)
- RPG (Report Program Generator)
- "C"
- BAL (Basic Assembler Language)
- DBASE

Data administration

The *data administration (DA)* function is responsible for implementing, maintaining, and controlling access to the corporate data bases. In a small company, only one person might perform these duties. In a large firm, the DA function might be made up of a group of people who specialize in certain areas.

RELATIONSHIPS WITH OTHER DEPARTMENTS

The functions of the typical IS department and the way in which this department interacts with other departments in the company have changed substantially over time. For many years, the IS department was staffed by computer specialists—operators, programmers, and systems analysts—who spoke a language that others in the firm could not easily understand. Thus, communication with other areas of the company was difficult and generally infrequent.

However, insurance companies began using computers not just as support systems, but as integral parts of the daily working environment. The need for strong lines of communication grew accordingly. More people in the company needed to tap the company's electronic capabilities. People who were computer novices needed the technical advice and experience of IS personnel to help them achieve their business goals.

To provide such support, some companies assign a computer expert to each functional area or product line. More commonly, though, a company establishes a specific unit within its IS department to help people in various areas of the company use computer technology. In this way, IS experts can provide training and assistance and act as internal consultants on computers and computer applications. End users are thus trained formally and informally in the use of the computer, advised about possible applications of computer technology, and aided in their selection of computer equipment. These activities also help business and systems professionals feel that they are working toward similar goals.

Training

Generally speaking, the IS department offers three types of training: (1) formal instruction, (2) walk-in assistance, and (3) "hot-line" assistance. Formal instruction generally takes two forms: classes and computer-based instruction. Classes may be held to teach fundamental applications when people who have similar needs are identified, such as when a group of new employees is hired at one time and needs to learn about the company's word processing system. On-line, computer-based training developed by the computer or software vendor or by the IS staff may also be made available to individuals or groups who need training. Walk-in assistance is provided to end users on a one-to-one, as-needed basis. "Hot-line" assistance is given over the telephone. IS staff members provide end users with answers to basic questions that can be answered quickly, such as, "How do I change my password?" or "How do I make a back-up copy of a disk?"

Technical Assistance

Desktop computers, also known as personal computers (PCs), can help people and entire companies perform their work more efficiently because of the number and variety of computer applications that are available to PC users. The purpose of technical assistance from the IS staff is to answer the end user's question, "How can I use my desktop computer or terminal more efficiently?" The technical assistance offered by an IS department covers a wide range of topics. These topics include advice about how to gain access to the various types of data available in internal and external data bases, and how to create charts and graphs on the computer.

Decision support systems

Another aspect of technical assistance provided by the IS staff is the creation of decision support systems. A *decision support system (DSS)* is an information system designed for use by a company's decision makers. DSS's are gaining in popularity because they provide a wide variety of timely and crucial information about conditions inside and outside an insurance company.

The scope of a DSS is limited only by the creativity of IS personnel and the requirements set by company executives. A decision support system typically includes information on company performance, operations, and personnel. In addition, a DSS may include access to external data bases, decision support programs, economic reports, news retrieval services, stock and bond market reports, and information about the company's competition. Compiling all this information into a single, accessible system enables executives and managers to make better informed decisions about the company's operations and strategic direction.

An important feature of a successful DSS is that decision makers find it easy to use. Many managers and executives do not have time to learn the ins and outs of a complex information systems package. As a result, the time required to learn the system must be kept to a minimum.

Expert systems

The IS staff provides assistance with respect to the purchase and installation of expert systems. An *expert system,* also known as a *knowledge-based system*, is a configuration of computer equipment and programs designed to make decisions or solve problems according to predetermined standards. Expert systems perform like humans do—that is, the decisions made by an expert system are based on the same information and logic that a well-trained employee would have. However, a computer can make many more decisions in a shorter period of time than an employee can.

An expert system is particularly suited to functions in the life and health insurance industry that require repetitive applications of corporate policies and procedures. The functions for which expert systems are used include

- risk selection
- claim administration
- financial planning and portfolio analysis
- commission calculation
- travel expense forms processing
- information system selection

For example, at its most basic level, an expert system can be designed to evaluate an application for insurance, assess the risks presented by the proposed insured, assign a rating to that proposed insured based on the risk, and determine the premium to be charged for that policy. Given the proper input regarding medical information, levels of risk, and premiums assigned to different classes of policyowners, an expert system can perform such risk selection at a rate many times faster than an employee. Using expert systems to evaluate fairly straightforward applications for insurance enables experienced underwriters to work on more complex applications that do not fall within the strict constraints imposed on expert systems. Cost savings result because many more simple applications can be processed in a shorter period of time than if people were used to perform the same function. Also, the results of expert systems underwriting are more consistent than if a number of different people were performing the work.

Assistance in Equipment Purchase Decisions

The IS department helps end users decide which types of equipment or programs to buy. Information systems specialists talk with end users about the type of work the end users expect to do, and then suggest products to meet the end users' needs. Thousands of computer products are available at various price and performance levels, and an end user cannot be expected to make an informed decision alone in an area that is as rapidly changing as the field of computer technology. Part of the job of IS technical specialists is to keep up with the latest developments in computer technology and applications. Thus, the IS department acts as a clearinghouse for information about computer technology and helps people throughout the company make informed decisions when computer-related purchases are necessary.

Some IS departments also have computer equipment available for temporary use by employees in other areas. Although some companies have one—or even two—terminals for each employee, not every company can justify the expense of having computer equipment for every employee.

Therefore, some IS departments have one or more on-line terminals available for those end users who do not have their own equipment.

TYPICAL INSURANCE COMPANY SYSTEMS

A core group of operational information systems is common to most insurance companies, although each insurance company tailors computer systems to its own operation. (Read INSIGHT 16-2 for an example of how one company reconfigured its computer systems to improve company operations.) In this section, we will describe some systems used in putting a typical life insurance policy in force. We will also discuss the information systems used by each of a company's functional areas.

INSIGHT 16-2

Managing the Future through Technology

The insurance companies that will be successful in the next decades are the ones that take control of their own technological futures. That doesn't mean that everyone in the company needs to become a technologist, but it means making a greater effort to learn how work happens in the company and how technology can make work happen faster, more reliably, more accurately, and more cost-effectively.

Today, if a company invests millions of dollars in a packaged solution and the latest hardware to run it—or develops a similar solution in-house—that solution will be at least somewhat out of date before it's completely installed. Programmers of years past produced programs that were so complex and idiosyncratic that no one else could understand or maintain them. That was logical when hardware was more expensive than programmers, but now

hardware is less expensive and people's time is more precious than ever.

The elegant hardware-efficient programs of the 1960s no longer make sense. Why tie a company's future to a single vendor or computing architecture when hardware has become the least important element in the solution? Elegant, solidly built applications quickly become labyrinths of millions of lines of code with thousands of loose and dead ends. Over time, documentations for all those changes will disappear. In the insurance industry, there are a lot of administrative systems where the only documentation is the system itself.

Is it any wonder maintenance of existing systems has become a full-time job, service is so difficult, and new products cannot get to the street quickly enough? Worst of all, when the time comes to introduce a new information-based product—and that time comes about weekly, it seems—it's a daunting task. It's so daunting some companies don't even bother. The result: another potential competitive edge lost.

What is the answer? At Phoenix Mutual Life Insurance Company, there was no clear solution, so analysts started with what was clear: the work the company does and the work needed to be done. Work processes were broken into the smallest possible components to see what was necessary and what wasn't. The team charged with this included business staff, not just information systems people, because it's the business staff that does the work.

A team of analysts charted the existing work flow in the individual insurance line. They found some amazing things. As a policy moved across the chart, data such as names and addresses were keyed into computers as many as five times. Calculations on premiums were performed more than 20 times. The staff was so dependent on paper files that often weeks were lost mailing pieces of paper from one office to another.

To redesign the process, the team looked at their charts and identified 40 items as "key business events." They isolated only the tasks that add value—ordering blood tests, evaluating risks, checking state regulations—the guts of what it takes to get from application to policy issuance. Everything else was deleted.

As the work flow was defined, it became obvious that a different approach was needed for computing work in this way. A solution built around the key business events was not the answer. Those events change as business changes, plus the company could not afford to replace those parts of the system that were working.

So in building the new business structure, The Phoenix decided to take some risks to get the desired productivity breakthroughs. A way to spend less money developing new systems while maintaining existing ones was needed.

The new work platform designed for The Phoenix allowed for the integration of the new processes with the existing computer system that held data. Since the idea was to gain flexibility to change and revise applications without rebuilding systems, the focus was on a layer of function between the operating system and application. The result was a new kind of control software. The software controller lets the staff create an environment in which work flow can be defined, executed, monitored, and administered across an enterprise. This controller brings together all events, including people and data, that are parts of the goal. It's a two-part strategy to make applications movable, task-specific, interchangeable, and reusable companywide. A separate software program, called an agent, can be written for one or more of those key events, then another layer of software tells the involved parties how to work together to produce a specified outcome. This kind of application platform is where technology is heading in every kind of industry.

What will this new approach achieve? A drastic reduction in system maintenance. When managers want to change work flow, they simply redefine the order of tasks. They can balance the work load to avoid bottlenecks and, with the software controller, a new work process can be prototyped in a day.

Instead of a paper trail crossing in the interoffice mail, the new system provides a single audit trail—a pipeline everyone has access to. Any of Phoenix Mutual's 100 field offices can check policy status from a terminal. Soon, when underwriters need a physician's review, their notes will be added to the computer file.

The productivity benefits are obvious. Simple policies, which represent 70 percent of the total, can be issued overnight—not in days or weeks. The competitive benefits are just as important. A level of customer service has been restored that hasn't been seen since the turn of the century, when policy-owners dealt with a single underwriter, not an assembly line of people.

Source: Adapted with permission from Robert W. Fiondella, "The Era of Open Application Platforms," *Insurance and Technology,* April 1991, pp. 36, 38.

Producing Ledger Proposals

For many types of life insurance sales, an agent contacts a prospect and discusses that prospect's insurance needs. After getting a general idea of the prospect's needs and resources, the agent requests one or more ledger proposals. A *ledger proposal* is a printed illustration of a policy's rates, cash values, and applicable dividends over a specified number of years.

In past years, when almost all life insurance products had fixed premiums and values, a preprinted rate manual was often used to show the prospect how the policy values would grow. Preprinted rate manuals are not useful with investment-based products because of the many variables involved. Ledger proposal systems that allow these variables to be input on a case-by-case basis are absolutely necessary for a sales presentation of these product lines. A ledger proposal system shows a prospect how the product can be expected to perform under a variety of economic conditions and interest rate scenarios, and with premium payments of various amounts. These proposals can be produced on an agent's laptop computer, on a personal computer in the agent's office, or on a mainframe system in the home office of the insurance company.

Processing Insurance Policy Applications

After obtaining a signed application from the prospect, the agent submits the application to the home office for underwriting. In some cases, the application is sent to the field office, which takes information from the application and transmits it electronically to the home office computers. When the application information is received in the home office, the information is entered into the new business system, and the prospect's name and date of birth are entered into an alphabetical index system. These alphabetical index systems are generally referred to as *alpha systems.*

An *alpha system* maintains data on (1) each person insured by the company, (2) recent applications that have been received and either issued or declined, and (3) other relevant records that the company may have collected in doing business. These records are connected using a number of identifiers, such as the person's name, age, and date of birth. If an applicant has other insurance with the company, or has been declined coverage recently by the company, the alpha system alerts the underwriter in the home office. In a large company, an alpha system may contain records on millions of people.

Once the application is approved, the file in the new business system is updated to reflect this transaction. The *new business system* produces policy pages containing rates and values as they will apply to the policy as issued and sends a master record to the *daily cycle system,* also called the *policy administration system.* The new business system may also notify the alpha system that the policy has been issued.

Daily Cycle System

The **daily cycle system** maintains records and processes the daily transactions involved in administering insurance contracts. Premium billing and collection, policy changes, loans, and maturity and death claims are examples of these transactions. They are entered by means of terminals, optical scanners, and other electronic data entry devices.

A daily cycle system usually has a large master record for each policy. The individual master records are stored in a policy master file. The master record for each policy typically contains the insured's name and address, age, date of birth, and other information related to the insured. It also contains data pertaining to the policy itself, such as the plan, amount of insurance, existence of any riders, dividends on deposit, cash value, and premiums payable. A third portion of the record usually contains data pertinent to actuarial functions, such as the cash value and dividend codes used for calculating the actual cash and dividend values, a reference to the mortality table used when the policy was developed, and the insured's risk classification.

The most common functions performed by the daily cycle system are premium billing and collection. This system also updates address information and calculates policy loan values and dividend values. The daily cycle system does any processing needed to keep the policy master record up-to-date. Even if, instead of one consolidated system, a company has several subsystems that process this information, it is easier to think of them as one large system.

Other Information Systems

In addition to processing transactions and keeping policy master records up-to-date, computer systems in insurance companies perform a wide variety of other functions. The remainder of this chapter gives a brief overview of the types of information systems that help various insurance company functional areas do their work efficiently and effectively. Each functional area usually maintains some form of an operational information system and a management information system.

Marketing

Computer technology helps the marketing area do marketing research and product design (in cooperation with other areas of the company). A *marketing information system* is an interactive system of people, equipment, and procedures designed to provide managers with a continuous flow of information that enables them to direct marketing activities. A marketing information system includes information on

- segmentation and target marketing
- consumer behavior
- the marketing environment
- the company's competition
- the company's distribution channels
- the effectiveness of various sales promotions
- product pricing and expenses

Maintaining this information electronically gives companies a greater ability to study and manipulate it so as to develop the most appropriate marketing programs and to introduce products with the greatest potential for success.

Actuarial

Perhaps no other insurance company functional area is as calculation-intensive as the actuarial area. Actuaries constantly analyze and monitor the premium and claim data used to determine prices for the company's products. Their analysis affects the success of the company's products and influences recommendations on how the company should alter its course in case of significant deviations from projected performance. Because such evaluations consider a myriad of variables—including performance of the company's investments, projected policy lapses, and number and extent of claims made against the company—an information system is essential. Computerized information systems allow actuaries to compile and analyze this data as quickly as possible; if operational changes are warranted based on actuarial analysis, the company can implement such changes without delay. Actuaries are also ultimately responsible for the policy liabilities information presented in the financial statements filed with federal, state, and provincial regulatory authorities, which in many cases can now be transmitted to those authorities electronically.

Underwriting

As mentioned earlier, information systems and expert systems are used in the underwriting area to screen applications. Also, the Medical Information Bureau (MIB) is an external information system that provides computerized input used by underwriters. Companies also maintain statistical information on their underwriting experience for reference by their underwriters. With this information, a company can assess the effects of various underwriting impairments on the mortality of their policyowners. Because this data base may be small, insurers may also merge their data bases with other insurers to achieve the benefits of a larger statistical sample.

Customer service

In one way or another, virtually all information systems are created to help the company provide better service to its internal and external customers. Systems that are essential to effective customer service include systems designed to (1) provide customers with timely information on the values of their life insurance or annuity policies; (2) verify information such as beneficiary changes, address changes, or projected death benefits; (3) issue claim or commission checks in a timely manner; and (4) issue accurate financial statements. On a more specific basis, though, as mentioned in Chapter 10, the customer service area is responsible for the extensive recordkeeping required of insurers. Information systems make these records more accessible and help keep them up-to-date.

Claim administration

Computerized claim systems help calculate complicated claims quickly and accurately. This feature is important to providing a high level of customer service, particularly in the health insurance business (see INSIGHT 16-3). Information systems that include a large data base are also used in the claim area to

- screen for limitations of benefits payable, such as when a policyowner still has a deductible to meet or has reached the maximum benefit payable for a covered expense

INSIGHT 16-3

Systems Improve Paul Revere's Service on Disability Claims

Advanced artificial intelligence systems at Paul Revere Insurance Group are helping to improve service and customer satisfaction in the disability income area. According to Charles E. Soule, executive vice president-insurance operations at Paul Revere, the company is the first to apply the artificial intelligence technology to claims handling for income replacement business.

The disability income claims department recently implemented systems that offer an "on-line interactive claims consultant," said Stephen Rutledge, director of claims systems and administration. Paul Revere's examiners are able to simultaneously handle individual cases on the terminal and incoming telephone inquiries, explained Mr. Rutledge, through the use of Procedures for Automated Claims Examining (PACE), an advanced automation system, and its attendant artificial intelligence system, Resource Information for Claims Handling (RICH).

The PACE system, he explained, uses a multiwindow terminal called "quad-screen," which provides up-to-the-minute information, eliminating the need for examiners to sift through paper files or obtain information through a data bank. "Examiners should not do a lot of data processing," commented Mr. Rutledge.

Consequently, the relationship between Paul Revere's examiners and claimants had improved through the increased level of personal contact. The company's "emphasis was on the claimant," he commented, adding "we were moving ahead with the customer in mind."

The RICH System assists the examination process by

- determining the proper level of examiner to handle the claim based on potential total liability, age of claim, reserve amount, etc.
- evaluating the claim, looking at such items as contestability, late notice, length of disability in relation to predicted disability
- making recommendations such as: refer to manager, send claim to a field examiner, send to legal, contact the claimant's physician, obtain an item

Although the recommendations follow defined claim examination practices, they are only recommendations; the examiner always has the final say and may choose other alternatives. The system can also recommend more qualified examiners to handle specific cases.

The PACE and RICH systems serve as training programs for novices, a support system for making decisions, and as a decision verifier for senior examiners. The system also points out fraud situations.

Source: Adapted with permission from Dorine Bethea, "Advanced Systems Improve Insurer's Service," *National Underwriter,* August 1, 1988, p. 19; and Lynn Ganim, "Expert Systems Move from Theory to Application," *Resource,* July/August 1989, p. 33.

- screen for claims incurred prior to policy effective dates
- prevent payments of benefits for ineligible services
- print large numbers of documents, such as signed checks, quickly

Perhaps the greatest efficiencies in a computerized claim payment system are realized in those systems designed to handle a large volume of claims, such as occur in group insurance plans.

An example of a large external information system and data base used by the claim area is the Medical Information Bureau, which was discussed earlier in relation to underwriting. The MIB maintains a claim-tracking system that allows participating insurers to note possible cases of overinsurance and fraud in disability claims and to evaluate the coverage amounts and claim histories of insureds.

Investments

Information systems help investment personnel keep track of the performance of the company's portfolios and project the status of these portfolios under a wide variety of possible economic conditions. For example, computers allow investment specialists to determine quickly and accurately what the company's investment assets are presently worth, as well as what they would be worth given a number of different stock market, real estate market, and interest rate scenarios. Without computers and information technology, the time required to perform such calculations would be prohibitive. Using computers, investment specialists can quickly make these calculations, which affect the design of new products and the investment strategy of the company.

Accounting

The first insurance company applications of automation and information systems typically involved the accounting function, because of this area's need for fast, accurate, and cost-effective processing of large amounts of data. The accounting information system works in cooperation with the information systems of many other company areas. It handles policy-related transactions, calculates and pays agent commissions, provides data needed to produce the Annual Statement and other financial reports, and provides various types of management information.

An accounting information system is one part of a larger financial information system, which gives information on both the flow of money through the company and the ways the money is being used to achieve the company's objectives. As such, this system helps company managers plan, allocate, and control the company's financial resources. The accounting information system also handles many of the day-to-day financial transactions of an insurance company, such as accounts payable and receivable, premium billing and collection, check writing, bank statement reconciliation, and payroll preparation.

Using properly designed information systems, accountants can code the company's accounts so that they are tied directly to the reporting requirements of federal, state, and provincial authorities, thus making compilation of these statements easier. Also, with the aid of computerized systems, accountants can transform these statements into a format that can be used by management and stockholders. Without information systems, such tasks would be much more time-consuming.

Legal

Although an insurance company's legal department may not be as concerned with internal and day-to-day data as other company functional areas, the legal staff still has a great need for information. The search for legal information has been made much easier because of data bases that are now commercially available to lawyers. Two examples of such electronic data bases are LEXIS and WESTLAW, which offer legal staff members a method of searching for information on specific cases, court decisions, and statutory provisions.[1] Conducting research through an electronic data base is much faster than manually paging through thousands of pages of reference books.

A company's legal staff benefits also from having direct access to information in the company's data base and other departments' information systems. For example, if a company lawyer needs to know the claim history of a particular policyowner, the lawyer can use the company's claim information system to access the data base, rather than having claim personnel spend the time finding and transmitting the information.

Human resources

Information systems are vital to the efficient operation of an insurer's human resource function because of the immense amount of information that HR departments must have at their disposal. Information systems help human resources personnel keep track of the company's employees, including their education, skills, and experience. Electronic storage and retrieval of such information makes succession planning easier than if such planning had to be researched and done manually. In addition, an information system handles payroll and benefits information. The automation of such a system is particularly important in an insurance company that employs thousands of workers.

KEY TERMS

information system	image processing
input	electronic publishing
processing	end user
output	systems analyst
control	programmer
operational information	data administration (DA)
management information	decision support system (DSS)
data base	expert system
nonredundant data	ledger proposal
data communications	alpha system
dumb terminal	daily cycle system
intelligent terminal	marketing information system
automated office systems	

NOTE

1. LEXIS® is a registered trademark of Mead Data Central, Inc. WESTLAW® is a registered trademark of West Publishing Company.

Chapter 17

International Operations of Life and Health Insurers

After reading this chapter, you should be able to

- Describe different approaches to international insurance operations
- Discuss motivations that an insurer would have to market its products internationally
- Describe staffing, marketing, and organizational issues that an insurer has to face when beginning to operate internationally
- List and explain some potential benefits and drawbacks of international insurance operations

As we've seen in this text, insurance companies can choose to operate in a wide variety of ways. For example, methods of marketing products and underwriting policies can differ among companies, and different methods of doing business may exist even within a single company. Companies also can choose *where* they do business. An issue that is becoming increasingly important for many insurance companies is choosing whether to conduct business on an international basis, and if so, how.

Operating internationally has traditionally been the province of manufacturing companies with products more tangible than insurance, such as automobiles and soft drinks. Only a handful of North American life and health insurers have a significant history of overseas operations. However, for a number of reasons, more and more North American life and health insurers are now expanding their operations to foreign countries or investigating the possibility of foreign operations. Similarly, insurers from Asia and Europe are finding opportunities to enter the North American marketplace.

International business involves three main entities: the company doing business, the host country, and the home country. The company doing the international business is usually called a multinational corporation. A *multinational corporation (MNC),* also known as a *transnational enterprise,* can be described as either

- an international corporation that has major operations in one or more foreign countries, or
- a corporation that participates in several types of international business, with local affiliates that are treated as separate enterprises and that may not be totally owned by the company.

For a multinational corporation, a **host country** is a foreign country in which the MNC does business. The MNC's **home country,** or *parent country,* is the country in which the company's chief executive officer and senior managers are located—that is, its headquarters.

Three attitudes can exist among companies with international operations: an ethnocentric attitude, a polycentric attitude, and a geocentric attitude.[1] An **ethnocentric attitude** exists when company managers believe that the home country's ideas and policies with respect to business operations are superior to those of the host country. Such an attitude can contribute to ease of operations and consistency among policies and products at home and abroad. However, ethnocentricity can also lead to resentment among the citizens of the host country and eventual failure of operations, because the particular needs and desires of the host country market are not taken into consideration.

A polycentric attitude is the opposite of an ethnocentric attitude. When a company's management has a **polycentric attitude** toward its international business, it operates under the assumption that people in the host country know what is best for their local markets. Such a method of operation requires extensive use of host country employees. A polycentric outlook may help an insurer's product offerings and operations fit local conditions more closely, but cooperation between the home country and host country staffs may be difficult because of language or cultural differences. In addition, control of international operations is harder for the home office when local managers are in command.

Another approach to operating an MNC takes a geocentric attitude. Managers who conduct business with a **geocentric attitude** have a worldwide operational view. They consider the objectives of both international and domestic operations, and they view the company's markets as both international and national in scope. Managers with a geocentric attitude accept similarities and differences between the home country's ideas and those of the host country, and they focus their efforts on using the most effective techniques and practices, regardless of where they originated.

Insurers have many incentives to operate on an international basis. In INSIGHT 17-1, you can read about a company that has been operating internationally for many years. In this chapter, we will discuss the reasons an insurance company may want to operate internationally, the issues involved in foreign operations, and the potential benefits and drawbacks of such operations.

INSIGHT 17-1

ALICO—Pioneer in the International Market

Today, many North American life and health insurance companies are interested in the international market. However, one U.S. company—American Life Insurance Company (ALICO) of Wilmington, Delaware—has been successfully operating internationally for almost 70 years, long before it became popular.

According to Richard R. Collins, ALICO's president, ''We are very at ease operating in foreign markets. It's part of our culture. In my view, we have a tremendous advantage over other North American companies and other foreign companies as well because there isn't another life insurance company around that operates in the number of countries that we do.''

Over the years, ALICO has developed three principles that guide its marketing efforts: (1) understanding the foreign market; (2) behaving in a market according to the practices of that market; and (3) bringing to that market the best North American (and other) practices, principles, and thinking.

ALICO's operating strategy or focus, notes Collins, includes developing multidistribution systems. That means the company looks at all methods of distribution—career agency, brokerage, direct response, mass merchandising, and working with other financial institutions.

ALICO also makes a point of hiring locals for the majority of its positions, from the top to the bottom. ''We do this for two reasons: service should be provided in the country where you do business and expenses should be incurred in the currency in which you do business,'' Collins explains. This approach, in turn, enables the company to operate successfully in both very sophisticated insurance markets (e.g., United Kingdom) and not so sophisticated markets (e.g., Bangladesh).

''Traditional types of insurance still continue to be the foundation of good financial planning for a family. Needless to say, the majority of our business is individualized business, although we do emphasize benefits and risk business also,'' Collins explains. While traditional whole life products form the nucleus of ALICO's selling efforts, it also markets health and hospitalization insurance, group insurance for large and small organizations and businesses, pensions, annuities, variable insurance, and unit-linked life insurance. Marketing these products on a global basis is done through a network of over 12,000 licensed agents and brokers, branches, subsidiaries, and affiliates in more than 60 countries.

Knowing how to adapt and adjust to the needs of a country is a key to successful global marketing for ALICO, notes Collins. For example, because of Bangladesh's poor economy and numerous natural disasters, there aren't many investment opportunities except real estate. Therefore, life insurance is a popular method of savings. For those reasons, Collins says, endowment policies are very popular in Bangladesh.

Collins believes future challenges for his company will come "not so much from the globalization of financial services as it will from our own record—our ability to be creative, aggressive, innovative, and down-right different on a continual basis."

Source: Adapted with permission of the publisher from Tim Kelley, "ALICO: Pioneer in the International Market," *Resource,* March 1990, pp. 15-17.

MOTIVATIONS TO OPERATE INTERNATIONALLY

For any business, the basic motivation for operating is to offer an acceptable return on the money invested by the company's owners or stockholders. Within this context, international operations offer a number of attractive opportunities for insurers. Generally, an insurer enters into the international arena to take advantage of marketing and financial opportunities (see Figure 17-1). Some other factors that motivate insurers to expand their business overseas are also discussed below.

Figure 17-1
Reasons insurers give for expansion to other countries.

	Expansion by international member companies	Expansion by U.S./Canadian member companies
New markets	86%	93%
Spread sources of income geographically	70%	46%
Improve return on equity	52%	57%
Establish other financial products	19%	7%
Take advantage of favorable regulations	15%	14%
Other	20%	36%

Source: LIMRA International, *International Company Global Expansion* (Hartford, CT: Life Insurance Marketing and Research Association, Inc., 1990), p. 7.

Marketing Opportunities

Because of the length of time insurers have operated in countries such as Canada, the United States, Great Britain, the Netherlands, and Germany, the market for insurance in such countries is said to be a *mature* market. Insurers operating in a mature market often look for additional marketing opportunities outside their home countries. An insurer's motivation to expand its operations internationally may also be based on competitive factors.

New markets

When an insurer's markets in its own country have matured, the insurer may look to other countries for business opportunities (see Figure 17-2). These opportunities may range from marketing some of their existing products in one or more foreign countries to acquiring the business of a foreign insurer. Insurers around the globe are taking advantage of such opportunities.

Because of local economic and political conditions at the time, countries or entire regions may emerge as good new markets for foreign insurers. Foreign insurers may find success in a country in which the government is

Figure 17-2
Reasons for choosing most recent expansion country.

	Expansion by international member companies	Expansion by U.S./Canadian member companies
Marketing opportunity	95%	90%
Reasonable match with own operations	45%	45%
Partnership or acquisition opportunity	40%	39%
Open door to another country	30%	35%
Legal reasons (barriers opened)	20%	29%
Language	20%	13%
Other	25%	29%

Source: LIMRA International, *International Company Global Expansion* (Hartford, CT: Life Insurance Marketing and Research Association, Inc., 1990), p. 7.

moving away from a centrally managed economy. Mexico, which is moving toward a more open economic system, is one example of such a country. Poland, Hungary, and other Eastern European nations began attracting foreign insurers in the early 1990s because of favorable economic and political changes there. The European Community (EC), which many European nations have joined to create a common market, also offers a large new customer base. The EC gives insurers a potential market of more than 320 million consumers who can be reached more easily than if a foreign insurer had to enter each country's market independently. INSIGHT 17-2 discusses the climate for insurers operating in and wanting to enter into the Asian insurance market.

INSIGHT 17-2

Pacific Rim Opportunities

James C.H. Anderson, ASA, MAAA, FCA, former managing principal, Tillinghast, recently addressed a group at LOMA's Strategic Management Conference in Singapore about challenges and opportunities for life insurance companies in the Pacific Rim countries.

Anderson said that opportunities in the Pacific Rim are most likely to be found in those countries with rapidly developing economies, such as South Korea, the Republic of China (Taiwan), Hong Kong, and Singapore. "It must be recognized that in all but the last of these four countries, there are significant political risks which must be assessed in the light of a business that hardly can be expected to break even in less than 20 years." And since these four markets stand out, they are also likely to become crowded unless entry is restrained by regulation.

Anderson said the only way insurers can survive in these already overcrowded and competitive markets is to build a "better mousetrap"—aimed at lowering costs and

improving margins. Such an innovation, however, is unlikely to be product-driven because imitation is relatively easy, he said. To illustrate this, he gave the example of U.S. insurers who were among the first in the introduction of universal life. Those companies enjoyed a first-entrant advantage for only three to four years.

A service-based advantage—one that emphasizes sharper focus on particular market segments—could be longer-lived, and possibly permanent. "But the most dramatic advantage of all would be the development of a much more efficient system of distribution, promising the possibility of a reduction in distribution costs of perhaps 50 percent and a reduction in overall costs of perhaps 33 percent," Anderson observed. He said this possibility has attracted the interest of certain banks in entering the life insurance industry, and their operating plans are modeled along these lines.

Anderson gave special mention to the life insurance market in Japan, stating that it is the most successful in the world and, among the developed countries, it is one of the youngest. "The Japanese life insurance industry is very large, very concentrated, and capitalized at levels that are beyond the imagination of life insurance companies based elsewhere."

Japanese companies present a major challenge for companies wanting to enter the Japanese life insurance market. On the other hand, Japanese companies, which for the most part have not yet expanded overseas, might decide to enter other markets where their capital resources could make them formidable competitors in a relatively short period of time. Potentially,

the major Japanese life insurance companies, and even some of the minor ones, could have the most profound influence upon the future development of the life insurance markets of the Pacific Rim.

In conclusion, Anderson told the audience that further rapid economic progress for most of the countries of the Pacific Rim, particularly those in Asia, is expected. This growing prosperity will probably spill over to some extent to neighboring countries, excepting those with population growth problems. "There are reasons to be selectively optimistic in economic terms, but there are also reasons to be cautious in political terms."

Source: Adapted with permission of the publisher from Sara Carlin, "Opportunities and Challenges in the Pacific Rim," *Resource,* December 1990, pp. 6-7, 10.

Demographic changes may combine with economic changes in a country to offer insurance marketing opportunities. Spain, for example, is becoming more of an urban society with an economy that features increased personal income and lower inflation.

General educational and demographic trends that are occurring in the United States and Canada are mirrored in many countries overseas. People worldwide are becoming more sophisticated consumers of financial products, and medical advances have resulted in an aging population. Both developments contribute to a positive outlook for globalization of the insurance business.

Gaining a competitive edge

Insurers are constantly looking for a competitive edge in a rapidly changing insurance environment characterized by aggressive competition, advanced technology, and more educated and sophisticated consumers. Insurers can use an expansion of their business into one or more foreign countries to gauge the market potential for new products and to learn more about other insurers that may currently or in the future represent their competition.

By expanding operations into other countries, insurers sometimes have the opportunity to market products that have not been made available in their home country. An insurer may be able to offer a life insurance product that, because of legal constraints, cannot be sold domestically. For example, an insurer may develop a product line that is supported by investments that are not permitted in its home country.

Foreign countries also provide the chance to test marketing strategies and techniques, perhaps on a smaller scale, before using them in the insurer's home country. One U.S. company, for instance, began advertising its products on television in Australia—the first time it used TV advertising for its products anywhere. If a marketing strategy or technique is successful in a foreign country, it can then be tried in the insurer's home country.

Alternate distribution methods can be tested in host countries. If the tested distribution method is later permitted in the home country, life and health insurers with such foreign experience can transfer elements of that experience to the domestic market. Some U.S. companies, for example, are experimenting with sales of life insurance through banks and retail outlets abroad.

By operating on an international basis, an insurer can keep up with competition that has already opened up in foreign markets. Greater activity in foreign markets helps an insurer avoid takeover of its domestic business by foreign insurers. Insurers can also learn about foreign marketing and find out how companies overseas operate before such foreign companies enter the insurer's home country market.

Financial Opportunities

As we mentioned earlier, a company's typical overriding motivation to expand into foreign markets is the opportunity to improve its financial performance, either directly or indirectly. A company operating overseas has the chance to increase its overall profits or additions to surplus, thus leading to an increase in financial resources that could help all of the company's operations, including its domestic business. Improved financial performance can come from an increase in sales, lower operating or compensation costs abroad, or the lenient tax policies of some foreign governments. A company may also realize lower costs of producing business overseas because its fixed costs of operating the entire business are spread over a larger customer base.

Another aspect of international operations that can help a company's financial position is the ability to diversify a number of types of risk. By investing in a variety of assets with different risk levels, a company lessens the chance that any one investment's poor performance can significantly affect the company's portfolio. Similarly, by operating in a number of different countries, an insurer can diversify its underwriting risk, its economic risk, and its political risk.

- *Underwriting risk* is diversified because an insurer is selling policies to more people and to a wider variety of people. An insurer underwriting policies in several countries can spread its risk over a larger customer base, thus taking greater advantage of the law of large numbers.
- Diversification of *economic risk* occurs because a company that operates internationally is not as affected by the economic conditions in a single country. If Country A's economy is faltering and the insurance business there is slumping, those conditions could be offset by Country B's economic upswings.
- Once a company begins to operate internationally, the need to diversify its *political risk* becomes more important. **Political risk** is the probability that political events and actions could negatively affect business investments in a given country.[2] For example, once an insurer begins to do business in a certain country, the company runs the risk that restrictions will be placed on its employees there, that its assets could be frozen in a tense political environment, or that terrorist acts could endanger the company's resources. By operating in a number of countries, an insurer's political risk is diversified and thus diminished.

Other Incentives to Operate Internationally

For some insurers, international operations provide testing grounds not just for new markets, products, or marketing strategies, but also for managers and employees who want to rise in the company ranks, especially if the company has long-term plans for the international market. Also, for more entrepreneurial managers and chief executive officers, the challenge and adventure of operating overseas provide enough of a reason to test foreign markets. However, as we will see in the next section of this chapter, it is important that company executives consider more than their own desires for intrigue when deciding whether to enter the international market.

FACTORS TO CONSIDER IN STARTING INTERNATIONAL OPERATIONS

As with any new business venture, many questions must be answered before an insurer's policies can be marketed in a foreign country. Because years may pass before international operations become profitable, an insurer must conduct extensive research in a wide variety of areas to be prepared for the many challenges that international operations pose. Typical factors that an insurer must consider include:

staffing	information systems
labor laws	compensation and benefits
site locations	financing
capitalization	currency exchange rates
projected volume of business	investment management
customer service	distribution channels
tax and securities laws	currency withdrawal restrictions
language	

More specifically, an insurer's research should focus on the aspects of the business environment shown in Figure 17-3.

Once questions such as those posed in Figure 17-3 are answered to the best of the company's ability and the company determines that it wants to pursue international operations, organizational issues must be addressed more specifically. The first such issue is the type of venture that would best suit the company. In the next section of this chapter, we will discuss the different types of ventures available, as well as some structural, staffing, and marketing issues that insurers face.

Methods of Undertaking Foreign Operations

The primary methods life and health insurers use to operate internationally are the establishment of branch offices or subsidiaries, joint ventures, and acquisition of foreign companies (see Figure 17-4). Although other methods are available, these three approaches are the most practical in the current marketplace and thus are the basic focus of discussion in this chapter.

Branch offices and subsidiaries

Of the methods of establishing international operations, setting up branch offices to operate overseas gives the home office the most control over its company's international activities. Policy and product decisions are made and implemented primarily by home office personnel. Another option that allows a considerable measure of control of international activities is to establish a subsidiary company overseas. In that case, the parent company provides direct oversight of the subsidiary's activities. One company opened a subsidiary in Florida to develop a market among Latin Americans, both in the United States and abroad. Its efforts are the focus of INSIGHT 17-3.

Figure 17-3
Questions to research in preparing for international operations.

Market potential. Does social security coverage exist, and, if so, what portion of the population is covered? How large is the local insurance market and how does it operate? How does the population view life insurance? Given the country's demographic profile and cultural orientation, where are the company's best opportunities for selling life insurance?

Administration. Are experienced local people available or will training be necessary? Will it be difficult to recruit personnel for a foreign company? Can home office personnel obtain work permits and transfer to the new operation? How expensive will this be? What can the company do about any language barrier?

Regulatory climate. What statutory deposits and/or minimum capital and surplus amounts are required? Are the valuation standards conservative or liberal? Are reporting requirements onerous? Must local auditors be used? What types of corporate structures (e.g., branch office, wholly owned subsidiary, minority interest in a local company) are permitted?

Taxes. How does the country raise money: through income, premium or payroll taxes; stamp duties; sales taxes; import duties; excise taxes; estate duties; mandatory contributions toward social security; or other government programs? How are foreign companies taxed relative to local companies? How will local taxes and profits affect the company's domestic taxes?

Exchange control. What limitations does the country impose on exporting funds? Can the company repatriate enough money through dividends, management service fees and reinsurance profits, net of any taxes, to cover home office expenses incurred in managing the foreign operation and to provide a reasonable return on investment? If not, does it make sense to do business in this location? What delays have other companies experienced in transferring money? Are delays an ongoing problem? Could the company sustain significant losses as a result of currency fluctuations in the time it takes to complete a currency exchange?

Investments. Is there a statutory limit on the amount the company can invest in certain types of assets? Must local liabilities be covered by assets held locally, as is the case in most countries? Are there sufficient local investments that offer adequate yields and security?

Source: Adapted and reprinted with permission from "Beyond Our Borders," *Best's Review* 88, no. 1 (May 1987), pp. 28-29, 121.

Figure 17-4
Structure used in most recent foreign expansion.

	Expansion by international member companies	Expansion by U.S./Canadian member companies
Subsidiary	30%	13%
Acquisition	25%	16%
Joint venture		
with an insurance company	10%	3%
with a noninsurance financial		
services company	10%	6%
with a nonfinancial services		
company	5%	6%
Branch office	15%	36%
Other *	15%	20%
	**	100%

* For international companies, "other" structures include an affiliate brokerage service, a managing general agency, and an agency agreement with an insurance company of the country being entered.

For U.S./Canadian companies, "other" structures include use of an existing property/casualty sales force, a general agency operation, and using two or more types of structures.

** One company used several structures.

Source: LIMRA International, *International Company Global Expansion* (Hartford, CT: Life Insurance Marketing and Research Association, Inc., 1990), p. 9.

INSIGHT 17-3

Best Meridian Targets Latin American Market

While some insurance companies are seeking business in other countries, Best Meridian Insurance Company has foreign insurance business coming to it. Founded in 1986, the company filed a charter to oper-ate in the state of Florida so that it could develop a market in the United States, while establishing strong ties to Latin America.

These ties are being established by Latin Americans who conduct business in the

United States. Strategically based in the Miami area, a U.S. hub for Latin American businesspeople, Best Meridian is able to attract a large part of this market.

"It seemed natural to form a company to provide insurance for the Latin American businessperson who is constantly coming back and forth to the U.S.," says Leonard Pelletiere, president of Best Meridian. "That's where most of our business comes from."

Best Meridian, a wholly owned subsidiary of BMI Financial Group Inc., a Florida-based life insurance holding company, began operations in August 1987. The company sells life insurance and annuity products, targeting the personal and business needs of upper-middle-income executives and professionals. The company markets its products through a sales force of about 250 small independent agents. Its business comes from both Central and South American countries, although the company is careful to distance itself from the more volatile countries.

To further increase its Latin American business, the company recently entered into a joint marketing venture with Denver-based Massachusetts General Life Insurance Company to market and issue that company's interest-sensitive products in selected Latin American countries. The companies will share in resulting business through reinsurance agreements. "We do front end work for them—underwriting and issuing policy

functions," explains Pelletiere.

The agreement allows Best Meridian to perform Massachusetts General's new business function, and provides the Latin American businessperson with the security of working with the larger, more established Mass General. In this way, the joint venture is a combination of Best Meridian's expertise and Mass General's products.

Pelletiere credits much of the success of the young company to a combination of staff experience and effective cost control. "We are able to produce these products and services because we are able to maintain very tight cost control," he says. This cost control is, in part, due to the company's automation. "We made a substantial investment in systems before we took our first application," says Pelletiere. "And that's paid off for us very handsomely."

Staff experience has also brought an edge. "Because we have seasoned people who had a lot of experience, they know how to avoid some of the operating pitfalls," says Pelletiere. "We're operating very efficiently. The turnaround time is as good as any major company selling insurance, and we're very proud of that."

In terms of the future, Best Meridian recently added a new sales manager in hopes of expanding sales operations in Florida, especially in the southern part of the state. The company also plans to expand its annuity capabilities with a new annuity product that is currently in the development stage.

Source: Adapted with permission of the publisher from Sara Carlin, "Best Meridian Targets Latin American Market," *Resource,* August 1990, pp. 27-28.

Setting up branch offices and subsidiaries can be risky if the home office or parent company is unfamiliar with ways of doing business in the host country. Also, the initial costs of beginning operations can be high. For these reasons, some insurers choose to enter into joint ventures with companies already operating in the foreign market.

Joint ventures

A *joint venture* is a partnership agreement in which two or more firms undertake a business project together, usually for a specific length of time. In the international insurance arena, a domestic insurer would join forces with an insurer from another country for the purpose of entering the insurance business in that other country. The primary motivation for the domestic insurer is obvious: to sell insurance in a new market. However, the host company's motivation for helping a new company gain entry into the host's own market may be less obvious. The host country insurer may want to

- benefit from the technological or marketing expertise of the home country insurer
- introduce into the host insurer's market new products that the home country insurer sells
- have an opportunity to reciprocate and enter into a joint venture in the other insurer's home country
- share in the profits of the joint venture
- strengthen its distribution system and increase total market share in the host country

Benefits that can result from joint ventures include possible *economies of scale*, which are the savings in overhead expenses that can take place when companies combine their operations; theoretically, fewer resources are required to perform the business of the two companies because overlap among the functional areas of the companies can be eliminated. Also, in a joint venture, the two parties share the risk involved in the alliance. The home country's insurer stands to lose less than if it entered the new market on its own. In addition, a home country insurer faces less stringent regulation upon entering the new market when it is paired with a company that is already doing business in that market. From a cultural viewpoint, joint ventures can be quite beneficial to a home country insurer because working with a host country partner reduces the chances of making social or linguistic mistakes with the host country's consumers.

A joint venture is not risk-free, however. The companies may not be compatible once they start trying to do business together. One or the other partner may not keep the promises made at the outset of the agreement. The two companies may discover that their objectives are different from those stated when their negotiations started. The companies may find that they are partners in one arena and competitors elsewhere. Another drawback of a joint venture is the lack of a single source of management control. A home country insurer operating in a joint venture overseas may be frustrated that it is not in complete control of its own business. Finally, the costs of organizing a joint venture can be great, so a company must carefully weigh potential benefits against potential drawbacks before entering into a joint venture.

Acquisitions

In order to establish a presence in a foreign country, some insurers choose to purchase companies already based in the host country. Foreign ownership of local companies has a number of benefits and drawbacks.

Among the benefits of acquiring an existing firm is that the insurer establishes an immediate presence in the foreign market. Although costs of acquisition exist, the risk of losing this investment may not be as great as with setting up a branch office, because the insurer is typically buying a company with established operations.

Some countries do not allow foreign ownership of insurance companies, so operation of a subsidiary in those markets is not an option. Also, in countries where the insurance market is not yet well developed, targets for acquisition may not be available.

Organizational Structures

A variety of organizational structures are available for the international division of an insurance company. The type of structure used is often dictated by the insurer's needs. Four typical organizational structures that can be used are geographical, functional, product-based, and matrix. Charts depicting each of these structures are shown in Figure 17-5.

- A *geographical* structure is organized according to each country or region in which the company does business. This structure is most appropriate when a company has a nondiversified product line featuring a single product or class of products. In this organizational structure, upper-level managers are assigned all functional operations within a geographical region. For example, the senior vice president of the "Western Region" would be responsible for all the activities—marketing, actuarial, underwriting, accounting, claims, IS, etc.—that take place in an insurance operation. A variation of the geographical structure could be used for a company with multiple product lines. Products would be handled by separate units under an upper-level manager responsible for a particular geographical area.
- A *functional* structure groups departments by function rather than

Figure 17-5
Basic organizational structures for international operations.

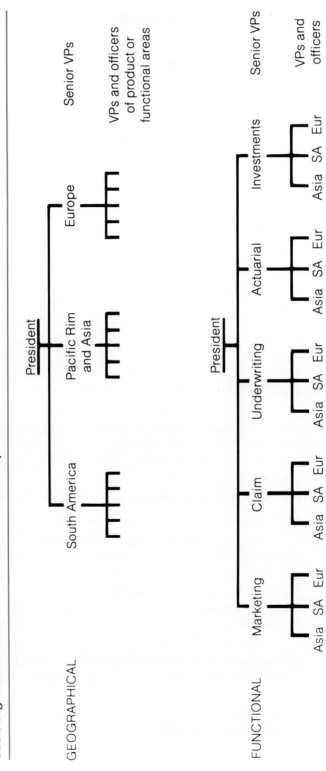

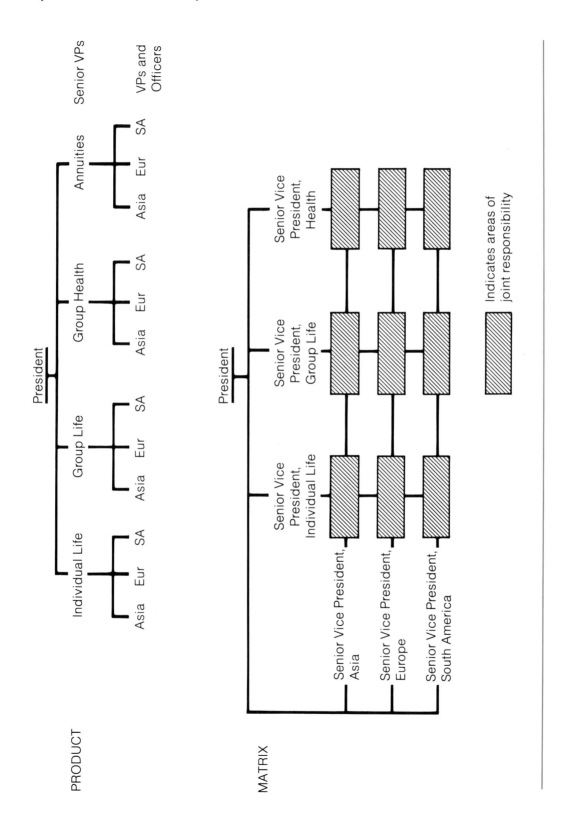

location. In this structure, each functional area handles the responsibilities for that function regardless of either the location of the activity or the product generating the activity. For example, the underwriting function would be handled in a single location for business written in any geographic location. Employees can thus be specialists in their tasks and benefit from co-workers' expertise. Coordination of activities is also easier in a functional structure.

- A *product-based* structure is suited to a company that has diverse product lines developed for specific geographical areas. In this structure, one division would be responsible, for example, for all whole life products marketed in a number of countries, and departments within the division would concentrate on the different countries.

- A structure with a *matrix* design can also be constructed for international operations. In a matrix organizational structure, two or more managers are responsible for the operations of a particular area. The matrix could include either product and geographical responsibilities or functional and geographical responsibilities. Although such an organizational design can make response to certain problems and situations easier, problems can arise when employees report to two different managers. Also, communications can become difficult in a matrix organizational structure.

Staffing Considerations

How an insurer staffs an international operation usually depends on whether the insurer follows an ethnocentric, geocentric, or polycentric approach to business. An insurer can staff its operation with people from the host country, people from the home country, or a combination of the two. A fourth option entails recruiting personnel from a third nation. Each of these approaches has its benefits and drawbacks.

Host country staffing

Host country staffing employs citizens of the host country as managers and staff members for the insurer's operations in that country. This approach has the overall effect of improving relations with the host country by increasing employment opportunities for its citizens and by allowing those people to become more familiar with the business of insurance. In host country staffing, the work force is already adapted to local manners and ways of doing business, which helps the company become acclimated more quickly.

A host country work force is less expensive to hire and maintain because no extra expenses are incurred for moving, educating staff members' children abroad, or providing acculturation training for employees. Also, the company reduces its risk of losing employees who do not adapt to the host country.

Some drawbacks are also present when using host country staffing. Communication between home office personnel and host country staff is more difficult, especially when language barriers must be overcome. Also, the culture of the host country's workplace may not mesh with the home country's corporate culture. For example, if the host country's culture does not allow promotion of women into decision-making positions, men employed on the host country's staff may resist taking direction from female executives in the home office.

Home country staffing

Home country staffing involves placing staff members from the home country into the host country's workplace. For example, a Canadian company setting up operations in India would send Canadians to manage and staff the operations in India. The primary benefit of home country staffing is that it ensures greater home office control over international operations. The corporate culture can be consistent among company operations in a number of nations, and language barriers are less likely to exist within the workplace. Home country staffing might be particularly important, for example, for a Japanese company operating internationally, because of the work ethic, culture, and approach to operations that Japanese firms instill in their employees. Home country staffing also provides an opportunity for employees to gather overseas experience. Such experience is particularly important in companies that are trying to choose and train potential company executives who may eventually be responsible for international operations.

A number of problems can arise with home country staffing. First, selecting and moving members of the home office staff is an expensive undertaking. Part of the expense involves replacing home office personnel in order to keep domestic operations fully staffed. Also, perhaps the most prevalent factor in the failure of overseas operations is the difficulty home country staff members often have in adapting to living in a foreign country. A staff member's family may not be willing to adapt to a foreign environment; even if the family does not accompany the employee overseas, the stress of living apart from one's family may sufficiently distract the employee from performing up to his or her capabilities.

Another problem with home country staffing arises when home country staffers are not provided with adequate cultural training. Managers who are not sufficiently trained in the customs and culture of the foreign country may not understand why their efforts constantly meet with disapproval, even though their actions would have worked well in the home country. For example, a manager from a country in which an autocratic managerial style is acceptable may, by using that style, alienate lower-level staff members if a participatory relationship between managers and staff is more common in their country.

A fourth problem with home country staffing is that domestic performance is not necessarily a good indicator of how staff members will perform in the international arena. This situation poses a difficulty for human resources personnel: the methods for evaluating the performance of home country staff members working in a foreign office often differ from the performance evaluation methods used at the home office.

Other methods of staffing international operations

Another approach to staffing a host country office uses ***third-country nationals:*** managers and personnel from neither the home country nor the host country. Although such people may be hard to find and expensive to relocate, they provide additional international experience from which the company can benefit. However, third-country nationals may be resented by both host country and home country staff members who feel that hiring people from a third country reflects unfavorably on their own skills and abilities.

Perhaps the most sensible approach to staffing an international operation that is expected to be a long-term venture is ***polycentric staffing,*** which finds the best available people for the positions, regardless of their nationality. Start-up of an operation staffed with people from different cultures and nationalities may proceed slowly, but if the people are the best for their positions, the quality of their work and their commitment to the task should eventually overcome any barriers to their interaction.

Marketing Considerations

Marketing concerns are basically the same in the international and the domestic markets. The "four Ps"—product, promotion, pricing, and place (physical distribution)—must be considered, with attention to the unique characteristics of foreign operations.

Among the many questions to be asked is, should the same *product* be sold abroad as at home? For example, an insurer must decide if the host country's market is better for term life insurance than for a life insurance product that contains an element of savings. Other questions include: How much financial risk are foreign customers willing to accept? Is it profitable to market health insurance products in countries in which such benefits are largely government-provided?

What will be the company's *promotional* strategy in foreign markets? If operations are conducted in a number of different countries, to what extent will its strategies be standardized? Operating abroad raises certain other promotional questions: What type of advertising should be used, given the country's literacy rate, level of television ownership, or responsiveness to sales agents' presentations? How does a company market life insurance benefits in Asia, for example, where many cultures feel that profiting from the death of a loved one is unacceptable?

Pricing can be difficult at first for overseas insurance operations if management is unfamiliar with local markets. Unlike many manufactured items, an insurance product's prices have long-term effects for the company, such as their impact on the accumulation of reserves. Pricing may also be regulated by the government, and the MNC may have to pay local tariffs on money that it earns abroad. Distribution costs may turn out to be higher abroad than they are at home, but the effect of many of these variables is not known until the product is actually on the market. A pricing mistake can be a hard one to correct.

The *physical distribution* of an insurance product overseas involves a number of elements. To what extent is a local sales force available? What types of compensation does that sales force expect, and to what degree can the home office control sales force activities? Another factor in the physical distribution of products overseas involves potential or ongoing changes in a host country's culture. For example, in Japan the agent force historically was made up primarily of female, part-time workers. However, because the nature of life insurance products and the demands of consumers have changed, more agents are working full-time and because "life insurance agent" is now a full-time occupation, more and more agents are men. How does a home country insurer prepare for and adjust to such host country changes?

EFFECTS OF INTERNATIONAL INSURANCE OPERATIONS

Entering the international insurance arena not only impacts the company trying to develop foreign business, but such business activity also affects both the home country and the host country involved. The next two sections discuss the effects of an international insurance operation on both countries.

Effects on the Host Country

An international insurance transaction can improve the host country's economy. This improvement can result from several types of activity. First, the host country may experience an inflow of capital because of taxes collected on the sales of insurance products and (if applicable) on the income of host country employees working for the insurer. Also, the country may charge certain tariffs and licensing fees to the MNC setting up operations there. If the host country has not yet experienced certain aspects of the technological revolution that has occurred over the last few decades, as may be the case in some Eastern European nations, that country could experience an inflow of technology that would benefit not only the local insurance industry, but other ventures as well.

Other possible benefits can result from the entrepreneurial attitude that foreign operations foster, particularly in countries that formerly relied on centrally planned economies. The creation of career opportunities for host country staff members and improved competition for the local insurance market are two examples that would also lead to better insurance products and services.

Some drawbacks of international operations can result from interference with local politics and the local economy. The regulation and supervision of foreign companies may be a problem for host country governments, and the operations of foreign companies may result in a decrease in the amount of business placed with local insurers.

Cultural problems can also arise. Home country personnel may be unaware of local customs and needs. This can lead to bad feelings between the local residents and the foreign company. Such social and cultural disruption can also make the host country reluctant to allow future international ventures and perhaps hamper the growth of a competitive environment in the host country. Resentment may also result if the MNC refuses to transfer technology or responsibility for local operations into the host country's hands.

Effects on the Home Country

Although the effects of international operations are typically more significant in the host country, some effects are also felt in the home country. One of these effects is that good overseas business brings some wealth into the home country and thus its economy. Further, the home country work force may be given increased opportunities to broaden its work experience through overseas employment.

Some drawbacks of developing business on an international basis are (1) the possible loss of a technological advantage at home once technology is exported overseas, (2) the possible loss of domestic jobs if too much focus is placed on international business, and (3) the acceptance of dual ethical standards by having one value system for the home country work force and another for international employees.

KEY TERMS

multinational corporation (MNC)   joint venture
host country   economies of scale
home country   host country staffing
ethnocentric attitude   home country staffing
polycentric attitude   third-country national
geocentric attitude   polycentric staffing
political risk

NOTES

1. Portions of this discussion are based on concepts expressed in Howard V. Perlmutter, "The Tortuous Evolution of the Multinational Corporation," *Columbia Journal of World Business* (January-February 1969), as cited in Richard M. Hodgetts and Donald F. Kuratko, *Management*, 3rd ed. (San Diego: Harcourt Brace Jovanovich, 1991).
2. Portions of this discussion are based on concepts expressed in M. Fitzpatrick, "The Definition and Assessment of Political Risk in International Business: A Review of the Literature," *Academy of Management Review* 8 (1983), as cited in Lloyd S. Baird, James E. Post, and John F. Mahon, *Management* (New York: Harper and Row, 1990).

BIBLIOGRAPHY

Albanese, Robert. *Management*. Cincinnati: South-Western Publishing Co., 1988.
Arthur Andersen & Co. and LOMA. *Insurance Industry Futures: Setting a Course for the 1990s*. Atlanta (LOMA) and Chicago (Arthur Andersen & Co.), 1988.

Baird, Lloyd S., James E. Post, and John F. Mahon. *Management: Functions and Responsibilities*. New York: Harper & Row, Publishers, 1990.

Braunschvig, David, and Jeffrey L. Schwartz. "The Time Is Right for U.S. Life Insurance Companies in Europe." *Journal of the American Society of CLU & ChFC* 44, no. 6 (November 1990): 74-79.

Collins, Richard R. "Go Global." *LIMRA's MarketFacts* 8, no. 7 (September/October 1989): 24-25, 48-50, 56.

Dunham, Randall B., and Jon L. Pierce. *Management*. Glenview, IL: Scott, Foresman and Company, 1989.

Gora, Jean Crooks. "Strategic Alliances in the Life Insurance Industry." Atlanta: LOMA (Life Office Management Association, Inc.), 1991.

Hodgetts, Richard M., and Donald F. Kuratko. *Management*. 3rd ed. San Diego: Harcourt Brace Jovanovich, Publishers, 1991.

Life Insurance Marketing and Research Association. *Exploring the International Marketplace*. Hartford, CT: LIMRA, 1989.

Life Insurance Marketing and Research Association. *International Company Global Expansion*. Hartford, CT: LIMRA, 1990.

Mondy, R. Wayne, Judith R. Gordon, Arthur Sharplin, and Shane R. Premeaux. *Management and Organizational Behavior*. Needham Heights, MA: Allyn and Bacon, 1990.

Rawlins, Patricia. "Exploring European Expansion." *Best's Review Life and Health Insurance Edition* 91, no. 9 (January 1991): 43-44, 95-96.

Resource. Atlanta: LOMA, 1989-1991 (numerous issues).

Schoderbeck, Peter P., Richard A. Cosier, and John C. Aplin. *Management*. 2nd ed. San Diego: Harcourt Brace Jovanovich, Publishers, 1991.

sigma, Swiss Reinsurance Company. "World insurance 1988: Asia and the EC continue to grow." Zurich: Swiss Reinsurance Company, 1990.

Skipper, Harold D. Jr. "Why U.S. Life Insurers Should Expand Internationally." *Journal of the American Society of CLU & ChFC* 45, no. 4 (July 1991): 46-49.

Chapter 18

Professionalism in the Insurance Industry

After reading this chapter, you should be able to

- Describe the difficulties inherent in defining ethical behavior
- Discuss the importance of corporate ethics and the establishment of ethical codes
- Describe types of professional education and training available to employees in the life and health insurance industry
- Identify associations that serve the life and health insurance industry

An insurance company is only as good as the people who work for it. The high quality of a company's products and services can be attributed to the professionalism of its employees. In this chapter, we will talk about professionalism in the life and health insurance industry—the ethical basis for professionalism and ways in which the life and health insurance industry encourages professionalism among its employees.

Professionalism can usually be identified by certain characteristics. These characteristics include

- a commitment to high ethical standards
- a commitment to education and training
- membership in associations and societies that encourage professional behavior

Each of these characteristics is discussed in this chapter.

ETHICAL BEHAVIOR

Ethical behavior is behavior in accordance with accepted principles of right and wrong. These principles of right and wrong behavior, however, vary from group to group according to the values of each group. People from different parts of the world or from different social or political backgrounds may disagree about the type of behavior that is considered ethically correct.

In the business world, companies and professional societies judge ethical behavior on a variety of levels. A person's actions may meet the requirements of ethical standards, but those actions may not conform to the spirit of the ethical standards. For example, a life insurance agent who encourages a client to replace one policy with another is acting within the law. Whether or not his actions are also ethically acceptable depends on the reason for the replacement. Agents who encourage replacement only so that they can collect extra commissions are engaging in *churning*, which is an unethical sales practice. Despite the difficulty involved in establishing broadly accepted standards of ethical behavior, most companies and professional societies consider such ethical standards to be necessary. Therefore, companies and societies typically establish ethical standards for their employees and members.

Importance of Corporate Ethics

Generally, we tend to think of ethical behavior as it pertains to each of us individually, but the whole area of corporate ethics and values receives a great deal of attention. Most business observers believe that successful, well-managed companies set guidelines for appropriate values and standards of ethical behavior. Figures 18-1 and 18-2 show the results of a recent survey of U.S. life insurance company chief executive officers concerning ethics policies, training, and procedures.

Well-managed companies keep in touch with customers' needs and strive to meet those needs. This kind of relationship with customers is built on trust and good faith, both of which depend on a strong ethical base. If a company does not act ethically, its relationships with its customers can be damaged, often beyond repair. Therefore, a company must demand high ethical standards of its employees. A company that does not set such standards or fails to censure employees who do not meet those standards is putting itself in jeopardy.

Well-managed companies are also committed to motivating employees to be as productive as possible. To keep employees motivated, a company must treat employees with respect and maintain the highest ethical standards in all employee relations. Furthermore, if a company asks its employees to do something unethical or tolerates unethical behavior, the employees' motivation and trust could be undermined. From this perspective, ethical behavior makes good business sense. Ethics as a business consideration is the topic of INSIGHT 18-1.

Figure 18-1
Communication of company policies on business ethics.

Practice	Percent of companies
I. Distribution of ethics policies to	
All employees	93.8%
Some employees/departments	6.3%
All new employees	12.5%
II. Training in ethics issues for	
All employees	12.5%
Some employees/departments	37.5%
All new employees	12.5%
III. Methods other than training for relating corporate ethics to company employees	
Videotapes	6.3%
Articles in company journals	31.3%
Informal discussion between employees and supervisors	56.3%
Public talks by executives	31.3%
Other	37.5%

Source: Journal of the American Society of CLU and ChFC, May 1991. From a report by the Ethics Resource Center, survey of CEOs of 25 of the largest U.S. life insurance companies, based on insurance issued in 1988; 16 respondents.

Figure 18-2
Existence of a written statement of company policies on business ethics and conduct.

	Percent of companies
Written Code of Ethics	68.8%
Similar policy statement on ethics	18.8%
Guidelines for proper business conduct	18.8%
Code, policy statement, or guidelines under development	12.5%
Company doesn't plan to have a written statement	0%

Source: Journal of the American Society of CLU and ChFC, May 1991. From a report by the Ethics Resource Center, survey of CEOs of 25 of the largest U.S. life insurance companies, based on insurance issued in 1988; 16 respondents.

INSIGHT 18-1

Increasing Ethical Considerations

Volatile economic conditions confront the financial services industry with increasingly difficult ethical dilemmas, according to Robert H. Moore, senior vice president of Alexander & Alexander Services, Inc. (A&A). "In the financial services industry, the integrity and professionalism of employees determine the company's image and its ultimate success in the marketplace," Dr. Moore said. "The facts are—ethics have become a strategic business consideration."

Dr. Moore remarked that the climate for ethical conduct has become much more volatile. A confluence of forces has put the entire financial services industry under intense scrutiny. National, as well as worldwide, financial services are under siege:

1. Wall Street continues to be shaken by various criminal allegations leading to trials and imprisonment.
2. The savings and loan debacle has proven to be a virtual sinkhole.
3. Major insurer insolvencies, especially among life companies, are front page news.

In the current inhospitable economic climate, some believe sensitivity to ethical considerations is a luxury they cannot afford. This is a tragically myopic view, according to Moore. Qualitative considerations, such as professionalism and integrity, are critical bottom-line factors in the services business.

Encouraging public dialogue is important because a company's primary "capital" is its employees. Their integrity and professionalism determine the company's image and its ultimate success in the marketplace. In addition, as business sectors consolidate through shakeouts and mergers, a critical distinction between the survivors will be the propriety of their business conduct. Thus, ethics will increasingly become a strategic business consideration.

Identifying ethical problem areas is clearly useful, but it is essential to recognize that proper conduct can be effectively encouraged through ongoing discussions with one's peers. For instance, developing and reinforcing an in-house process for addressing ethical issues is far more valuable than requiring employees to memorize a code of conduct.

Discussions need to take place among an insurance company's buyers, brokers, and underwriters, as well as at professional meetings and public forums, including trade publications and the general business press. While the growing complexity of insurance ethics will not make our tasks any easier, it is imperative that we continue to work for the highest professional standards.

Source: Adapted with permission from "Ethical Dilemmas—A Growing Concern," *Insurance Advocate,* September 28, 1991, pp. 6-10.

Ethical Codes

Because ethical standards vary from person to person, many corporations, including life and health insurance companies, have formulated ethical codes that reflect commonly accepted values and standards of conduct. In addition to stating broad ethical standards and guidelines, such codes often include examples of ethical dilemmas that may be encountered in the course of the company's work. Each ethical dilemma is then followed by an explanation of what the company believes would be a proper response to the dilemma. These codes can help employees evaluate the appropriateness of various responses to a given situation.

Professional societies and government regulators also identify standards of conduct for members of certain professional groups. For example, the NAIC in the United States has adopted a Model Claims Settlement Practices Act that cites activities that are considered unethical for claims personnel. Selections from this NAIC Model Act are shown in Figure 18-3.

Figure 18-3
Excerpts from the NAIC Model Claims Settlement Practices Act.

(Unfair claim settlement practices include) committing or performing with such frequency as to indicate a general business practice any of the following:

(a)   misrepresenting pertinent facts or insurance policy provisions relating to coverages at issue;

(b)   failing to acknowledge and act reasonably promptly upon communications with respect to claims arising under insurance policies;

. . . .

(d)   refusing to pay claims without conducting a reasonable investigation based upon all available information;

. . . .

(f)   not attempting in good faith to effectuate prompt, fair and equitable settlements of claims in which liability has become reasonably clear;

. . . .

(i)   attempting to settle claims on the basis of an application which was altered without notice to, or knowledge or consent of the insured. . . .

EDUCATION AND TRAINING

Another essential step toward developing a high level of professionalism is taken when a company encourages its employees toward further education and training. By adding to their knowledge throughout their careers, employees increase their value to their companies and customers while advancing their own business careers and enriching their personal lives. As we mentioned in Chapter 15, there are a variety of ways to obtain further education in insurance and general business subjects. Besides the numerous university and in-house programs available to insurance company employees, many organizations provide continuing education and training for the insurance industry. A few of the largest and best-known insurance education programs are described below.

Insurance Education Programs

The FLMI Insurance Education Program

Administered by the Education Division of LOMA, the FLMI program provides courses on insurance and functional operations of insurance companies as well as areas of general business interest. FLMI courses are designed for independent study, although many companies and FLMI Societies provide classroom instruction for some of the courses. After studying the program's courses and passing the required examinations, participants are awarded the professional designation of Fellow, Life Management Institute (FLMI). People who have earned the FLMI designation can continue their professional education by passing specified additional examinations, including an examination on strategic management, and earning the designation of Master Fellow (FLMI/M).

CLU and ChFC professional education programs

In the United States, the CLU and ChFC professional education programs provide professional education for people involved in financial planning and life insurance sales. Like the FLMI program, the CLU and ChFC programs are designed for independent study. A participant in either the CLU or ChFC program must pass 10 examinations in order to earn the professional designation of Chartered Life Underwriter (CLU) or Chartered Financial Consultant (ChFC). These two programs are administered by the American College, which was established in 1927 to provide professional education for people involved in life insurance sales.

In Canada, the Life Underwriters Association of Canada (LUAC) offers a separate series of courses that lead to the Chartered Life Underwriter (CLU) or CHFC (Chartered Financial Consultant) designation for Canadians. LUAC also offers several other educational opportunities, primarily for life insurance agents.

ASA and FSA professional education programs

Among its many other activities, the Society of Actuaries provides a rigorous program of studies leading to the professional designations of Associate, Society of Actuaries (ASA), or Fellow, Society of Actuaries (FSA). The program of study covers a variety of subjects, including general mathematics, probability and statistics, life contingencies, pricing of insurance products, principles of pension funding, economics, investments, and valuation of assets. After completing the first series of examinations and any additional requirements of the Society, the participant is designated an Associate (ASA). After passing a second series of examinations, in which the student can focus on a particular area of actuarial study, and completing any necessary additional requirements, the participant is designated a Fellow (FSA).

The HIAA Education Program

The HIAA Education Program is sponsored by the Health Insurance Association of America. Its main purpose is to help individuals increase their knowledge of group life and health insurance and individual health insurance. The program consists of five courses designed for independent study. Participants who complete the program by passing the required examinations are awarded the HIA (Health Insurance Associate) designation.

The ICA Claims Education Program

The ICA Claims Education Program, which is sponsored by the International Claim Association (ICA), is designed to provide individuals with an introduction to life and health insurance and a thorough understanding of claim administration. The program consists of six parts designed for independent study. The first two parts include material on general life and health insurance subjects. The last four parts include courses on medical and dental aspects of claims, life and health insurance law, claim administration, and claim operations management. Participants who complete the program by passing the required examinations are awarded the designation of Associate, Life and Health Claims (ALHC).

The AALU/FALU education program

The AALU/FALU education program provides a series of courses and examinations on general insurance, business, and home office underwriting topics. After passing the first series of required examinations, participants are awarded the designation of Associate, Academy of Life Underwriting (AALU). After passing the second series of required examinations, participants are awarded the designation of Fellow, Academy of Life Underwriting (FALU). The program operates under the auspices of the Home Office Life Underwriters Association (HOLUA) and the Institute of Home Office Underwriters (IHOU).

Career Counseling

The educational programs described above and all the other educational opportunities that are available to employees of insurance companies are most useful when they are pursued in the context of a career plan. A training specialist in a company's human resources department or an employee's manager can help an employee plan a program of continuing education and training to assist the employee in achieving his or her full potential in the company. Such counseling is usually intended to help employees foresee the roles that they may play in the company over a period of 10 to 15 years. The company and the individual employee together develop a career plan based on such counseling. When used in conjunction with a skills inventory, career counseling allows a company to assess current skill levels and guide its employees to develop the necessary skills to assume increasing degrees of responsibility. Career counseling also demonstrates to employees the company's commitment to their continuing professional development.

COMPANY ASSOCIATIONS AND PROFESSIONAL ASSOCIATIONS

The professionalism exhibited by an industry as a whole is affected by the associations related to that industry. Such associations can be divided into two categories: *company associations*, which are organizations whose members are companies with similar interests, and *professional associations*, which are organizations established for individuals who have similar occupational backgrounds and who meet certain membership requirements.

Company Associations

Company associations are established as forums for a particular industry. They provide the companies in that industry with opportunities to communicate with one another, share information, learn about new developments in the industry, improve performance, and present their views to consumers and regulators. A few of the major company associations of the life and health insurance industry are described below.

American Council of Life Insurance (ACLI)

The ACLI represents the life insurance business in legislative and regulatory areas at the federal, state, and local levels of government. It provides the public with information about the purpose and uses of life insurance, maintains research facilities to record the performance of the industry, and measures the attitudes of the public on issues concerning the life insurance industry.

Canadian Life and Health Insurance Association (CLHIA)

The CLHIA is an association of most of the life and health insurance companies in Canada. It conducts research on insurance issues and promotes the best interests of the insurance industry. The CLHIA is the primary source of information about the life and health insurance industry in Canada.

LOMA (Life Office Management Association)

LOMA is an international association founded in 1924. Through education, training, research, and information sharing, LOMA is dedicated to promoting management excellence in leading life and health insurance companies and other financial institutions. LOMA conducts research on various company operations, including expense management, human resources, and information management. LOMA also conducts a variety of seminars and workshops that help company employees improve their skills and increase the productivity of their organizations. As mentioned earlier, LOMA is also responsible for the FLMI Insurance Education Program.

LIMRA (Life Insurance Marketing and Research Association)

LIMRA works to improve the efficiency of life insurance distribution, conducts research on insurance issues, provides marketing management educational services, offers consulting services, and prepares a wide range of publications. LIMRA has approximately 600 member companies throughout 50 countries.

Health Insurance Association of America (HIAA)

HIAA is an association of more than 300 insurance companies in the United States and Canada. Its purpose is to help its member companies promote and develop voluntary health insurance to protect people from loss of income and other financial burdens resulting from sickness or injury.

National Association of Life Companies (NALC)

The NALC is an association of small- and medium-sized stock life and health insurance companies that keeps its member companies informed about issues affecting the insurance industry and presents the position of its member companies to insurance regulators.

Professional Associations

Professional associations are designed to give individuals with similar interests, training, and credentials the opportunity to meet, exchange information, increase their knowledge, and express their views about developments in their professions. They also promote high standards of ethical conduct in their chosen field. Many companies encourage employee membership in job-related professional associations. In fact, some companies pay membership dues so their employees can belong to professional associations. Both the company and the employee can benefit from employee membership in a professional association. Benefits of membership include

- increased employee competence resulting from the educational opportunities provided by professional associations
- greater opportunities for the employee to develop industry contacts who may be valuable both to the employee personally and to the employee's company
- increased identification of the employee with his or her field of work
- increased visibility for the company through employee participation
- information gained from studies conducted by the professional association
- opportunities for the employee to learn leadership and organizational skills by taking on responsibilities within the professional association
- reinforcement of high ethical standards through the example of other association members

As we did with company associations, we will describe a few of the many professional associations that are important to life and health insurance companies and the people who work in those companies.

The *Society of Actuaries* and the *Canadian Institute of Actuaries* are organizations of individuals who have passed the required examinations and have become either Fellows or Associates in the Society or the Institute. The Society and the Institute provide continuing education and development programs, promote and publish actuarial research, and enforce a professional code of ethical conduct for their members.

The *National Association of Life Underwriters (NALU)* and the *Life Underwriters Association of Canada (LUAC)* work through local groups of life insurance agents to sponsor sales meetings and seminars, promote high ethical standards, participate in community service projects, and support public policies in the interest of their members.

The *Association of Life Insurance Counsel (ALIC)* is an organization of life insurance attorneys, seeking to increase its members' knowledge of life insurance law and to promote high standards of ethical behavior.

The *American Society of CLU and ChFC* is composed of individuals who have earned either the CLU or ChFC designation. It has more than 200 chapters that promote continuing education, recognition of the CLU and ChFC designations, and high standards of ethical behavior.

Found in some three dozen insurance centers around the world, *FLMI Societies* are local organizations chartered by LOMA and composed of individuals who have earned the FLMI designation. FLMI Societies foster continuing professional development for their members, promote recognition of the FLMI designation, and provide assistance to students earning that designation. The FLMI Society Committee has adopted the following statement of ethical guidance:

> "A Fellow of the Life Management Institute (FLMI) continually strives to master all aspects of his or her business. The FLMI discharges all duties with objectivity and fairness, applying to the business environment standards of integrity and professionalism. The FLMI carries his or her professional designation proudly and seeks to enhance its reputation in every way."

THE IMPORTANCE OF PROFESSIONALISM

As the life and health insurance industry moves into greater competition with other providers of financial services, insurers will place an even greater emphasis on employee professionalism. Employees who have high ethical standards, pursue continuing education, seek to meet the needs of others, and exhibit other characteristics of professionalism enhance a company's reputation for professionalism, a reputation that can prove to be a major advantage in a competitive marketplace.

KEY TERM

ethical behavior

Glossary

absolute assignment. A procedure in which a policyowner transfers all rights of policy ownership to another person or organization.

accident risk. A classification of risk used by health insurance underwriters to indicate the type and degree of risk of accident represented by a particular occupation.

account. A record of the transactions involving a particular asset, liability, or owner's equity item.

accountability. The characteristic of being answerable for how one's authority as an employee is used and how one's responsibility for achieving goals is handled.

accounting. A system for collecting, analyzing, and summarizing financial data.

accrual-basis accounting system. An accounting system in which income items are recorded when they are earned and expense items are recorded when they are incurred, even if cash has not actually changed hands.

acquisition. One company's purchase of a controlling interest in another company, usually by buying a percentage of the acquired company's stock.

actuary. A person in a life and health insurance company whose job is to apply the theory of probability to calculate mortality rates, morbidity rates, lapse rates, premium rates, policy reserves, and other values.

adjustable-rate mortgage (ARM). A type of mortgage that allows the interest rate to rise or fall with prevailing interest rates in the national economy.

administrative law. The body of law that deals with the interpretation and application of regulations established by state, provincial, and federal agencies with regard to company operations; applies to areas such as policy forms, rates, and advertising materials.

advance and arrears accounting. A premium accounting method used in industrial insurance premium collection. Under this method, the home office charges an agent with the amount of all premiums due on the policies that the agent services. When the agent sends the collected premiums to the insurance company, the agent is credited with the amount of premiums collected.

agency law. The body of law that governs the rights, duties, and liabilities that arise among parties when an agent represents a principal in contractual dealings with third parties.

aggregate claims. The product of multiplying the claim frequency rate per insured by the average dollar amount per claim by the number of insured lives.

alien corporation. In the United States, a corporation that is incorporated under the laws of another country.

alpha system. An alphabetical index system that maintains data on (1) each person insured by the company, (2) recent applications that have been received and either issued or declined, and (3) other relevant records that the company may have collected in doing business.

alternation ranking method. A performance appraisal method in which the appraiser compares employees with one another and ranks them, from best to worst, based on specific characteristics of their work or behavior.

amortization. The process by which a loan is gradually paid off by making periodic payments of principal and interest throughout the life of the loan.

annual claim costs. The product of multiplying the expected number of claims for one year by the average amount payable for each claim.

annual report. A financial document containing a balance sheet, an income statement, and any other data that a company's management is required to or chooses to include.

Annual Statement. A financial document filed with insurance regulators. The Annual Statement contains detailed accounting and statistical data that authorities need to evaluate a company's solvency and compliance with insurance regulations.

antiselection. The tendency of people with a greater-than-average likelihood of loss to apply for or to continue insurance coverage to a greater extent than do other people.

application form. A document designed or adapted for each company that requests the specific information which the company needs to identify appropriate job applicants.

aptitude test. A test that is designed to predict a person's ability to learn a specific job if sufficient training is provided.

asset-liability matching. The process of determining the best way to invest and adjust a company's asset holdings so that cash is available as it is needed to meet the company's liabilities.

assets. Things of value owned by a company.

asset share. The amount of assets that any block of policies will accumulate at any given time.

asset share calculation. A calculation that simulates the way in which the assets supporting a block of policies should grow, depending on various assumptions about future interest rates, mortality expenses, lapse, etc.

Attending Physician's Statement (APS). A report from a physician consulted by the proposed insured either for routine physical examinations or for a specific health problem.

auditing. The process of examining and evaluating company records and procedures to ensure the reliability of accounting reports.

authority. The right of an employee to make decisions, take action, and direct others in order to complete assigned duties.

automated office system. A system that uses computers and other electronic equipment to improve productivity by increasing the speed, accuracy, and efficiency of information transfer among the various offices of a company.

automatic binding limit. Under an automatic reinsurance treaty, the dollar amount of risk a reinsurer obligates itself to accept without making its own underwriting assessment of the risk.

automatic reinsurance treaty. A legal document between a ceding company and a reinsurer in which the reinsurer agrees to provide reinsurance automatically for all amounts in excess of the ceding company's retention limit up to some specified amount.

back pay. All of the payments—including wages and fringe benefits—that a victim of discrimination would have received had he or she not been discriminated against.

balance sheet. A document that shows a company's financial condition as of a particular date.

bar examination. A licensing test that a person must pass before practicing law.

basic mortality table. A mortality table without a safety margin built into it.

behaviorally anchored rating scale (BARS). A performance appraisal method that is similar to the graphic rating scale, but which contains job-related characteristics that are more specific to the job and more fully described. *See also* **graphic rating scale.**

benefits budget. A type of budget indicating the amount of money a company expects to pay for claims, cash surrenders, policy dividends, and policy loans in the upcoming year.

bilateral contract. A type of contract in which if either party fails to do what it has promised, the other party can sue for damages.

biodata. Information about an employee's or job applicant's education, previous employment, and other past experiences that relate to a desired position.

blended rates. Rates that are based partly on manually rated data and partly on the company's experience-rated data.

board of directors. The primary governing body of a corporation.

bond. A debt investment that represents a promise on the part of its issuer to repay the borrowed money to the bondholder at a stated time in the future and, in the meantime, to pay interest to the bondholder at either a specified rate or a floating rate.

bond certificate. The evidence of the issuer's debt to the owner of the bond.

bond rating. The letter grade that indicates the credit quality of bond issues.

bond yield. The rate of return that a bond is expected to earn.

branch manager. An individual in charge of a field office in a branch office system.

broadcast media. Radio and television, which can be used to market insurance products.

broker (n.). An agent who sells insurance products for more than one insurance company.

broker (v.). To submit insurance applications to companies other than the agent's own company.

brokerage manager. A salaried insurance company employee or an independent agent whose responsibility is to encourage agent-brokers to sell the company's products.

brokerage shop. A field office operated by a general agent who is under contract to a number of insurance companies.

brokerage system. A distribution system that relies on commissioned agents who sell the products of more than one company.

budget. A detailed plan showing how resources should be allocated during a specific period.

calendar-year deductible. A type of deductible that applies to any eligible medical expenses incurred by the insured during any one calendar year.

callable. A characteristic of bonds in which the issuer has the right to pay a bond off before the maturity date at a price specified on the bond.

capital. The amount of money invested in a company by its owners or stockholders.

career agent. A full-time commissioned salesperson who holds an agent contract with one or more insurance companies.

case study. A training technique in which trainees must evaluate descriptions of conditions or problems that must be solved.

cash-basis accounting. An accounting system in which entries are not made until cash actually changes hands.

cash premium accounting. A premium accounting system used for industrial insurance under which the agent informs the home office of the amount collected on each policy. The home office then updates the policy records to reflect these collections and prepares new route collection records.

cash value. The amount of money that an insurance company guarantees to a whole or universal life insurance policyowner if the policyowner cancels the coverage and surrenders the policy to the insurance company.

catastrophic reinsurance plan. A type of nonproportional reinsurance plan in which the reinsurer pays losses in excess of the plan deductible when a specified minimum number of claims result from a single accidental occurrence. *See also* **nonproportional reinsurance.**

ceding company. In a reinsurance transaction, the insurer seeking to reinsure a risk.

charter. A legal contract that creates a corporation and contains the terms specified in the articles of incorporation.

claimant. The person who submits a claim. This person may be the policyowner, the beneficiary, or a person acting on behalf of the policyowner or beneficiary.

claim examiner. An insurance company employee whose job is to consider all the information pertinent to a claim for insurance benefits and make decisions about the company's payment of the claim.

claim fluctuation reserve. A special reserve whose purpose is to provide for possible unfavorable claim experience in future years.

claim form. An application for payment of benefits under an insurance policy.

claim frequency rate. The expected percentage of insured people who will file claims.

claim investigation. The process of obtaining necessary claim information in order to decide whether or not to pay a claim.

closed contract. A type of contract under which the terms of the insurance policy constitute the entire agreement between the policyowner and the insurer.

coinsurance (health insurance). A provision of a medical expense insurance policy that requires the insured to pay a percentage of all eligible medical expenses, in excess of the deductible, that result from a sickness or injury.

coinsurance (reinsurance). A type of proportional reinsurance plan in which the ceding company pays the reinsurer part of the premium paid by the insured, minus an allowance for the ceding company's expenses.

collateral assignment. A procedure in which a policyowner transfers some ownership rights in a contract from one party to another, generally for a temporary period.

collateralized mortgage obligation (CMO). A type of bond backed by investments in mortgages.

collection report. A report that shows total premiums collected, premiums paid in advance, and premiums overdue.

collective bargaining. A process in which a company negotiates with a labor union to reach an agreement about the pay, work hours, benefits, and working conditions for company employees who are represented by the union.

combination company. A company that markets both ordinary and industrial insurance products.

common stock. The most prevalent type of ownership shares in a corporation.

compound interest. Interest earned on the amount of money originally borrowed or invested and on the interest previously earned.

computer-based training. Programmed instruction that is presented in a computerized format.

computer screening. The use of automated systems to perform simple underwriting tasks.

conference method. A training method in which trainees interact in small groups with a trainer present to provide feedback and guidance.

conglomerate. A group of unrelated businesses under the control of a holding company.

conservation. The efforts a company makes to prevent a policy from lapsing.

consolidation. The formation of an entirely new company by merging two or more companies.

contestable period. The time limit during which an insurer may contest or challenge the validity of a policy because of misrepresentation in the application.

continuance table. A compilation of morbidity statistics that indicate the distribution of claims according to the duration of illness or amount of expense involved in the claims.

contract. A legally binding agreement between two or more parties.

contract law. The body of legislative enactments and previous court decisions that governs the interpretation of the rights and duties of the parties to a contract.

contribution to surplus. In a mutual insurance company, the income that results when the insurance company makes more money than is needed to pay the cost of providing insurance.

contributory. A feature in a group plan in which members must pay a portion of the insurance premium. Enrollment is voluntary.

controlling interest. Ownership of more than 50 percent of an acquired company's stock.

conversion privilege. A provision in a group insurance policy that gives an insured group member the right to convert his or her group coverage to coverage under an individual insurance policy.

convertible. A characteristic of bonds in which the bond can be converted into shares of the bond issuer's common stock at a stated conversion rate.

convertible preferred stock. Preferred stock shares that can be converted into shares of common stock.

coordination. The orderly arrangement of a company's activities so that the company's goals can be achieved.

coordination of benefits (COB) clause. A clause contained in most group medical expense policies and some individual policies that integrate benefits payable under more than one group medical expense insurance policy so that the insured's benefits from all sources do not exceed 100 percent of eligible medical expenses.

corporate bond. A secured or unsecured bond issued by a corporation.

corporate culture. The attitudes, values, perceptions, and experiences shared by a company's employees and management.

corporate income tax law. The body of laws and regulations that defines income for a corporation and how that income is taxed.

corporation. A legal entity separate from its owners, who are not personally liable for its debts.

credit (accounting). An entry made on the right side of an account.

credit (underwriting). In the numerical rating system, a credit is used to represent underwriting factors that have a favorable effect on an individual's mortality rating. Credits are assigned negative values.

credit life insurance. A type of life insurance designed to pay off a debt to a creditor if the debtor-insured dies.

creditor. A person or organization that has loaned money or extended credit to another business or person.

critical incident technique. A performance appraisal method in which a supervisor keeps a record of an employee's especially good or bad work behavior.

cross-selling. The act of selling property/casualty insurance products, life and health insurance products, and other financial services products to the same customer.

cumulative preferred stock. Stock on which the amount of any stated dividend that is not declared in one period is added to the dividend due in the following period.

current profit-sharing plan. A type of profit-sharing plan that pays employees a share of the profits as the profits are earned.

customer service. The broad range of activities that a company and its employees undertake in order to keep customers satisfied so they will continue doing business with the company and speak positively about the company to other potential customers.

daily cycle system. A system that maintains records and processes the daily transactions involved in administering insurance contracts.

data administration. The process of implementing, maintaining, and controlling access to a company's data bases.

data base. A collection of data organized for easy access, updating, and retrieval.

data communications. The transmission of data from one point to another through a transmission link.

debenture. An unsecured bond that is backed only by the full faith and credit of the issuer—that is, by the issuing corporation's promise to pay.

debit (accounting). An entry made on the left side of an account.

debit (underwriting). In the numerical rating system, a debit represents underwriting factors that have an unfavorable effect on an individual's mortality rating. Debits are assigned positive values.

debiting. In the home service distribution system, the practice of charging an agent with the amount of premiums to be collected in that agent's territory.

decision support system. An information system designed for use by a company's decision-makers. *See also* **expert system.**

deductible. The portion of medical expenses that the insured must pay before the insurance company makes any benefit payment under a health insurance policy.

default. A financial condition in which a bond issuer is unable to make either payments of interest or repayments of principal to bondholders.

deferred profit-sharing plan. A type of profit-sharing plan that puts each employee's share of the profits in a trust fund where the money earns interest or dividends.

delegation. The act of assigning to one employee the authority to make decisions and act for another employee.

demographics. The characteristics of a population such as the numbers of marriages, births, divorces, two-income families, single parent households, retirements, and the age of the population in general.

demotion. The act of assigning an employee to a job at a level of the organizational hierarchy lower than his or her present job.

demutualization. The process of changing a mutual insurance company to a stock insurance company.

detached agent. An agent who works out of a personal office located in or close to his or her home rather than in a field office.

development. An activity directed toward learning and improving the skills needed for future job performance.

direct-response distribution system. A distribution system that uses advertisements, telephone solicitations, and mailings to generate sales.

direct-response marketing. A distribution system that permits the supplier and the consumer to make transactions directly with each other.

disability income insurance. Health insurance that provides for benefits to be paid in regular installments to an insured person in order to replace some of the insured's income when he or she is disabled by sickness or accident.

discharge. The dismissal of an employee who does not otherwise wish to leave an organization.

disintermediation. The process of removing money from one financial intermediary in order to earn a higher yield somewhere else, generally with another financial intermediary.

disparate impact. Discrimination which occurs when an employer has an employment policy or practice—not justified by business necessity—that appears to be neutral but results in a disproportionately negative impact on a group of people who are protected by law from employment discrimination.

disparate treatment. Intentional discrimination involving the creation and application of different rules concerning hiring, promotion, and compensation of people based on factors such as sex, race, age, and national origin.

distribution system. A network of organizations and individuals that perform all the marketing activities required to convey a product from the insurer to its customers.

diversification. An investment strategy through which companies purchase many different types of investments to lessen the chance that the poor performance of any single investment will have a significant negative effect on the company's portfolio.

dividend (insurance). (1) A refund of excess premiums paid to the owner of an individual participating life insurance policy. (2) The portion of a group insurance premium that is returned to a group policyholder whose claims experience is better than had been expected when the premium was calculated.

dividend (investments). A periodic payment paid by a business to a stockholder.

divisible surplus. The amount of money available to a life and health insurance company to be distributed as dividends to participating policyowners.

domestic corporation. From the point of view of a particular state in the United States, a business that is incorporated under the laws of that state.

downstream holding company. A holding company that is formed by a parent company and which remains under the control of the parent company.

dumb terminal. A video display terminal that cannot process data without being connected to a computer.

economies of scale. The savings in overhead expenses that can take place when companies combine their operations; theoretically, fewer resources are required to perform the business of the two companies because overlap among the functional areas of the companies can be eliminated.

electronic publishing. An office automation technology that uses computer programs and equipment to produce professional-quality visual and printed material without expensive typesetting and graphics equipment and in significantly less time than is required by traditional printing technologies.

employee stock ownership plan (ESOP). A type of profit-sharing plan in which the company contributes money to a trust fund that is used to buy shares of the company's own stock for the employee.

employment interview. An interview, or a series of interviews, in which the purpose is to provide the manager and the candidate with the chance to decide if the candidate is qualified for the job and if the job is suited for the candidate.

employment standards law. The interpretation and application of legislative and regulatory requirements that are concerned with a variety of issues, such as minimum wage rates, overtime pay, and, in Canada, required amounts of paid vacation, and required amount of parental leave.

endorsement. A document that is attached to an insurance policy and that subsequently becomes a part of the contract.

endorsement method. A beneficiary change procedure in which the policyowner returns the policy to the insurance company, and the endorsement with the name of the new beneficiary is attached to the policy. Alternatively, the policyowner requests the change by letter, and the company sends the policyowner an endorsement that can be attached to the policy.

end user. A company employee who uses a computer to perform his or her work.

Equal Employment Opportunity Commission (EEOC). A U.S. government agency that investigates job discrimination complaints.

equity. Ownership of a business or property.

equity-based life insurance product. An investment-based life insurance product in which the investments underlying the policy are in equities, or ownership shares in a company.

escrow account. A special account in which a mortgagor holds the money collected from a mortgagee to pay for property taxes and property insurance on the mortgaged property.

essay appraisal. A performance appraisal method in which managers and supervisors write a report about each of their subordinates, indicating the subordinates' job performance, strengths, weaknesses, accomplishments, and potential for promotion.

estate planning. A type of total-needs programming that not only provides funds for the prospect's dependents upon his or her death, but also tries to conserve, as much as possible, the personal assets that the prospect wants to bequeath to heirs.

estate tax law. The sections of the tax code that specify the types of taxes levied on a person's assets at the time of death.

ethical behavior. Behavior that is in accordance with accepted principles of right and wrong.

ethnocentric attitude. A belief among company managers that the home country's ideas and policies with respect to business operations are superior to those of a host country.

exclusive agent. An agent who represents the products of only one company and who is not permitted to sell the products of another company.

exclusive territory. Under a general agency distribution system, a territory in which no individual other than the general agent is permitted to offer the insurer's products.

executive search firm. A company that locates and places executives, upper-level managers, and specialized technical staff, such as underwriters and actuaries.

exit interview. A meeting between a manager (or a human resource director) and an employee who has resigned or who has been laid off, retired, or discharged.

expense ratio. A mathematical comparison that shows the proportion of expenses to a certain level of production or to the level of a certain marketing-related activity.

experience rating. The process of using a group's own claim experience to develop premium rates.

experience rating refund. A premium refund sent to nonparticipating group insurance policyholders based on the claim experience of the group.

expert system. A configuration of computer equipment and programs designed to make decisions or solve problems according to predetermined standards.

external audit. An audit conducted by a regulatory body and/or a private accounting firm.

external customer. Any person or business who is not on the insurance company's employee payroll and who is in a position either to (1) buy or use the insurance company's products or (2) advise others to buy or use its products.

extra-percentage tables. The most commonly used plan for computing premiums for substandard risks. Extra premiums are calculated for the average extra percentage of mortality anticipated for each class.

facultative-obligatory (fac-ob) reinsurance treaty. A variation of a facultative reinsurance treaty which combines the features of automatic and facultative treaties. *See also* **facultative reinsurance treaty** and **automatic reinsurance treaty.**

facultative reinsurance treaty. A type of reinsurance treaty in which the reinsurer makes an independent underwriting decision on each risk sent to it by the ceding company.

field force. The collective term for agents who work out of field offices.

field underwriting. The process of an agent gathering pertinent information about a proposed insured and recording that information on the application for insurance.

financial analysis. The process of evaluating financial records to determine a company's profitability and stability.

first-year commission. A commission that is based on a policy's first annual premium amount.

flat extra premium. A method of rating a substandard life insurance risk when the extra risk is considered to be constant or temporary.

floating rate preferred stock. A class of preferred stock that does not have a fixed dividend rate.

foreign corporation. From the point of view of a particular state in the United States, a corporation that is incorporated under the laws of another state.

fraternal benefit society. An organization that is formed to provide social and insurance benefits to its members.

fraudulent claim. A type of claim that occurs when a claimant intentionally uses false information in an attempt to collect policy benefits.

free-fall advertisements. Preprinted ads that are stuffed in, but not bound to, newspapers or magazines.

friendly takeover. An acquisition in which (1) an acquiring company makes an offer to purchase a company, (2) the company to be purchased agrees to the acquisition, and (3) both companies settle on a buying price.

fulfillment kit. A package sent to a telemarketing respondent which contains an application and, usually, more information about the product.

general agent. An individual in charge of a field office in a general agency system.

general and administrative expense budget. The document that shows the amount of money a company expects to pay for certain operating expenses in the company.

general obligation bonds. A bond that is backed by the credit and taxing power of the government unit that issued it.

geocentric attitude. For a multinational corporation, a managerial approach that incorporates a worldwide operational view.

going-concern concept. A method of measuring a company's financial condition which assumes that the company will remain in business in the future.

good distribution of risk. A concept which holds that the good health of a large number of individuals offsets the claim experience of the unhealthy group members.

graphic rating scale. A performance appraisal method in which the appraiser is provided with a list of basic characteristics that relate to job performance and then must determine the degree to which the employee exhibits the characteristic being rated.

gross premium. The amount that policyowners actually pay for their insurance.

group representative. An insurance company employee who finds group insurance prospects, designs proposals, installs the group product, and renegotiates the policy at renewal.

guaranteed-issue. A method of offering direct-response products in which an applicant for insurance cannot be turned down for reasons related to health status.

health maintenance organization (HMO). An organization that provides comprehensive health care services for people in a specified geographic area; people enrolled in an HMO pay fixed, periodic dues in return for the right to health care services.

hearsay evidence. Evidence based on what someone has been told but has not actually witnessed.

help-wanted advertising. An external recruitment method in which advertisements are placed in newspapers, magazines, and professional and trade journals.

historical comparison. A method of comparing expenses in which the current performance of an agency is measured against its performance or the performance of other agencies in previous years.

holding company. A company that owns and has a controlling interest in a subsidiary.

home country. The country in which a multinational corporation's chief executive officer and senior managers—that is, its headquarters—are located.

home country staffing. A staffing method that involves placing staff members from a company's home country into its host country's workplace.

home service distribution system. A personal-selling distribution system that uses full-time agents to sell products and provide customer service to a block of policyowners in an assigned geographical territory.

host country. A foreign country in which a multinational corporation does business.

host country staffing. A staffing method that employs citizens of the host country as managers and staff members for the insurer's operations in that country.

hostile takeover. The situation that exists when the management of a company refuses an acquisition offer, but the acquiring company continues with its takeover attempt despite the wishes of the target company's management.

human resource planning. The process of determining the number of qualified people who are now available or should be available in the future to fill positions needed in a company.

human rights law. The interpretation and application of legislative and regulatory requirements that are concerned with protecting the personal rights of the individual worker.

illness risk. A classification used by health insurance underwriters to indicate the type and degree of risk of illness represented by a particular occupation.

image processing. The ability to capture, store, retrieve, display, process, and manage visual and printed images electronically.

impairment rider. A rider that excludes or limits coverage for a specific health impairment.

income statement. A document that reports on a company's profitability for a given period by summarizing the company's income and expense accounts during that time.

industrial life insurance. A type of insurance traditionally characterized by (1) death benefits of $2,000 or less; (2) a weekly, biweekly, or monthly premium payment schedule; (3) minimum underwriting requirements; and (4) the collection of premiums at the policyowner's home by an agent.

inflation. A condition of rising prices.

information system. A system that processes data and makes the resulting information available to the people who need it.

input. Data entered into an information system.

inside director. A board member who holds a position in the company in addition to a position on the board.

inspection report. A report prepared by a consumer reporting agency that contains information about a proposed insured's occupation, personal habits, hobbies, driving record, health, and finances.

installation. A term used to include all the activities from the time a prospect decides to purchase a group insurance policy to the time the master group policy and its individual certificates are issued and delivered.

institutional advertising. Advertising that promotes a company's image rather than a specific insurance product.

insurable interest. A condition in which the person applying for an insurance policy and the person who is to receive the policy benefit will suffer an emotional or financial loss if the event insured against occurs.

Without the presence of insurable interest, an insurance contract is not formed for a lawful purpose and, thus, is void from the start.

insurer-administered billing plan. A billing plan for group plans in which the insurance company performs the administrative work—which includes computing the amount of the premium due—and mailing a statement to the group policyholder, usually on a monthly basis.

intelligent terminal. A computer terminal that can process information without being connected to a computer.

intercompany comparison. A method of comparing a company's or an agency's expenses with industry averages.

interest. Money that is paid for the use of money.

interest test. A test that identifies a person's general interests.

internal audit. An audit conducted by a company's own accountants.

internal customers. Employees who receive service from other employees of the company.

interpleader. A legal remedy that allows an insurance company to pay policy proceeds to a court for the court to determine their distribution.

intracompany comparison. A method of comparing the expenses of one agency with other agencies in the same company.

investment-based life insurance product. A life insurance product in which the cash value and benefit level can fluctuate according to the insurer's investment earnings and in which policyowners accept the risk of sharing in the insurer's investment gains and losses. *See* **equity-based life insurance product.**

irrevocable beneficiary. A beneficiary whose rights to the proceeds of a life insurance policy cannot be canceled by the policyowner unless the beneficiary consents.

jet screening. The process of evaluating simple applications for insurance as quickly as possible according to strictly defined underwriting criteria.

job aid. A checklist, procedure guide, manual, or other item that employees can use for reference at work.

job posting. An internal recruitment method in which the human resources department announces a new job opening by placing a position description on the company's bulletin boards.

job rotation. The act of moving an employee from one position to another at regular intervals in order to enable the employee to develop expertise in a variety of jobs.

joint venture. A partnership agreement in which two or more firms undertake a business project together, usually for a specific length of time.

lapse. Termination of a policy because of nonpayment of renewal premiums.

lapse rate. The number of policies that lapse during a given policy year divided by the number of policies in force at the beginning of that policy year.

lateral transfer. The act of moving an employee from a position at one level in an organization to another position at the same level of hierarchy.

law of large numbers. A statistical concept which states that the greater the number of opportunities for an event to occur, the more likely it is that the event will occur as indicated by the mathematics of probability.

layoff. A separation action taken by an employer when not enough work is available for employees. In a layoff situation, the employer expects to call the employees back when work becomes available.

learning objectives. Specific statements of the desired outcomes or results of training and development activities.

lecture. A presentation of information to employees who attend class sessions.

ledger. The collection of all of a company's accounts.

ledger proposal. A printed illustration of a policy's rates, cash values, and applicable dividends over a specified number of years.

lessee. An individual or organization that is leasing a building from an owner.

letters patent. In Canada, a procedure used by insurance companies wishing to incorporate through the federal government or in the provinces of Quebec, New Brunswick, Prince Edward Island, and Manitoba.

level premium. A premium that remains the same for each year of the premium payment period.

level-premium whole life insurance policy. A type of life insurance policy that provides a specific amount of insurance protection for as long as the insured lives in exchange for a level premium.

leveraged buyout (LBO). An acquisition in which one company purchases another company in a transaction that is financed primarily through borrowing.

liabilities. A company's debts and future obligations.

line authority. Direct authority over subordinates.

line unit. The areas of an organization that produce the company's products or services.

liquidity. The ease with which an investment can be converted into cash quickly and at a reasonable price.

litigation. The act or process of resolving a dispute by means of a lawsuit.

loading. The additional charge added to a net premium to pay operating expenses.

location-selling distribution system. A system that distributes insurance products by locating insurance offices and agents in places where consumers generally shop for other items or take care of other business matters, such as department stores, grocery stores, and banks.

lock-box banking. A premium collection system in which the insurer's bank opens premium payment envelopes and immediately deposits the payments to the company's account.

mail kit. Sales literature used in a direct-response mail campaign.

management information. Information that managers need to formulate company objectives, to determine if these objectives are being met, and to support the decision-making process.

manual rates. Standard rates that are developed independently of the mortality experience of a particular group and which are based on the experience of an average group.

market. A group of people who, either as individuals or as members of organizations, are the actual or potential buyers of a product.

marketing. The process of identifying customers, determining the types of products those customers want, and distributing those products to the customers in a convenient, timely, and economical manner.

marketing information system. An interactive system of people, equipment, and procedures designed to provide managers with a continuous flow of information that enables them to direct marketing activities.

marketing mix. The product, pricing, distribution, and promotional strategies that a company adopts in order to satisfy its overall objectives.

marketing plan. A document that specifies a company's marketing objectives, the strategies needed to achieve those objectives, and the particular goals for each critical product or line of products.

marketing territory. The geographical area in which a company distributes its products.

market segment. In a large, basically similar market, a smaller market that has certain characteristics in common.

market segmentation. The process of dividing large, basically similar markets into smaller markets that share certain characteristics.

master contract. A legal document between an insurance company and a group insurance policyholder. A master contract insures a number of people under a single contract.

matrix structure. A type of organizational structure that operates by forming ad hoc committees or teams of qualified employees from various disciplines to work on projects.

maturity date. The date on which a bond's principal amount will be repaid to the bondholder.

medical expense insurance. Health insurance whose purpose is to pay for part or all of an insured's health care expenses.

Medical Information Bureau. An organization that serves as a clearinghouse for medical information for the life insurance industry.

memorandum of association. In Canada, a document of incorporation used by insurance companies wishing to incorporate in the provinces of British Columbia, Alberta, Saskatchewan, Ontario, Newfoundland, or Nova Scotia.

merger. The legal joining of two or more corporate entities.

minimum deposit business. A block of insurance policies in which the policyowners instruct the insurance company to pay premiums out of their policies' cash value and to bill the policyowners for premiums only if the cash value is insufficient to pay the premium.

misrepresentation. The act of deliberately making false or misleading statements to induce a prospect to purchase insurance.

modified coinsurance (modco) plan. A type of proportional reinsurance plan in which the reinsurer receives its share of the gross premium minus an allowance for the ceding company's expenses.

morbidity rate. The likelihood that a person of a given age will suffer an illness or a disability.

mortality curve. A line graph that represents the mortality rate as it changes from age to age.

mortality rate. The frequency with which death occurs among a defined group of people.

mortality table. A table that presents the probabilities of living and dying for a large group of people.

mortgage. A legal instrument under which a lender can claim the real property pledged for a loan if the borrower does not make loan payments when due.

mortgage correspondent. Mortgage bankers and brokers who act as correspondents between borrowers, such as building contractors, and lenders, such as insurance companies.

multinational corporation (MNC). (1) An international corporation that has major operations in one or more foreign countries. (2) A corporation that participates in several types of international business, with local affiliates that are treated as separate enterprises and which may not be totally owned by the company.

multiple-line agency system (MLA). A type of a personal-selling distribution system that uses full-time agents to distribute life, health, and property/casualty products for groups of financially interrelated or commonly managed insurance companies.

municipal bond. In the United States, government bonds other than those classified as federal bonds.

mutual insurance company. An insurance company that is owned by policyowners rather than stockholders.

mutualization. The process of changing a stock company to a mutual company.

net amount at risk. A policy's death benefit minus that policy's reserve at the end of the policy year.

net lease. A lease arrangement in which the lessee is required to pay the taxes and insurance on the property.

net premium. The amount of money needed to provide life insurance benefits for a policy.

net single premium. The benefits that are expected to be paid on a block of policies.

nonadmitted assets. Assets that, according to government regulations, are not acceptable for inclusion on a life insurance company's balance sheet.

noncontributory. A group plan characteristic in which the premium is paid entirely by the employer; enrollment of group members is automatic.

nonexclusive territory. Under the general agency system, a territory in which more than one general agent may represent the same insurer.

nonledger account. An account used in cash-basis accounting to record assets and liabilities that are not affected by cash transactions.

nonparticipating policies. A life insurance policy under which the policyowner does not receive policy dividends.

nonproportional reinsurance. A category of reinsurance plans in which the proportions of the risk to be carried by each company are not specified in the reinsurance treaty.

nonredundant. A description of data that appears a minimum number of times in a data base.

nonresident corporation. In Canada, a company incorporated under the laws of another country.

numerical rating system. A method of classifying risks in which each medical and nonmedical factor is assigned a numerical value based on its expected impact on mortality.

on-the-job training (OJT). Training provided while participants remain in the workplace and which involves performing the actual work to be done on the job.

open contract. A type of contract under which a society's charter, constitution, and bylaws become a part of the insurance contract, and any amendments to them automatically become amendments to the insurance contract.

operating budget. A part of an agency's operating plan that forecasts the levels of new and renewal business that the agency is expected to produce.

operational information. Data from a company's source documents that the various functional areas of the company need to perform their work.

ordinary agency system. A type of personal-selling distribution system that uses career and part-time agents to sell and service all types of individual and group insurance and annuity products.

organization chart. A diagram that visually depicts various jobs performed in a company and the lines of authority and responsibility among company units.

orientation. The process of introducing new employees to an organization's procedures, policies, and other employees.

orphan. A policyowner whose agent has retired, left the company, or died, leaving the policyowner without a local contact with the company.

outplacement counseling. A program offered by a company providing career counseling, vocational testing and skills evaluation, and information about job searches to laid off employees.

output. The data or information generated when an information system processes input.

outside counsel. Lawyers who are members of a private firm that has been hired to represent or provide advice to an insurer.

outside director. A board member who does not hold another position in the company.

overlapping territory. Under the general agency system, a territory in which some portion of the territory is open to an agent other than the general agent, while the rest of the territory is the exclusive domain of the general agent.

owner's equity. The difference between a company's assets and its liabilities, representing the owner's financial interest in the company.

paired combination method. A performance appraisal method in which each listed employee is compared to all other listed employees one at a time to determine which employee is the better of the two with respect to the particular job characteristic under consideration.

paralegal. A person specially trained in techniques of legal research and the formalities associated with various legal transactions.

partial disability. A condition that prevents an insured from working full-time or completing one or a number of important job duties.

participating policy. A type of insurance policy under which policy dividends may be paid to the policyowner.

participating preferred stock. Stock that grants stockholders the right to receive dividends above the stated rate if the company has good earnings and declares an extra dividend.

partnership. A business that is co-owned by two or more people.

pass-through certificate. A type of mortgage-backed security that represents fractional ownership in a pool of mortgages.

pension benefits law. The interpretation and application of legislative and regulatory requirements that are concerned with the terms and operation of private pension plans used by employers for their employees.

per cause deductible. A type of deductible that applies to all eligible expenses resulting from a single sickness or injury.

performance test. A type of test designed to measure the work that a person can do and relate it directly to the job for which the person is applying.

perpetuation of past discrimination. The intentional or unintentional continuation of a discriminatory practice.

persistency. The measure of how long a policy or a block of policies remains in force.

persistency rate. The number of policies in force at the end of a given year divided by the number of policies in force at the beginning of that year.

personal income tax law. The sections of the tax code that specify the types of income that are taxable to individuals, as well as the expenditures that can be deducted from taxable income.

personality test. A test that identifies a person's motivational, emotional, interpersonal, and attitudinal characteristics.

personal producing general agency (PPGA) system. A distribution system that uses personal producing general agents who hold agency contracts with several insurance companies and who spend most of their time selling insurance rather than managing an agency.

personal-selling distribution system. A distribution system in which commissioned or salaried sales personnel sell products by making oral presentations to prospective purchasers.

plateau. The career level at which an employee has no opportunity for upward movement within the organization.

point factor comparison system. A job evaluation method in which points are assigned to each job based on the specific requirements and characteristics of the job.

policy accounting. The branch of accounting that is responsible for premium billing and collection, commissions, policy loans, and policy dividends.

policy dividend. (1) A refund of excess premium paid to the owner of an individual participating life insurance policy. Such a dividend is paid out of an insurer's divisible surplus. (2) The portion of a group insurance premium that is returned to a group policyholder whose claims experience is better than had been expected when the premium was calculated.

policy reserve. A liability account that identifies the money that an insurance company expects to pay out in future claims.

political risk. The probability that political events and actions could negatively affect business investments in a given country.

polycentric attitude. A belief among a company's management that people in host countries know what is best for their local markets.

polycentric staffing. A staffing method which finds the best available people for the positions, regardless of their nationality.

portfolio. A group of investments managed or owned by an individual or organization.

position description. A document that lists a job's title, the duties and responsibilities of the position, and the qualifications that a candidate must have to be considered for the position.

preauthorized payment. A premium collection system in which the policyowner signs a two-part authorization form allowing the insurance company to withdraw future premiums from the policyowner's savings or checking account as they become due, and authorizing the bank to honor such withdrawals.

pre-existing condition. An injury that occurred or a medical condition that first appeared before an insurance policy was issued.

pre-existing condition provision. A provision in a health insurance policy which states that until coverage is in force for a specified period—usually one or two years—no benefit is payable if the condition that produces a claim (1) manifested itself before the issue date and (2) was not disclosed on the application.

preferred beneficiary. In Canada, a class of beneficiaries applicable to policies issued before June 30, 1962, and consisting of the spouse, children, parents, and grandchildren of the insured.

preferred provider organization (PPO). A group of hospitals and physicians that contract with employers, insurers, and other organizations to provide comprehensive health care services to individual members at discounted fees.

preferred stock. Stock that usually carries a fixed, specified dividend payment.

premium receipt book. A book given to a policyowner when the agent makes the policy sale. When the agent collects a premium, he or she signs one of the receipt forms in the receipt book, and the policyowner keeps the receipt.

present value. The amount of money that must be invested at the beginning of a period in order to increase to a predetermined amount at a specified later date.

principal. The amount of money that is originally borrowed or invested.

print media advertising. All advertising placed in newspapers and magazines.

prior claim. The right of certain investors to collect the assets of a failed business before other investors can have their claims to those assets met.

private employment agency. A company that helps employers find qualified people to fill jobs and help individuals find the types of jobs they want for a fee that varies from 10 to 30 percent of a job candidate's first-year salary.

private placement. Investments which are offered by the issuer directly to specific financial institutions and that do not need to be registered with government agencies.

probability. The likelihood of some event's occurring.

processing. The act of performing specified operations on an information system's input to produce meaningful results.

production bonus. An individual pay incentive—usually a percentage of the employee's hourly wage or annual salary—which is a reward to an employee for achieving certain prescribed goals.

profit. In a stock company, extra income that is not needed to pay for the cost of providing insurance.

profit center. A segment of an organization that controls its own revenues and expenses and makes its own decisions regarding its operations.

profit-sharing plan. A form of a group pay incentive in which each employee receives a stated share of the company's profit.

programmed instruction. The use of educational devices—such as textbooks, workbooks, and computers—to provide trainees with (1) information about a subject, (2) opportunities to apply their knowledge, and (3) feedback about their progress in gaining knowledge.

programmer. An information systems employee who is responsible for writing computer programs that fill the company's needs.

projection method. A method for keeping annuity tables up-to-date which assumes that the mortality rate at any given age decreases, or improves, by a constant percentage each calendar year.

promotion. The act of awarding an employee a job at a level of the organizational hierarchy higher than his or her present job.

proportional reinsurance. A category of reinsurance plans in which the different proportions of the risk that will be carried by the ceding company and by the reinsurer are specified when the reinsurance treaty is made.

prospect. A potential purchaser of insurance products.

prospecting. The act of identifying, contacting, and qualifying potential customers.

prudent investor rule. A rule which mandates that companies must exercise sound and reasoned judgment in making their investment decisions.

public offering. Investments in stocks and bonds that are offered for sale to the general public.

punitive damages. Fines that are awarded over and above the amount of the actual loss and that are designed to punish a litigant for its behavior.

pyramid-shaped organization structure. A graphic depiction of a company's chain of command that shows the authority and responsibility in a company, starting with one person or group of key people and then being distributed to ever larger numbers of people within the company.

rate making. The establishment of premium rates for an insurance company's products.

rate of return. The expected return of an investment expressed as a percentage of cost or purchase price.

ratio analysis. An analysis that shows the proportional relationship between two different amounts.

real property law. The body of laws and regulations that deals with ownership and transfer of rights in real estate.

rebating. The act of offering a prospect a special inducement to purchase a policy.

recording method. A method of changing a beneficiary designation in which the policyowner merely notifies the insurance company of the change in writing.

reinsurance. Insurance that one insurance company buys from another insurance company to cover part or all of a risk that the original company will not or cannot undertake itself.

reinsurance treaty. A legal document between a ceding company and a reinsurer that specifies the risks to be reinsured and the terms and conditions of reinsurance, including the reinsurance plan.

reinsurer. An insurance company that accepts a risk transferred from another insurance company in a reinsurance transaction.

reliability. The extent to which a test gives the same results on repeated administrations of the same or an identical test.

renewal commission. A commission paid for a specified number of years after the first policy year.

replacement. The act of surrendering an insurance policy or changing the coverage of that policy in order to buy another policy.

rescission. The legal process of canceling an insurance contract because of material misrepresentation in the application.

resident corporation. In Canada, a company that is incorporated under Canadian law.

residual benefit for partial disability. A disability income benefit payment that is made to a partially disabled insured.

resignation. The act of an employee leaving an organization in order to pursue work with another organization or to take up an alternative occupation, parenting, or education.

responsibility. An employee's obligation to perform assigned duties.

retention limit. The maximum amount of insurance that a company carries at its own risk on any individual.

retirement. The act of an employee withdrawing from a position or an occupation, usually concluding his or her career or profession.

retrocession. The process of one reinsurer's ceding its excess risk to another reinsurer.

retrocessionaire. A reinsurance company that accepts the excess risk of another reinsurer.

revenue bond. A bond that is backed only by the income the issuer expects to receive from the project for which the bonds were issued.

revenue budget. A document detailing the amount of income that a company expects to receive in the upcoming year.

rider. An amendment to an insurance policy that expands or limits the benefits payable and that becomes a part of the insurance contract.

risk class. A group of insureds who present a substantially similar risk to an insurance company.

role playing. A simulation technique in which learners act out specified roles.

salaried sales distribution system. A distribution system that uses salaried employees of an insurance company to sell and service policies.

sale-and-leaseback transaction. A method of investing in real estate in which the owner of a building sells the building to an investor but immediately leases back the building from the investor.

sales expense budget. The amount of money a company expects to pay for expenses incurred in selling insurance.

screening interview. A preliminary interview that is almost always conducted by a human resources employment specialist, and which is intended to eliminate those applicants who are obviously not qualified for the available position.

secured bond. A bond whose issuer pledges to meet bondholders' claims by using some or all of its assets or properties if necessary to make payments when due.

securities law. The interpretation and application of legislative and regulatory requirements regarding the sale and purchase of investment vehicles, especially stocks and bonds.

segmentation of accounts. A process in which asset portfolios are organized so that they support specific lines of business and specific products.

segregated account. *See* **separate account.**

select group. Applicants who are accepted for insurance at standard rates.

select period. The length of time, normally 5 to 15 years, during which the effects of risk selection are assumed to be observable and significant.

self-administered billing plan. A billing plan for group plans in which the policyholder performs most of the administrative work.

separate account. An account maintained separately from a company's general accounts for the purpose of managing the funds used to support nonguaranteed insurance products.

separation. The resignation, layoff, retirement, or discharge of an employee from an organization.

service center. A segment of an organization that provides support services for profit centers.

service fee. A form of agent compensation that constitutes a small percentage of the premium and that is usually payable only after renewal commissions on a policy have ceased.

simple interest. Interest payable only on the amount of money originally borrowed or invested.

single-need selling. A mode of marketing insurance products in which an agent isolates a particular financial need that can be met by insurance.

situation management test. A type of performance test in which the job applicant is asked to respond to a particular work-related situation. The situation can be presented on paper, verbally, or on videotape, and the applicant is evaluated on the basis of his or her response to the situation.

skills inventory. A manual or computerized data base of the education, training, and experience of each person working for an organization.

sole proprietorship. A business that is owned, and usually operated, by one person.

solvency. The ability to meet financial obligations as they come due.

span of control. An indicator of the number of people a manager directly supervises.

spin-off. A former unit or department of a company that operates as an independent company whose primary customer is the parent company.

staff authority. Indirect authority that staff personnel have over personnel in other departments.

staffing schedule. A part of an agency's operating plan that estimates the number of agency and office personnel needed to produce the projected amount of business, the cost of salaries and training for office personnel, as well as the time and money needed for recruiting, hiring, and training new agents.

staff referral. An external recruitment method in which a current employee suggests a job candidate to the human resources department.

staff unit. The areas of an organization that support line units by providing advice, information, or the physical materials that the line units need to complete their work.

stock. An investment that represents an ownership share in a corporation.

stock exchange. The place where brokerage firms carry out stock market transactions.

stockholder. A person who owns stock in a company.

stock insurance company. An insurance company that is owned by people who purchase shares of the company's stock.

stock market. A network of intricate relationships through which stockholders, potential stock investors, and stockbrokers gather information about stocks, look for potential buyers and sellers, and make stock trades.

stop-loss provision. A provision in medical expense policies which states that after an insured has paid a specified maximum amount of medical expenses, the insurer pays 100 percent of the balance of medical expenses for the year, up to the contract limit.

stop-loss reinsurance plan. A type of nonproportional reinsurance plan in which the reinsurer agrees to pay a percentage of all claims paid by the ceding company during a specified period that, in total, exceed a specified amount.

strategic alliance. A prolonged relationship involving risk and reward sharing by two or more independent firms that are pursuing individual strategic goals.

strategic business unit (SBU). An area of a business that is operated as a separate profit center, has its own set of customers and competitors, generally has its own management and support functions, and is capable of having its own plan of operations.

strategic planning. Long-range planning which studies the company's current performance, identifies the company's position in the insurance market, predicts future trends, and creates a plan of development for the company's future.

subsidiary. A company that is controlled or acquired by another company.

substance abuse. The excessive use of drugs or alcohol.

succession charts. A graphic illustration of the likely candidates for promotion to various key positions in a company.

supplementary benefit rider. A rider that is added to insurance policies in order to provide additional benefits.

surplus. The amount by which a life and health insurance company's assets exceed its liabilities and capital.

suspense account. An account that is used in cash-basis accounting to record transactions that cannot be credited immediately to a permanent account.

systems analyst. A person who designs computer systems to meet the operational needs of the different functional areas or product lines of a company.

target market. A group of individuals or organizations with which a company seeks to do business.

target marketing. The process of evaluating the attractiveness of market segments and selecting the markets on which the company is going to concentrate.

telemarketing. Direct response marketing performed by telephone.

temporary help agency. A company that provides companies with part-time and temporary workers—usually for clerical, office services, systems, or accounting positions—to fill immediate or seasonal demands for workers.

tender offer. A procedure in which an acquiring company tries to buy a controlling share of a target company directly from the target company's stockholders.

test marketing. The process of introducing a new product and its marketing program on a limited scale in the product's target market.

third-country nationals. Managers and personnel from neither the home country nor a host country.

total disability. A disability that prevents an insured from performing the essential duties of his or her regular occupation.

total-needs programming. A mode of marketing insurance products in which the agent brings together all the prospect's life insurance needs, calculates the amount of money required to take care of each of those needs, evaluates the assets that will be available when the prospect dies, and determines the amount of life insurance and types of policies required to cover any shortfall.

training. An activity directed toward learning, maintaining, and improving the skills necessary for current job performance.

trend analysis. Studying data from past periods in order to predict future trends.

twisting. A specific form of misrepresentation that occurs when an agent induces a policyowner to discontinue an insurance contract with another company and to use the cash value of the original policy to purchase a new policy, without clearly informing the policyowner of the differences between the two policies and of the financial consequences of replacing the original policy.

underwriting. The process of assessing and classifying the degree of risk that a proposed insured represents.

underwriting impairment. A factor that tends to increase a proposed insured's risk of death above that which is normal for his or her age.

underwriting manual. A summary of the guidelines used by a particular company to evaluate and rate risks.

unilateral contract. A type of contract in which only one party promises to do something.

unity of command. A management principle which states that each employee should receive authority from only one person and be accountable only to that person.

universal life insurance. A life insurance product that provides for variable interest-rate assumptions and flexibility in the premium and death benefit amounts.

upgrading. Educating, developing, and training a current employee to perform work duties more effectively or to take on new duties.

upstream holding company. A holding company that is formed by a parent company, which in turn is controlled by the holding company.

validation period. The amount of time that it takes for a product to become profitable or begin adding to surplus.

validation point. The point at which a product becomes profitable or begins adding to surplus.

validity. The degree to which a test is correlated with job-related criteria.

valuation mortality tables. Mortality tables developed and published as industry-wide standards for computing the value of policy reserves.

vocational rehabilitation. Rehabilitation that is intended to help a disabled person return to an occupation that provides some income.

waiting period. A prescribed amount of time following policy issue during which the insured's medical expenses are not covered by the policy.

work sample test. A type of performance test in which the applicants perform a task, such a typing a letter, that is a necessary part of the job they want.

worksheet. A printout of all available information about a proposed insured and, in some companies, pertinent information about the agent who submitted the application.

yearly renewable term (YRT) plan. A type of proportional reinsurance plan in which the ceding company purchases yearly renewable term insurance from the reinsurer.

Index